Technological Reflections

By

Anab Whitehouse

© Anab Whitehouse

Interrogative Imperative Institute

Brewer, Maine

04412

All rights are reserved. Aside from uses that are in compliance with the 'Fair Usage' clause of the Copyright Act, no portion of this publication may be reproduced in any form without the express written permission of the publisher. Furthermore, no part of this book may be stored in a retrieval system, nor transmitted in any form or by any means – whether electronic, mechanical, photo-reproduction or otherwise – without authorization from the publisher.

Published 2024

Published by One Draft Publications in Conjunction with Bilquees Press

Table of Contents

Chapter 1: Framing Analysis and Technocracy -- page 7

Chapter 2: Climate Delusional Syndrome – page 41

Chapter 3: The Geoengineering of Humans – page 77

Chapter 4: PCR and Models – page 123

Chapter 5: Memory, Mind, and Neuroscience – page 133

Chapter 6: NIST and 9/11 – page 155

Chapter 7: Emergent Properties – page 173

Chapter 8: Facebook - page 179

Chapter 9: Tractatus Technologicus – page 219

Chapter 10: Devil's Dictionary – page 291

Chapter 11: Targeted Individuals: Five Questions – page 337

Chapter 12: Some Evolutionary Considerations – page 389

Chapter 13: The Sovereignty Project – page 425

1. Framing Analysis and Technocracy

Although I am not a sociologist by trade, nonetheless, I have some degree of familiarity with, and appreciation for, the work of Erving Goffman, a Canadian researcher who was born in 1922 and died in 1982. I especially have been attracted to his notion of "framing analysis" that -- in somewhat altered and piecemeal forms -- appeared in many of his earlier writings such as: *Presentation of Self in Everyday Life* (published in 1959), *Asylums* (released in 1961), *Stigma* (published in 1963), and *Interaction Ritual* (released in 1967), but which did not become more fully delineated until *Framing Analysis* was published in 1974.

While, hopefully, the idea of framing analysis will shortly become a little more concrete and visible, one should note that even though that idea can be applied to the dynamics of social interaction – for example, as a way in which a psychiatrist might evaluate (or frame) the behavior of patients in mental asylums -- nonetheless, Goffman clearly indicates that framing analysis ultimately has to do with a broader process of organizing experience in general. Therefore, framing analysis should not be limited to just the phenomena of social dynamics.

As such, one might describe 'framing analysis' as the process of reflecting on the ways in which we – both individually and collectively – attempt to understand, interpret, create, and critique the dynamic perceptual/conceptual/linguistic/emotional/intentional structures that are used to bring organization to, and confer meaning upon, our experiences as we seek to figure out the nature of our relationship with reality at any given juncture of our experiences – whether considered individually or collectively.

Ideas, concepts, perceptions, assumptions, beliefs, values, emotions, motivations, theories, hypotheses, principles, paradigms, world views, interpretations, and methodologies all give expression to frames of organizing experience that can be used to analyze and critically reflect on the nature of experience. The question that haunts all of the foregoing possibilities is the following: What do such ways of framing experience have to do with coming to grips with, or understanding, what is taking place at any given instance of on-going experience?

Frames of experience can be given to us by others, such as during formal modalities of schooling or through articles that are published via one media outlet or another (e.g., television, the internet, magazines, radio, newspapers). Frames of experience also can be created by us as, for example, when we generate interpretations concerning what we believe might be happening during an on-going experience.

The framing process can be active or passive. In other words, on the one hand, we might passively – that is, do so without objection and, perhaps, not even with conscious consent – accept frames of experience that are imposed on us (such as might be done through various modes of education, indoctrination and propaganda), or which we are induced to adopt through the dynamics of undue influence when power relationships, of one kind or another, are used in unethical ways by individuals for purposes of manipulating someone's behavior ... individuals who might be in the form of parents, neighbors, peers, teachers, doctors, scientists, religious figures, corporations, employers, and/or government agents. On the other hand, frames of experience also can be actively constructed by us – whether done individually or done in co-operation with others during formal and informal inter-subjective projects such as science, education, religion, medicine, commerce, sports, and politics.

There is no guarantee that any frame of experience, or the analysis of such a frame of experience, will be correct. Goffman, sometimes, uses the term: "fabrication," in order to refer to framing processes during which we – whether considered individually or collectively – generate false beliefs or mis-framings concerning the actual nature of what is transpiring at any given moment (or series of moments).

Such 'fabrications' need not be intentional – although they might be. However, 'fabrications' also might be forthcoming via the most sincere of intentions (despite being incorrect).

Seen from the foregoing perspective, the sorts of iatrogenic fatalities which were discussed somewhat in the Introduction – that is, deaths caused by the medical industry despite following protocols involving established standards of care – could be construed as "fabrications" in Goffman's foregoing sense. In other words, whatever the theories, ideas, understandings, or standards of care that might have been playing an essential role while governing or shaping the manner in which patients were being treated prior to their deaths, those fatalities were due to the fact that the doctors and medical establishment had no idea that their protocols would be the very thing that led to the deaths of such individuals, and, consequently, what can one call such false or mistaken ideas, if not delusional thinking, concerning their way of medically treating such soon-to-be-dead patients except as a form of 'fabrication'. In short, the reason such patients died is because the individuals treating the former were operating on the basis of one, or more, fabrications that the medical personnel had accepted and which they were treating as truths, but were not, in fact, actually true, and, as a result, led to tragic results.

Frames of experience sometimes have the capacity to conceal the truth in certain ways via, for example, the previously noted process of 'fabrication'. Alternatively, when done appropriately, frames of experience can, in a sense, unmask the character of what is taking place and, in the process, reveal (within certain degrees of freedom and constraints) different facets of the truth.

Frames of experience are the focus of our exchanges with ourselves as we reflect about on-going phenomenology. In other words, these frames of experience are forms of conscious awareness that gives expression to modalities off existential streaming that are taking place in the present or which involves memories – frames – concerning the past that are playing out or being recalled in the present.

Frames of experience also give expression to the character of our communications with other human beings. We use such frames of experience to convey something of ourselves to others or to ourselves – for example, as a function of the role or roles that we play in different social contexts -- and, in addition, we use such frames of experience to convey something about our understanding of the nature of the relationship between human beings and the Ocean of Being within which such framing processes take place.

Framing analysis is also a means of trying to distinguish – to whatever degree this is possible – between, on the one hand, one's essential self that might be at the heart of one's capacity for personhood, and, on the other hand, one's social self as given expression through the roles, rules, rituals, and so on that are learned in order to be able to navigate one's way through the highways and byways of the social milieu that tends to vary from one society to the next – although there might be some degree of commonality or overlap with respect to the nature of such social highways and byways that exist within various societies. Framing analysis is also the attempt to distinguish between, on the one hand: (a) the sorts of frames that are being imposed upon experience – and experience is, by default, one's point of contact with reality or Being – and which, in the process, obscure or obfuscate the nature of that reality, and, on the other hand: (b) the sorts of frames of experience that seem to unmask or reveal or reflect or resonate with some 'real' dimension of that which makes such experiences possible.

Framing analysis is the process of critical reflection that seeks to engage, consider, understand, question, evaluate, and organize all of the foregoing considerations. The purpose of such a dynamic process is to work toward being able to grasp – to whatever extent this is possible – the degree to which such forms of framing analysis are capable of uncovering or reflecting the nature of our relationship with both social as well as, possibly, even more fundamental physical and metaphysical dimensions of experience, Being, or reality.

Thus, every instance of medical diagnosis and/or treatment protocol is an exercise in framing analysis in the foregoing sense. Every medical practitioner is engaging their experience – including patients – through the manner in which their process of framing analysis induces the practitioner to pay attention to some aspects of experience to the exclusion of other facets of experience – a framing analysis that when considered in its entirety defines how any given individual – medical practitioner or otherwise – is oriented toward what they consider the truth to be with respect to the nature of their experiential relationship with the universe, Being, or Reality.

A simple example of framing analysis might involve a painting. More specifically, paintings are framed by different materials in ways that are intended to orient a viewer with respect to the qualities of a painting as well as to separate that particular painting from other properties of the surrounding environment – such as the wall on which the painting hangs, as well as other, near-by paintings.

However, such a framing process can involve more than the molding materials that are used to mark the visible boundaries of a painting. For example, the lighting that is used to illuminate a given painting could be considered to be part of the framing process, and depending on the character of the light which is shining on a painting, different facets of the painting might be given emphasis over other aspects of that same painting.

Furthermore, molding materials that "frame" a painting could be hiding defects along the edges of that artwork. If so, the painting would have to be de-framed in order for those defects to be discovered, and without such a process of de-framing to unmask the true nature of the painting, the molding material serves as a form of fabrication because it conceals various hidden facets of the painting that might lead an observer to have a different impression of the painting than if such defects were also visible to the observer.

Similarly, lighting also can both reveal and hide different aspects of a given painting. Change the nature of the lighting that illuminates a painting, then the features of a painting to which a viewer's attention is being drawn might also change, and, in fact, artists have long indicated that the time of day in which something is painted will affect how and what a painter sees, and, therefore, even the act of creating an artwork is a process of framing what is experienced at the times that an artwork is being rendered.

Whistleblowers in the medical industry are, to use the term provided previously, de-framers. In other words, medical whistleblowers are individuals who talk about the defects which are present in the medical industry despite the best efforts of the medical industry to frame over and, thereby, hide those defects from the public.

For example, Dr. William Thompson is such a whistleblower or de-framer. He revealed that the CDC had been hiding data for more than a decade indicating that the thimerosal -- a mercury based preservative -- which was present in certain vaccines was, despite the denials of the CDC, indeed, responsible for the emergence of autism in certain demographics (e.g., young black males).

Or, consider the perspective of Dr. Marcia Angell who has served as another de-framer – that is, a person who discloses defects that lie hidden beneath the forms of framing analysis that are used by the medical industry to, among other things, cover up its faults and short-comings. She was the first woman ever to be appointed to serve as the editor-in-chief of one of the most prestigious medical journals in the world – namely, the *New England Journal of Medicine*.

In her 2004 book: *The Truth About the* Drug Companies, she documented how the corporate world has financially corrupted the processes of both medical research and education, not only in the United States but all over the world. She also once stated that: "It is simply no longer possible to believe much of the clinical research that is published, or to rely on the judgment of trusted physicians or authoritative medical guidelines. I take no pleasure in this conclusion, which I reached slowly and reluctantly over my two decades as editor of the *New England Journal of Medicine*" – which is as about as severe a form of de-framing as one might offer.

One might also consider the 2018 book *Dopesick* by Beth Macy as an exercise in the dynamics of de-framing – that is, an exposé concerning the ways in which different aspects of the medical industry (including an array of hospitals and doctors, as well as the FDA and a pharmaceutical company,) colluded together for several decades to ignore, if not actively resist and hide, information concerning the destructive impact which OxyContin was having on Americans. Thus, for instance, while tens of thousands of Americans were dying as a result of problems surrounding the use of OxyContin -- deaths about which the FDA had been apprised of on many occasions -- certain FDA officials were, nonetheless, busy with generating an official labeling profile for the drug that hid the actual truth concerning the drug's addictive, debilitating, and lethal potential ... not to mention the impact the drug was playing in pushing crime statistics higher and higher as users who became hooked on the drug looked for ways to subsidize their addiction. Furthermore, when the FDA subsequently was provided with a second opportunity to properly re-label the drug with respect to the drug's actual dangers, the federal organization once again just continued on with its enabling activities and provided a form of labeling that, apparently, helped the drug to achieve increased sales.

Many more examples of the foregoing sorts of de-framing activities could be provided here, but, perhaps, enough has been said to indicate that the sorts of problematic framing processes which have been actively pursued through different facets of the medical industry within the United States are not a matter of isolated cases that don't accurately describe the "normal" manner in which the medical industry operates, but, instead, tend to paint a picture of a corrupt, systemic dynamic in which many doctors, hospitals, pharmaceutical companies, universities, media outlets (both technical as well as general), and government agencies such as the CDC, the FDA, and the NIH have become entangled within a set of conflicts of interests, and other kinds of unethical practices which have had, and continue to have, devastating effects on the well-being of American citizens.

A further complication concerning the foregoing considerations concerns how the process of framing analysis might spill over into the notion of a 'palimpsest'. Although normally speaking the term "palimpsest" refers to contexts in which what previously had been written on a piece of parchment has been completely or partially scraped off from that piece of parchment in order to free-up space for some new form of text to be placed on the parchment, nevertheless, one could apply the palimpsest notion to artists when they take an old canvas on which something previously had been painted and, then, proceeded to paint over the earlier creation.

Sometimes the foregoing process is done in order to free-up space on a canvas in order to be able to have an opportunity to give expression to, or unmask, some new artistic creation. Sometimes, however, something of value is concealed – whether intentionally or unintentionally – by painting over some artwork, and the earlier artwork will only be discovered – if at all – by a painstaking process of removing the paints that have been used to cover up the earlier artwork.

As such, intentions are capable of becoming part of a framing process. For instance, if, for whatever reason, someone deliberately decided to cover up some earlier artwork that had been recorded on a given canvas, then such intentions become part of a framing process and such processes were undertaken in order to hide something from view.

Without wishing to try to argue that all forms of alternative medicine are necessarily reliable and, in addition, keeping in mind that there are unprincipled individuals who populate virtually every strata of society who seek opportunities that are amendable to the exploitation of unsuspecting people who are seeking medical assistance of some kind, nevertheless, a very strong case can be made (and constructing such a case will be attempted in some of the subsequent chapters of the present work) that following the Carnegie Foundation-supported, but Rockefeller serving, *Flexner Report* published by Abraham Flexner in 1910, a power-struggle ensued in which an allopathic approach to medicine sought to erase from competition, if not existence, any form of medical practice that was inconsistent with what the *Flexner Report* indicated medicine should be and the manner in which doctors ought to be trained.

The sort of allopathic medicine which was being promoted in the *Flexner Report* constituted – allegedly -- a science-based system of medicine. However, what was actually being promoted was the establishment of a power system for controlling what could and couldn't be considered to be acceptable forms of medical education and practice, and, therefore, what was meant by the idea of a science-based system of medicine was left to be worked out by the individuals who either were in, or who soon would be in, positions of power within government, corporations, hospitals, the media, as well as educational institutions, and, as such, allopathic medicine was not necessarily so much science-based as it was to become power-based and the ones in power got to determine what the notion of being "science-based" did and did not mean.

In other words, allopathic medicine sought to create a palimpsest in which all forms of previously existing medical ideas were to be painted over because those idea or practices were deemed to not comply with what the new overlords of medicines insisted was to constitute how everyone needed to understand the nature of medicine and, therefore, outlined how new medical images, ideas, and textual accounts should be laid down. Moreover, the foregoing new way forward for medicine was to be established irrespective of whatever constructive elements earlier medical ideas and practices might have entailed, as well as irrespective of whatever problematic, if not unsuccessful, elements might be introduced through allopathic medicine.

Although, initially, what follows might seem to have nothing to do with the issues at hand, I would like to offer a more complicated and personal example concerning the issue of framing analysis that is drawn from the life of my spiritual guide. More specifically, when he was doing doctoral work in England back in the 1950's and 1960s – and prior to when I met him for the first time in the early 1970s -- the occasion had arrived for him to give an oral defense of his doctoral thesis. His dissertation was on, among other things, the life and teachings of Shaykh Ahmed Sirhindi (may Allah be pleased with him) a Sufi saint who lived in India during the 16th and 17th centuries.

One of my future spiritual guide's examiners was Professor A.J. Arberry, who was considered, by a general consensus of experts at that time to be one of the leading academic authorities on, among other things, the Sufi mystical tradition. During the process of translating the Qur'an into English, Professor Arberry had converted to Islam, and for a time, that conversion was hidden from his fellow academics through a process of social framing due to the existence of stigmatizing prejudices concerning Muslims and Islam that existed at the time – and, unfortunately, continue to exist -- in the institution of higher education where Professor Arbitrary taught.

Following the aforementioned oral examination of my future spiritual guide's dissertation, Professor Arberry indicated that the thesis which he, along with others, had been examining was the best work on the Sufi tradition that Professor Arberry had seen in the English language up to that point in time. For a number of years after receiving his doctorate, my future teacher had sought to publish his doctoral thesis, but, due to various biased machinations – jealously being one of those dynamics -- that were taking place within the academic department to which my future spiritual guide belonged, the thesis was not published even though, at one point, a prominent English publisher of such textual materials had indicated its interest in publishing the work but that interest was undermined subsequently by the activities of some of the individuals who belonged to the same academic department as my future spiritual guide.

When my future spiritual teacher was informed by his own Sufi teacher in the late 1960s that my soon-to-be teacher had been given the responsibilities of being a shaykh or spiritual guide, he began to observe some of the more rigorous forms of practice entailed by the Sufi path, including the discipline of spiritual seclusion. During this form of observance, the individual goes by himself or herself into a room from which all the distractions of modern society have been removed while wearing the two sheets of cloth known as Ihram (worn during the Hajj) and, then, spends one's time engaged in constant remembrance of God, prayer, and other acts of worship.

In addition, the individual fasts from two hours, or so, prior to sunrise until sunset, and, as well, the person keeps the night vigil. Adhering to such a discipline also requires that an individual refrain from interacting with other human beings.

The structure of seclusion is such that an individual eats less, drinks less, sleeps less, and spends less time with people. As a result, a person's time is freed up to concentrate on God more, and one does so through the processes of fasting, ritual prayers, remembrance or zikr, night vigils, reading the Qur'an, as well as through meditation and contemplation.

The foregoing set of observances may last for a day, three days, five days, seven days, eleven days, nineteen days, twenty-one days, and forty days. Almost invariably the length of the seclusions observed by my spiritual guide lasted 40 days, although, occasionally, the foregoing 40-day seclusion --which was usually done during the summer months when the university's regular programs were not in session – would be augmented by a shorter period of seclusion lasting 19 or 21 days on other occasions during the year (for example, during Christmas break).

Spiritual experiences of one kind or another sometimes are undergone during such periods of seclusion. Furthermore, quite irrespective of whether those experiences take place, the time spent in seclusion tends to be an intense time of learning about oneself and the nature of one's relationship with Reality or Being.

Every time that my spiritual guide came out of seclusion, he would, at some point or other in the following weeks and months, begin to think about revising his doctoral thesis in the light of what had been learned during his period of seclusion. The problem with such an idea was that following the next round of seclusion, he would have had, by the Grace of Allah, further spiritual experiences and/or additional intense forms of learning, and, as a result, he, once again, would be faced with the prospect of having to revise whatever he might have previously revised in his thesis based on experiences and learning that had taken place in conjunction with earlier periods of spiritual seclusion.

Eventually, after a number of periods of spiritual retreat, my shaykh gave up, altogether, on the idea of revising his doctoral thesis. He understood that no matter how many times the dissertation might be revised, those revisions would not be able to keep up with what was being learned during various subsequent periods of seclusion.

During the time that I knew him, he observed some 15 or 16 periods of 40 day seclusions as well a number of lesser 19 and 21 day periods of seclusion, and, in addition, prior to the time when I first met him, he already had observed a number of 40-day periods of spiritual retreat. So, by the grace of Allah, a great deal of learning is likely to have taken place during those many instances of seclusion.

In a sense, despite the dissertation of my future shaykh having been described by Professor A.J. Arberry as being the best text on the subject of the Sufi mystical tradition in the English language that the professor had encountered, nonetheless, my spiritual guide's original doctoral thesis was, to a considerable extent -- a conceptual process of framing analysis involving the life and teachings of Shaykh Ahmed Sirhindi (may Allah be pleased with him). However since each period of spiritual seclusion through which my guide went gave rise to newer mystical forms of framing analysis, then, as his conceptual understanding was opened up to an expanded set of experiential modalities of learning, then, so too, did the way in which he understood the nature of his relationship with Being also undergo transitions.

With each instance of seclusion, the process of framing analysis which was taking place within my guide was turned back on itself in a critically reflective manner. Consequently, as a result, whatever that process of framing analysis might have indicated previously changed as a result of subsequent experiences and learning that took place during ensuing periods of seclusion.

The foregoing process went on until my spiritual guide was informed, in a vision that took place in India, that his work on Earth had been completed. He had been on sabbatical when the foregoing event occurred and was not expected to return to Toronto for a number of months, but he returned to Toronto unexpectedly, spent the month of Ramadan with his initiates (of which I was one), and, then, passed away nineteen days after the month of fasting had concluded.

The term "fitra" is the Islamic/Sufi term that refers to the inherent, essential potential of a human being. In a sense, whether one approaches the idea of fitra from the perspective of framing analysis or through the notion of 'palimpsest', the purpose of the Sufi path is to assist an individual's journey back to one's original nature and its concomitant potential in order -- through a complex dynamic of interacting experiences – to discover the essential character of one's relationship with Being or reality.

Therefore, the practice, observance or discipline of seclusion can be understood as a rigorous form of a reflexively reiterative process in which one seeks -- over time and God willing -- to remove (through fasting, prayer, keeping the night vigil, remembrance, reading the Qur'an, mediation, contemplation, and so on) all of the different kinds of framing analysis or modalities of palimpsest that have been superimposed on fitra, or one's essential nature, due to the beliefs, values, ideas, motivations, understandings, feelings, roles, rituals, rules, methods, theories, systems, and interpretations that arise as a result of maturation, schooling, acculturation, peers, parenting, as well as imagination, and in the process have come to obscure, or generate, an array of 'fabrications' – or false beliefs -- concerning, the nature of what or who one, in essence, is.

Every time that my shaykh went into seclusion, he was engaged in an exercise of seeking to remove – or have removed -- more and more of the fabrications or false systems of understanding that tend to build up in us over time due to the way we engage experience as a function of different kinds of theories, theologies, presuppositions, likes, dislikes, and so on. As such, he was seeking to remove – or have removed, God willing -- forms of framing analysis and palimpsest that led away from truths entailed by one's fitra or essential nature because such fabrications induced one to wander away from fundamental truths or to become distracted away from such truths despite – when properly unmasked or unveiled -- their very palpable presence.

I can attest to some of the foregoing considerations, because in my own very limited way, I have gone into spiritual seclusion for – compared to my spiritual guide – only relatively short periods of time. Nevertheless, I have observed the discipline of seclusion and the intense manner in which it helps a person, if God wishes, to begin to learn how to differentiate, at least within certain parameters, between various fabrications and truths concerning one's way of having engaged experience prior to such observances or practices.

Notwithstanding the foregoing considerations, I also can truthfully say that I am far from being a realized human being. In other words, I am a work in some sort of, God willing, progress through which I continue to try to critically reflect -- via an array of different spiritual practices -- on the different forms of framing analysis and palimpsests that have been, and are being, imposed on (sometimes by others and quite often by me) my own essential nature or fitra that emerged due to various experiential forms of socialization, acculturation, schooling, propaganda, parenting, as well as individual choices that, each in their own way, have helped – in part or completely – to conceal, obfuscate, distort, and mis-frame one's essential nature, and, therefore, have gotten in the way of trying to understand the nature of my relationship with Being or Reality.

Socialism, communism, feudalism, mercantilism, capitalism, democracy, fascism, corporatism, anarchy, monarchy, oligarchy, plutocracy, legalism, constitutionalism, trans-humanism, methodology, scientism, schooling, artificial intelligence, militarism, spiritualism, philosophy, journalism, mythology, science, banking, medicine, economics, politics, rationalism, empiricism, materialism, evolution, education, and religion are all ways of framing experience. Furthermore, seeking to induce people to engage reality – or advocating that people should pursue such forms of engaging reality -- through the foregoing sorts of framing processes or dynamics has the potential for obfuscation that is rooted in the understandings, ideas, emotions, hermeneutical renderings, and perspectives to which the aforementioned systems of framing and palimpsest formation give expression.

The current portion of the present presentation is also an exercise in framing, as is the topic on which this part of the current presentation is about to critically reflect – namely, technocracy. Framing is not necessarily inherently evil or immoral – although it can be -- but, instead, framing analysis seeks to draw attention to the manner in which almost every – if not every -- way that we engage reality imposes various kinds of conceptual, hermeneutical, emotional, and epistemological obfuscations onto reality (that is, so many layers of fabricated conceptual palimpsests), and, in the process, even when such understandings accurately convey certain aspects of the truth, nonetheless, we are required to realize that various facets concerning the nature of reality are simultaneously being concealed, if not distorted, as a result of the different forms of the conceptual, emotional, epistemological, and experiential frames or palimpsests through which we engage, perceive, and analyze Being, or Reality, or experience.

The process of trying to understand ourselves is like – to state a mouthful that requires unpacking -- a multi-leveled reverse palimpsest dynamic. The French philosopher Paul-Michel Foucault would likely refer to such a dynamic as an expression of the "archaeology of knowledge", whereas the German existential phenomenologist Edmund Husserl might employ the notion of a series of phenomenological and cognitive bracketing processes that were intended to enable a person – or, so, the hope went -- to work his, her, or their way down, or back, to some semblance of experiential apodicticity, or necessary certainty, concerning the nature of experience and what the result of such a bracketing process might have to say, if anything, about the character of one's relationship with Being or reality.

In other words from the perspective of the Sufi path, human beings begin life with an original manuscript page – namely, our fitra or essential nature. However, as we go through life, we begin to paint over, re-text, or re-frame our original nature, or fitra, so that the manuscript of original potential can be repurposed, instead, to give expression to the imprint of some other set of individual and/or social modalities of – metaphorically speaking – existential expressions of texting over, painting over, or re-framing the character of our essential nature ... the source of our personhood ... our true selves.

Instead of removing what has been imposed on -- and, therefore, does not belong with -- the original manuscript page (in other words, our essential relationship with Being), we become busy with developing or acquiring new conceptual and emotional texts, images, and imaginings to the existential parchment that covers up or obfuscates fitra or original nature. Such texts, images, and creative efforts may allow some facets of the potential of the original manuscript to shine through, but, on the whole, such frames and palimpsests tend only to add new forms of conceptual and emotional texts, images, and imaginings that are inclined to obscure – rather than reveal -- the nature of the original manuscript page ... that is, the true nature of our experiential relationships with Being or reality.

The foregoing overview of several aspects of mystical science has to do with the Sufi spiritual tradition. However, one can find counterparts to all of the foregoing methodological features in a variety of spiritual traditions such as: The Vedanta, Yoga, Taoism, Buddhism, Judaism, Christianity, Janism, and any number of other kinds of indigenous spiritual traditions that can be found in North America, South America, Australia, New Zealand, and so on.

All of the foregoing spiritual traditions have at least one commonality. The discipline and methods entailed by those systems of understanding are all geared toward helping the individual to undergo a series of de-framing exercises through which one seeks to undergo an archaeological exploration concerning the palimpsest layers of understanding (many of which are self-imposed or other-imposed "fabrications" in Goffman's sense) that have been laid down previously and, in the process, covered over or covered up one's essential potential and, thereby, have served to obstruct one's search for the truth concerning the nature of one's relationship with Being, Reality, or the Universe.

Many people today believe that science and religion stand at opposite ends of any process of inquiry. For example, many individuals might claim, among other things, that science is rooted in methodology whereas religion is a function of theology. Or, alternatively, many people maintain that science seeks to provide hard evidence and work out rigorous proofs in support of various claims, whereas religion bases its assertions on professions of blind faith and speculation.

While I am quite willing to concede that there often is a great deal of truth in the foregoing ways of characterizing and comparing science and religion, I don't feel that such a perspective necessarily does justice to the discipline of authentic mysticism. Although the impression of some people concerning the nature of mysticism is that it tends to be entangled in notions of flights of fancy of one kind or another, the essential nature of authentic mysticism is, I believe, quite different from those sorts of considerations.

For instance, the previous discussion concerning the nature and rigors of the spiritual practice of seclusion – which is just one of many practices that might be mentioned – indicates that such a methodology is far more advanced and demanding than anything which medical school or medicine has to offer as a way of cleansing, calibrating, activating, and learning how to use different facets of the instrument that is primary to any sort of endeavor – medical or non-medical -- and this has to do with the instrument of the self. While medical school and the practice of medicine might involve, in some minimal fashion, engaging the occasional course, seminar and/or text concerning the idea of medical ethics, none of those courses, seminars, or texts actually require a person to go through a demanding, methodological discipline, such as spiritual seclusion, in which a fundamental emphasis of the exercise, is to not just to induce one to think about ethics but to actively engaged in purifying the instrument – namely, the self – through which an ethical or moral perspective is to be expressed and applied to everyday situations.

I am wondering how many medical doctors and medical practitioners there would be if they had to go through just one extended exercise of seclusion in order to be able to obtain a medical license, and, as well, were required to participate every year, or so, in additional exercises of a like nature in order to be able to keep their medical license. Any doctor who claims objectivity with respect to the practice of medicine and who alludes to various principles of ethics which, supposedly, govern medical practice, but who is unwilling to undertake a rigorous set of methods, like spiritual seclusion, to help purify the primary instrument – namely, the self – that is to be engaging in allegedly objective and ethical activities, is really doing little more than whistling past the cemetery and, while doing so, engaging in an elaborate form of fabrication.

If one were to characterize scientific methodology, one might indicate that it consists of the following sorts of procedures or protocols: (1) empirical observation; (2) the use of instrumentation; (3) recursive methodology; (4) objectivity; (5) a community of expertise; (6) experimental replication, and (7) reliable prediction. Surprisingly, to some extent at least, such a methodology is not the exclusive preserve of so-called material sciences, but actually represents the essence of authentic mystical methodology of whatever traditional form of spirituality one might wish to mention.

However, unlike material sciences, the thrust of authentic mystical sciences of whatever species (and, yes, to complicate matters there are some counterfeit forms of such spiritual sciences) is that the entire methodology is directed toward cleansing, calibrating, and learning how to use the only instrument which matters, and that instrument is the self and its associated faculties. In the absence of a purified and calibrated self, then, in many ways, science begins at no beginning and works toward no end, and, instead, for the most part, becomes little more than an exercise in self-posturing irrespective of how dazzling, in some respects, that posturing might appear to the uninitiated.

My spiritual guide not only engaged in steps 1-6 of the foregoing procedures for scientific methodology in every single spiritual seclusion which he entered in order to be in a position to become open to spiritual possibility if, God willing, something in that regard might be offered. However, he engaged in the discipline of spiritual seclusion as a rigorous way to continue to hammer away at whatever fabrications that might be lurking in his understanding of the nature of his relationship with Being or Reality.

To be objective, one needs to eliminate as many sources of bias, prejudice, distortion and error as is possible. The search for truth must be freed from all forces which would compromise the integrity of that search.

Thus, through an exacting process of empirical observation, my spiritual guide sought to purify and calibrate the instrument of the self by means of the process of spiritual seclusion again and again (i.e., recursively), in order to whittle away at whatever biases might be present. Such attempts at achieving objectivity would, then, be measured against the standards that have been evinced by the community of those (for example, authentic spiritual guides) who have, by the Grace of Allah, been able to achieve various levels of knowledge, and, in the process would (via steps 1-5) work toward replicating the experiment that constitutes the dynamics of spiritual seclusion and which every member of the community of those who have real knowledge also have replicated again and again.

Just as the goal of a mystic is to de-frame experience and understanding so that one might gain access to one's essential potential and, thereby, discover the nature of the truth concerning one's relationship with Reality or Being, so too, the goal of a medical practitioner is to de-frame experience and understanding in order to try to discover the actual nature of health and disease with respect to the essential potentials of the body. As different chapters in the present book will attempt to indicate, allopathic medicine appears to fail miserably with respect to such a quest, and, as a result, its understanding of health and disease is, quite frequently, a function of fabrications rather than being a function of a rigorous de-framing process that seeks to bring one closer to more essential truths concerning the nature of health and disease.

Before delving into a few considerations concerning the nature of technocracy (see Chapter 3) in which much of allopathic medicine seems to be deeply ensconced, perhaps being able to take a look at some of the meanings to which religion supposedly gives etymological expression might be instructive. The reason why this might be instructive is because I believe that when the notion of technocracy is properly understood it can be seen as a form of theocracy, and since much of allopathic medicine plays a fundamental role in that theocracy, one needs to have some appreciation for the way in which allopathic medicine has many of the qualities of a religious, evangelical activity.

Words are ways of linguistically and conceptually parsing reality or the universe. Therefore, trying to understand the structural character of the logic that is inherent in different ways of engaging and parsing experience might prove to have heuristic value.

To begin with, various individuals claim that the etymology of religion rests with the Latin word **re**-li-gare. The central sense of the foregoing Latin word refers to a process of tying or binding oneself to something.

The obvious questions are: What is being tied, and what is the nature of the tying process? The foregoing questions might be best engaged through another Latin word: "re-li-gi-o-nem" that conveys a sense of reverence for that which is considered sacred.

When combined together, the foregoing two etymological possibilities give expression to the idea of becoming bound or tied to that for which one has reverence or that which one considers to be sacred because one believes that that to which one is binding oneself is true in some sense. At the heart of this condition of being tied or bound is a state of belief, understanding, commitment, knowledge, and/or faith concerning one's relationship with that which is considered to be sacred or worthy of reverence.

Another etymological possibility involves the term "religion" that comes from the Old French and refers to a process of devotion or piety, as well as refers to communities in which that devotion and piety plays a central role. Devotion and piety both give expression to a sense of being bound or tied to that which is sacred or worthy of reverence, but, as well, piety alludes to a set of behaviors, some of which are moral in nature, that are intended to manifest conscientiousness concerning the presence, and requirements that emerge in relation to the realm of the sacred.

When discussing the meaning of religion, some individuals make reference to Cicero's use of the word *"re-le-gere"*. This term refers to a process of going through a text or a textual reading more than once.

Perhaps, the idea of reading something again is intended to make reference to a process of taking care with, and critically reflecting on, the possible meanings inherent in a text. In other words, one goes through a reading again and again in order to make sure that one understands what is being said ... and, perhaps, in order to try to be certain that one has arrived at the truth of a given text.

The foregoing sense of things might be relevant in contexts in which the texts being studied have to do with issues considered to be sacred in nature. One wants to bind oneself or tie oneself to the truths – assuming there are some -- that are being given expression through various sacred themes contained in a given text or practice, and one does not want to become bound or tied to some distorted or false understanding concerning those matters.

Consequently, there is a need to exercise care in how one reads a given text or parses a given experience. One engages the material again and again to work toward a correct understanding of, on the one hand, what is being said, and, on the other hand, the possible nature of the relationship between what is being said and the nature of Being or Reality.

The *Oxford English Dictionary* indicates there are some question marks surrounding the etymology of the word: "religion". Nonetheless, one should keep in mind that etymological factors have to do with how certain root ideas associated with this or that word were used in the past and, in the process, shaped the way in which language was used to parse experience.

Nonetheless, while etymology can help create a sense of some of the possible meanings that might be woven into the semantic and syntactic fabric of a word, one might note that words tend to evolve or change over time. As this occurs, words become used in a variety of ways that often juxtapose, if not blend, older senses of a word with newer nuances, leading to different understandings and ways of describing experience.

Today, there are a growing number of people who are of the opinion that the general idea of "religion" has acquired what they consider to be a deserved aura of negative connotations ... if not problematic denotations. Those individuals seem to believe there is something inherently defective in the process of binding or tying oneself to a sense of the sacred in a manner that establishes parameters of piety and moral behavior for purposes of engaging the sacred in an appropriately reverential manner.

An obvious question that arises in conjunction with the foregoing considerations is what -- if anything -- is the relationship between "the sacred" and "the nature of reality"? Does that which is considered to be sacred necessarily give expression to some dimension of the real or is the notion of sacredness merely a human construction that, ultimately, tends to obfuscate the nature of the truth concerning what one's relationship with Reality, Being, or the Universe?

If there are dimensions of reality that are worthy of reverence and, thereby, give expression to the sacred, then, identifying the actual nature of those dimensions becomes a very important process. If one reads or parses reality in the wrong way, then, one's sense of the sacred will be skewed or tarnished.

Consequently, one must be careful to distinguish between, on the one hand, what, if anything, reality actually requires of us, and, on the other hand, what, if anything, we are imposing on reality through inappropriate hermeneutical dynamics. If there is a sacred dimension to reality, then binding or tying oneself to that dimension in a manner that distorts the nature of that sort of a reality, is likely, sooner or later, to lead to problems of one kind or another, both for oneself as well as for others.

Perhaps Cicero was on to something when he mentioned the idea of going through the reading of a written text or reality (which is a text of another kind) more than once. Becoming bound to the sacred should be done in accordance with the nature of the sacredness to which reality actually gives expression – to the extent that it does this -- rather than in accordance with some human construction that is arbitrarily imposed on reality.

In many ways, the general idea of religion might carry a lot of negative connotations for so many people precisely because all too many individuals have done such a poor job of: Reading reality, understanding its dimensions of sacredness, and determining what, if anything, the idea of sacredness requires from us. In and of itself, the idea of binding oneself to the sacred and developing a sense of reverence in that regard is not necessarily the problem.

After all, everyone binds himself or herself to a hermeneutical orientation or set of beliefs that they consider to be sacred and deserving of reverence, and, therefore, commitment. Consequently, the essential issue is: What, if anything, does one's sense of the sacred have to do with the actual nature of reality?

The foregoing question can be translated into the manner through which framing analysis might address that query. More specifically, framing analysis is the attempt to distinguish between: (a) the sorts of frames that are being imposed upon experience by oneself or others (experience, as the default point of reference, is one's point of contact with reality or Being), and which, as a result, obscure or obfuscate one's understanding of such experiences, and (b) the sorts of frames of experience that seem to de-frame, unmask, reveal, reflect or resonate with some dimension of that which makes such experiences possible, and which some might refer to as "Reality"..

In other words, framing analysis is the process of critical reflection that seeks to engage, consider, understand, question, evaluate, and organize all of the foregoing considerations. The purpose of such a dynamic process is to work toward being able to grasp – to whatever extent this is possible – the degree to which such forms of framing analysis are capable of uncovering the nature of our relationship with both social as well as, possibly, even more fundamental physical and metaphysical dimensions of experience, Being, or Reality.

Consequently, someone's conception of medicine or medical practice gives expression to that person's beliefs about how one ought to bind or connect to what is considered to be an appropriate framing of reality (that is, without what is believed to be any obfuscations) and, as such, is worth binding to and, therefore, being treated as something which is sacred (that is, something which should be treated with deference and reverence), and because it is sacred (that is worthy of being bound to conceptually, emotionally, socially, and so on), then, that form of framing analysis constitutes a way of orienting and informing oneself when it comes to one's sense of duty and obligation that should govern one's actions medically and in other ways as well.

Medicine – as is true for any kind of science, philosophy, political theory, theology, spirituality, or conceptual system – is an attempt by an individual or group of individuals to seek that which is considered to be the truth in relation to the nature of an individual and/or a collective relationship with the Universe, Reality, or Being ... however one wishes to state the matter. As heretical and distasteful as the foregoing sort of claim might appear to some – perhaps many -- that medicine is a species of religion, nonetheless, such an observation is not without its merits. In other words, I don't believe one is unnecessarily distorting the nature of medicine to indicate that -- just as is the case with any sort of understanding concerning reality -- medicine is a species of parsing dynamic which frames the way one understands how, or believes that, one is bound to the nature of reality, and, in the process, not only establishes one's sense of the sacred, obligation, duty, and the like, but, as well, might come to motivate one to become quite evangelical concerning one's willingness to spread that perspective to, if not impose it on, others.

In addition, one might suppose that -- and this would be in line with the ideas of Cicero mentioned earlier -- medicine as theology becomes something that one reads over and over again. This process is not only a means of trying to make sure that one understands what is being said, but it also induces the one who is going through the review process is seeking to inculcate and reflect on the theological fabrications that are being taught concerning one's alleged relationship with Reality as understood by or through the framework of medicine.

Just as religious theologies exist, so too, do medical theologies tend to exist. Medical theology is the body of beliefs that tend to shape and orient many facets of medical understanding and practice, and while the notion of "objectivity" tends to serve as a watchword which supposedly protects medicine from descending into a system of blind beliefs concerning official medical doctrine, how can one honestly speak of "objectivity" or morality when so much of medicine is – as previous examples have pointed out – caught up in a systemic process of corruption, conflicts of interest, bribery, indoctrination, desire for power, influence-peddling, propaganda, palimpsest activity, and "fabrication?"

According to Patrick Wood in his work: *Technocracy: The Hard Road To World Order*, (and Patrick Wood has written a number of other works on the issue of technocracy prior to the aforementioned book), one of the primary shaping forces that operates in conjunction with various manifestations of technocracy that have been taking place, and are continuing to take place, in the world can be traced to the creation of the Trilateral Commission by David Rockefeller and Zbigniew Brzezinski in 1973. The essential purpose of the Trilateral Commission is to create a new, globalized economic system that will replace the sovereignty of nations, states, and individuals with the economic system that is being given expression through the Trilateral Commission.

Prior to the formation of the Trilateral Commission, Brzezinski had written a book that was published in 1970 which was entitled: *Between Two Ages: America's Role in the Technetronic Era*. The term "Technetronic" refers to the manner in which societies are shaped politically, legally, economically, financially, psychologically, and culturally by the impact of technology, especially electronic technology. However, instead of having the foregoing sorts of impact occur in unpredictable and uncontrolled ways, the Trilateral Commission was created in order to bring order to the process of change that was to take place through the use of technology.

Brzezinski believed that systems such as socialism and communism were merely stop-gap measures that arose on the way to the sort of economic system that needed to emerge in conjunction with the impact of technology. Some people – for example, Klaus Schwab, the founder and Executive Chairman of the World Economic Forum – refer to the aforementioned economic system as the "Fourth Industrial Revolution"

The first industrial revolution concerned the emergence of the steam engine and the impact which that discovery and its various applications had upon society. The second industrial revolution arose with the advent of the electrification of businesses, societies, and individuals. Finally, the third industrial revolution became established through the digitalization of many aspects of life that occurred in conjunction with the introduction of computers and other related forms of electronic technology.

The fourth industrial revolution seeks to fuse quantum computing, artificial intelligence, robotics, genetic engineering, nanotechnology, medicine, and other kinds of physical and biological technology into a unified, ordered framework of economic, social , legal, and political connectivity within which human beings will be induced to move and exist. Moreover, this fourth industrial revolution will operate in accordance with an array of partnerships involving private entities (i.e., corporations) and public agencies (i.e., various forms and levels of governance).

In the book, *Technocracy:: The Hard Road To World Order*, Patrick Wood indicates that the notion of technocracy predates, on the one hand, Brzezinski's aforementioned work which, as indicated previously, introduces the term: "Technetronic Era" and, on the other hand, the idea of technocracy also predates the advent of the Trilateral Commission. Thus, Patrick Wood notes that in 1932 Nicholas Butler, who at the time was President of Columbia University, released a public statement announcing the intention of the university to lend its full support to a new economic system that was being, and would continue to be, designed as well as implemented by an array of engineers and scientists and that the forthcoming system would replace all previous systems of economics, including socialism, communism, and capitalism.

The system would be known as "technocracy". Brzezinski's notion of the "Technetronic Era", Klaus Schwab's Fourth Industrial Revolution, and the Trilateral Commission's notion of economic globalism were just variations and elaborations of that original concept of technocracy. Irrespective of the term or terms that have been used, the operating system that is held in common by each of the foregoing treatments of technocracy is the idea that scientists and engineers would, supposedly, solve the political, legal, economic, and social problems of the world within a framework of unified government that was to be directed by the dynamics of technocratic understanding and organization.

In effect, technocracy was a system of social engineering. According to technocracy, one of the ways in which society could be engineered would be through the manner in which goods and services would be generated by, and distributed among, the people of the world, and, therefore, seen from that perspective, technocracy was an economic theory that would use the methods and discoveries of scientists and engineers to determine not only how goods and services would be produced and distributed, but, as well, the purposes to which such goods and services should be directed.

Although what Patrick Wood says in his aforementioned book is in line with some of the historical sources that he cites in his work, nonetheless, Patrick Wood tends to restrict, if not reduce, the idea of technocracy to being merely a system of economics, and doing so seems to distort and obfuscate the extent of the social engineering which modern proponents of technocracy appear to have in mind. In other words, however technocracy might have been conceived of originally, nonetheless, currently, technocracy gives expression to a system of dynamic organization that seeks to fuse corporations and legal/constitutional agencies into a network of fascist rule that seeks to take the ideas, beliefs, values, theories, methods, and creations of scientists as well as of engineers and impose those conceptual products onto the members of society without the informed consent of the latter and, in the process, technocrats seek to re-shape, in fundamental ways, the understanding, existential orientation, and activities of people concerning what they believe to be the nature of their relationship with Being and Reality.

As such, technocracy seeks to control what and how people think, feel, and act. Indeed, the extent of the social engineering that is entailed by technocracy transcends the production and distribution of goods and extends into issues of purpose, belief, values, aspirations, motivations, psychology, philosophy, religion, law, governance, culture, and society.

Technocrats wish to re-fashion human beings in accordance with the way in which such technocrats wish to fuse an array of digital, physical, and biological considerations. For example, the transhumanist dimension of technocracy maintains that the present state of the human species is not an end point but, instead, is merely a way station along an evolutionary path through which human beings can be transformed into a novel species that is augmented in different ways through applying to the human condition various techniques of genetic engineering, nanotechnology, pharmaceuticals, artificial intelligence, and other forms of technology to human beings.

The foregoing possibilities give expression to what might be technically possible, either now, or in the future. However, neither technocracy, nor its transhumanist dimension, nor any of the other facets of technology which various technocratically-inclined individuals are advocating, actually rigorously address whether any of the foregoing technocratic aspirations should be pursued, or whether such would-be social engineers have a viable way of justifying (that is, by means of something that is other than through methods which are tautologically self-serving) their desire to impose their philosophical, religious, political, economic, financial, medical, pharmacological, psychological, and legal system onto others through a fascist system of control that undermines the sovereignty ability of people – both individually and collectively – to place limits on what is being done to the general population.

Even more importantly, technocrats are inherently incapable of resolving the problem of how to deal with the unforeseen consequences of their actions – which there always are – because the very nature of such consequences is that they are unforeseen, and, therefore, cannot be planned for ahead of time. The foregoing sorts of unforeseen consequences tend to give expression to Black Swan events that evade, in catastrophic ways, one's ability to predict and control, and the collateral damage that ensues from such events is just one of the forms of pollution that are generated by technocracy ... forms of environmental damage (including damage to human beings) for which technocracy has an extremely poor record of handling in ways that do not just add to environmental problems rather than resolve those issues in a constructive fashion that is to everyone's benefit.

According to Patrick Wood, ideas such as "sustainable development," "Technetronic Era," "global warning," "one world government," "globalization," "Transhumanism," "Agendas 21 and 30," as well as the "Fourth Industrial Revolution" are all different manifestations of the notion of "technocracy". The foregoing ideas have been, and are being, pushed by a variety of organizations such as: The League of Nations (introduced in 1920), the United Nations (first instituted in 1942), The Bilderberg Group (established in 1954), The World Economic Forum (founded in 1971), the Trilateral Commission (formed in 1973), The William J. Clinton Presidential Foundation (originally formed in 1997 but in 2013 was renamed the Bill, Hillary, and Chelsea Clinton Foundation), The Open Society Foundation (established by George Soros in 1998), The Bill and Melinda Gates Foundation (launched in 2000), as well as a number of corporations involving Big Tech (e.g., Google), Big Finance (e.g., BlackRock, Vanguard, or State Street Bank), Big Pharma (e.g., Pfizer, Moderna, Johnson and Johnson, AstraZeneca, etc.), as well as a variety of organizations/corporations that are involved in different aspects of security – including biosecurity – along with an array of activities involving intelligence gathering, data crunching, and surveilling human beings (e.g., via social media, facial recognition, digital passports, and so on).

The methodologies of technocracy are intended to measure – in arbitrary and, therefore questionable ways (for example, as a function of the notion of 'efficiency') everything which human beings: Produce, buy, consume, use, desire, observe, communicate, learn, feel, think, and do. Such information will be used by technocrats to induce human beings (through a combination of rewards and punishments) to comply with all aspects of technocracy, and, thereby, cede their agency to a system that wishes to dictate to human beings what the nature of our relationship with Being or Reality is or can be. The foregoing agenda will be generated through the Internet of Things as well as codified within so-called Smart Cities that are intended to be made tractable and capable of being processed by algorithmically-driven technologies like 5G and beyond.

From technocrats arises the web of permissible degrees of freedom and constraints that will define the sort of existence that human beings will be permitted to have. From technocrats emerge -- in best tradition of Orwellian forms of Newspeak -- the arbitrary definitions, characterizations, and meanings that words and thoughts can assume for human beings. One's understanding of existence, reality, Being, life, identity, purpose, justice, morality, duties of care, law, and potential will be assigned to those who manage to survive the transition period through which technocracy becomes established, and as far as the issue of managing to survive is concerned, a number of proponents of technocracy are calling for the elimination of nearly 7 billion human beings.

Given the foregoing considerations, technocracy and its web of technological pathways will become the only sort of reality with which human beings will be permitted to develop a relationship. The Reality that makes life and human potential possible, as well as makes possible the lives and potential of all other beings, phenomena, and dimensions of existence will become only what technocracy and technocrats say it is or can be.

During the course of Patrick Wood's book -- *Technocracy: The Hard Road To World Order* – he details many of the twists and turns that the unfolding of technocracy has taken since the 1930's when the term first came into currency – details that are far too extensive in number to be able to encompass within the present, relatively abbreviated work -- and to that end, the aforementioned book is well worth reading. However, there is one further idea that Patrick Wood touches on during the course of his foregoing work which is important and actually ties the idea of technocracy back to the discussion with which the current conceptual journey began, and this concerns the ideas of framing analysis and palimpsest.

About half way through his book, Patrick Wood mentions the term "infrastructure" in conjunction with the issue of Supply Chain Management. According to him, infrastructure has two important functions to perform: namely: (a) it must be able to efficiently move resources and necessary materials to places that manufacture and assemble such resources and materials into finished products of one kind or another, and (b) the infrastructure must be able to deliver such goods in a timely and efficient manner to consumers.

Patrick Wood points out that when governments communicate to their citizens about the issue of infrastructure, this is done in a context where people are induced to believe that those types of projects have to do with building highways and bridges, or fixing potholes, or improving sewage systems, or providing enhancements to the delivery of clean water. However, Patrick Wood goes on to say that when globalists and technocrats refer to infrastructure they tend to mean something that is very different from the way in which citizens have been led to understand the notion of infrastructure.

More specifically, technocrats and globalists see infrastructure as the system that ties the world together in a functionally efficient way that is capable of serving the needs of chain supply management with respect to the resources and materials that need to be gathered and delivered to places of manufacture and assemblage so that finished goods can be delivered to consumers in a timely fashion. In order to be able to accomplish the foregoing infrastructure functions, resources, corporations, financing, workers, manufacturing, transportation, consumer outlets, communication, legal issues, and different levels of governance must all be controllable.

As such, infrastructure is not just about manufacturing, transportation, and consumption. Rather, infrastructure functioning has to do with the entire network of social institutions (both private and public) that make the foregoing sorts of functions possible. Allowing nations and/or individuals to have sovereignty tends to interfere with the efficiency with which such an infrastructural system works, and this is why technocracy and technocrats seek to undermine and eliminate any potential for sovereignty among nations and/or individuals because the presence of such sovereignty is perceived by technocrats as having the potential to interfere with the efficient functioning of infrastructure as a global system of control which takes resources from raw materials to finished, manufactured products that can be made available to consumers in a timely fashion.

In light of the foregoing considerations, infrastructure is not just about highways and potholes, but it is also about the form of the global system that the technocrats consider necessary for society to be able to function effectively and efficiently. Moreover, in order to engage the notion of infrastructure in terms of its more global system for managing the supply chain of resources, manufactured products, and modes of distribution to consumers as outlined previously, one begins to realize that, for the technocrat, the notion of infrastructure encompasses all manner of: Scientific, educational, financial, political, philosophical, legal, methodological, environmental, social, cultural, militaristic, religious, medical, and media forms of activities.

In order for technocrats to be able to do what they want to do, everything must become an efficient, working, compliant cog within infrastructure operations so that the supply chain of goods and services can be properly – that is efficiently – run. Anything which undermines or interferes with such infrastructure operations will adversely affect efficiency.

By necessity, technocrats must impose their understanding of infrastructure on everyone and everything if their system is to operate in the way that they envision. This means that the infrastructure which the technocrats wish to impose on people must become a Leviathan-like palimpsest that covers over, obliterates, and obfuscates every trace of the original existential manuscript with which human beings came into this world.

Technocrats need to set the degrees of freedom and constraints that are available for the sorts of framing analysis that can be used by any individual or group of individuals, for if they do not set such limits, their system cannot function in the way they wish the system to function. Under technocracy, framing analysis can never be permitted to be pursued to a sufficiently rigorous extent that would enable a person to work toward discovering the possible character of one's essential nature independently of the infrastructure palimpsest and systems of framing that technocrats insist be imposed on every human being and through which their experiences are to be forcibly filtered.

Technocracy – and, therefore, technocrats -- will not permit human beings to explore any modality of framing analysis that would enable individuals to come to understand the differences between possible fabrication and possible truth. As noted earlier, fabrication has to do with the generation of mis-framed instances of experience that lead to false beliefs about the character of one's relationship with reality, whereas truth is what the actual nature of reality gives expression to and which we try to engage, to varying degrees, through our conceptual, emotional, behavioral, psychological, social, and spiritual activities.

Unfortunately, technocrats cannot see, or do not tend to have insight into, anything which lies beyond the boundaries that are set by what technocracy requires for its system to be able to effectively continue in order to be able to control what people think, feel, say, and do. All that technocrats can perceive is in accordance with the quality of the light that is given off by technocracy's notion of economic efficiency, along with its quantitative, arbitrarily construed, utilitarian notion of whatever is considered to constitute the greater good.

As such, to say that arbitrary conceptions of economic efficiency or the alleged greater good should become the only permissible modalities for engaging – whether individually or collectively -- the nature of our relationship with reality is like saying that the only form of music that should be permitted as a metric for evaluating the quality and worth of the melodies and instrumentation entailed by classical, jazz, rock and roll, pop, rap, hip hop, blues, religious, spiritual, or musical offerings from different cultures must be some sort of elevator Muzak. Reality is calling to us to explore its complex potential as well as is calling us to explore our complex relationship with it, but all technocracy has to offer is an existential and epistemological cul-de-sac enclosed within a dazzling – but toxic -- array of technological sweet nothings whose only purpose is to control, oppress, and destroy whatever comes into its spheres of influence.

Day after day, technocracy is busily going about its mundane business of generating newer and newer modes of oppressive and controlling technological palimpsests that are being imposed on human beings in the attempt to erase the message of our original, essential nature or fitra and replace it with a counterfeit message that serves the interests of the technocratic overlords. To preserve one's humanity in the face of such a destabilizing assault upon our souls – both individually and collectively -- one has no choice but to become equally busy in the search for whatever tools of 'framing analysis' that one can find (whether scientific, methodological, philosophical, medical, psychological, political and/or spiritual in nature) which might offer one some kind of constructive assistance with respect to developing a capacity for acquiring the quality of discernment or de-framing that is necessary to be able to constructive meet the challenge of learning how to tell the difference between frames of understanding that are fabricated (by ourselves and/or others) and frames of understanding that resonate in essential ways with the properties of reality, and as such, are important way stations in the human journey toward realizing, in part or more completely, the nature of one's relationship with reality.

Contrary to the claims of Patrick Wood, technocracy is not just an economic system. Rather, technocracy is a system of total control in which economics of a certain kind has a role to play as part of that system's dystopian sense of order. Within that system of oppression, human beings (at least those who are not in control) are nothing more than deposable resources, of a sort, whose sole function is to maintain, protect, promote, repair, and serve such a system in order to ensure that it continues on in the prescribed manner.

Technocrats often seem to believe they are deriving order from chaos. In reality, however, technocracy is merely an elaborate, technologically based and algorithmically driven form of coping mechanism that, among other things, seeks to limit the unknown nature of future experiences as well as to limit where the latter might lead if those experiences were engaged by minds, hearts, and souls that aspired to seeking the truth concerning the nature of their relationship with reality rather than being forced to comply with an oppressive system of technocratic delimitation that exists only to serve the existential insecurities, impoverished set of interests, and psychological deficits of the overlords who have assigned to themselves the task of ensuring that everyone operates in accordance with the notion of order with which the technocratic overlords -- in a completely self-serving manner -- feel most comfortable.

Allopathic medicine has come to play a fundamental role in the technocrats desire to establish a theocracy in which all that is considered to be sacred, deserving of reverence, worthy of being bound to -- and the ultimate, absolute source of one's sense of duty, obligation, and morality -- is a function of a technology that is to be imposed on individuals quite independently of any considerations of informed consent. The proof of the foregoing claim can be found in the details of the alleged COVID-19 pandemic in which medical technocrats sought to claim that everyone should treat unjustifiable proclamations of the alleged medical "experts" concerning PCR tests, the wearing of masks, social distancing, lockdowns, as well as their forced mandates involving treatments (whether through mRNA jabs or the use of remdesivir and respirators in hospitals) that were shown, again and again, to be agents of unsafe, ineffective, and averse, if not fatal, outcomes [for further details in support of the foregoing claims, please see my book: *Observations Concerning My Encounter With COVID-19 (?)* In addition, in order to provide a somewhat broader perspective concerning allopathic medicine and a few related issues, one might take a look at: *Explorations in Medicine, Evolution, and Mind*].

During the course of the so-called COVID-19 pandemic, fundamentalist proponents of, and evangelical shills for, allopathic medicine have managed to turn the two-weeks that were said to be needed to flatten the curve into a three-plus year adventure in which such intellectually and emotionally challenged individuals sought to exploit every: Institutionally rooted, media-based, governmental-related, corporate-oriented, educationally biased, and arbitrary form of medical science to engage in a process of fabrication that has unnecessarily destroyed the lives, finances, and sovereign rights of millions of human beings in order to protect society from an alleged "virus" which – even if one granted them their fairy tales concerning so-called infectious diseases – constituted a potential (but not necessarily an actual) threat to a miniscule part of less than one percent of the people.

2. Climate Delusional Syndrome

In 1957, my family moved from a city of some 10,000 people in Western Maine to a small, rural community in north-central Maine which was less than one-tenth the size of my previous home city. The move took place in the summer prior to my entering the eighth grade.

In order to make some money, I took over a paper route that delivered the *Bangor Daily News* to individuals in my new rural area. The newspaper was one of the major dailies for the state of Maine.

The year after I began delivering the paper, the *Bangor Daily News* ran a contest for its newspaper carriers. The winners would be those individuals who were most successful in increasing the subscription base for their respective routes over a given period of time – and, I seem to recall there were five, or so, youngsters from seven or eight Maine counties who were subsequently announced as winners of the competition.

To make a longer story much shorter, I was one of the winners. The winning prizes involved receiving an all-expense paid trip to Boston for a few days to attend a Boston Celtics basketball game and, thus, have an opportunity to watch a number of future Hall of Famers play, including Bob Cousy, Tommy Heinsohn, Sam Jones, Frank Ramsey, Bill Russell, Bill Sharman, Arnie Risen, and Andy Phillip.

As exciting as the foregoing aspect of the trip was, it does not play a prominent role in why the present anecdote is being transmitted. This latter dimension of the trip arrived around 2:00-3:00 a.m. in the morning following the night of the aforementioned game.

The television in the hotel room was on. We had been watching a science fiction film and the other kids had fallen asleep.

I was the only one awake when a second feature -- "*Invasion of the Body Snatchers*" -- began to run. I was intrigued by the movie and stayed up to watch it while the other kids were sleeping.

For those who are unfamiliar with the movie, it begins with a psychiatrist being called in to consult on a case in which an individual has an incredible story to tell, and the task of the psychiatrist is to determine whether, or not, the individual is crazy, delusional, or sane. The person being examined is a medical doctor -- Miles Bennell (played by Kevin McCarthy) – who has been living in a small California community by the name of Santa Mira.

The movie is mostly devoted to the doctor's recounting of his story concerning the alleged invasion of his community by an alien form of life (pod plants) which, supposedly, has the ability to replace the bodies of humans and retain all the memories of the humans that are being "snatched" through this transformation process. However, the alien life forms seem to lack the capacity for certain emotions such as love.

Toward the end of the movie, when the doctor has finished his story, a doctor from the hospital privately confers with the psychiatrist who has been asked to offer a professional opinion concerning the case. They both have come to the conclusion that Miles Bennell is suffering from some sort of psychotic break with reality.

As the two doctors are about to discontinue their conversation, casualties from a highway accident are being wheeled down a corridor near to where the two doctors have been talking. One of the two doctors makes inquiries concerning what has happened.

The doctors are told that a truck had overturned on a nearby highway and had spewed the strangest looking pods all over the highway – the sort of pods about which Miles Bennell had been describing in his tale, When one of the doctors asks where the truck was coming from, they are told: "Santa Mira," and, almost immediately, the two doctors realize the significance of what they are being told when considered in the context of the story which they just have been told by Miles Bennell.

Human beings often operate on the basis of a dynamic which is known as "consensual validation". In other words, if a person has doubts about the nature or reality involving some aspect of experience, then, quite frequently, the tendency of human beings is to seek out the opinions of fellow human beings with respect to what the latter individuals might think concerning the nature of the experiences which are being filtered through an individual's retelling of certain life events as allegedly experienced by the account-giver.

The two doctors who listen to the experiences that are being related by the character, Miles Bennell, proceed to subsequently arrive at their diagnosis concerning the mental state of the story teller, not on the basis of facts but, rather, on the basis of their own previously developed sense of "consensual validation" concerning the nature of reality that has been built up over the course of their lives via interactional experiences involving: Parents, siblings, relatives, neighbors, school mates, friends, work colleagues, professional people of one kind or another, processes of formal education, books read, radio programs heard, television news shows watched, and so on.

The consensual validation out of which the two consulting doctors were operating in the aforementioned movie had no room for the possibility of alien life forms (pod plants) which could take over or replace a human being. As a result, initially, they discounted the story of Miles Bennell until they were introduced to certain facts – namely, the highway accident involving a truck carrying strange pod plants coming from Santa Mira that independently appeared to corroborate certain aspects of the story which they had just heard.

Of course, if the two consulting doctors in the movie had been provided with additional script-time through which they were enabled to come into contact with new information that emerged after being told about the highway accident, and if the new data was, in some way, inconsistent with the information that had come into play at the end of the movie, then, the two doctors might have reached some conclusion other than one involving the idea that, indeed, human beings were, indeed, being invaded by alien body snatchers and which brought the movie to a close. For example, perhaps, the pod plants which seemed so strange to one person might have been common knowledge and not considered to be all that strange to someone who knew about certain kinds of exotic agricultural crops which were being grown in the area or who knew that a legitimate, plant-based industry of some kind had sprung up in the Santa Mira area relatively recently.

Alternatively, while the direction in which the ill-fated truck had been travelling in the movie might have been moving away from the area where Santa Mira was geographically located, nonetheless, there could have been any number of other routes in the area between the accident and Santa Mira which were linked to towns and cities other than Santa Mira and which fed into the highway where the accident took place. However, given that the person who has been watching the movie has been living the invasion of the body snatchers through the eyes of the Kevin McCarthy character, then, the information about the highway accident involving strange pod plants which were said to have been coming from Santa Mira tends to be interpreted by the two consulting doctors as constituting a form of confirmation of the story that the Kevin McCarthy character has been telling.

Finally, one should also leave a few degrees of freedom for the possibility that although the viewer of the body-snatcher movie has been witnessing things from the perspective of the central character in that film -- namely, Kevin McCarthy (actor) aka Miles Bennell (movie character) – and, in the process, the viewer has been led -- by the script writer and movie director -- to believe that everything being recounted by the central character is an accurate depiction of events as they happened. Notwithstanding the foregoing considerations, perhaps, one should leave room for the possibility that one is being manipulated by the script writer and director to adopt an invented worldview which, in actuality, gives expression to someone's psychotic break with reality (whatever that might be) and, therefore, none of what is being described by that character actually took place or didn't take place in the way in which it is being remembered by the Kevin McCarthy character – sort of like the way in which the viewing audience is, for a time, taken for an illusory ride by Ron Howard in the movie: *A Beautiful Mind*, and, as a result, one is led to believe that what the Russell Crowe character – John Nash – is experiencing in the first part of the movie actually took place in a world which has been framed or presented as having been "real" when this was not the case (the experiences were real, but they were hallucinatory delusions and had no actual counterpart in the world outside of the mind of John Nash.)

The fact that many of us tend to seek out sources of consensual validation as a way of allaying whatever doubts we might have about a given set of experiences does not mean that the process of consensual validation will necessarily give expression to the truth or help one arrive at the truth in relation to any given topic. Seeking consensual validation is a form of coping mechanism which is intended to help one deal with whatever uncertainties, reservations, anxieties, concerns, fears, and doubts that might have arisen within one in conjunction

| Technological Reflections |

45

with a given set of circumstances, and, consequently, that dynamic is not necessarily geared toward uncovering the truth but, instead, is directed toward acquiring some sort of existential and/or hermeneutical stability concerning one's relationship with experienced reality.

If the individual (or individuals) whom one approaches during the process of consensual validation has (or have) a problematic relationship with reality (maybe, for example, they are addicts or are part of a cult or are involved in perpetrating -- in some way, such as a prank -- the very issues about which one is discussing), then, while what is said during such interchanges might alleviate the fears, anxieties, uncertainties, and so on which have arisen within one in relation to a certain experience or set of experiences one has encountered, then, one might be no closer to the truth of a matter at the end of such a conversation than one had been prior to seeking some form of consensual validation. The fact a group of people believe 'something' to be true does not necessarily make that something true, which is why science is not about consensus, per se, but involves a much more complex process of on-going: Observation, experimentation, methodology, instrumentation, measurement, analysis, critical reflection, and replication.

Let's assume that you – the reader – have been called in as a consultant to make a judgment about a rather incredible story that is being told by various individuals who have come to your place of work in order to try -- like the Miles Bennell movie character -- to warn the world about an impending disaster. The individuals with whom you are speaking indicate that the world is at a tipping point which -- unless human beings collectively take the appropriate sort of corrective actions -- will lead to: Increasing atmospheric temperatures, extreme forms of weather, melting ice caps and glaciers, as well as rising oceans – all of which could lead to the destruction of much, if not most of, life on Earth, and that the apocalypse which is about to descend is the result of human-caused activity.

More specifically, so-called "greenhouse gases" – especially carbon dioxide, but including, as well, methane and nitrous oxide – are being generated to such an extent by various forms of human activity (e.g., via industry, recreation, agriculture, economics, transportation, culture, technology, as well as energy generation and consumption) that the aforementioned greenhouse gases are reaching untenable levels which already are causing considerable damage, with more to come in lethal forms of global warming, rising oceans, extreme weather, as well as playing a role in the emergence of new forms of pandemic diseases. One is being told that the situation is so dire that if constructive steps are not taken immediately to counter the aforementioned generation of greenhouse gasses, then, within ten years, human beings and much of the rest of life on Earth might well become extinct, and if not extinct, then, they will become extremely compromised with respect to the kinds of lives that might be lived by their offspring.

According to the hypothetical story that is being related to the reader, every human being has a moral responsibility to reduce his, her, or their carbon footprint – that is, the extent to which a person's lifestyle (including: Work, entertainment, hobbies, dietary habits, traveling, energy use, and medical condition) generates either carbon dioxide or some equivalent form of greenhouse gas which, for ease of computation and establishing a common form of measurement, can be converted into a carbon dioxide equivalency figure. Furthermore, the foregoing situation is so fraught with danger for all life on Earth, that if people are not willing to freely observe their ecological responsibilities to one another, then, different forms of: Political, economic, medical, military, financial, and/or social sanctions must be used to ensure that people do the things that are necessary to save the Earth's inhabitants, whether human or non-human, and such actions, should they be needed, will require various levels of government to: (1) Establish a one government world; (2) re-organize community life into a series of fifteen-minute cities in which one's movements, activities, and sovereignty will be closely surveilled and severely restricted; (3) introduce central bank digital currency as a way of keeping tabs on how people spend money as well as a way of regulating how money is spent (using one's carbon footprint as an index measure), and, consequently, will serve as the method through which to modulate the lives of those who say or do socially, politically, or medically discordant things; (4) provide forms of public health based on whatever medical procedures are deemed to be appropriate by ruling authorities in order to protect the community, and this will be done without people's informed consent; (5) arrange an array of private-public forms of association from which most people will be excluded and which will entitle those institutional arrangements to have total authority and control over every aspect of the lives of individuals; (6) place all of the foregoing considerations under the supervision of different forms of artificial intelligence into which certain people will be assimilated, via transhumanist methods, in order to serve the needs of such a network of public-private arrangements.

At the epicenter of the conceptual earthquake which is being described is a shifting set of tectonic-like plates involving the alleged relationship between the amount of carbon dioxide which is present in the atmosphere and the purported impact of that gas's presence on environmental temperatures. Supposedly, increases in levels of carbon dioxide lead to increases in environmental temperature, and once a certain tipping point is reached, global warming and destructive forms of climate change will – allegedly -- become unstoppable and irreversible.

What follows is the equivalent of being told that there has been an accident on the highway and some strange pod plants have been strewn about at the scene of the accident and, furthermore, the truck, supposedly, was coming from the direction of Santa Mira. The task of the reader is to try to make sense of the information which is about to be provided when considered in relation to the story that has been told about global warming and determine whether, or not, this new information is consistent with the global warming story and, in addition, whether, or not, that information lends credibility to the global warming narrative as well.

The atmosphere consists of: 78% nitrogen, 21% oxygen, .93% Argon, and approximately .07% greenhouse gases (that is, just 7 hundredths of one percent). 95% of the foregoing .07% greenhouse gas figure is in the form of water vapor (100% - 99.93 = .07 x .95 = .0665% of total set of atmospheric gases), and water vapor is rarely, if ever, mentioned in global warming models even though it accounts for 95% of the greenhouse gasses in the atmosphere.

The percentage breakdown of the remaining 5% of greenhouse gasses is as follows: 99.44% CO_2 (or .9944 x .07 = .00696% of total atmospheric gases); .47% methane (or .0047 x .07% = .000329% of total atmospheric gases); .08% N_2O – nitrous oxide – (.0008% x .07% = .000056% of total atmospheric gases). So, according to the account being given, if the % of CO_2 were to increase – which, currently, is being measured at .00696% of the total amount of atmospheric gases – – then, this would bring about an increase in environmental temperature of some amount.

Rather than using percentages, let's measure the amount of a greenhouse gas in terms of ppm (or parts per million). For instance, in 2017, the amount of CO_2 in the atmosphere was measured to be roughly 406 ppm.

Water vapor -- which accounts for 95% of all greenhouse gases -- measures approximately 30,000 parts per million in atmospheric samples. Water has more than 70 times the effect on atmospheric temperature as does CO_2, and, yet, no one talks about the problematic nature of our "water vapor footprint" and no one has gone to the trouble of developing a trading system of water vapor credits which can be swapped among governments, companies, institutions, and individuals.

The individual who is seeking to warn people about the perils of global warming indicates that if the parts per million of carbon dioxide continues to increase, and, in the process, brings about a temperature increase of 2-3 degrees Centigrade, then we all will be faced with a runaway greenhouse effect that will have catastrophic consequences for all life on Earth. Yet, studies have shown that over the last 570 million years, temperatures were, on average, ten degrees hotter than today, and, yet, life did not disappear, and, consequently, why should one suppose that even if a 2-3 degree increase in average temperature did occur (as a function of whatever set of forces), nonetheless, there is no historical evidence to suggest that this would bring an end to life.

Moreover, although CO_2 levels climbed between 1998 and 2015, there was no increase in average global temperature during that period of time and, in fact, if anything there was a slight cooling which took place. Therefore, if an increase in atmospheric CO_2-levels is supposed to lead to higher temperatures, then, why did the foregoing 17 year period not show any increase in average temperatures given that CO_2 levels increased throughout this period.

Technological Reflections

Moreover, the decade between 1930 and 1940 was among the hottest periods over the last 100 years. Yet, the levels of atmospheric CO_2 were much lower than they are currently.

On the other hand, during the 1960s and 1970s, average global temperatures were going down. Nonetheless, atmospheric levels of CO_2 increased throughout this period.

In order to identify something as the cause of something else, then, whenever the former "something" is present, then, there should be some corresponding change in the phenomenon that, supposedly, is being affected by the alleged causal agent. However, the foregoing data indicates that there have been times when, on the one hand, atmospheric levels of CO_2 have increased, and, yet, average global temperatures went down, while, on the other hand, there also have been periods when the average global temperature went up despite the fact that the levels of atmospheric CO_2 went down, and, therefore, in neither of the foregoing instances is there any evidence to indicate that atmospheric levels of CO_2 have a clear-cut causal impact on whether average global temperatures will go up or down.

If one takes a step, or two, back from the climate timeline in order to get a more inclusive historical view of what has gone on for millions of years, one finds that the evidence clearly indicates that, in general, there is no long-term data which is capable of establishing that increases in atmospheric levels of CO_2 lead to increases in atmospheric temperature. In fact, the opposite tends to be true – that is, increases in atmospheric CO_2 often follow – by 800 years or so – relatively lengthy periods of elevated atmospheric temperatures.

The 800-year differential has to do with the way in which water has a high specific heat (the amount of heat which must be added to one gram of a substance in order to raise the temperature of that substance by one degree Centigrade). As a result, because of its high specific heat, water tends to heat up and cool down much more slowly than do land masses which have been subjected to naturally caused, extended periods of elevated temperatures.

The rise in ocean temperatures which recently have been recorded gives expression to an 800-year time lag following the extended period of elevated temperatures which occurred during the Medieval Warm Period (approximately 900 CE to 1300 CE). The oceans – because of their high specific heat -- have taken this long to react to, or reflect, what transpired on land (i.e., higher temperatures) approximately 800 years ago.

Over a number of years, the recent heating up of the oceans in response to the extended period of relatively elevated temperatures which occurred during the Medieval Warm Period has resulted in an increase (in addition to the carbon dioxide which is normally released by the oceans) in the amount of CO_2 which have been released into the atmosphere from the oceans.

Only a very small amount of the aforementioned CO_2 that is being released by the oceans into the atmosphere is due to human activity. Furthermore, one should keep in mind that irrespective of whatever amounts of CO_2 that are being generated through human activity and, subsequently, are being released into the atmosphere via the heating up of the oceans, nevertheless, atmospheric temperatures went down in the 1960s and 1970s despite an increase in atmospheric levels of CO_2 and there was a period from 1998 to at least 2015 in which temperatures held steady despite increases in atmospheric levels of CO_2

The absence of any increase in average global temperatures during this interval was one of the reasons why there was a transition in vocabulary which emerged during this time frame – from: "global warming," to: "climate change." This is because (as will soon be demonstrated) when scientific evidence is properly used, it does not support the notion of global warming, while the idea of "climate change" is a much more nebulous term that could be used to help lend a certain amount of obfuscating camouflage to problematic theories since everyone agrees that climates change over time, but there are differences of opinion concerning what causes those changes.

One might also note that ice core samples are able to introduce some interesting data which reflects some of what took place climatically during the aforementioned Medieval Warm Period (approximately from 900 CE to 1300 CE). More specifically, various ice core samples indicate that atmospheric CO_2 levels during the aforementioned 400-year interval actually declined to a level that is less than is the case today even as the overall average temperatures during that period of time increased by several degrees.

Consequently, the whole notion of referring to certain gases as being greenhouse gases is essentially misguided. 'Greenhouses' are relatively closed-system structures consisting of a roof and walls made of glass which trap sunlight in the form of, among other things, heat.

The Earth's atmosphere, however, is a relatively open system in which much of the heat from the sun is reflected back into space. While some of the solar energy striking the atmosphere is retained for a relatively short period of time by atmospheric gases such as methane, water vapor, and carbon dioxide, nonetheless, this energy is eventually released.

In addition, if the aforementioned solar energy were not retained for a relatively short period of time and, in the process, translated into a certain amount of heat, then, the Earth's average temperature would be about 28 degrees colder than it currently is (i.e., 15 degrees Centigrade versus -13 degrees Centigrade) and, as a result, life would either have had to be very different than what is presently the case or life might never have come into existence in the first place because environmental conditions would have been antithetical to life's emergence. Consequently, referring to gases such as water vapor, carbon dioxide, and methane as greenhouse gases is, on several levels, inappropriate and misleading.

As touched upon earlier, many of the models that are used to support the idea of global warming omit water vapor despite the fact that this gas makes up 95% of all so-called atmospheric greenhouse gases and despite the fact that it has more than 70 times the impact on atmospheric temperatures than does carbon dioxide. Furthermore, there are a number of other factors that tend not to be present in global warming models which could affect both the levels of CO_2 in the atmosphere as well as average global temperatures.

For example, many global warming models only take into account the activity of volcanoes which are visible above ground while ignoring the fact that 85% of all volcanic activity (there are approximately 1,500 active volcanoes) occurs beneath the oceans, and this underwater activity leads, eventually, to considerable out-gassing, including CO_2, as the latter gas is released from the Earth's mantle through fissures in the tectonic plates. Moreover, many of those global warming models don't appear to give appropriate consideration to the way in which cosmic rays, ocean dynamics, earthquakes (there are more than 10,000 earthquakes a year which generate, among other things, CO_2), different modalities of cloud coverage (low and high cloud formations have different impacts on atmospheric temperatures), and aerosols (such as soot) affect either atmospheric temperatures or CO_2 levels, or both.

Oftentimes, a missing element from various global warming models – and is most glaring in its absence -- concerns the dominant role which the sun plays in climate formation and change. This would include the way in which orbital angles of our planet relative to the sun tend to vary over time and, as a result, affect what goes on in the Earth's atmosphere.

If one hopes to develop a model which accurately reflects the dynamics of climate change, then, that model needs to factor in all of the forces and phenomena which will affect climate change in different ways. By leaving out the aforementioned sorts of dynamics from a model that purports to provide an account for why global warming is allegedly taking place, then, such models can hardly be expected to yield anything but distorted and errant conceptions of what is supposedly being modeled ... i.e., climate change, global warming, and what impact, if any, that increases or decreases in atmospheric levels of CO_2 are having on global warming.

Over the last 150 million years, a variety of sampling techniques have indicated that atmospheric levels of CO_2 have been steadily decreasing. Those levels have ranged from a high of 6000 parts per million to a low of 180 parts per million (and a number of scientists have pointed out that if the parts per million content of CO_2 fell below 150 ppm, plants could not survive, and if plants could not live, then, neither could a great many kinds of other life forms).

The foregoing data establishes several points of reference. First, notwithstanding the existence of a high level (6000 parts per million of atmospheric CO_2) which occurred at some point during that 150 million year period, life did not end due to the presence of such elevated levels of CO_2. Therefore, when various individuals today busy themselves with issuing apocalyptic pronouncements concerning humanity's future because the amount of CO_2 in the atmosphere is 400-plus parts per million and increasing somewhat, then, such pronouncements need to be tempered with some degree of emotional moderation which comes from the realization that during the last 150 million years, there was a period of time when atmospheric CO_2 levels were more than 15 times greater than conditions today and, yet, all manner of life did not come to an end.

The second point of reference to be established in relation to the foregoing considerations is that levels of CO_2 go up and down over time as a result of a variety of factors – many of which are not even represented in many, if not most, of the global warming models. The levels of atmospheric CO_2 which exist today (400-plus parts per million) are substantially below the much higher levels of atmospheric CO_2 (6000 parts per million) which existed tens of millions of years ago and which did not lead to the end of life on Earth, nor is there any indication that such high levels of atmospheric CO_2 were related to near-extinction level events.

The climate.gov web site stipulates that there was an increase of 2.8 parts per million which took place between 2022 and 2023. The aforementioned web page also indicates that this is the 12th successive year in which the increase in atmospheric CO_2 has increased by more than 2 parts per million.

In 2017, the measured amount of atmospheric CO_2 was 406 parts per million. Therefore, if one were to add in the increases in atmospheric CO_2 that took place between 2017 and 2024 (and lets be generous and say that atmospheric levels of CO_2 increased by 3 parts per million per year), the atmospheric levels of CO_2 are now 427 parts per million, and, so, the moral of the government story is what?

There is no moral to the government story that is based on science. Given the aforementioned historical realities, documenting data concerning slight increases in atmospheric levels of CO_2 is relatively meaningless.

As shown previously, the atmospheric levels of CO_2 (irrespective of their source) CANNOT be causally tied to increases in global atmospheric temperature. However, increases in atmospheric temperatures CAN be demonstrated to be causally related to subsequent increases in levels of atmospheric CO_2, and, therefore, the

2-3 parts per million increases in CO_2 levels that are being noted by the government climate web page might well be the effect of increases in atmospheric temperature which are due to something other than elevated levels of atmospheric CO_2.

Furthermore, considerable scientific evidence exists which indicates there have been times when levels of atmospheric CO_2 were 15 times higher than presently is the case. Yet, all manner of organisms (both simple and complex) continued to live in the presence of such historically high levels of atmospheric CO_2.

In addition, scientific evidence has shown that during the last 400,000 years, average atmospheric temperatures have been measured to be anywhere from 9 degrees Centigrade colder than the average global temperatures of today, to 3 degrees Centigrade hotter than the average global temperatures of today. Moreover, scientific evidence also has indicated that the foregoing range of temperatures have been cycled through every 100,000 years, or so, during which time there have been four ice ages lasting some 50,000 years, or more, each, and that our current average global temperature is about 3-5 degrees Centigrade less than higher temperatures which were reached on five separate occasions previously during that 400,000 year period, and none of these latter periods of elevated temperature led to extinction level or near-extinction level events.

Moreover, when considered in the context of the last ten thousand years, the average atmospheric temperature of today is 1-2 degrees Centigrade cooler than the average atmospheric temperature for the rest of that ten thousand year period. To be sure, there are short periods of time during the last thousand years for which evidence exists that indicates how atmospheric temperatures have been slightly warmer than other periods during the modern era. Nevertheless, none of what is taking place currently falls outside the natural variability in atmospheric temperature that can be observed across thousands of years and which have extremely little, or nothing, to do with the levels of atmospheric CO_2 that might be present at any given time.

The "official" investigation into the issue of global warming began in 1988 with the emergence of the Intergovernmental Panel on Climate Change. The IPCC began with a biased mandate.

More specifically, the IPCC's understanding of "climate change" was tied arbitrarily – by members of the United Nations -- to the way in which human activities (especially in relation to the issue of atmospheric levels of CO_2) supposedly were altering the character of the Earth's atmosphere. As a result, IPCC researchers and scientists were only permitted to pursue the topic of climate change from the limited perspective of human activities related to greenhouse gases and were not permitted to investigate natural, non-human dynamics which might be contributing to changes in the properties of the atmosphere that were affecting climate in various ways, and, this is why – as noted previously – IPCC and global warming climate models are often missing – to the detriment of those models -- considerations involving natural phenomena such as: Solar cycles; earthquake dynamics; cosmic ray effects; volcanic activity; natural aerosol contributions – such as soot; orbital angles of the Earth relative to the sun; as well as the chemistry and physics associated with ocean dynamics.

The first report of the IPCC was released in 1995. After seven years of research involving many researchers and scientists (as noted earlier, the IPCC began in 1988), the initial report stipulated that although the climate was changing in various ways, nevertheless, there was no hard evidence to suggest that such transitions in climate could be traced to human activity.

Unfortunately, an ethically challenged and politically motivated member of the IPCC who had been given the responsibility to write a summary of the final report deviated substantially from what researchers had actually discovered and stated. Without providing evidence to back up such claims, this individual claimed there is a growing body of data which is demonstrating that human activity (in the form of greenhouse gases and sulfur aerosols) is responsible for certain changes in climate activity that were being observed.

Similar sorts of data manipulations, disinformation, and misinformation "tricks" have been performed in conjunction with the attempt to induce people to believe, for example, that a consensus of scientists or 97% of all scientists agree that on-going climate changes can be directly tied to the activities of human beings involving the generation of greenhouse gases. The foregoing 97% figure and associated "Consensus"-meme is based on four reports: (1) Naomi Oreskes -- "The Scientific Consensus on Climate Change: How Do We Know We're Not Wrong?" (2005); (2) Peter T. Doran and Maggie Kendall Zimmerman -- "Examining the Scientific Consensus on Climate Change," (2009); (3) William Anderegg, et. al., -- "Expert Credibility in Climate Change," (2010); (4) John Cook, et. al., -- "Quantifying the Consensus on Anthropogenic Global Warming in the Scientific Literature" (2013).

In 2014, a non-profit Canadian organization, *Friends of Science* -- whose membership consisted of retired earth and atmospheric scientists -- released a 51 page report entitled: "97% Consensus? No! Global Warming Math Myths & Social Proofs". Among other things, this study contained a critical examination of the four "Consensus" reports mentioned earlier in this essay.

The *Friends of Science* report provided a detailed analysis of how each of the four reports noted previously suffered from fatal methodological flaws that failed to properly reflect the views of a considerable number of individuals who were seriously engaged in climate research. In fact, on the basis of one, or another, questionable sampling or methodological decision, the four reports (each in its own manner) either failed to take into account, or significantly underrepresented, the views of climate scientists who were skeptical of the global warming claims and, as a result, the perspective of the latter researchers tended not to be properly represented in the aforementioned reports and, consequently, a distorted understanding of climate science was advanced through those four reports.

In short, the aforementioned *Friends of Science* study indicated that <u>none of the four reports</u> being critiqued <u>had put forth credible data or evidence</u> which was capable of tenably demonstrating: (a) There was a <u>consensus</u> among scientists concerning the alleged anthropogenic cause of global warming, or (b) the claims concerning the idea that <u>97% of scientists</u> had agreed that global warming was being caused by human beings were justified ... in fact, while there are researchers and scientists who do believe that global warming is caused by human activity and that such warming is due to the quantities of CO_2 which allegedly are being released into the atmosphere by that activity, nonetheless, the actual percentage of the foregoing sorts of researchers and scientists is far, far smaller than the aforementioned 97% figure.

For example, 31,487 scientists and researchers signed a 2007 petition which gave expression to an initiative that was seeking to counter the idea of human-caused global warming. Among other things, the foregoing petition stated that there is no credible evidence which has been brought forth within the scientific community that is capable of demonstrating how human-generated greenhouse gases -- such as carbon dioxide and methane – have caused, or will cause (in the future), catastrophic increases in atmospheric temperatures or bring about problematic changes in climate dynamics.

In 2008, The U.S. Senate Environment and Public Works Committee published a *Minority Report*. Among other things, the foregoing report took issue with a claim which had been made in an earlier report prepared by the House Select Committee on Energy Independence and Global Warming that there was a consensus among scientists with respect to the idea that human activity was causing an increase in greenhouse gases which was causing global warming to an extent that was capable of destroying the world.

The Senate *Minority Report* indicated how claims made with respect to the idea that a consensus existed among scientists concerning the manner in which human beings were responsible for the global warming that was capable of destroying the world were false. For example, the *Minority Report* pointed out that the contention of the IPCC that a consensus existed among scientists about the human cause of global warning was actually based on the activity of just 52 individuals who had engaged in a series of disinformation campaigns which used propaganda techniques to create the impression that their view was the view of most of the climate researchers and scientists in the world.

The Senate *Minority Report* countered the propagandized disinformation of those 52 individuals with the views of more than 650 international scientists and researchers who rejected the IPCC position that global warming existed or that human beings were responsible for having created something that did not exist. Many of the 650-plus individuals referred to in the *Minority Report* were neither Republicans nor Democrats, but, rather, they were scientists and researchers from countries such as: Japan, India, Canada, Russia, Norway, as well as from a number of other nations.

Furthermore, in 2012, 49 former employees of N.A.S.A. sent a letter to the foregoing agency indicating that a number of the agency's decisions were being made on the basis of climate models which were flawed in fundamental ways and, as a result, were leading to predictions that had turned out to be incorrect. Chances are that the reason why the foregoing 49 individuals felt sufficiently free to attach their names to such a letter is precisely because they were "former" employees rather than current employees because current employees who might have wanted to criticize their employers in conjunction with the climate models being used by N.A.S.A. that were leading to incorrect predictions might very likely have found themselves becoming former employees for voicing their professional opinions on matters that stepped on politically vested interests rather than scientific toes.

Finally, the previously mentioned *Friends of Science* report that was critical of the contention that there is anything remotely approaching a consensus concerning the cause of alleged global warming also indicated that there was a fundamental theme missing from each of the consensus articles as well as from many other studies which sought to demonstrate that human beings were the primary cause of global warming. More specifically, the studies to which reference was being made in the 2014 *Friends of Science* report seemed to be completely devoid of any understanding of, or insight into, the principle that the primary driver of climate change on Earth is the Sun, not humans, nor CO_2, nor other so-called greenhouse gases.

Another analytical report on the issue of consensus with respect to the issue of alleged human-caused global warming was released just prior to the 2014 *Friends of Science* study. This critical analysis was entitled: "Climate Consensus and Misinformation" and was authored by David Legates et. al.

Among other things, the Legates report indicated that following a review of the abstracts for nearly 12,000 scientific articles that had been published over a 21 year period (1991 to 2011) and which dealt with climate-related issues, only 3/10ths of one percent of those publications indicated any kind of support for the ideas that global warming had been taking place since 1950 and that such climate dynamics were caused by human activity. The foregoing data suggests that the 97% consensus figure might be overstated to a considerable degree, and, as such, gives expression to the property of agnotology – that is, the manner in which systemic ignorance tends to give expression to not only a basic lack of knowledge with respect to a given topic but tends to exhibit the dynamics of willful blindness as well as acts of intentional deception.

One might note in passing that issues of: Reliability, credibility, and validity do not occur only in conjunction with climatology. Similar sorts of problems exist in other fields as well, including virology (see *Follow the What? - An Introduction*, by Anab Whitehouse) and medicine.

For example, Marcia Angell served as the first woman editor-in-chief of the *New England Journal of Medicine*. She has stated that: "It is simply no longer possible to believe much of the clinical research that is published, or to rely on the judgment of trusted physicians or authoritative medical guidelines. I take no pleasure in this conclusion, which I reached slowly and reluctantly over my two decades as an editor of the *New England Journal of Medicine*."

Consequently, politics, money, ideology, and ego have corrupted many areas of research. The IPCC is only one small part of the problem.

The aforementioned "97%-consensus" notion resonates with two additional meme-like promotions that have played important roles in several other crises that temporally overlap, somewhat, with the global warming issue. Like the "97%-consensus" idea, these two other meme-like ideas give expression to perspectives that are constructed in deceptive, if not untrue, ways.

First, consider the following sentence: "The rate of addiction for patients who are treated by doctors is much less than 1%." The foregoing words were voiced by Alan Spanos, a medical doctor, during an advertisement for OxyContin.

That statement is based, in turn, on a four sentence 'letter-to-the-editor' which appeared in a 1980 issue of *The New England Journal of Medicine*. The letter had been written by Dr. Hershel Jick and Jane

Porter in reference to an informal study that had been conducted through the Medical Center affiliated with Boston University and which indicated that there had been only four cases of addiction-related issues associated with opioid usage among 12,000-plus patients who had been prescribed opioids by a doctor.

There are several problems with the way in which Purdue Pharma used information contained in the aforementioned four sentence letter. To begin with, whatever opioid medications were being prescribed through the Boston University Medical Center prior to 1980, those medications were not OxyContin (which hadn't, yet, been "invented"), and, therefore, there was no evidential basis for implying – as Purdue Pharma did in some of its promotional material -- that people would respond to OxyContin in the same way that the people who had been treated elsewhere had responded to opiates that were not OxyContin.

Secondly, the dosage of the opiates being prescribed for patients being treated through the Boston University Medical Center is unknown. Purdue Pharma, on the other hand, was manufacturing products that ranged in dosage from 10 mg up to 80 mg.

Therefore, one does not know what role, if any, dosage level played in the Boston University Medical Center report. Consequently, one is in no position to conclude that such dosage levels were comparable to the Purdue Pharma array of product dosages and whether, or not, products containing 20 mg, or more, in the Purdue Pharma line of products would have led to addiction issues.

So, when a television commercial for OxyContin has a medical doctor say that Purdue Pharma products "should be used much more than they are for patients in pain," such a statement is irresponsible. The foregoing statement is completely irresponsible because the basis of comparison which supposedly underlies the claim that the alleged "much less than 1% addiction" rate can legitimately be tied to Purdue Pharma OxyContin products is devoid of any evidence which can be shown to be clearly rooted in empirically demonstrated facts.

Thirdly, the aforementioned four sentence letter-to-the-editor was not making reference to a formal, double blind, control group study that had been conducted in relation to prescribed opiate use at the Medical Center affiliated with Boston University. However, even if that letter had been referring to the results of such a formal study, nevertheless, Pharma Purdue would have had to run a separate series of controlled studies to justify being able to make claims that its own line of opioid products was also less than 1% addictive, but Purdue Pharma never carried out such studies.

In 1992, *Time* magazine published an article entitled "*Less Pain, More Gain*" which referred to the Boston University Medical Center report on opioid addiction as being a "landmark study." Yet, Dr. Jick -- who referenced the foregoing informational exercise in his (and Jane Porter's) four sentence letter to *The New England Journal of Medicine* -- has difficulty remembering much about how the Medical Center report was put together, and, therefore, one can't help but wonder about the evidential basis for, or credibility of, the *Time* magazine claim that the aforementioned Medical Center report or study was landmark in some way.

The New England Journal of Medicine acknowledges that the foregoing letter-to-the-editor has been cited at least 400 times. Google Scholar indicates that the four sentence letter-to-the-editor had been cited more than 1,200 times.

For what is the aforementioned letter-to-the-editor being cited? Who is doing the citing and have any of those individuals actually engaged, and, then, critically examined, the data contained in the original report or study or whatever it was in relation to the opioids being prescribed to 11,000-plus patients at the Boston University Medical Center?

The less than 1% addiction rate being used in conjunction with OxyContin is like the 97% consensus figure being used in relation to global warming. Neither has any relation to real science, but both percentages are being cited as if the information to which they give expression is true, and, in the process, a lot of people's lives are being (and have been) either destroyed or are being upended in fundamental ways.

The 97% consensus figure in relation to the claim that the greenhouse gases being generated by human activity is causing global warming also resonates with another meme-like three word sentence: namely, "HIV causes A.I.D.S.". At one point during his career, Kary Mullis -- who had been awarded a 1993 Nobel Prize in chemistry for his invention of the PCR protocol -- was tasked with writing an article about HIV and A.I.D.S. and, as background for the paper, he began asking all manner of scientists and medical doctors about where one might find an article, study, or reference which demonstrated that HIV causes A.I.D.S. because he wanted to begin his paper with such a statement and be able to provide an appropriate citation.

The list of people whom he asked for such a reference (i.e., one which showed that HIV caused A.I.D.S.) included a future, fellow Nobel laureate, Luc Montagnier, who had been honored in 2008 for his alleged, earlier discovery of HIV. Montagnier couldn't provide Mullis with a reference concerning the alleged relationship between HIV and A.I.D.S. and, according to Mullis, Montagnier actually got upset with the question and abruptly walked away.

Later on, Montagnier appeared to distance himself from the idea that HIV caused A.I.D.S. . Instead, he adopted a fallback position which maintained that HIV must combine with some other, unknown, factor in order to bring about A.I.D.S., but this other, unknown co-factor has never been found, and, therefore, no one has been able to provide Kary Mullis with a citation or reference indicating that HIV causes A.I.D.S. .

Yet, despite a complete lack of evidence to justify making such a statement, the sentence – "HIV causes A.I.D.S." – is ubiquitous throughout the world. Similarly, statements to the effect that: "There is a 97% consensus among scientists that global warming is caused by the way in which human activity is generating increases in greenhouse gas emissions (such as CO_2), and this activity is contributing substantially to global warming" are ubiquitous throughout the world despite the fact there is no actual evidence which is capable of demonstrating that claims concerning a 97% consensus figure among scientists in conjunction with climate change are true.

In 2009, person, or persons, unknown hacked into the e-mail system for the Climate Research Unit at the University of East Anglia in the United Kingdom. More than a thousand e-mails were made public.

The hacked e-mails entailed considerable evidence indicating that various members of the IPCC (including members of the CRU at the University of East Anglia) were attempting to fraudulently convince the world that a consensus of scientists supported the claim that human activity was responsible for increasing the levels of greenhouse gases in the atmosphere. The narrative being manufactured by such people indicated that human-caused increases in greenhouse gases (especially CO_2) were inexorably leading the world toward an irreversible tipping point that would result in an apocalyptic future in which: Atmospheric temperatures would shoot-up precipitously and lethally; ocean levels all over the world would rise and inundate coastlines where the majority of the world's population live; extreme weather events (floods, hurricanes, droughts, tornadoes, blizzards) would become the norm and wreak havoc on civilization everywhere.

The hacked e-mails also contained evidence that various members of the IPCC were attempting to make sure that opposing viewpoints would not find their way into professional publications – that is, they were engaged in an array of activities that were directed toward censoring anyone who disagreed with the aforementioned "consensus narrative." In addition, those same members of the IPCC also were involved in attempts to make sure that any information which might have the potential to undermine their consensus-narrative would not become accessible to the public.

For instance, to accomplish data hiding, they talked about using "Mike's trick" in conjunction with various issues involving climate change. The "Mike" to whom reference is being made in the previous sentence, is Michael Mann, who, at the time, was on staff at Penn State University, and the "trick" to which reference is being made is the manner in which Professor Mann had decided to leave out tree ring data from 1961 onward that were inconsistent with his perspective (i.e., such data actually showed a decline in temperature) and, instead, replaced that data with thermometer readings which tended to be consistent with his position (i.e., that temperatures were rapidly increasing).

Professor Mann had used various statistical methods when preparing a 1999 paper which contained a graph in which average temperatures in the Northern Hemisphere were shown to be sharply rising within a very short period of time in the 20th century. Supposedly, this sharp rise in average temperatures was taking place before our very eyes and was occurring following a thousand year period in which available data (from indicated that average global temperatures had been fairly steady despite being interspersed, here and there, with occasional, slight upticks or downturns in average global temperatures.

The graph which Mann presented resembled, to some degree, a hockey stick in which the long handle part of that stick was a relatively horizontal straight line running along, but above (on the y-axis), the x-axis (representing time elapsed) which gave expression to a period of relatively stable temperatures. The stable temperature part of the hockey stick was, then, linked -- a short while later on the y-axis -- to the blade portion of the stick which rose sharply upward and represented, supposedly, a rapid increase in average temperatures in the Northern Hemisphere.

However, within the first three or four years that kicked off the 21st century, Richard A. Mueller, a professor of physics, later revisited Mann's original research and concluded that there were a number of problems with the statistical techniques and forms of analyses which were present in the Mann paper, and that Professor Mann's conclusions did not follow from the data he was using. In short, Professor Mueller indicated that while he agreed that the Earth had been going through a warming period for the last 100 to 150 years, nonetheless, this already had been known since 1980 and, therefore, Mann had not actually demonstrated anything new or different in this regard, and, perhaps, most importantly, Mann had not demonstrated that average temperatures in the Northern Hemisphere had risen in the way in which Mann claimed had been the case in his 1999 paper.

Furthermore, one might want to keep in mind that there are various problems inherent in the process of gathering raw data in relation to the issue of determining average global temperature. People in different locations go about measuring temperatures in different ways with different kinds of instruments, and, consequently, determining where, how, and under what circumstances such measurements are made will affect what sorts of meanings, significance, or weight can be assigned to those measurements.

For instance, if one takes temperature measurements near sources that are likely to radiate high heat – such as is generated through the urban heat island effect or in proximity to an airport where jets are taking off and landing all day long -- then one has to try to separate out the heat which is being generated by those sorts of surroundings from the heat that is being naturally generated as a result of climate. In addition, while there are proxy forms, or indirect modes, of measuring temperature -- such as when one uses data from, for example, ice cores, lake sediments, stalagmites, coral, glaciers, and so on to try to find temperature-related forms of data which are, to varying degrees, independent of one another and, therefore, can be used to either discount or corroborate other kinds of temperature measurements -- nonetheless, the downside to such proxy forms of indirect measurement is there can be considerable variability in how different people go about measuring and/or interpreting the significance or value of those sorts of proxy measurements.

Furthermore, there are some 40,000 temperature measuring stations around the world. If one is using only some of those stations, while ignoring measurements from other locations that might be inconsistent with the station measurements one is using, this, obviously, raises questions about the reliability of whatever conclusions one arrives at based on an unduly limited and/or biased sampling of those 40,000 stations.

There have been a number of attempts to replicate Mann's 1999 work and, as well, there have been claims that quite a few of those attempts at replication have been successful and, as a result, some individuals have concluded that Mann's "hockey stick" research has been vindicated. Professor Muller indicates, however, that he (i.e., Professor Muller) was a referee on a National Research Council (National Academy of Sciences) panel which studied a variety of issues entailed by Mann's work, but the panel had come to the conclusion that none of Mann's original research claims have been validated or corroborated.

In addition, as noted earlier, Professor Mann's findings were inconsistent with tree-ring data which appeared to indicate there had been a slight downturn of temperature at the same time that Professor Mann's graph indicated temperatures were rising precipitously. The "trick" which had been performed involved – as noted earlier -- eliminating data which was inconsistent with Professor Mann's perspective and replacing that data with readings from other kinds of measurement which were more favorable to the perspective which Mann was trying to advance.

However, let's assume that Professor Mann's claims were true – namely, that we have entered into an era of extraordinary climate warming (and Professor Muller stipulates that the National Research Council panel of which he was a member had found that Professor Mann's foregoing claim was not warranted). Even if one were to grant the foregoing conclusion, nevertheless, none of Professor Mann's presentation is capable of demonstrating that such warming had been caused by anthropogenic activity involving increases in the generation of greenhouse gases.

Six, or so, months ago, I watched a movie on PBS entitled "The Trick" which provided a dramatization of some of the problems that arose in conjunction with the hacking of e-mails at the Climate Research Unit at the University of East Anglia in the United Kingdom. Phil Jones – who was the head of the CRU at the time of the hacking episode – was depicted in the movie as someone who seemed to be so outraged and incensed by the allegations being made in conjunction with the hacked e-mails that he couldn't bring himself to talk about the issue other than to say that he had done nothing wrong.

Unfortunately, in my opinion, the sorts of information that were being disclosed through the hacked e-mails indicated that quite a few things were being done by various members of the IPCC which did not seem to be ethical or in the spirit of real science. At the end of the aforementioned movie, indications were given that the actions and perspective of Phil Jones, head of the CRU at the University of East Anglia, supposedly had been fully exonerated of any wrong doing.

Yet, I am having difficulty reconciling the idea of such exoneration with the manner in which various members of the IPCC were acting. They were actively engaged in: Trying to censor anyone who disagreed with them; or, were attempting to prevent people from being able to have papers published that dissented from the views of the CRU or the IPCC; or, were engaged in discussions that entertained methods for hiding relevant data; or, were resistant to the idea of sharing scientific data and information with individuals who held different views on climate change from the CRU and the IPCC; or, were referring to "Mike's trick" as if it were a legitimate form of objectively rigorous science rather than a way to ensure that one's conclusions would already be aligned, before the fact, with the data which was being selected.

Before the events of November 2009 had unfolded via the hacked e-mails of the Climate Research Unit at the University of East Anglia, Judith Curry had been chairperson of the Schools of Earth and Atmospheric Sciences at the Georgia Institute of Technology. She was a climatologist with interests in, among other things, climate and atmospheric modeling, and she had written over a hundred papers that were published in peer-reviewed journals.

She indicates that prior to November 2009 she had believed that there was a consensus among scientists concerning the issue of human-caused global warming. However, after she had an opportunity to peek behind the Oz-like curtain which had been made possible through the November 2009 e-mail hacking of the Climate Research Unit at the University of East Anglia and, as a result, she learned about the unethical and unscientific activity which was taking place through the IPCC, she realized that prior to the 2009 Climategate scandal she had been operating in accordance with a group think sort of mentality in which a person simply adopts a conceptual perspective without having exercised due diligence simply because one had been induced to believe, based on false testimony, that such a perspective was the consensus of thousands of scientists and researchers when, in fact, this was not the case.

Judith Curry was not the only individual who had to escape from an atmosphere of IPCC-oriented group think. Many other individuals – whether due to the revelations of the 2009 Climategate scandal or as a result of trying to resolve various issues related to climate research – also began to question the narrative which was being promulgated through the IPCC that human beings were responsible for global warming as a result of so-called greenhouse gases that collectively were being generated by humanity.

For example, Klaus-Eckert Puls – a German physicist who specializes in meteorology – indicated that, for a time, he had been a member of the IPCC choir with respect to singing the praises of the man-made global warming cantata. Nonetheless, at a certain point, he began to engage in some independent research and critical reflection concerning the IPCC perspective and discovered that much of what the

IPCC was proclaiming to be true was irreconcilable with a great deal of scientific data, especially in conjunction with the alleged relationship between CO_2 and the problematic notion of global warming.

Two years after the initial, 2009-release of hacked e-mails involving the Climate Research Unit at the University of East Anglia, a second batch of hacked e-mails was unleashed upon the world. This time around, there were more than 5,000 e-mails which were being disseminated (nearly five times as many e-mails as the first go around), and what was being revealed through this second batch of e-mails concerning the unethical and unscientific activities of various members of the IPCC were described as being even more unsettling than the first batch of hacked e-mails had been.

The communications in the second batch of e-mails indicated that the Intergovernmental Panel on Climate Change, which was a United Nations agency, was continuing to be deeply involved in a process of deception concerning the claim that human activity – in the form of so-called greenhouse gases such as CO_2 – was not only the predominate shaping force in the emergence and development of global warming which required immediate action if the world was not to be destroyed. Yet, despite the damning evidence concerning the manipulation of data, the censorship of opposing views, and the attempt to discredit anyone who opposed the IPCC position that was contained in the released e-mails, nevertheless, politics and money trumped science. As a result, the underhanded, duplicitous activities of various members of the IPCC were covered up and buried, and a massive propaganda program continued to be implemented which was intent on inducing people everywhere – scientist or non-scientist – to submit to the claim that human beings were the cause of global warming and that unless radical, dire actions were immediately undertaken, human beings would be in jeopardy of apocalyptic consequences.

One might point out in passing that the IPCC (which is an agency of the United Nations) is pushing an agenda which dovetails with the activities of another agency that is closely associated with the United Nations but is not actually an UN agency -- namely, the World Health Organization. The latter group's current full-court press activities are seeking to impose a draconian set of public health requirements and restrictions on the rest of the world through the amendments to the

International Health Regulations (amendments which entail degrees of freedom that will enable climate change to become a public health issue over which the W.H.O. has control).

Despite the fact that the group within W.H.O. (the International Negotiating Body) which is responsible for developing the amendment process has not abided by its own stated rules and, as a result, has failed to give nations sufficient advanced notice concerning amendment issues, the foregoing amendments are to be: Discussed, if not voted on, and, possibly, passed, during a forthcoming set of meetings (77th World Health Assembly) in Geneva that is taking place during the last few days of May 2024 as well as during the first few days of June 2024. Both the IPCC and the W.H.O. are seeking – each in its own manner -- to help establish a one-world government form of health religion, and the 77th World Health Assembly is part of that dynamic.

Both the IPCC and the W.H.O. have many, rabid, cult acolytes in different countries that are assisting the two aforementioned agencies in unethical and unscientific ways to realize their goal. This goal is rooted in a desire for world conquest and domination, and if one pays attention to what the IPCC and W.H.O. are doing, then, one can clearly see the presence of oppressive and tyrannical inclinations in their activities that are directed toward controlling, if not abolishing, the God-given sovereignty with which every human being is born.

Before bringing this essay to a close, a few words should be devoted to the strange fascination which many proponents of climate alarmism seem to have with the number 10. For instance, before global warming was the buzz word, there was concern about the issue of global cooling (which also was being blamed on CO_2 emissions).

Thus, during his 1970 observance of Earth Day, Dr. Kenneth Watt predicted that if chilling trends present at that time continued to assert themselves, then, one not only would witness a 4 degree drop in average global temperature over the next twenty years, but, there would be a further 7 degree plunge in average mean temperatures around the world during the ten year period between 1990 and 2000. Neither of the foregoing predictions turned out to be true.

In June of 1989, the New York director of the U.N.'s Environment Program declared that the governments of the world had just a ten-year period within which to successfully resolve the climate crisis or nations would be destroyed as a result of the consequences of global warming. To date, not one nation on the face of the Earth has suffered such a fate.

Approximately six months later, on December 5, 1989, the *Dallas Morning News* claimed that making certain predictions for the next decade (1989-1999) would be easy to make. The paper proceeded to indicate that the advent of global warming during that ten year period would "rekindle interest in cooler climates," but the prediction turned out to be more problematic and difficult than originally had been believed to be the case.

Meryl Streep served as host for a 1990, 10-part PBS series entitled: *Race to Save the Planet*. The program maintained that the average mean temperature of the world would increase by four degrees during the next ten years, and, spoiler alert, the prediction turned out to be incorrect to a considerable degree.

In the spring of 2001, CNN analysts claimed that the nine South Pacific islands of Tuvalu would all be beneath water in just ten years as a result of global warming. Nearly 17 years later, not only were the Tuvalu islands still above water but there was evidence to indicate that the surface area of the coral atolls had expanded in size.

ABC News jumped onto the ten-year meme bandwagon in 2007. It claimed that "we have ten years" to avert a global warming catastrophe. Once again, the prognostications turned out to be incorrect.

None of what has been said in the foregoing pages should be construed as indicating, suggesting, or implying that there are not a plethora of serious environmental problems which are threatening human existence as well as threatening the ecological systems where we participate in the gift of life. One major contributor to such environmental problems are the militaries of every single country on Earth, each of which claims to exist for the protection of the people but, in reality, all of them exist for the protection of financial institutions, corporations, and other vested interests that are antithetical to human sovereignty, and all of them are major sources of pollution and release of hazardous, toxic materials.

Another major contributor to environmental problems are the manufacturers and consumers of the many electronic devices, satellites, and systems of dirty electricity which have created an electromagnetic smog that envelops the Earth and is responsible for undermining life – both human and non-human. To the former modality of ubiquitous pollution, one can add the issue of micro-plastics which have seeped into nearly every facet of life on Earth (a recent study found that one liter of bottled water contains a quarter of a million nano-sized plastic materials).

Furthermore, increasingly, both the medical system and those who are pushing a transhumanist agenda are involved in projects and activities which are flooding life on Earth with all manner of: Meta-materials, bio-convergence dynamics, so-called synthetic biological processes, molecular communication, optogenetic forms of control, directed energy devices, self-assembling systems of nanotechnology, and energy harvesting protocols which, without informed consent, are polluting, interfering with, attacking, destroying, undermining, transforming, exploiting, and/or jamming, the biofields of human beings. The aforementioned biofields are sovereign expressions of human existence, and, as such, should be treated with sanctity rather than with experimental arrogance, indifference, curiosity, and/or self-indulgence.

Having made the foregoing observations and critically reflecting on a number of considerations relevant to those observations, let's return to the point from which this essay was launched – namely, the *Invasion of the Body Snatchers* movie. Or, more accurately, let's return to the problem which faced the two doctors who were listening to the tale being related by the Miles Bennell character played by Kevin McCarthy.

The problem that was initially raised is what are the two doctors to make of a narrative which is warning that humanity is at risk? Is Miles Bennell psychotic, delusional, or sane?

The nightmare of the Miles Bennell character ends when a highway accident provides evidence which, to some extent, appears to corroborate his story. Thus, the aforementioned movie offers an artificially scripted way of resolving questions concerning issues of psychosis, delusion, or sanity.

In the present essay, the Miles Bennell character is being played by an unnamed proponent of the idea that anthropogenic-caused global warming (due to greenhouse gas-generating forms of activity) is bringing the world to the brink of destruction. The lengthy discussion during the current essay parallels, to a degree, the information which was received toward the end of the aforementioned movie when the two doctors who were tasked with the decision of deciding whether, or not, Miles Bennell was sane and/or telling the truth were informed about some strange pod plants that had been carried by a truck which was travelling away from Santa Mira.

The reader and I are comparable to the two doctors in the movie who were being required to make a decision about the mental status of the individual who has just related a fantastic story as well as whether, or not, that story was true. The reader, of course, will have to arrive at that person's own decision concerning the problem being posed in this essay.

However, I feel free to state my professional judgment that the individual whose story the reader and I have been considering appears to be suffering from a rather severe case of: *Climate Delusional Syndrome* which requires some sort of corrective treatment. However, I feel that the prognosis for such a diagnosis is uncertain because the person who has been relating the story is, like Miles Bennell, convinced that the events being related are true and, therefore, such a person is likely to interpret my diagnosis as evidence that global warming deniers have been able to snatch my awareness and replace it with an alien form of understanding.

The very nature of a delusion is that it gives expression to a false belief or false set of beliefs. Removing oneself from a delusional system of thought is an extremely difficult challenge, and, unfortunately, not everyone is able to successfully resolve such a conundrum because one comes face to face with a fundamental question: What and/or whom should we trust ... and this issue of trust even extends to one's own hermeneutical and epistemological activities.

At one point during the *Invasion of the Body Snatchers* movie, Dr. Miles Bennell says: "In my practice, I've seen how people have allowed their humanity to drain away. Only it happened slowly instead of all at once. They didn't seem to mind... All of us - a little bit - we harden our hearts, grow callous. Only when we have to fight to stay human do we realize how precious it is to us, how dear."

What does being human entail? Raising, critically engaging, and seeking to resolve the issues given expression in this essay and doing so in a tempered, judicious, balanced, reflective, and wise manner is, one might assume, part of what is meant by the idea of being human.

However, there appear to be an array of forces at work within us and around us which are seeking to deny us this right to be human. This sounds frighteningly like the scenario being presented through the *Invasion of the Body Snatchers* movie in which there are alien, non-human entities which are seeking to infiltrate and take control of the essential sovereignty of human beings, and, if so, then, as unsettling as it might be to realize, then, perhaps, the Miles Bennell character might well have been correct as he was trying to warn the people who were driving past and becoming annoyed with him as he yelled to them in desperation while bouncing from car to car: "They're here already! You're next! You're next! You're next!"

Bibliography

Angell, Marcia – "Drug Companies & Doctors: A Story of Corruption," *The New York Review*, January 15, 2009 Issue.

Allis, Sam – "Less Pain, More Gain," *Time*, October 19, 1992.

Anderegg, William R.L. – Prall, James W. - Harold, Jacob Christopher, and Schneider, Stephen H. - "Expert Credibility in Climate Change", *Proceedings of the National Academy of Sciences*, July 2010.

Badamasi, Hamza – "Explainer: What Is the Carbon Footprint and Why Does It Matter in Fighting Climate Change," Earth.org, February 9, 2023.

Balzer, Lynne – *Exposing the Great Climate Change Lie*, Faraday Science Institute, 2023.

Bell, Larry – "Climategate II: More Smoking Guns from the Global Warming Establishment, *Forbes*, November 29, 2011.

Cook, John - et.al. - "Quantifying the Consensus on Anthropogenic Global Warming in the Scientific Literature," Environmental Research Letters, 8 (2013) 014024, 7pp.

Detrano, Joseph – "The Four-Sentence Letter Behind the Rise of OxyContin," Center of Alcohol & Substance Use Studies, May 23, 2024.

Doran, Peter T. and Zimmerman, Maggie Kendall -- "Examining the Scientific Consensus on Climate Change," Eos, Vol. 90, No. 3, January 20, 2009.

Friends of Science – "97% Consensus? No! Global Warming Math Myths & Social Proofs: The Science of Statisticulation," February 17, 2014.

Koenig, Peter – "The WHO Health Tyranny – Or Not?," *Global Research*, May 12, 2024.

Legates, David R. – Soon, Willie – Briggs, William M. – Monckton, Christopher - "Climate Consensus and 'Misinformation': A Rejoinder to Agnotology, Scientific Consensus, and the Teaching and Learning of Climate Change," *Science & Education*, (2015), 24: 299-318.

Mann, Michael E. Mann - Bradley, Raymond S. - Hughes, Malcolm K. - "Northern Hemisphere Temperatures During the Past Millennium: Inferences, Uncertainties, and Limitations", *Geophysical Research Letters*, Volume 26, No. 6., pages 759-762, March 15, 1999.

Mann, Michael E. – "Beyond the Hockey Stick: Climate Lessons from the Common Era," Proceedings of the National Academy of Sciences, 2021, Vol. 118, No. 39, 9 pages.

Mainwaring, Daniel – *Invasion of the Body Snatchers*, Produced by Walter Wanger, Directed by Don Siegel, based on a 1954 story by Jack Finney, Released by Allied Artists, 1956.

Muller, Richard A. – "Climategate 'hide the decline'" YouTube, February 27, 2011.

Mullis, Kary – "Kary Mullis Testimony on Why He Began Questioning the 'HIV Causes AIDS' Theory," https://www.youtube.com/watch?v=y68ugCb2z60 .

Nass, Dr. Meryl – "Why the WHO's New Plan Should Worry Everyone", The Epoch Times, Jan Jekielek, Senior Editor, 2024.

Oreskes, Naomi – "Beyond the Ivory Tower: The Scientific Consensus on Climate Change", *Science*, Volume 306, Issue 5702, page 1686.

Qian, Naixin – Gao, Xin – Lang, Xiaoqi – and Min, Wei – "Rapid Single-Particle Chemical Imaging of Nanoplastics by SRS Microscopy," Proceedings of the National Academy of Sciences, January 8, 2024.

Sheers, Owen – *The Trick*, BBC, Director Pip Broughton, 2021.

Smith, C. Paul – *The Climate Change Hoax Argument*, Frederick Printing, 2021.

Taylor, James – "Climategate 2 Reveals More Destruction of Evidence, Scientific Flaws, *Climate Change Weekly*, #29, December 1, 2011.

U.S. Senate Environment and Public Works Committee Minority Staff Report, "More Than 650 International Scientists Dissent Over Man-Made Global Warming Claims," 2008.

Wallace, Sabrina Dawn – Odysee.com/@psinergy:f, Psinergy, 2024.

3. The Geoengineering of Humans

Geoengineering is a term that refers to a set of processes – which might entail atmospheric, biological, chemical, and/or environmental changes of some kind -- that are intended to modulate, re-shape, or completely re-fashion different dimensions of the world in which we live. The motivations for undertaking such processes are not always clear, but they often have to do with some combination of various inclinations toward profits, control, hubris, self-serving delusions of one sort or another, and/or a technocratic, religiously-flavored compulsion to impose one's ideas on others no matter what the cost of doing so might be for the world or those that inhabit the world.

I first encountered the foregoing term – that is, geoengineering – when I came across a documentary approximately ten years ago on the topic which was entitled: 'What In The World Are They Spraying?' The DVD was put together by Michael Murphy, G. Edward Griffin, and Paul Wittenberger.

After finishing the aforementioned DVD, I remember investigating the matter further, and during this process of research, I subscribed to a few newsletters on the subject. At some point – and, this did not take place right away – I began receiving strange e-mails which were critical of Michael Murphy, one of the creative forces responsible for putting together "What In The World Are They Spraying," and, in addition, whoever was writing to me – and others – was making various allegations concerning Michael Murphy.

Among other things, the foregoing messages indicated that while it was unfortunate that what was being said with respect to Michael was being said – especially given how much Michael had accomplished with respect to rallying people's interest in, and informing them about, the topic of geoengineering -- nonetheless, the issue of geoengineering was too important to let the matter concerning Michael Murphy slide and that, somehow, what was being done was for the greater good.

I had no way of knowing whether, or not, what was being said about Mr. Murphy was true. Although, for a time, I continued to do a bit more investigation concerning geo-engineering, my research activities soon carried me in other directions, and the foregoing was, more or less, set aside even as, from to time, I found myself wondering about what had happened to Michael Murphy because I had found the documentary that he, G. Edward Griffin, and Paul Wittenberger had helped to put together to be quite interesting and informative as well as raised a lot of important questions concerning the high level of heavy metal toxicities that were being dumped on the Earth.

Flash-forward another ten, or more, years, and my research brought me back to the issue of geoengineering. Furthermore, such exploration also introduced me to another set of controversies, some of which touched upon the Michael Murphy issue.

During my second round of research directed toward the subject of geoengineering, I came across an interview that Michael Murphy had done with, I believe, Kim Moore, but I might be incorrect with respect to the second name. During that interview, a very different story emerges from the one which I had been led to believe was the case some ten years earlier, and it doesn't take very much effort to locate, via the Internet, the various source materials concerning the dispute at issue, and not withstanding such information, I still found myself in no better of a position to determine what the truth of things is with respect to the aforementioned dispute.

However, I did come across an article dated August 31, 2014 that had a byline bearing the name Dane Wigington that had been published on geoengineeringwatch.org (a web site which, I believe, Dane Wigington operates and controls), and the article was entitled: "Setting the Record Straight for Those Who Truly Care about the Battle to Stop Climate Engineering." In the article, Mr. Wigington is critical of, and makes various charges in relation to, three individuals: Michael Murphy, Kim Moore, and someone who goes by the moniker of "weatherwar101."

As far as Michael Murphy and Kim Moore are concerned, I have no way of determining where the truth lies concerning the allegations that are made by Dane Wigington during the course of the essay. However, when it comes to the work of 'weatherwar101', it is possible to uncover, at least to a degree, some of the truth, and in doing so, one can't help but wonder what is going on.

More specifically, in the aforementioned article by Dane Wigington, one finds the following passage:

"I have indeed made clear my disagreements with WW101 and I stand by everything I have stated in this regard. WW101 has put out some good and I believe accurate information about NEXRAD radar, but other videos put out by WW101 are completely unhelpful and untrue. Some of the WW101 videos blame all the weather disruptions on the sun without so much as mentioning the climate engineering issue. Other videos state that all the moisture for storms is coming from power plant cooling towers. This conclusion is so far from reality that it does not even deserve a response."

To date, I have spent hours working my way through more than 50 videos on the weatherwar101 YouTube site, and, so far, in stark contradistinction to Dane Wigington's statement in his previously cited article, I have not come across even one reference to the idea that weather disruptions on Earth are caused by the sun. In fact, 'weatherwar101' is quite repetitive (and this is not a criticism) in indicating that the weather disruptions on Earth are largely, if not entirely, the work of human beings.

Furthermore, while Mr. Wigington is of the opinion in the previously cited article that 'weatherwar101's contention that disruptive weather on Earth is, in part, a function of the massive amounts of superheated moisture that are being released from the cooling towers of power plants "... is so far from reality that it does not even deserve a response," nevertheless, Mr. Wigington not only responded – despite having claimed that a response was not deserved -- but, as well, he missed a perfect opportunity to provide a teaching moment by failing to offer any actual evidence as to why the perspective of 'weatherwar101' was , supposedly, " so far removed from reality" as far as the purported role that superheated moisture from power plant cooling towers is concerned in relation to the possibility of assisting extreme weather storms to be generated.

A declarative sentence, with no evidence to back it up, is nothing more than an unsupported claim. It is an argument based on the alleged authority of the one making such a declaration – in this case, Dane Wigington -- rather than being an expression of the sort of rigorous examination of data that is required by reliable research.

Mr. Wigington follows up the foregoing, unverified claim with an ad hominem argument on 'weatherwar101' by asserting:

"Now it seems that WW101 is branching out to personal attack videos in the effort to try and extract revenge from those who don't agree with his "it's all just the sun" or his "cooling tower" theories."

Mr. Wigington is attributing motives to 'weatherwar101' for which no corroborating evidence is being offered, and, in fact, Mr. Wigington not only fails to provide any evidence to back up his charges concerning 'weatherwar101's' alleged motives for making videos, but in the process of making those allegations, Mr. Wigington proceeds to distort 'weatherwar101's' perspective once again by repeating the earlier unproven allegations involving the sun and cooling towers which misrepresent the actual position of 'weatherwar101'.

In the section of the Wigington article that follows the foregoing considerations – a section entitled "Bottom Line" -- one also finds the next set of statements -- namely:

"When people mix their theories about multicolored aliens and the coming ice age into the climate engineering issue, it does not give credibility to our cause ... rather such inappropriate and incorrect information moves the cause backwards. I again stand by my position on refuting these subjects when others try to blend them with the fight against climate engineering."

Although I have not gone through every video published by 'weatherwar101', nonetheless, so far – after hours of research -- I have not seen anything in those videos – nor in the short introductory book which 'weatherwar101' wrote (called *No Natural Weather*) that discusses, let alone mentions, the idea that "multicolored aliens" have anything to do with weather disruptions on Earth, and, consequently, one can't avoid the following question: Why is Dane Wigington mentioning something in his article's conclusion that has nothing to do with the conceptual position of the individual whom he is seeking to criticize?

As far as Mr. Wigington's dismissive references in the conclusion to his article is concerned that touch on the idea of a possible, forthcoming ice age that has been predicted by those who are exploring some of the issues that are entailed by the notion of the Grand Solar Minimum and which revolves about certain dynamics of the Sun, once again, this has nothing to do with the point of view to which the work of 'weatherwar101' is giving expression. I have no idea what opinion, if any, 'weatherwar101' holds concerning the issues surrounding the Grand Solar Minimum model, but even if he fully subscribed to that idea, it has nothing to do with the heart of 'weatherwar101's' perspective that is being given expression through the more than 50 videos that I have studied on the relevant YouTube site, and if Dane Wigington had actually done any research into the actual perspective of 'weatherwar101' rather than engaging in what seems to be a fabricated narrative, then Mr. Wigington would have known that what I am saying is true, and, therefore, the fact that Mr. Wigington mentions the issue of a possible forthcoming ice age tends to help one to realize that he is engaged in a process of misdirection by introducing a straw man sort of argument in which one idea is dismissed – i.e., the notion of a possible forthcoming ice age -- which has nothing to do with the subject at hand – namely, the actual position of 'weatherwar101` concerning the issue of geoengineering in order to try to make it seem as if the latter subject has been addressed when this is not the case.

Dane Wigington goes on to conclude his article in the following manner:

"Though many will likely speculate that all this turmoil is somehow the work of government operatives trying to create division, in my opinion there is no truth to this in this particular case. There is so much strain on people -- as the walls close in on us all -- that some are simply snapping. The end of our former paradigm, which this period certainly qualifies as being, requires a steadfast holding to truth and facts. We need to be in this together, and not allow ill behavior or egos to divide us from making progress. We all suffer the results of geoengineering's ill delivery, and fighting this means we don't have time for any nonsense."

The foregoing consists of nothing more than "nonsense" in the form of a series of ad hominem attacks. Mr. Wigington appears to be claiming that 'weatherwar101' is merely someone who has snapped under the strain of the weather and climate issues that are closing in on all of us and, in addition, Mr. Wigington seems to be asserting that 'weatherwar101' is someone who does not "hold steadfastly to truth and facts." Finally, according to Dane Wigington, 'weatherwar101' is someone who, apparently, is guilty of either "ill behavior or ego" or both and, as a result, supposedly prevents people from making progress with respect to the problems presented by the issues of geoengineering.

Unfortunately, absolutely no evidence is advanced by Mr. Wigington to support any of the foregoing innuendoes concerning the alleged character of 'weatherwar101' or the alleged quality of the latter's research. Given the extent of the problems with various aspects of the unsubstantiated series of character assassination that appear to be directed against 'weatherwar101' and which have been outlined in the foregoing discussion, one can't help but question the veracity of the allegations that were made by Dane Wigington earlier in his article concerning either Michael Murphy or Kim Moore.

The purpose of this presentation is not to adjudicate the foregoing matters. Rather, I have put forth some considerations that run contrary to the sort of narrative that Mr. Wigington seems to be trying to spin with respect to 'weatherwar101' and which, therefore, carry – potentially -- problematic implications with respect to other things that Mr. Wigington has said not only about Michael Murphy and Kim Moore, but, as well, about geoengineering in general.

Although the foregoing dispute took place quite a few years ago, it is not irrelevant to events that are transpiring today ... events that, on the surface, might not appear to have anything to do with geoengineering, but which, when engaged with the right degree of rigorous consideration and understanding, could be seen to be giving expression to another facet of the process of geoengineering that is taking place in the world today and which has been going on for quite some time – that is, the geoengineering of human beings.

A little later in this presentation, I plan to provide an overview of my understanding of 'weatherwar101's' perspective – the perspective that, for unknown reasons, Dane Wigington seems to want to criticize because, apparently, he never took the time or made the effort to examine what was actually being said by 'weatherwar101' or, alternatively, Mr. Wigington could actually have taken the time and made the effort to look at what 'weatherwar101' was saying, and, for whatever reason, might have felt threatened by those ideas and, as a result, decided to engage in innuendo, as well as ad hominem and straw man arguments rather than put on his big boy pants and seek to settle the matter with well-reasoned and evidentially rich arguments concerning whatever it is that he seems to be so averse to addressing and, unfortunately, appeared to resort, instead, to engaging in inappropriate forms of argument that obfuscate and distort, rather than illuminate, the relevant issues. I do not know if the perspective being put forth by 'weatherwar101' is right, but I do know that the evidence and arguments that are being put forth through various videos that have been published by that individual, as well as through the aforementioned short book on the topic, have a quality that resonates with my sense of where the truth might lie, and, most importantly, that individual – or individuals -- does this in a way that is rooted in the sorts of evidential considerations that – for me, at least -- are quite compelling.

However, before moving on to the overview of the work of 'weatherwar101' that has been promised previously, I would like to retrace my steps and return to the video "What In the World Are They Spraying" that was mentioned at the beginning of this presentation. This decision should not be seen as a deviation from the 'overview' project that is being promised, but, instead, should be understood as helping to set the stage a little with respect to that which is to come in this essay.

When I first watched the aforementioned video, I was fascinated, but it was entirely foreign to my own experience. At the time of viewing the video – which was around 2011, or so -- I lived in Maine. None of the chemtrails that were being shown or discussed in the documentary seemed to be in the skies above me, and, so, I wondered whether what was being explored in the video was something that affected a few places on the West Coast of the United States as well as Hawaii and, maybe, a few places in Europe as was being depicted in that DVD.

To be sure, I might not have been paying proper attention to what may have been going on in the skies over Maine, but I did the empirical thing and looked, yet, at the times that I looked, nothing anomalous seemed to be taking place. However, all of this changed about six or seven years ago, and, suddenly, there in the skies above me were the same sorts of chemtrails that I had seen on the DVD ... running in a series of roughly parallel strips from one horizon to the other, or crisscrossing with one another at various points, or forming huge 'V's' and 'X's' in the sky.

One often could see jet planes – three and four at a time -- laying down the chemtrails. Often this occurred in the late afternoon.

Initially, the "official" position was that the effluent streaming from the planes was nothing more than contrails that were a natural chemical reaction which occurred when jets flew at certain altitudes and in certain temperatures. Anyone who took a little time to research such claims soon discovered that contrails and chemtrails are entirely different phenomena, and, as a result, one encountered the first of many lies that were issued out of the mouths of people who, apparently, were seeking to hide the reality of what was actually taking place.

Eventually, the official narrative changed from "nothing going on here folks but contrails" to a narrative in which a heroic battle was being fought to defend against the impending catastrophic impact of global warming generated by the effects of greenhouse gases such as: CO_2 and methane that were being created by human beings ... a heroic battle in which chemtrails were being used to reflect or divert incoming radiation from the Sun in order to help cool the planet. Toward the beginning of: "What In the World Are They Spraying," a fair amount of time is spent covering a symposium that occurred in San Diego during 2010 concerning the topic of geoengineering, and it might be instructive to take a look at some of what transpired during that gathering of geoengineers.

One of the geoengineering specialists who spoke at the symposium and also was featured, to a certain extent, in the documentary being made by Michael Murphy, G. Edward Griffin, and Paul Wittenberger was a fellow by the name of David Keith who taught at the University of Calgary in Canada. During the course of his presentation, Professor Keith started to talk about the possibility of using alumina or aluminum oxide in aerosols as a way of dealing with global warming.

After mentioning that alumina had four times the reflective volume surface area of some other aerosol candidates and, that, as well, alumina possessed 16 times the coagulation rate when compared with certain other aerosol candidates, and after noting how this latter property of coagulation is very important when it comes to issues of removal, Professor Keith proceeded to indicate how easy it would be to spray alumina into the atmosphere via either a new jet aircraft that were built to be able to handle such a project or by retrofitting existing jets to perform the function of spraying alumina or aluminum oxide into the atmosphere. While Professor Keith felt the cost of undertaking such a spraying project would not be expensive, he acknowledged that the possibility that in the not-too-distant future researchers were likely to discover that the issue of aerosol spraying from jets might not necessarily be as easy or as uncomplicated as initially supposed by many researchers, and, especially, this might be the case in conjunction with the problem of managing possible side-effects that could be associated with such aerosol spraying.

During the question and answer session that followed different presentations, one of the individuals in the audience – Dane Wigington – pointed out that he hadn't heard anything during the various presentations that addressed the potential of a highly reactive heavy metal like aluminum to "toxify soils and waters" and, in the process, adversely affect the health of human beings and the surrounding environment. He wanted to know whether, or not, this dimension of aluminum toxicity had been studied by any of the geoengineers.

David Keith from the University of Calgary took the question. He claimed that the individuals who were working on the aerosol issue were from Carnegie Mellon and that one of the very first things they did was to address whether, or not, the use of alumina would affect human health, and, in addition, he noted that while various toxicological issues needed to be addressed, nevertheless, even though

| Technological Reflections |

the group had not, yet, published its results if one were "just thinking about the sheer number of particles ... the human health impact of small particles ... the answer is that it's not even close to being an issue."

Dane Wigington followed up on his original question and asked: "... so, ten megatons of aluminum dumped into the atmosphere would have no human health" aspects?

At that point, David Keith responded by saying:

" ... let me be more careful here ... to separate out the toxicological ... so, the alumina that we have just begun to research and published nothing ... and, so, there could be something terrible that we find tomorrow that we haven't looked at."

Professor Keith's answer was rather disingenuous. In fact, considerable research already had been done elsewhere indicating that aluminum does have a toxic impact on life.

Furthermore, why would Professor Keith want to separate out – or set aside -- toxicological considerations from the rest of his answer? The whole point of the question being asked was whether, or not, geoengineers had undertaken the sorts of studies that would indicate whether, or not, using aluminum in jet aerosol spraying would have a toxic impact on human health and the environment in general.

Moreover, while it might have been true that the Carnegie Mellon research group was just beginning to undertake such research, perhaps someone should have informed Professor Keith that such spraying already had been going on for a number of years. In addition, there was a growing body of evidence indicating that such spraying was posing a health hazard on a variety of levels.

For example, Francis Mangels -- a retired, U.S.D.A. biologist -- indicates that when the presence of aluminum in a given location exceeds 1,000 parts per billion, the federal government is supposed to be called in to address the situation. Samples have been taken, among other places, from the snows of Mt. Shasta in California, and these samples have been shown to be at 61,000 parts per billion – 61 times greater than what the government indicates is safe, and, this was more than 12 years ago.

Similar results to the foregoing were present in nearly 30 other tests that have been run in conjunction with air, water, and soil samples. All of these studies indicated that there was a growing amount of toxic heavy metals being dumped on the Earth that, in addition to other problematic ramifications, were destroying microscopic life forms in the soil.

Aluminum, barium and strontium – which like aluminum are heavy metals -- have also been found in samples that exceed levels that are considered to be safe -- and even when a substance is deemed "safe", this does not necessarily mean that such substances do not continue to be cumulatively toxic even at such "safe" levels. In point of fact, all heavy metals have toxic ramifications for human beings as well as for the environment in general, and such toxic samples have been traced to the nano-particles that are inherent in the chemtrails that are being rained down upon the Earth.

According to the previously mentioned, former government biologist, Francis Mangels, gardens grow best when the pH of the soil is between 5.5 and 5.6. Somewhere around 2005 he started a garden that had measured the soil's pH value and discovered that the soil in the garden had the necessary pH properties for growing things, but five years later, the pH of the soil in the garden had been pushed in a more neutral or even alkaline direction of 6.8, and this change in pH values was due to the heavy metal nano-particles that were falling to Earth from chemtrails.

Deborah Whitman took samples from the silvery bark that had begun to appear on dying trees in her area. The tests came back positive for a variety of heavy metals including aluminum, barium, and titanium – all of which have been documented to be present in chemtrails.

The presence of aluminum has been implicated in the rapidly rising number of Alzheimer cases. Furthermore, aluminum also is a fire accelerant, and its presence in the trees throughout California suggests that it might be playing a role in the way forest fires have been spreading so quickly and intensely in conjunction with the increasing number of those kinds of catastrophic events that are taking place in California.

When Michael Murphy and Paul Wittenberger travelled to Hawaii to see whether, or not, chemtrails were present in what many consider to be a relatively pristine environment, they were told that the bark of coconut trees had undergone a change since chemtrails had begun to be dispersed near the islands, and, as a result, such bark had become soft and easily could be stripped from those trees, something that had not been the case prior to the advent of chemtrails being dispersed near Maui.

The documentarians also talked with a mother who had been raising her daughter on an organic farm. A friend of hers suggested that she should have her daughter's hair tested for possible heavy metal contaminants.

Because her child had been raised within what was considered to be a completely organic lifestyle, and, in fact, the child never even had been vaccinated, the mother believed that any such tests would be negative. Nonetheless, she discovered that her daughter's hair tested positive (in amounts that exceeded allegedly safe reference limits) for the presence of heavy metals such as: aluminum, antimony, arsenic, cadmium, Gadolinium, lead, tin, and tungsten, and most – if not all -- of the foregoing ingredients have been found in samples of chemtrail nano-particles.

To try to claim that officials have not been, and are not, aware of the foregoing issues is rather problematic. After all, and to give just one example, Patent #7582809, which dealt with an aluminum-resistant gene was granted on September 1, 2009, a full year prior to the previously mentioned geoengineering symposium that was held in San Diego in 2010 and at which David Keith had sought to evade questions concerning the possible toxicity of the aluminum for human beings and the environment that he was proposing might be sprayed from jets into the atmosphere.

Why would someone want to patent an aluminum-resistant gene if aluminum was not already considered to be a toxin that was present in the environment in quantities that were known to be capable of interfering with crop growth and viability? Apparently, the foregoing sort of information is precisely the kind of thing to which Professor

Keith alluded when he said that "… there could be something terrible that we find tomorrow that we haven't looked at" since, obviously, something terrible already had been found yesterday – not tomorrow – and either Professor Keith was clueless concerning what already was known about the toxicity of aluminum or, maybe, the reason why he was being so disingenuous with respect to evading the question he was being asked concerning the toxicity of the aluminum that he was proposing could be sprayed from jets is because, perhaps, he already knew the answer to the question being asked, and such an answer would not be able to be used to spin chemtrails as being, potentially, a good thing to do.

More than twelve years have passed since all of the foregoing events transpired, and, yet, since that time, there has been a relentless drive on the part of various forces -- which, at best, are nothing more than exercises in demagoguery and, at worst, constitute sources of destructive malevolence -- to pour more and more toxic heavy metals as well as other toxic substances upon the world's ecologies despite the fact that evidence has also been accumulating at a rapidly increasing rate which demonstrates toxicity inherent in all that is being done via chemtrails.

Toward the end of the "What In the World Are They Spraying" documentary there is footage of Michael Murphy going to Washington, D.C. and meeting with – or trying to -- members of Congress – both Senators and Representatives, as well as both Democrats and Republicans – in an attempt to inform those individuals and get their commitment to work toward some sort of coherent, concerted plan to gain substantive government and public control over toxic heavy metals that are being dispersed into the environment. In a series of visual and auditory vignettes involving the alleged bastions of the American Republic that would be hysterically comical if the bottom line were not so disturbingly monstrous, the aforementioned documentary records the responses of numerous members of Congress concerning the overtures of the individuals making the documentary, and those responses were frighteningly reminiscent of what cockroaches do when light shines upon them – namely, scurry for cover and seek to disappear into anonymity.

According to David Keith – in his aforementioned talk in 2010:

"... implementation decisions will be risk to risk ... the risk of doing it [that is, spraying chemtrails] against the risk of not doing it."

Given the considerable evidence that CO2 might not be quite the villain that global warming advocates have claimed it to be since, among other considerations, (1) elevated CO2 levels do not automatically indicate that temperatures will become elevated because high CO2 levels also have been recorded in conjunction with lowered temperatures as well, and given the fact that (2) there is a great deal of evidence – at least according to Grand Solar researchers -- that the near future might give expression to an ice age rather than to an era of global warming – and (3) putting aside the falsification of research results that appear, on the basis of hacked e-mails, to have been committed in England by the Climate Research Unit of East Anglia University in 2009, as well as similar falsification of data that was uncovered in 2011 that attempted to lend credence to the global warming narrative when evidence actually indicated otherwise, and given the fabrication of data by the NOAA (that is, National Oceanic and Atmospheric Administration) to induce countries to sign the Paris agreement on climate change, one is not exactly sure what the nature of the risk is to which Professor Keith alluded in his talk if one were to refrain from spraying tons of heavy metal nano-particles -- as well as other toxic substances – on the Earth.

In an equally revealing communication, Ken Caldera, a geoengineer who also participated in the previously mentioned 2010 San Diego meeting of geoengineers concerning climate change, responded in the following way when asked about the motivation or rationale for dropping toxic heavy metals on the world:

"Maybe, I'm putting a particle in the atmosphere because I'm trying to make money, or, maybe, I'm putting a particle into the atmosphere because I'm engaged in scientific research and trying to understand cloud physics, or, maybe, I'm putting this particle into the atmosphere because I'm trying to make it rain locally ... to seed the cloud and get more snow on our ski slopes."

To begin with, since chemtrails have never been about dropping single particles into the atmosphere, Ken Caldera's foregoing manner of phrasing things is, at best, a poorly chosen and euphemistic way of speaking that substantially downplays the fact that tons of particles are being dropped into the atmosphere through chemtrails and not just single particles. Secondly, Dr. Caldera might be well advised to stop thinking about what his motivations for doing anything are and to begin considering how his motivations for proceeding with the dropping of his ludicrous one particle into the atmosphere might entail problematic ramifications for people besides himself and, yet, his whole manner of speech seems to convey the idea that, somehow, he has the right to do such things without the informed consent of other people who might be adversely affected by what he is doing.

Of course, everybody can identify with Ken Caldera's previous reference to a profit motive, but making money at the expense of the safety and health of other individuals seems to be a rather reckless and self-serving way of going about life. Furthermore, while one can appreciate his wish to carry out the sort of scientific research that seeks to determine the dynamics of cloud physics, nevertheless, individuals cannot carry out such research – at least not in any ethically justifiable manner -- if that research is likely to have negative consequences on individuals and/or the environment -- especially if the research is being conducted without the informed consent of the individuals who, at least potentially stand in harm's way. It's almost like Dr. Caldera had never read Mary Shelley's 1818 book or seen any of the various film adaptations of that work or failed to understand why the townspeople might be prepared to take pitchforks in hand and lay siege to the laboratory of Herr Doctor Frankenstein because he was responsible for releasing a dangerous entity into the world that inflicted damage, and while that damage might have been unintended by Dr. Frankenstein, nonetheless, the damage occurred because the good doctor lacked the necessary foresight or insight to appreciate that he had created something which had a substantial potential for destruction.

Ken Caldera ends his relatively short answer to a question concerning his motivation or justification of spraying chemtrails with the following words:

"This obviously raises all kinds of questions ... its usually risky ... it likely will negatively impact some people, but we might find ourselves in a situation where these risks seem worth taking."

Quite frankly, I find the foregoing words to be quite disturbing. Who is the "we" that is finding themselves "in a situation" which is fraught with danger, and what, precisely, is the nature of that situation that supposedly warrants taking risks, and what sorts of risks are "we" talking about and what is the metric for evaluating what constitutes a "worthy" risk, and how does one propose to justify the use of such a metric?

An assortment of academic figures, together with various alleged research "experts", as well as elected and unelected government officials, different military authorities, and select representatives of the media all -- at one time or another and in one way or another – have lied about the issue of climate change. While the current presentation is not intended to be a venue through which to resolve the problem of climate change, one really doesn't have to be an expert in geoengineering to have good grounds for wondering if the people who want to rush to judgment on such matters have all their cognitive and ethical marbles in working order.

The foregoing considerations help set the stage for taking a look at the perspective of 'wearherwar101'. Although there are hints, here and there, in the works of that person or persons that I have seen which indicate that the world is warming up, this position does not necessarily give expression to a greenhouse gas theory of global warming, and, actually, irrespective of whether, or not, 'weatherwar101' does adhere to some version of global warming, this issue actually has nothing to do with the facets of his perspective that I would like to explore in the present part of my presentation ... facts that are quite important in their own right and which, if true, carry a variety of grave implications for humankind and our planet.

There are a number of different components that form the basis of the paradigm that 'weatherwar101' is putting forth concerning the nature of man-made weather. As the title of his book: "*No Natural Weather*" indicates, 'weatherwar101' does not believe that a great deal of the weather that occurs – especially in relation to extreme weather events, but, quite possibly, in conjunction with all weather – is man-made.

While acknowledging that attempts are still being made to try to pin down precisely when and how the breakdown of the hydrological cycle might have occurred, the reason why 'weatherwar101' believes there is no natural weather anymore is because that cycle has become dysfunctional. However, although the precise nature of the how and when of such a breakdown is somewhat elusive at the present time, nonetheless, from time to time, 'weatherwar101' does clearly state that human beings have caused the aforementioned breakdown in the natural hydrological cycle, and, consequently, 'weatherwar101' is of the opinion that weather constitutes an anthropogenic issue ... that is, a problem that has arisen due to the acts of commission or omission – or both -- on the part of human beings,

Irrespective of exactly how the natural hydrological cycle has been disrupted and rendered dysfunctional by mankind, we are confronted with the possibility that we no longer have an autonomously operating natural hydrological cycle that is capable of sustaining, in any reliable manner, the dynamics associated with: Slowly evaporating water systems that get transformed into water-bearing clouds that, when sufficiently saturated, release their moisture which -- depending on conditions – is manifested as rain, snow, sleet, hail, or becomes part of different storm systems. Instead, the broken hydrological system has been replaced with a man-made system that has changed over time as new technology emerges and permits.

As alluded to earlier, 'weatherwar101' believes that at least three components are needed to make weather: (a) a source of water; (b) a way of making clouds that can absorb water, and (c) a means of inducing the clouds and their water to do what one wishes them to do. According to 'weatherwar101' (a) -- the source of water that is necessary for making weather -- comes from the superheated water vapor that is released everyday from the cooling towers affiliated with more than 11,000 power plants in the United States and 70,000 power plants that exist worldwide, while (b) chemtrails contain materials that can assist with cloud formation as well as help enable weather to be shaped, and, finally, (c) the nexrad (short for Next Generation) Doppler radar stations that have been put up since 1988 provide the sort of technology that is capable of modulating what takes place in any given weather system that is being maintained through clouds made up of fast evaporating water and nano-particles of, among other things, heavy metals. Let's take a look at each of the foregoing three components.

Dane Wigington has gone on record as saying the following:

"I have had a number of people request [via geoengineeringwatch.org and elsewhere] that I address the completely ridiculous information being put out by some stating that power plant cooling towers are being used for climate modification."

Before pushing on to the rest of Mr. Wigington's public statement concerning the issue of cooling towers, one might note that the issue being addressed by 'weatherwar101' is not a matter of climate change per se – as Dane Wigington seems to imply -- but, rather, the focus of 'weatherwar101' is on the process of weather formation. While climate and weather obviously are interconnected, nevertheless, I have not come across any indication -- at least not in the materials I have covered – that 'weatherwar101' claims that climate is a function of weather.

To be sure, one might reasonably suppose that whatever weather is possible is, in part, a function of a given set of climatic conditions, but one also might simultaneously contend that climate gives expression to a broader set of considerations than does weather involving, for example: The, rotation of the Earth, the nature of ocean currents, the electro-magnetic properties of our planet, the relationship between the Earth and the Sun – both in terms of varying distances between the two as well as in terms of the diagonal disposition of Earth's poles relative to the Sun, along with the dynamics entailed by cosmic rays from deep space and the amount of energy possessed by those rays, together with the dynamics of plate tectonics, volcanic activity, and a host of other considerations. To be sure, weather formations take place within the context of the former, climatic forces, but while all of the aforementioned factors might impact weather in different ways, the nature of weather tends to constitute a set of dynamics that is somewhat different from, and somewhat more narrowly conceived (in which the hydrological system plays a primary role) than the more complicated dynamics that give rise to climate.

While attempting to address the issue of cooling towers, Dane Wigington goes on to contend that:

"I have personally worked on cooling towers for Bechtel power over three decades ago. The facility I was involved with was the 'Cool Water Coal Gassification Project' located in Daggett, California.

"Daggett is in the middle of the Mojave Desert. How much available water is there in this desert? Not much, and for this reason, these cooling towers were a 'closed loop system.'

Many power plants use this type of system to conserve water. To believe that isolated steam cooling towers could magically put this volume of water into the sky from water sources that often are only ponds fed by wells is beyond ridiculous."

One wonders about the nature of the process for conserving water to which Dane Wigington alludes in the foregoing statement. Given a power plant system that supposedly operates through a completely closed loop process, one wonders why there is any need at all for a ready supply of water from a well unless water is somehow being lost during the process of generating power along with the on-going dissipation of heat which that process produces, and, if this is the case – and it is – then, this would raise the question of just how much water is lost to superheated water vapor that helps dissipate the heat that arises during the generation of power and, thereby, cools the power generating system, which one might suppose is the reason why some of the towers associated with a power plant are known as "cooling towers."

Dane Wigington fails to mention what the heat load was for the cooling equipment that was used at the Bechtel power plant in Daggett, California. Moreover, he didn't specify how much evaporation took place in the cooling towers associated with the aforementioned power plant in order to be able to handle the heat load that arises during the generation of power.

Generally speaking, thousands of gallons of water per minute per tower tend to evaporate during the cooling process. Furthermore, how many thousands of gallons of water evaporate per minute will depend on the extent of the heat load that develops during the generation of power.

Furthermore, as 'weatherwar101' points out in a number of video presentations, the only part of the power generation process that is closed has to do with the water that is needed to turn a turbine. On the other hand, the water that is used to help cool and re-condense the water/steam in that closed-loop facet of the power generating system is part of what is known as a "wet surface air cooler or WSAC" which consists of a combination of sprayed water and air induction being run through a network of bundled tubes, and this cooling process is part of an open-loop system that, eventually, releases water into the atmosphere in the form of superheated water vapor.

How it is that Dane Wigington who worked for Bechtel at a power plant in the Mojave Desert doesn't seem to understand any of the foregoing dynamics is something of a mystery. Whether done intentionally, or unintentionally, Dane Wigington has misled his audience with respect to the nature of how a power plant operates.

Dane Wigington also is misrepresenting the cooling tower issue by trying to argue that 'weatherwar101' claims that any set of cooling towers associated with a single power plant would be sufficient to generate the amount of water vapor necessary to feed a storm system. 'Weatherwar101' has been very clear that weather systems are fed and grow through the successive contributions of numerous power plants that twice a day release thousands of gallons per minute of superheated water into the atmosphere and which is capable of helping weather system develop that are in the vicinity of a given group of contributing power plants.

| Technological Reflections |

Contrary to the seemingly sarcastic verbiage used by Dane Wigington in the previous quote, there is nothing "magical" about the way in which groups of power plants are not only capable of supplying enormous amounts of superheated water vapor into the atmosphere, but, in addition, for more than 50 years such superheated water vapor have been known to have had the capacity to affect weather. Indeed, in 1971, the State of Illinois conducted a water survey study in conjunction with the 2200 megawatt nuclear power plant being built by Commonwealth Edison Company in Zion which is located near Lake Michigan in North-east Illinois.

The aforementioned report contained a literature review covering previous research. For example, a 1968 paper by Changnon indicated that precipitation increased anywhere from 20 to 40 percent in areas that were located downwind from the urban-industrial effects of the city of Chicago, and therefore, one had to seriously entertain the possibility that superheated water vapor from cooling towers might be able to affect the amount of precipitation that fell downwind from such effluents.

A 1970 study concerning tower plumes in Keystone, Pennsylvania that was conducted by Visbisky and others found that, depending on atmospheric conditions, effluents from towers were capable of contributing to the formation of clouds. Another study by Carson in 1971 reported that the heat and water vapor that were released by cooling towers were able to contribute to the formation of cumulus clouds and that such effluents had the potential to serve as triggers for the release of precipitation miles downwind from those towers.

In addition, 'weathewar101' notes that research concerning cloud physics has indicated that rain showers and thunderstorms have been known to be triggered by the introduction of relatively small amounts of energy into a developing weather system. Thus, the possibility that thousands of gallons per minute per cooling tower from a number of power plants might be capable of supplying the energy needed to trigger such weather events is not necessarily as "magical" as Dane Wigington seems to suppose is the case.

The aforementioned Illinois Water Survey report offered a few figures which could be used to roughly calculate the amount of water vapor that would evaporate from a power plant the size of the 2200

| Technological Reflections |

megawatt nuclear facility in Zion. The report worked on the assumption that there would be a heat load for cooling equipment in the order of 14.3 times 109 BTU/hour and that this would require an evaporation rate of 18,000 gallons per minute,

Given the foregoing figures, if one were to consider just a two hour period, the amount of evaporated water required to help cool the facility would be 120 (i.e., two hours converted to minutes) times 18,000 gallons per minute which results in a total of 2,160,000 gallons for each cooling tower. So, if one multiplies 2,160,000 gallons by 2 (the number of cooling towers present), one arrives at the figure of 4,320,000 gallons of superheated water vapor that would be released into the atmosphere during a two hour period from two cooling towers at a power plant like the 2200 megawatt facility at Zion, Illinois.

Estimates were also given in the foregoing report that were based on a lesser loss to the atmosphere than the foregoing figures depending on whether the loss took place in winter (11,000 gallons per minute) rather during spring, summer, or fall (14,700 gallons per minute). If one were to use the lower figures, the basic point that is being made here would not be altered in any substantial way.

On the basis of the 11,000, or so, power plants that are distributed across the United States, or the 70,000, or so, power plants that are located all around the world, then, one is able to calculate that every day, billions and billions of gallons of superheated water vapor are being released into the atmosphere twice a day in the United States as well as in the rest of the world. If studies conducted back in the 1960s and 1970s indicated that cooling tower effluents were capable of affecting weather systems downwind from those towers, then, what data and/or reasoning does Dane Wigington wish to employ to try to justify his contention that the superheated water vapor emanating from cooling towers could not possibly affect weather systems that are in the area of those towers, and, moreover, if one were to take into consideration the potential of a group of such cooling towers in a given area to be able to affect weather system via their combined release of effluents, then, the only thing that seems ridiculous concerning the possible active role of superheated water vapor in conjunction with weather is Dane Wigington's continued inclination to deny the relevant evidence concerning cooling towers.

As warm, moist air – i.e., water vapor from cooling towers – rises up through the atmosphere because it is less dense than the air through which it is rising, the rising water vapor begins to cool. As a result, tiny drops of water begin to form through the process of condensation, and from this condensation process clouds begin to form.

According to 'weatherwar101,' the foregoing dynamic of artificially created precipitation is easily identified by the manner in which there are sudden, massive, bursts of superheated water vapor in an area with atmospheric properties that should not be able to generate the foregoing sorts of bursts, but what is otherwise inexplicable on the basis of natural phenomena can be traced to power plant cooling towers that are in, or near, the region where the sudden burst of superheated water vapor occurs, and this whole dynamic is easier to detect and follow when one views that process via infrared imaging.

One of the videos that had been put together by 'weatherwar101' took a look at the 2017 eclipse which was the first eclipse to cross the United States since 1918. 90 minutes were required for the shadow of the moon eclipse to travel from the Washington/Oregon area on the West coast to South Carolina where it was last visible in America.

As spectacular as the eclipse was, 'weatherwar101' points out that most people missed the opportunity to see something very important in conjunction with that phenomenon. More specifically, GOES-16 satellite imagery – GOES stands for Geosynchronous Operational Environmental Satellite – was following the progress of the eclipse across the country, but that imagery also depicted something else taking place.

In Carbondale, Illinois – where the longest period of eclipse totality occurred – sudden cloud cover arose as the shadow was about to pass over the city and it obscured the eclipse. The crowd can be heard booing during the video because of the way the cloud cover interfered with being able to clearly see the eclipse.

'Weatherwar101' indicates that the generation of the cloud system in Carbondale that was captured by GOES-16 imagery can be traced to the superheated water vapor plume that was released from the cooling towers of a nearby power plant. Furthermore something similar occurred in Charleston, South Carolina when a thunderstorm took place as the totality was taking place, and 'weatherwar101' provided video evidence that tied the thunderstorm to the activities of about 16, or so, power plants in the Charleston area that had, and were, releasing millions of gallons of superheated water vapor into the atmosphere which helped to create and feed the storm system.

A second component that is at the heart of the human-made weather perspective being described in the videos and writing of 'weatherwar101' involve WSR-88D technology. The designation "WSR" stands for Weather Surveillance Radar, while the 88D portion of that moniker refers to the year – 1988 – in which the 'D' (that is, Doppler) form of radar was deployed.

WSR-88D is the latest edition in a line of technological enhancements concerning radar dating back to 1957. Prior to the appearance of WSR-88D, there were similarly labeled versions of the technology in the guise of WSR-74C and WSR-57.

In addition, there were other, earlier generations of the technology that emerged prior to 1957. These were known as: WSR-1, WSR-1A, WSR-3, and WSR-4.

'Weatherwar101' maintains that evidence exists which seems to indicate that the frequency of tornados began to increase with the deployment of the aforementioned radar technology. Such data not only serves as a hint concerning what might have begun to take place more than half a century ago, but, as well, the correlation between the increased frequency of tornados and the deployment of various generations of the Weather Surveillance System technology suggests that the aforementioned correlation might not be coincidental but causal in nature.

For some time, a number of individuals have sought to connect the increasing number of extreme weather events with the HAARP facility near Gakona, Alaska (population 169 in 2020, down from 218 in 2010). "HAARP" stands for 'High-frequency Active Auroral Research Program.'

The one billion watt facility consists of 180 antennas spread out over 33 acres that are capable of directing focused forms of electromagnetic radiation into the ionosphere. The ionosphere is the outermost layer of the Earth's atmosphere that begins at about 30 miles and extends out to, approximately, 600 miles above the Earth's surface.

The ionosphere contains many particles and molecules that have become ionized as a result of being stripped of electrons through the impact of ultraviolet rays from the Sun, as well as from the impact of cosmic rays coming in from other parts of the Milky Way galaxy. The physics of the ionosphere was of interest to researchers – especially the military -- because, among other reasons, what takes place in that region of the atmosphere plays an important role in the process of communication.

Before being taken over by the University of Alaska at Fairbanks, HAARP was run, first, by the Navy, and, then, by the Air Force. Furthermore, DARPA – the Defense Advanced Research Projects Agency, a division of the Defense Department – also engaged in extensive research at the Alaska facility.

As noted earlier, quite a few people believe that the secret research activities that took place at HAARP since the early 1990s – and there were a series of upgrades to the facility over several decades – were responsible for modifying, if not creating, the weather in a variety of ways. 'Weatherwar101' contends that there is really no hard evidence demonstrating that HAARP plays any role in the modification of weather, and, as a result, speculation concerning the nature and purpose of HAARP have distracted people from looking at what 'weatherwar101' maintains is taking place all around them via the 200 nexrad Doppler facilities (i.e., the WSR-88D technology) that have been deployed around the country, along with the many other facilities employing similar kinds of technology that have been constructed in numerous, if not most, nations of the world.

If one looks at imaging characteristics of those facilities when they are operational – and 'weatherwar101' provides many instances of such images in various videos – one discovers that those facilities produce an extended ring of heat/energy that is capable of interacting with pulsed energy from other such facilities to form a phased array network. A phased array network is a set of antennae involving different facilities which produce signals that can be coherently focused, through computer algorithms, to send directed energy toward specific areas of the atmosphere while simultaneously suppressing other signals that would run counter to that sort of electromagnetic focus.

'Weatherwar101' has been criticized by some individuals who claim that nexrad, or next generation, Doppler radar facilities, which consume about 50.8 kilowatts of power, are not sufficiently powerful to be able to have much, if any, impact on weather systems. However, 'weatherwar101' indicates that each nexrad facility is equipped with a klystron unit which is capable of converting standard commercial power to more powerful forms of coherent of energy.

Therefore, while the radar transmitter itself only requires 15 kilowatts to operate (a relatively modest portion of the total power -- i.e., 50.8 kilowatts -- that is being consumed by the nexrad facility as a whole), nonetheless, thanks to the on-site klystron unit, the 15 kilowatts that is consumed by the radar transmitter can be converted into 750,000 watts of coherent energy with each pulse that is released. As a result, the peak power of the radar transmitted is 750,000 watts (750 kilowatts) and not 15,000 watts (15 kilowatts).

According to "official" documentation and reports, each nexrad facility is only supposed to transmit pulses of energy for just 7 seconds during each hour – that is, roughly 0.19 percent of the time. Nonetheless, 'weatherwar101' indicates that if one actually takes the time to watch what takes place with these facilities, one discovers that they are active far more often than 7 seconds an hour.

Early on during the research process, 'weatherwar101' would look at weather radar images and wonder what could be causing the storms that would show up on radar and would erupt out of what seemed to be dry air on a daily basis. Over time, he was able to determine that the storm bursts could be tied to the way in which power plants released superheated water vapor into the atmosphere but because such releases happened at different intervals, one had difficulty grasping the common source of such atmospheric bursts – namely, the 11,000 power plants that populate the United States.

Various critics of the work of 'weatherwar101' also were resistant to the idea that the radio frequencies generated by nexrad facilities might be capable of affecting the weather. Nevertheless, a decade, or more, ago, the Naval Research Lab reported that its researchers had been able to generate a plasma bubble that was a kilometer-wide and, in addition, were able to sustain that bubble for an hour by beaming a radio signal of a certain frequency into the atmosphere.

The frequency used by the Naval Research Lab people in the foregoing study was between 1.44 megahertz (i.e., 1.44 million cycles per second) and 4.34 megahertz (that is, 4.4 million cycles per second). Interestingly, the pulses sent out by nexrad Doppler radar facilities can run between 0 and 12.4 megahertz (i.e., 12.4 million cycles per second), and, therefore, as far as being able to generate the right sorts of frequency signals is concerned, nexrad facilities had the capacity to generate layers of plasma just as the Naval Research Lab had been able to do.

One should also keep in mind that the aforementioned Naval Research Lab studies were in conjunction with the ionosphere where there is already a great deal of ionized molecules and atoms roaming about in the roughly 570 mile-deep layer of atmosphere that makes up the ionosphere. In essence, among other things, those researchers were looking for frequencies that might be capable of helping the ionized materials that were naturally present in the ionosphere to coalesce together as one coherent bubble or layer.

The capacity to change frequencies has little impact on the atmosphere that is closer to the Earth because there are not sufficient ionized or ionizable materials to work on in so-called "pure" air. There must be something in the air for frequencies to be able to act on, and this is where the heavy metals that are present in the chemtrails come into play, for it is heavy metals which are being ionized by the pulses of energy that emanate from nexrad radar facilities that, according to 'weatherwar101', are being shaped into forms and forces that can be used to manipulate weather conditions in one way or another.

U.S. Patent #5041834 refers to a technology that is capable of generating an Artificial Ionosphere Mirror or AIM. This is another way of saying that such technology has the capacity to generate layers of plasma at various points within the atmosphere toward which such technology is actively directed.

Plasma involves the ionization of molecules and atoms. In effect, AIM technology constitutes a heater antenna that has the capacity to project power with certain frequencies into the atmosphere and, in the process, destabilize the portion of atmosphere toward which the heater is actively pointed and, as a result, set in motion an avalanche of ionization that leads to the formation of a layer of plasma in the atmosphere.

A tiltable AIM refers to a heater antenna array whose frequency and phase can be altered in ways that enable the technology to be able to create plasma layers that can be tilted in any desired direction by simply refocusing the frequency and phase of the beam to point toward slightly higher altitudes. Although the Naval Research Lab was able to generate a plasma bubble using the one billion watt HAARP facility, nexrad facilities are able also to accomplish similar goals with less power (750,000 watts) but use the same sorts of frequency and phase shifts in its antenna array, and, in addition, each nexrad facility is able to interact with other nexrad facilities and co-ordinate their efforts to create atmospheric destabilization through the creation of plasma layers that are capable of being tilted and modulated in different ways by altering the frequency, phase, and altitudes at which nexrad pulses are released or directed.

One of the ways in which nexrad facilities modulate plasma layers is through the use of the technique of heterodyning. Heterodyning was invented in 1901 by Reginald Fessenden, a Canadian engineer.

Heterodyning constitutes a radio signal processing technique that is capable of combining two different frequencies into a new mode of frequency with different sorts of dynamic properties from the frequencies from which the new frequency was derived which includes being able to modulate and demodulate the aforementioned plasma layers.

When nexrad facilities are sequentially activated, they can dynamically engage the bursts of superheated water vapor that have been, or are being, released by the cooling towers from an array of power plants. Furthermore, as previously indicated, given that various heavy metals are present in chemtrails and have become mixed with the clouds formed in conjunction with the aforementioned superheated water vapor plumes, then when one combines superheated water vapor with heavy metal chemtrail residues, and exposes that combination to the frequency, phase, and altitude shifts of sequentially activated nexrad Doppler facilities, then, one is in a position to generate and/or substantially modulate the behavior of a weather or storm system.

'Weatherwar101' has put together hours of images which disclose how all of the aforementioned three components interact with one another – that is, (1) superheated water vapor from power plants; (2) heavy metal residues from chemtrails that are sensitive to ionization dynamics generated by certain frequencies of heat/energy and have become part of the developing weather systems that are being fed millions of gallons per minute of superheated water vapor from the cooling towers of an array of power plants, and (3), the sequential, coherent pulses of energy from an array of nexrad Doppler facilities whose frequencies, phases, and other potentials (such as heterodyning) are capable of being used to modulate and demodulate the behavior of developing weather systems formed in conjunction with (1) and (2) noted previously. His work is not speculative in character but, rather, is empirical in nature.

For example, 'weatherwar101' indicates that the process of heterodyning frequency – that is, combining two frequencies to produce a new frequency with a different sort of impact on the atmosphere – is capable of generating slow wave patterns such as what are known as "gravity waves" that are capable of driving storm systems. When gravity waves in the atmosphere are created through the heterodyning process and the leading edge of those waves are sufficiently fed by superheated water vapor, then storm fronts are established in the form of, for example, 'shelf clouds' and 'roll clouds.'

GRITS -- which stands for 'Gravity Wave Interactions With Tornados]' – is a computer model developed by Tim Coleman that has been used to study how gravity waves interact with severe storm systems such as tornados, and he describes gravity waves as being similar to the waves that roll across the surface of oceans but, instead, such waves roll through the sky, and gravity is what maintains those waves as they are pulled up and pulled down by forces of gravity.

Gravity waves are initiated when, for whatever reason, the atmosphere is disturbed in some significant way. Thus, if there were a sudden change in the Jet Stream or if a wind shear of some kind occurred, or if there were a sudden updraft in a thunderstorm, these sorts of events would set gravity waves in motion much like a rock thrown into the water will generate ripples that extend out from the point of the rock's entry.

Nexrad Doppler radar facilities are also capable of setting gravity waves in motion and, therefore, can be used to induce severe weather systems to become manifest in the form of a tornado. In other words, sequentially programmed beams from a group of nexrad facilities are also capable of creating the sorts of gravity waves, wind shear elements, and vortex torque forces that are capable of inducing a weather system that also is being fed sufficient amounts of superheated water vapor from power plant cooling towers that, together, enable the storm system to begin to rotate with significant speeds – the sorts of conditions out of which tornados arise.

When a gravity wave (and gravity waves sometimes come in sets) is induced – say, by sequential pulses from various nexrad facilities – to push against a thunderstorm in rotation, the storm system becomes compressed. As a result, according to Tim Coleman, the storm system begins to spin faster like a skater who is in rotation and pulls in his, her, or their arms and begins to spin faster during the process of conserving angular momentum.

Gravity waves are also associated with the creation of significant forces of wind shear. Thus, if one were to use a set of phased sequential pulses from an array of properly situated nexrad facilities, then, gravity waves could be both generated and maneuvered to induce certain kinds of weather systems to begin to spin faster. Such sequentially pulsed rotating frequencies are sometimes referred to as "frequency scoops" which take heavy-metal chemtrail infused and artificially created water vapor clouds from power plant cooling towers and spin them up into huge vortices (super cells) through which various kinds of tornados and wind shear forces can be developed that can have a multiplicity of speeds, directions, and planes of on-going dynamics.

The foregoing considerations help explain why some 60 tornados formed in a 4 day period, including the Moore, Oklahoma F5 category tornado in May of 2013. Apparently, heavy metal chemtrails, plus millions of gallons per minute of superheated water vapor from power plant cooling towers, plus nexrad Doppler facilities are a potentially dangerous triad.

Aside from the previously noted point that the heavy metal aluminum, along with many other heavy metals and various other components to be discussed shortly, are being dispersed via chemtrails and that said aluminum can serve as an accelerant for the fires that have been ravaging many parts of California for a number of years and where high levels of aluminum have been found to be present in the barks of trees and in the soil, one also might keep in mind that gravity waves can be maneuvered to generate wind shear forces and that in a number of cases – for example, the Thomas Fire that burned from early December 2017 to late March 2018 – fires were, at times, accompanied by extremely high winds which helped to intensify those fires as well as assisted them to spread. In fact, the fires were said by officials to be caused by downed power lines that had been toppled by inexplicable winds.

However, 'weatherwar101' points out that research not only indicates that the winds that existed at the time the foregoing fires started were not remotely strong enough to topple power lines that were designed to withstand wind gusts greater than 56 miles per hour and, furthermore, photographs of the downed power lines where the fires were supposed to have started also show many surrounding trees that give no sign of having been touched by such allegedly initiating fires that led to massive forest fires. He also notes that GOES satellite imagery of the areas where the fires broke out show that the fires started within a short period of time relative to one another in locations that are quite disparate from each other, and, in addition, all of those fires began during the night in December – not exactly conditions that are conducive to producing massive fires in disparate locations.

Notwithstanding the foregoing considerations, 'weatherwar101' points out that once the fires got started – however that might have been – there were massive, inexplicable wind shear forces that arose and kept intensifying and spreading the various fires. Perhaps, a local, friendly nexrad facility or two provided some assistance by creating gravity waves that led to the generation of the sorts of wind shear and intense winds that were experienced during certain aspects of the Thomas Fire.

One might also note in passing that such fires release substantial amounts of carbon CNN – that is, Cloud Condensation Nuclei – into the atmosphere (as the result of hundreds of thousands of acres of carbon-based materials -- mostly trees and vegetation – having been burnt). When these CNN are combined with plumes of superheated water vapor from power plant cooling towers and, subsequently, shaped by pulses from nexrad stations that have the appropriate frequency, phase, and altitude, then, that dynamic, interacting triad of potentials will lead to the formation of storm systems involving gravity waves of one kind or another as such systems are pushed eastward from California across the United States.

In any event, apparently, prior to 1990, atmospheric gravity waves seemed to be fairly rare. However, with the advent of nexrad Doppler radar facilities in 1988, such waves can be detected on almost a daily basis, and, in addition, one might suppose that the question of how, for example, there could be more than 200 tornados that were reported during a two week period during April/May 2014 beginning with the F4 category tornado that hit Mayflower, Arkansas on April 27th might start to come into focus through the lenses of the role that nexrad Doppler facilities could be playing in the creation of those sorts of gravity waves.

The foregoing considerations lead to the next issue – namely, perhaps what can be created can also be shut down. For instance, in another video that appears on the YouTube site of 'weatherwar101', a two and a half minute long video clip is present in one of the videos that includes a sequence near the end which depicts the sudden dissipation of a tornado in just 15 seconds as it was headed toward Tinker Air Force base which is located near Moore, Oklahoma – a town that had just been flattened to a considerable extent by that same F5 tornado system which was a mile wide and had a two-mile wide debris field that stayed on the ground for 40 minutes before it suddenly dissipated .

| Technological Reflections |

'Weatherwar101' does an analysis of the 15 second period of tornado dissipation. He indicates that the foregoing termination event was caused by a dual-polarization beam which consists of both horizontally and vertically polarized pulsed beams, and during the video, 'weatherwar101' highlights the signature waveform which indicates the presence of such a beam as it cut through the trunk of the tornado.

The Moore, Oklahoma F5 tornado occurred on May 20, 2013 and killed 24 people. Interestingly enough, approximately 160 nexrad facilities in the United States either had been, or were in the process of being, upgraded with dual-pol technology (i.e., dual polarization technology) at the time of the aforementioned tornado and all upgrades were supposed to be completed by mid-2013 ... maybe someone decided to take a newly 'dual-pol' upgraded nexrad radar facility out for a test drive.

In another video, 'weatherwar101' explores the birth and development of Hurricane Harvey which was a category 4 storm that made landfall in Texas and Louisiana in late August of 2017. The storm had been trying to form since August 16th, 2017 but – and this is all shown in the aforementioned video – the storm had fallen apart and been re-started a number of times.

For much of its life, the storm consisted of little more than a collection of a series of sudden bursts of superheated water vapor that seemed to be emanating from cooling towers affiliated with power plants that populated many of the 13 sovereign island states and 12 dependent territories that were in the general vicinity of the weather system. Presumably, there also were a number of nexrad stations on some of the foregoing island states or territories that were equipped to modulate the weather system, but as 'weatherwar101' points out through a news clip, the U.S. government has one, or more, vessels known as SBX-1 -- a sea-based X-Band radar facility that is the big brother of the land-based nexrad facilities, and, therefore, even if no such nexrad facilities existed on those island states or territories, one, or more, of the SBX-1 vessels might have been able to fill the void in technology required for storm generation.

The SBX-1 is a self-propelled, floating radar array system that is operated by a crew of 86 individuals that is capable of operating in heavy seas and high winds. The vessel has been operational since 2006.

After several false starts, Harvey began to develop into, first, a tropical storm and, then, into a Category 4 hurricane that caused more than one hundred deaths and 125 billion dollars in damage. Once the false starts were done and Harvey began to be put together in a viable manner, Harvey only required 40 hours to go from a fledgling weather system to a tropical storm and, then, finally to a Category 4 hurricane.

According to 'weatherwar101', the storm system, apparently, was being fed millions of gallons per minute of superheated water vapor that helped energize and enhance the storm as it made its way toward its date with Texas and Louisiana. Moreover, he believes that once Harvey made landfall, it was further enhanced by the release of massive amounts of superheated water vapor from land-based power plant systems which helped transition the storm into a "prolonged rain and flood event."

Weatherwar101' did a similar analysis in conjunction with Typhoon Haiyan (known in the Philippines as Typhoon Yolanda) that took place in November 2013 and constituted one of the most powerful cyclones every recorded. As was the case with Hurricane Harvey, 'weatherwar101' shows via infrared imaging how there were bursts of superheated water vapor which were feeding the Haiyan weather system, and these appeared to be coming from power plants on land and not from the ocean.

Earlier, mention was made of some of the extensive fires that have taken place in California (e.g., 2003, 2007, and 2008, as well as 2015-16, 2017-2018 and beyond). During that portion of this presentation, the suggestion was put forth that, perhaps, nexrad Doppler facilities might have been used to generate atmospheric conditions that could have led to the emergence of wind shear forces and high winds that could have impacted and intensified and spread of some of those fires.

One might also note that the long-standing drought conditions that have existed in California could also be shaped by refraining from using nexrad Doppler facilities -- in conjunction with the superheated water vapor plumes being released and the chemtrails that have been dispersed across California for well over a decade – to create artificial forms of precipitation – that is, rain. In other words, if 'weatherwar101' is correct and the hydrological cycle is broken, then, if nexrad stations are not used to help direct clouds formed through superheated water vapor and metal-heavy chemtrail flotsam to generate the sorts of weather fronts that would lead to precipitation, then drought is another weather condition that is capable of being controlled by the nexrad Doppler system simply by not doing what needs to be done to terminate those drought conditions.

There are some who believe that the California drought has been brought about by the active use of HAARP facilities. However, 'weatherwar101' has demonstrated a method through which drought can be established by a passive use – or non-use -- of nexrad Doppler radar since all one has to do is let the broken hydrological cycle continue on as is – namely, broken -- in the areas where one wishes to create drought conditions.

Alternatively, if one wished to create flood conditions, all one would have to do is create what amounts to atmospheric scalar walls through the employment of heterodyning and gravity waves as a way of keeping a storm system relatively stationary as well as providing a means of continuing to fuel such storm systems with more and more superheated water vapor from power plant cooling towers. The storm systems could, then, be manipulated to continue to release massive amounts of artificial precipitation over a given area and, thereby, help to bring about flood conditions.

One further manifestation of manufactured weather involves so-called polar vortices and the process of ice-nucleation. 'Weatherwar101' makes references to the phenomenon of "heavy wet snow" falling in temperatures that run as high as 50 degrees Fahrenheit.

He indicates that the foregoing phenomenon is a function of artificial ice nucleation. In addition, he notes that, usually speaking, there are two ways of bringing about artificial ice nucleation: (1) through various kinds of chemical reactions; (2) by using certain species of bacteria.

For instance, one kind of chemical reaction that is capable of inducing the formation of ice would occur if one were to take two dry solids such as barium hydroxide and ammonium nitrate and, then, mix them together. The temperature of the mixture – which we will assume is in a beaker of some kind -- would drop sufficiently low to be able to freeze water if the latter were placed on a piece of wood and, then, one were to set the beaker with the mixture of chemicals on top of that thin layer of water.

The foregoing reaction is endothermic in nature – that is, it is a chemical reaction which absorbs heat/energy from the environment. The chemical reaction in the beaker is actually removing energy/heat from the water on the wood, and that is why the water freezes.

The second mode of artificial ice nucleation mentioned by 'weatherwar101' involves the use of certain kinds of bacteria which possess proteins that are capable of serving as catalytic agents that are able to change the phase of $H2O$ from liquid to solid ... in other words, from water to ice. This form of ice-nucleation is actually faster (it takes place almost immediately) or is more efficient than the chemical reaction which was described earlier and that usually requires a few minutes before it occurs.

A third way of inducing artificial forms of ice nucleation is through certain kinds of frequency interactions that are sequential in nature and act on residues contained in chemtrails that have become caught up in various developing weather systems. If such sequential cycling of certain frequencies occurs in circumstances that are conducive to the occurrence of artificial ice nucleation events in conditions that already are sub-freezing, then, not only will snow and ice be produced in those circumstances and conditions, but, as well, this will also be accompanied by a further lowering of the prevailing sub-freezing temperatures.

Some individuals refer to the foregoing sort of conditions as being due to a vortex of some kind that, somehow, inexplicably, has broken off from a region near the North Pole (in other words a "polar vortex"). However, 'weatherwar101' maintains that such a process of ice nucleation and accompanying lowering of temperature might be due to another process or set of processes altogether (in other words, chemical and/or bacterial components interacting with sequential frequency arrays of certain kinds), and if the conditions in which ice-nucleation takes place are warm, or even hot, then, nonetheless, hail, ice, and wet, heavy snow might, nonetheless, be precipitated.

| Technological Reflections |

Across more than a hundred videos prepared over a period of four or five years, 'weatherwar101' has rigorously broken down, in great detail, the considerable evidence that is available from, among other possible sources, infrared, satellite, and radar imagery ... evidence which is capable of demonstrating how some set of individuals of unknown numbers is, and has been, engaged in the manufacture of weather – not only in the United States but elsewhere in the world as well. 'Weatherwar101' has demonstrated how virtually every form of weather – from: Clouds, to: snow, hail, wind shear, torrential rain, cold, drought, gravity wave driven storm fronts, tornados, and hurricanes – can be manufactured through the interaction of: (1) superheated water vapor from cooling towers (11,000 of them in the United States and some 70,000 of them worldwide), (2) heavy metal laden chemtrails which include – based on air, soil, and water samples -- aluminum, barium, strontium, cadmium, titanium, chromium, copper, nickel, iron, and zinc, as well as (3) nexrad Doppler radar facilities which have the capacity to shoot pulses containing 750,000 watts of power that are capable of being modulated via an array of directed, programmable, sequentially changing frequencies, phases, and altitudes involving such pulses.

The nexrad radar facilities are operated under the authority of (a) the National Weather Service, (b) the Federal Aviation Agency – in other words, the FAA, and (c) the United States Air Force. The cooling towers which release billions of gallons of superheated water vapor into the atmosphere every day at varying times are operated by an array of power companies or corporations. And, finally, chemtrails – which have been discovered to contain many kinds of toxic materials, and not just heavy metals – have been dumped on billions of people without the informed consent of the latter by an array of pilots, technicians, and administrators – both military and civilian.

All of the foregoing services, agencies, corporations, and the like have a moral, if not legal, responsibility to address the entire array of issues that have been raised through the considerable research of 'weatherwar101'. If that perspective concerning the possible man-made nature of much of – if not all of – the weather is correct, then, the lives of hundreds of millions, if not billions, of people have been, and are continuing to be, placed in harm's way every single day of the year through the catastrophic impact that man-made or assisted hurricanes, tornados, floods, wind shear, droughts, hail storms, fires, cold, and blizzards are having on the lives of people around the world as well as on the environment in which we all live, and on the crops on which we rely for our food, and on the homes we rely on for our safety and comfort.

The research that is documented through weatherwar101wordpress.com, as well as a corresponding YouTube channel and a short book providing an overview of the work seems to have stopped in 2017. What this means is uncertain.

Perhaps, the individual passed away. Maybe, that person decided to move in a different direction and felt that undertaking new projects might best be done in a non public way because, quite frankly, there are all too many natural as well as ideological psychopaths in the world -- along with any number of paid trolls -- who have nothing better to do with their time than to seek to abuse, as well as to try to make things difficult for, those who might have something of value to say or to offer to others.

A Twitter account associated with 'weatherwar101' has also been suspended. However, since Twitter has suspended a lot of accounts for reasons that have nothing to do with anything but a desire to censor information and control the narrative or impoverish discussion, then, the upshot of such a suspension for me is that it merely eliminates one more venue through which one might have access to what 'weatherwar101' has been seeking to communicate to people.

I don't know who 'weathewar101' is. The foregoing moniker is a pseudonym of sorts.

Not knowing the true identity of 'weatherwar101' is neither here nor there for me. I have engaged him, her or them through the work that has been produced, and whatever conclusions I have arrived at as a result of studying a good portion of that work is not based on an identity but on the nature of what has been said or written.

Whoever that person or those persons might be, I feel the individual is sincere with respect to what she, he or they are doing or have done. Of course, I could be wrong about this, and, moreover, even if that person or persons is, or are, sincere, sincerity does not guarantee that an individual is necessarily correct concerning what is being sincerely explicated.

Ultimately, the views of 'weatherwar101' might prove to be true or they might be found to be false, or that perspective might entail some combination of being right about some things and wrong about others. However, such an ultimate determination has not, yet, been attained, but since that individual has – or those individuals have -- established a prima facie case of sufficient evidential and rational rigor and detail, I believe the ideas about the possibility that much, if not all, weather is man-made warrant further critical reflection and investigation by all of us and not necessarily just the services, agencies, corporations, and technocrats who are criminally implicated by 'weatherwar101's' findings.

Notwithstanding the foregoing considerations, I also need to remind anyone who is reading, listening to, or watching this presentation that whatever mistakes I might have made with respect to representing or characterizing the views of 'weatherwar101' are, of course, my responsibility and should not be attributed to 'weatherwar101' or any of the individuals that work with that person. I have tried to be as fair, impartial, and accurate as I could be with respect to the task of trying to capture the perspective of another human being or other human beings, but, sometimes, this doesn't always work out well, and I hope the current presentation is not one of those occasions.

Before bringing this essay to a close, there are a few further related items that should be discussed. 'Weatherwar101' touches on these subjects in a few of the videos that have been published, and if I do so as well, then, this will bring us back full circle to the subject matter with which the current presentation began – namely, chemtrails.

Although there has been a long-standing tradition on the part of some individuals to impugn the character and/or sanity of anyone who tries to engage the topic of chemtrails in a serious manner, nevertheless, a body of substantial evidence concerning the reality and nature of chemtrails has been accumulating for more than two decades. Furthermore, despite the efforts of government officials and other disinformation sleight of mouth impresarios to deny that chemtrails were anything other than contrails and despite the efforts of those individuals who sought to paint anyone who tried to communicate contrary evidence concerning the issue of chemtrails to the general public as being nothing more than tin-foil-hat zealots who ought to be committed to some sort of psychiatric facility, if not eliminated in some other fashion, nevertheless, such individuals might have finally retreated to another limited-hangout perspective which admits that while, yes, chemtrails are real and that while, yes, those effluents being dumped on people do contain some heavy metals which our best and brightest geoengineers have concluded are the most promising way discovered to date for resisting the onslaught of impending global warming, nonetheless, all there is to tell about chemtrails is that there is nothing more to the story beyond the existence of a few heavy metals which are really being dumped on us for our own good.

To begin with, whether, or not, dumping toxic heavy metals on human beings has had any significant impact on mitigating the alleged threat of global warming is a research issue for which supporting evidence is not as readily available as some individuals have claimed or as other advocates of that model might have supposed was the case. Furthermore, there has been a steadily accumulating body of evidence indicating how those toxic heavy metals have been changing the pH of soils in problematic ways and how those toxic heavy metals have had a devastating impact on the environment, and how those toxic heavy metals have been serving as accelerants in intense forest fires, and how those toxic heavy metals have found their ways into our bodies and are implicated in any number of diseases – from Alzheimer's to other kinds of neurological disorders, and, therefore, given such a strong body of evidence, one has to revisit the question raised by Professor Keith at the 2010 geoengineering symposium held in San Diego concerning just what are the risks of not dumping toxic heavy metals on human beings versus the risks of continuing to do so since the alleged "cure" seems to be worse than the disease it allegedly is treating.

Moreover, as the research of 'weatherwar101' seems to demonstrate, the idea that chemtrails are necessary for the struggle to mitigate impending climate warming might be nothing more than a

| Technological Reflections |

problematic cover story that has been created in order to hide a dual use purpose of those chemtrail effluents. One facet of such a dual-use purpose has to do with the possibility that chemtrails are designed to combat climate warming, while the other purpose entailed by chemtrails – which has, until the work of, 'weatherwar101' been hidden -- involves the capacity of the heavy metals which have been demonstrated to be present in chemtrails to be used as part of a process for directing the manufacture of weather systems that appear to be responsible for the deaths of thousands of individuals, as well as apparently being responsible for billions, if not trillions, of dollars in property destruction, together with seeming to be interfering with and undermining the ability of the farming industry to provide a reliable means of providing food for society.

As threatening as all of the foregoing might be, unfortunately, there is also considerable evidence to indicate that there might be much more in chemtrails than just the toxic heavy metals that could be being used to manufacture weather or attempt to mitigate global warming ... evidence which carries implications that official sources continue to naysay just as they initially did in conjunction with even admitting the reality of chemtrails being in the sky at all. For example, consider a study conducted approximately a decade ago by Analytika which is an independent center of research in France that specializes in organic chemistry.

The focus of the aforementioned study concerned some air samples that had been gathered from four disparate locations in France. Those samples bore traces of a number of organic compounds that are commonly present in jets: Fuels, lubricants, and reactors. The presence of these compounds suggested the possibility that the four samples which were being studied might have been part of the chemtrail residue that were been dispersed from jet aircraft if for no other reason than that there were no other plausible explanations for how the samples that were caught in the different air filters could have found their way into those filters with the jet-related properties that were observed in those samples.

In addition to the foregoing organic compounds, the four samples that were studied also contained a number of toxic synthetic compounds. These toxic compounds were known to have the capacity to serve as endocrine disrupters and involved, among other molecules, several kinds of phthalates [PHAL-lates] which are substances that often are added to plastics to increase the flexibility, transparency, and durability of those products, but which also can be found in some of the fuels and lubricants that are used in jet aircraft..

The endocrine system consists of an array of hormone-messenger molecules that are released into the circulatory system and help direct and regulate the functioning of a variety of biological process such as: Blood sugar, cellular differentiation, reproductive activity, as well as growth of the body in general. Obviously, anything which disrupts the foregoing sorts of processes – as, for example, what the sorts of phthalates [PHAL-lates] are known to do that were found in the aforementioned samples – constitutes a problem for human beings.

Endocrine disruptors are capable of leading to learning disabilities, developmental problems in the brain, attention deficit disorders, and various forms of cancer involving the thyroid and prostate glands. Tailliez Bernard, who is the founder and director of Analytika, believes that the foregoing findings indicate there might be a new form of biological hazard associated with the sort of pollution that arises from jet air traffic – both military and civilian – and which is showing up in soil, air, water, and blood samples.

There was a long list of identifiable compounds and molecules that were detected in the French samples being studied at Analytika, many of which pose hazards of one kind or another However, what was the most disturbing finding associated with the foregoing study of samples was the long list of non-identifiable, synthetic components that also were present in the four samples being studied … components which gave hints of being a function of various kinds of biotechnology and nanotechnology.

Twelve years prior to the foregoing French study, Clifford Carnicom gathered air samples at a relatively high altitude in New Mexico, and found filaments in those samples that were very similar – in terms of structure and properties – to the kinds of filaments that are found in those who suffer from Morgellons Syndrome … a disorder which is characterized by lesions that produce tubular filaments that are capable of being cultured, and when this is done, give rise to extensive networks of filament colonies.

Individuals who exhibit advanced symptoms of Morgellons Syndrome report that what had begun with just filament-like fibers coming out of lesions in their skin has progressed to forming strange crystalline-like and metallic-like, often multi-colored structures. Interestingly enough, according to Sofia Smallstorm, an independent researcher, tissue samples taken from individuals who do not exhibit any of the symptoms of Morgellons Syndrome have also have been shown to possess the same sorts of fibers that are found among those who suffer from Morgellons Syndrome ... fibers that can, subsequently, be cultured and which, eventually, also produce extensive networks of the same sorts of filaments that are present in individuals with Morgellons Syndrome.

Like the materials found in the 2012 French study mentioned earlier, the filaments discovered by Clifford Carnicom did not match anything that had been catalogued in the established data bases for compounds and molecules – whether synthetic or organic Moreover, in May of 2004 Clifford Carnicom found desiccated erythrocytes – that is, dried red blood cells – in some of the air samples he had been collecting, and when these erythrocytes were studied by a biologist who specialized in microscopy the dried blood cells were determined to have been bioengineered.

In addition, sub-micron – that is, nanometer (one billionth of a meter) – sized filaments containing bio-engineered red blood cells that were capable of replication outside of the body have been observed. These nano-structures proved to be quite resilient despite having been exposed to toxic levels of both bleach and acid.

Sofia Smallstorm talks about a woman by the name of Jan Smith who suffers from advanced Morgellons Syndrome. Jan has had the filament-fibers that emanate from her skin tested.

She learned that those filament-fibers consisted of synthetic, high-density substances. In other words, they were man-made.

More specifically, the filament-fibers were made from cellulose and GNA. GNA stands for glycol or glycerol nucleic acid.

GNA is similar to DNA and RNA except that the sugar-phosphodiester backbone of the former is made up of three-carbon sugars rather than five-carbon sugars. In addition, GNA is not known to occur in the natural world.

GNA is considered to be an ideal building-block for nano-technology structures because the units of GNA tend to self-assemble according to relatively simple rules of chemical attraction.

The first nano-structure that exhibited self-assembly properties was developed by the Biodesign Institute at Arizona State University. The nano-structures were made using only units of GNA.

The aforementioned research of Sofia Smallstorm indicates that an article based on research in Japan -- which was funded by the National Institute of Health in the United States – discovered that various conduction polymers and gold-nano particles are, sometimes, found entangled within self-assembling GNA structures. And, interestingly enough, when some of the filament-fibers from the previously mentioned Jan Smith were tested by subjecting them to an intense flame, little beads of gold in the form of either an orb or a tentacle bearing a golden head were observed to appear.

Do the foregoing synthetic filaments, GNA nano-structures, and/or bio-engineered, desiccated red blood cells – all of which are man-made -- come from the chemtrails that are being poured on humanity? After all, chemtrails already have been demonstrated to contain highly toxic heavy metals as well as various kinds of toxic endocrine disrupters, so, would one necessarily be entering the realm of the implausible to merely raise the question as to whether, or not, synthetic filaments, GNA-based nano-structures, and/or bioengineered erythrocytes might also be present in chemtrails and that just as the possible real reason for the presence of heavy metals in chemtrails has never been properly acknowledged (namely, that they seem to play a key role in making man-made weather possible), so too, the reason why such other man-made elements are present in the chemtrails that are being dumped on humanity might remain unacknowledged. Moreover, just as particles in the form of heavy metals are characterized by the property of being sensitive to certain kinds of frequencies that are capable of maneuvering such metals to perform different kinds of functions in the atmosphere, so too, perhaps the synthetic filaments, GNA-based nano-structures, and bioengineered, desiccated erythrocytes are also sensitive to, or dependent on, certain kinds of frequencies in order to become active to serve whatever unknown function they might have been designed to perform under the right set of circumstances.

Irrespective of whether, or not, any of the nanotechnology or bioengineered materials which – for several decades now – have been found to be present in various air samples can be shown to be related to the issue of chemtrails, the fact that such things have been found at all should be deeply disturbing. Furthermore, just as the issue of man-made weather should be pursued with rigor and critical reflection, so too, should the man-made synthetic structures that, somehow, have infiltrated human beings also be subjected to intense scrutiny.

On a variety of fronts, considerable evidence seems to indicate that human beings are, in one way or another, being subjected – directly and indirectly -- to different forces and dimensions of geoengineering in a manner that tends to suggest that we are seen by self-absorbed technocrats as entities which can be manipulated, modified, mitigated, or eliminated just like any other "object" in the universe … self-absorbed and self-serving technocrats who seem to believe that they have an inherent right to experiment with the Earth and its inhabitants – human and otherwise – in any way they deem necessary without any hint of informed consent to the rest of humanity. As was indicated in an earlier presentation of mine concerning the issue of technocracy, technocrats appear to consider human beings to be just another dimension of the infrastructure which they are seeking to overhaul in order to produce the sort of efficient, soul-less, authoritarian society with which they are enamored in such a delusional, self-aggrandizing, and compassionless manner.

4. PCR and Models

On October 29, 2021 an article appeared in the Australian National Review. The title of the article is: "Coronavirus Scandal Breaking in Merkel's Germany. False Positives and the Drosten PCR Test", and the article was written by William Engdahl.

The so-called Drosten PCR test was the alleged brain child of Christian Drosten. The test played a central role in advancing the policies of WHO, the CDC, the FDA, and the NIH with respect to many of their COVID policies – including lockdowns, the wearing of masks, social distancing, as well as the concerted, authoritarian march toward introducing gene therapy and passport mandates world-wide that were intended to control the movements of everyone in society according to the likes and dislikes of fascist governments, corporations, and various medical practitioners (a variation on the method of digitalized social credit scores that were, and are being, used to oppress people in China).

On January 20th, 2020, the journal *Eurosurveillance* (a department within the EU Center for Disease Control) published an article entitled: "Detection of 2019 Novel Coronavirus (2019-nCOV) by Real-time RT-PCR"

The paper was a collaboration involving the alleged work of Christian Drosten along with a number of his colleagues from the Berlin Virology Institute at Charité Hospital, as well as the head of a small biotech company located in Berlin. The paper claimed to have established a procedure which was capable of determining whether, or not, someone contained within them the virus that was supposedly at the heart of the initial Wuhan outbreak of illness in 2019. Interestingly enough, the Drosten paper also noted that the researchers whose work was being given expression through that article didn't have access to the actual virus which their test was supposed to be able to detect (more on this shortly).

Instead of basing their test on the specific properties of the SARS-CoV-2 virus (assuming it actually existed), the Drosten group used a surrogate marker for purposes of identification – namely, the 2003 SARS virus. However, this just raises the same sorts of questions all over again.

More specifically, if one does not have access to the SARS-CoV-2 virus, then, why should one suppose that claiming to have access to the 2003 SARS virus is – methodologically speaking -- any more sustainable? Surely, one can ask: Has anyone successfully been able to isolate and purify the alleged 2003 SARS virus, or is that virus just another entry into the theoretical sweepstakes that is being operated by virologists?

Moreover, despite the similarity in names, one still does not know what the nature of the relationship is between the base pairs that supposedly – if they actually exist – have a unique sequence with respect to 2003 SARS and how this differs from the sequence of base pairs that supposedly – if they actually exist – have a unique sequence in conjunction with SARS-CoV-2.

Furthermore, if the alleged detection-test -- which, allegedly, had been developed by Drosten et. al. – had been based on various, supposedly, synthetic fragments that, allegedly, had been derived from the structure of 2003 SARS, why should one accept – without independent confirmation of any kind – that what Drosten was proposing as a test would be capable of detecting the presence of SARS-COV-2? There is a lack of clarity concerning the nature of the relationship between 2003 SARS and SarsCoV-2 in much of what the Drosten paper asserts and claims.

Immediately – even perhaps sooner than immediately since there is evidence indicating that the paper was acknowledged and endorsed by WHO before the article had even been released for publication – the paper received the endorsement of the Director General of WHO, Tedros Adhanom Ghebreyesus. This marked the beginning of the time when the Drosten PCR test became the so-called gold standard for detecting whether, or not, someone supposedly had the SARS-CoV-2 virus.

The foregoing Corman-Drosten paper – as it is sometimes referred to – was submitted to *Eurosurveillance* on January 21st, 2020, accepted for publication by *Eurosurveillance* on January 22nd, 2020, and subsequently published on-line during January 23rd, 2020.

There is no evidence indicating that – according to usual standards of scientific publishing – the foregoing paper ever went through a process of critical, peer review. However, on November 27, 2020 --

some 10 months, or so, after the release of the Corman-Drosten paper – a group of 27 well-regarded microbiologists, virologists, and other scientists from related disciplines did engage in a critical review of the Corman-Drosten paper, and as a result of their review, indicated that the Drosten article should be removed from *Eurosurveillance* list of publications.

Among other problems, the foregoing group of 27 scientists and researchers indicated that both Christian Drosten, along with one of his co-authors – namely, Dr. Chantal Reusken – had failed to inform potential readers of their paper that they were both board members of the *Eurosurveillance* journal. Not only had their paper not undergone any sort of peer review process, but Drosten and Reusken appeared to be using their insider status at *Eurosurveillance* to have the paper accepted and published (without peer review) – an obvious conflict of interest that threatens the credibility of scientific journalism.

Another issue that was raised by the aforementioned 27-member peer review group had to do with the considerable degree of disconnect between the paper and what actually was taking place in real time during the paper's release. More specifically, why was the Corman-Drosten article recommending use of a RT-PCR test as a world-wide standard during a time when only 6 cases had been detected in Wuhan that might have some sort of SARS-CoV-2 related disease connection? Even more pointedly, why had the WHO been so anxious to acknowledge and endorse such a perspective even before that paper had been released to the public for publication and despite the fact that there were no more than 6 cases existing at that time for which the test – assuming it to have been valid and reliable – might be applicable.

Quite a few months ago, I remember listening to a very informative discussion on *"The Infectious Myth Podcast"* between the late David Crowe and Stephen Bustin (his PhD is in molecular genetics and was granted by Trinity College in Dublin) who is an expert in all aspects of what is known as 'Quantitative PCR". In fact Stephen Bustin is one of the founders and developers of the MIQE Guidelines that are used for reporting QPCR and digital PCR results.

Q (quantitative) PCR concerns real time dynamics to which various editions of quantitative PCR give expression. In addition, there is something that is known as RT-PCR which focuses on the use of Reverse Transcriptase processes in conjunction with PCR.

During the interview, Dr. Bustin indicated that the properties and characteristics of Real Time – PCR dynamics are the ones that are defined by the MIQE Guidelines. He contrasts the forgoing sort of dynamics with the end point assays that are done when one runs an appropriate form of gel, then observes, in real time, the nature of the florescence that arises in conjunction with that gel as a function of the PCR amplification process, and then, plots the progress of such growth by measuring the degree of florescence that is being manifested over time.

The MIQE Guidelines focus on issues and problems that take place prior to engaging in the end-point florescence process. The monitoring of the degree of florescence that might be present as an indication of the amount of amplification that is taking place is a separate issue.

Another distinction of importance involves the terms "probe" and "primer". A probe is used to help detect the character of the target in some original sample of RNA, whereas a primer tends to delimit the portion of the DNA that is being replicated during the PCR stage of the process.

Dr. Bustin noted during the interview that one can get a PCR reaction without benefit of a probe, and, as such, the primers are sufficient for generating a PCR product that can be detected with certain kinds of non-specific dyes. However, he goes on to indicate that the probe can serve as a sort of insurance policy that permits one to have confidence that whatever result emerges from the PCR process, it constitutes a real result which cannot be dismissed as a misleading artifact that might arise in cases where a non-specific dye might have attached itself to something that gave an erroneous sort of replication but, instead, probes can actually be tied to the product in which one is interested.

Probes tend to be optional. Dr. Bustin suggests that for a diagnostic assay, one often would be likely to use a probe, but one might not always use a probe in research settings because probes add to the cost of the assay.

Technological Reflections

At this point the David Crowe-Stephen Bustin discussion moved on to the issue of some of the many problems that surround being able to secure reliable replication of results within the scope of Quantitative PCR dynamics that occur when being assessed through the MIQE Guidelines. Dr. Bustin noted that there are many, many factors that can affect the sorts of numbers one gets when one carries out any given RT-PCR.

For instance, he indicates that one will arrive at very different quantitative outcomes depending on a variety of factors. Among these factors are: How one goes about preparing one's sample; which enzymes are used in the process; what protocols are used; as well as the methods one employs in order to interpret the data generated by the RT-PCR process.

One very important point that was noted early on by Dr. Bustin during the foregoing interview is the following. Although various sequencing issues do arise when one is engaged in techniques involving RT-PCR within the context of the MIQE Guidelines, nonetheless, the MIQE Guidelines do not cover issues and problems that involve procedures for determining what the genetic sequence might be or should be for a particular instance of bacterium or some alleged virus or other form of microorganism.

One could go on exploring a litany of possible idiosyncrasies and problems that surround the process of Quantitative PCR, but enough has been said in the foregoing to help give emphasis to the crucial issue that is at the heart of so-called PCR testing. Unless one's probe and/or primer can be shown to be capable of identifying some facet of the SARS-CoV-2 genetic sequence that is unique to SARS-CoV-2 and helps differentiate it from all other viral sequences, then, really, a PCR test begins at no beginning and works toward no end.

If tests of some kind are to be used to identify the presence of a specific kind of virus, then that test – whatever its nature – must be capable of reliably and credibly being able to disclose or discern the presence of such viral uniqueness. If the test cannot accomplish this, then, the test is useless.

The issue of unique identification has nothing to do with the number of rounds of amplification that take place during the PCR process. The probe and primer that are used must be capable of demonstrating that the RNA or DNA remnant for which one is searching in a given sample can not only be identified as representing, or giving expression to, a particular kind of species (for example, a coronavirus of some kind) but as well, such a sequence must be capable of being specifically tied to a unique genetic sequence within the SARS-COV-2 genome that indicates that the viral agent in question is, in fact, novel.

Returning to the issue of the previously mentioned Corman-Drosten paper, one of the many problems that the aforementioned group of 27 scientists who performed a peer review of the Corman-Drosten article discovered is the following set of ambiguities. Drosten et al. presented a number of unspecified primer and probe sequences in their article that, supposedly, were to be used by laboratories for identifying who did, and did not have – allegedly – COVID-19.

Due to the lack of specificity in those primer and probe sequences, one had no basis for identifying a sequence that could be shown to be unique to SARS-CoV-2. Labs could have used any one of the six, or so, primer and probe sequences that had been indicated for a testing process, but no one would be able to demonstrate that any of those sequences had anything to do with the SARS-CoV-2 genomic sequence ... garbage in, and garbage out.

If one looks into the research background of Christian Drosten, one finds as many disturbing research mistakes as exist in the background of Neil Ferguson of Imperial College, a epidemiologist and professor of mathematical biology, who came up with a model for the alleged lethality of SARS-CoV-2 that were wildly inaccurate, Ferguson had committed many similar kinds of mistakes of modeling.

For example, during the Mad Cow crisis that captivated England in 2001, Ferguson's model indicated that 150,000 people would die and, as a result recommended that millions of animals be slaughtered. Ultimately, only 200 people died, and because Tony Blair accepted Ferguson's recommendation based on the aforementioned inflated model, the farming community in England was devastated for years to come.

Ferguson was again at his inflationary – and completely inaccurate -- best when he generated a model for the 2005 Bird Flu that claimed 200 million people might die from that form of influenza. The actual number of deaths attributed to the alleged epidemic involved just a few hundred individuals.

In 2009, Ferguson came up with a model that predicted that at least 65,000 people would die from the Swine Flu. The actual number of deaths was in the order of 500 people

Drosten made the same sort of fear-mongering prognostications in Germany that Ferguson had made in England. For instance, in relation to the alleged SARS crisis that was being given prominent media space in 2003, Drosten had stated: "... if the epidemic cannot be pushed back in the near future, there may be repeated cases of SARS." However, according to WHO data, since the first appearance of SARS in 2003, there have only been 8,096 cases of SARS worldwide, 774 of whom died, and only nine of these deaths occurred in Germany.

For anyone to die of a given disease is tragic. Nonetheless, Drosten had been completely wrong about the idea that SARS constituted some sort of epidemic that was going to devastate economies.

Drosten's penchant for exaggerating or misrepresenting the actual character of a situation again showed up during the 2009 Swine Flu debacle just as Ferguson's inflationary rhetoric did. At that time, Drosten stated that: "The disease is a serious common viral infection that produces significantly more side effects than anyone can imagine from the worse vaccine," and he went on to urge everyone to get vaccinated against the Swine Flu.

The predicted pandemic never took place. Moreover, while millions of dollars worth of vaccines were eventually ordered, most people never took them despite Drosten's strong urging for the public to do so, and much of the foregoing resistance to the issue of taking a vaccine had to do with the fact that a great deal of evidence had accumulated which showed that the vaccines were causing far more damage to people than was Swine Flu.

One further facet of Christian Drosten's manner of conducting himself that pertains to the credibility – or lack thereof – of the alleged PCR test supposedly developed by Drosten concerns his business arrangement with Olfert Landt who is owner of the Berlin biotech company TIB Molbiol Syntheselabor GMbH.

Prior to the issue of Corona, they had jointly developed PCR tests to be used with SARS in 2002-2003. In 2011, they developed another PCR test for EHEC (Enterohemorrhagic Escherichia Coli). A further such test was developed in 2012 in conjunction with MERS. In 2016, they put forward another such test for Zika, and in 2017, they continued on the process and extended it to Yellow Fever.

According to a *Berliner Zeitung* article, Landt claimed that at the heart of their business model was the following principle (if one can call it that): "The test, the design, the development came from the Charité. We just immediately converted that into a kit form. When you don't have the virus, which was initially available only in Wuhan, we can make a synthetic gene (i.e., using computer modeling) to simulate the virus genome. We did that very quickly."

The foregoing is an extraordinary statement. In essence, it indicates that Drosten and Landt merely created or invented an arbitrary gene as a way of simulating an alleged virus genome, and, yet, there was nothing to indicate that the invention of such a synthetic gene had anything to do with the actual genomic structure of the viral genes which, supposedly, Drosten and Landt were trying to model.

Furthermore, Landt was quite wrong when he claimed that the virus was available only in Wuhan. As I will show a little later, no one – not scientists in Wuhan or anywhere else – had access to an isolated virus of the kind for which any of the artificial genes had been invented.

Depending on the quality – or lack thereof – that is, or is not, generated through a given computer modeling process and which is used to generate the aforementioned synthetic gene, the latter artificial gene could be an entirely arbitrary entity which has no empirical link to the actual character of the genomic sequence of the viral entity that, allegedly, is being modeled. If the foregoing sort of mismatch between invented synthetic gene and the genetic character of some given target organism turns out to be the case, then, the PCR tests that Landt and Drosten put together for SARS in 2002-2003, or EHEC in 2011, or MERS in 2012, or Zika in 2016, or Yellow Fever in 2017 or coronavirus in 2020 are all useless markers ... that is, those synthetic or artificial genes that are generated thorough the process of computer modeling to which Landt is alluding don't actually reflect the character of what is being measured or sought.

If the foregoing is true, then, the PCR test that was used by my wife in conjunction with her illness to determine whether, or not, she had COVID-19 was nothing more than a delusional artifact of an untenable testing methodology. If so, then, what the nature of the illness was with which my wife had been battling remains uncertain.

5. Memory, Mind and Neuroscience

Recently, I watched a 'TED' talk (TED is an acronym for 'Technology, Entertainment, and Design'). The talk was given by two neuroscientists, Steve Ramirez and Xu Liu, and took place in Boston, June 2013.

The presentation was based on research that led to several publications that appeared in the science journals, *Nature* and *Science*. The title of the *Nature* article is: 'Optogenetic stimulation of a hippocampal engram activates fear memory recall' and was published in early 2012, while the *Science* report was entitled: 'Creating a False Memory in the Hippocampus' and was published in July 2013.

All of the foregoing will be elaborated upon shortly. However, first, I would like to create a context for the critical reflection that will give expression to my comments concerning the research of the two aforementioned neuroscientists.

Toward the end of the June 2013 TED presentation, Steve Ramirez indicated that one of the purposes of their talk was to bring people up to date on the kinds of research that were taking place in neuroscience, as well as to acknowledge (even if only vaguely) the existence of various ethical issues raised by their research, and, finally, to invite people to join in the discussion with respect to their research. Steve's co-presenter, Xu Liu, also stipulated at one point near the end of the talk that their research was rooted in a philosophical principle of neuron science - namely, that, ultimately, mind is a function of physical stuff ... stuff that can be "tinkered with" and a tinkering process that is limited only by our imagination.

On the one hand, the following comments constitute my acceptance of the aforementioned invitation from Steve Ramirez during the June 2013 presentation for people to join in the conversation concerning their research. Consequently, part of my comments will address some of the ethical concerns that were alluded to by Steve Ramirez during the Boston presentation, while another aspect of my comments - perhaps the more central dimension of such comments -- will revolve around an exploration of the philosophical principle cited by Xu Liu that is at the heart of neuroscience and which, as indicated earlier, seeks to reduce mental phenomena to biological, material, or physical events.

Let's begin by providing an outline of the experimental model employed by Steve Ramirez and Xu Liu. Among other things, that model involves introducing mice to a few methodological bells and whistles.

Optogenetics (a word which appeared in the title of the aforementioned *Nature* article) is a term that - as the sub-components of the word might suggest - involves combining optical and genetic properties in certain ways. Essentially, microbial or viral genes are engineered to become receptive or sensitive, in some manner, to light or optical energies and, thereby, such genetic residues are enabled to, in effect, serve as a target for light sources (e.g., lasers) that will induce the target molecules to serve like switches that are capable of turning certain aspects of cellular functioning on and off when the genetically engineered concoction is injected into, say, mice and, subsequently, activated by laser stimulation.

In their presentation, Ramirez and Liu also point out that there is a biological marker or indicator present in cells that signifies certain kinds of activity have taken place in those cells. Therefore, part of the process of genetic engineering employed in the optogenetics technique is to take a molecular component that has a sensor-like capacity that is able to detect the presence of the aforementioned cellular indicator or marker signifying recent cellular activity and, then, splice that sensor component to the aforementioned molecular/genetic switch that, subsequently, can be activated and deactivated through the application of targeted laser energies.

In the case of the Ramirez-Liu experiments, the 'switch' portion of the genetically engineered component is channelrhodopsin. This is a membrane protein that controls the flow of certain ions (for example, sodium - $Na+$) into the interior of a cell. Modifying the flow of ions into a cell is possible because channelrhodopsin is a protein whose three-dimensional conformation can be altered when stimulated by, among other things, laser light and, in the process, open or close the membrane channel-way with respect to ion flow, thereby affecting the functioning of such a cell.

To sum up, the general idea employed by Ramirez and Liu in their experiments is to identify cells that are involved in, for example, memory formation through the manner in which those cells will leave an activity signature or marker. This marker can be detected by the genetically engineered sensor-switch component and, this, in turn, will transform the cell into a target that is believed to have something to do with memory formation and which -- when deemed appropriate by the researchers - can be activated by stimulating the switch side (i.e., the membrane protein channelrhodopsin) of the genetically engineered virus with laser light.

For quite some time, the hippocampus (a ridge section found along the bottom of the lateral ventricle portion of the brain - there are two such ridge sections) has been implicated (via an array of experimental and clinical evidence) as playing an important role of some kind with respect to memory formation. Thus, when one scans the title of the aforementioned *Nature* journal article - i.e., 'Optogenetic stimulation of a hippocampal engram activates fear memory recall' - and understands that the term "engram" is a way of referring to a memory trace that has arisen through a hypothesized change (temporary or permanent) in brain chemistry within the hippocampus, then one is being told by the *Nature* article title that the Ramirez/Liu experiment is one which uses optogenetic methods (outlined previously) to bring about the activation (or recall) of memories involving fear.

In 2000, Eric Kandel received the Nobel Prize for research that helped establish the nature of some of the physiological dynamics that are associated or correlated with memory formation/storage in Aplysia -- a sea slug whose relatively large nerve cells made it a good candidate for trying to scientifically analyze what happens biochemically when learning or memory formation occurs in those life forms. To make a much longer story somewhat shorter, Kandel and other researchers discovered -- while studying the gill-withdrawal reflex in Aplysia -- that sensitization and habituation (which are both forms of learning and, therefore, constitute instances of memory formation) were associated with the release of certain kinds of molecules -- [e.g., c-Amp - the so-called second messenger of the cell, serotonin (a neurotransmitter) , PKA (c-AMP dependent kinase) , and CREB (cAMP response element binding protein) -- that appeared to play important roles in short-term and long-term memory formation, as well as were implicated in the processes that converted short-term memory into long-term memory.

The generation of the foregoing sort of cascade of biochemical molecules also was correlated with increases in synaptic complexity or connectivity. As a result, Kandel came to believe that changes in synaptic connectivity were indications that learning/memory was somehow being established through those synaptic enhancements, and, in turn, those changes in synaptic connectivity were some kind of a function - although many of the details were lacking with respect to the precise dynamics of that function -- of the cascade of biochemical changes that were taking place within neurons.

Mice are more complex than Aplysia, and humans are more complex than either mice or Aplysia. Nonetheless, ever since the work of Kandel began back in the 1960s, a great deal more biochemical, physiological, cellular, and neuronal evidence has been generated that is consistent with the idea that when certain (a) biochemical changes in cellular physiology are correlated with (b) changes in synaptic connectivity that are correlated with (c) differences in behavioral activity over time, and when the foregoing three elements occurred in relatively close temporal (if not spatial) juxtaposition to one another, then the collective presence of those three elements was interpreted to indicate that learning or memory had been generated ... and, this remains the basic idea concerning the issue of memory formation irrespective of whether one is talking about Aplysia, mice, humans, or any other life form that is capable of exhibiting a capacity to learn or retain memories (short-term or long-term) with respect to on-going experience.

Naturally, the physical/material details of learning and memory might change as one moves from species to species. Nevertheless, a growing body of evidence lends support to the idea that learning/memory are entirely functions of physical/material events.

The Ramirez/Liu research that was outlined in the June 2013 TED talk is a continuation of the foregoing perspective. The two investigators took mice and surgically implanted a means of delivering laser stimulation to the hippocampus portion of a mouse's brain that also had been equipped with a genetically engineered 'sensor-switch' which could detect recent activity in cells that seemed to be involved in the formation of memories concerning fear in the experimental animals.

More specifically, the researchers placed a number of surgically altered, and genetically engineered mice into a chamber where an electrical shock was applied to the feet of the animals. As a result of this experience, certain cells in the hippocampus portions of the mice brains became active, and this activity left a biochemical footprint that was detected by the genetically engineered sensor-switch which had been injected into the mice through a viral host and, as a result, served as target candidates for subsequent laser stimulation.

The fact specific cells became active during the shocking process was interpreted by the researchers to signify that a memory had been formed. However, a number of questions can be raised concerning that kind of interpretation.

To begin with, what does it mean to say that a cell has left a marker indicating that the cell has been active recent? Active doing what?

The presumption of Ramirez and Liu is that the cellular activity gives expression to processes that are involved in learning or memory formation. However, one could ask in relation to such activity: Involved how?

How does a neuronal cell's activity generate learning or memory formation? Where, exactly, is the memory amidst such cell activity?

Is learning/memory in the cells that have been activated? If so, what is the form of the dynamic structure or process that is said to 'hold' the memory in the cells - whether considered either individually or collectively? Or, is the memory of fear to be found in the synaptic changes that follow from the changes in cell chemistry. Or, is it some combination of the foregoing two possibilities.

According to Ramirez and Liu, the process works as follows. First, the three-dimensional conformation of channelrhodopsin is induced to change. As a result, certain ions begin flowing into the interior of the cell.

In turn, the ion influx leads to a cascade of metabolic processes involving, among other things, c-AMP, serotonin, CREB, PKA, and other bio-molecules. Where is the memory or learning in all of this, and how did this cascade of cellular denizens come to signify or be interpreted to mean "fear"?

Kandel and others believed that the foregoing cascade of events was functionally related to changes in synaptic connectivity and that it was this transformation in synaptic connectivity and complexity which signified that learning had occurred or a memory had been formed. So, does the memory reside in the synaptic connections, and, if so, how is the memory instantiated in those connections, and if the memory is held through those synaptic connections, what determines the holding pattern and what 'reads' that pattern to understand that it is a memory which holds one kind of learning rather another?

What is the relationship between, on the one hand, cells (the sort of cells in which Ramirez and Liu are interested and for which they have genetically engineered their sensor-switch mechanism) that are active during memory formation and, on the other hand, changing synaptic connectivity (which people such as Kandel believed was central to learning and memory formation) ? If memory is in the cells - as Ramirez and Liu seem to believe - then what is the significance of the changes in synaptic connectivity and how does what transpires in the cell shape, color, and orient those synaptic changes?

Alternatively, one might ask what determines which cells will be initially activated to become part of the fear learning or fear memory process? Or, what determines which biochemical, electrical, and physiological changes will take place within cells that will permit an organism to differentiate learning/memory experiences over time. After all, if the same cellular components (e.g., c-AMP, serotonin, PKA, CREB, etc.) are thought to be at the heart of memory formation, then how are those components put together in distinct packages that would enable an organism to differentiate among memories? Or, what determines the pattern of synaptic connectivity that will take place and which can be said to hold - allegedly - this or that form of memory/learning, and what is it about the structural or dynamical character of enhanced synaptic connectivity that gives expression to memory?

One might also critically reflect on the nature of the differences between the original existential circumstances that led to the - alleged - formation of a fear memory, and the quality of that memory relative to the actual event. People who suffer from PTSD have vivid, intense, flashbacks, and, consequently, there seems to be a dimension of intensity associated with such flashback memories that is comparable to the original circumstances out of which the memories arose.

However, memories are not always as vivid and intense as the original circumstances from which they were derived or on which they are based. So, the fact that a given memory in a mouse is activated doesn't necessarily explain - in and of itself - why such a memory should necessarily lead to the response of freezing, and, therefore, one is left with the possibility that something might be going on in the experiment other than what Ramirez and Liu are hypothesizing to be the case.

Mice appear to have some degree of awareness or consciousness. How do cellular and synaptic changes generate phenomenology or how does phenomenal experience arise out of those changes?

When a mouse receives a shock to its feet, does the mouse experience fear or does it experience pain? Or, is the mouse experiencing stress?

There is a behavioral response in mice known as "freezing". This consists in a set of behavioral dispositions in which the mouse remains very still and, possibly, vigilant when immersed in a given existential situation that is considered threatening in some way.

Once a mouse has been shocked and, then, subsequently, exhibits, freezing, this doesn't necessarily mean that the mouse is experiencing fear or remembering fear while in the condition of freezing (although this might be the case) . Instead, the mouse might be exhibiting a form of coping strategy (which could be instinctual rather than learned) that is intended to either help avoid subsequent shocks or deal with the pain of having been shocked, and if so, perhaps the primary phenomenological component under such circumstances is merely heightened vigilance with an inclination in the mouse toward escaping or avoidance when possible.

Alternatively, freezing in mice might represent a state of shock. Possibly, a mouse that is exhibiting freezing behavior might not either be in pain or in a state of fear, but, rather, is just stunned and directionless with respect to how to proceed or what to do next ... somewhat like a prize fighter who has been rocked by a punch and is merely trying to stay on his or her feet but with very little focused awareness with respect to just what is going on around him or her.

A variation on the foregoing possibility is that 'freezing' in mice might be a response to stress rather than an expression of fear. Pulled in different direction by various internal and external forces, a mouse might freeze up, and, consequently, the associated phenomenological state is one of stress rather than fear.

The fact of the matter is that we don't know what is going on in the phenomenology of a mouse during the state of freezing. Is the mouse afraid, in pain, in shock, stressed, uncertain, vigilant, wanting to get away, remembering a previous, similar problematic experience, or is the mouse experiencing some combination of all of the foregoing possibilities? We don't know.

Freezing is a behavioral disposition that is exhibited by mice during certain circumstances. Freezing in mice is a coping strategy and/or an instinctual behavioral response.

Learning or memory formation might play some sort of modulating role with respect to how that behavioral response manifests itself within different circumstances. Nevertheless, we don't necessarily understand what is triggering the behavioral response of freezing or what the precise properties and dynamics of the triggering event are.

Is the freezing response being triggered by a memory? If so, how does the memory lead to the initiation of the behavior?

Moreover, mice have a more expansive repertoire of behavior than just freezing. Sometimes they fight and sometimes they take flight?

What if the freezing is an indication that the mouse is uncertain about whether to pursue fighting or fleeing? What if the freezing indicates indecision rather than fear, stress, pain, or shock?

Perhaps, freezing means different things to a mouse in different circumstances. On some occasions, it might be an expression of fear, but on other occasions it might indicate stress, indecision, or a vigilant wait for the sort of information that might push the mouse toward fighting or fleeing.

We don't know what, if any, phenomenology is associated with

Technological Reflections

that behavioral response. We don't know what, if anything, the cellular and synaptic changes that have been described by neuroscientists since the time of Kandel have to do with the generation of that phenomenology.

There is no neuroscientist on the face of the Earth who has yet been able to demonstrate how one goes from cellular changes in neurons to enhanced synaptic connectivity, and, then, is capable of proceeding on to demonstrate how the phenomenology of memories of a particular character and quality arise from those cellular and synaptic changes. All scientists have established so far is that there is a correlation between certain kinds of biological events and the appearance of the sorts of behavior that seem to suggest that learning has taken place or a memory has been formed, but, unfortunately, some scientists have jumped to unwarranted conclusions concerning the connection between biological activity and the phenomenology of experience.

Consider the following idea. One can probe the electronic intricacies of a television set all one likes - even down to the quantum level. However, such analysis will do nothing to tell one where the content and structure of the picture comes from that is made manifest through the television set.

As is the case with television sets, so too, biology, cell physiology, and synaptic connectivity might play a necessary supporting role with respect to the phenomenology of experience. Nonetheless, biology alone might not be sufficient to account for the character of the content that is given expression through the phenomenology of experience.

A television set plays a necessary supporting role with respect to being able to generate a picture on its screen but that same electronic device cannot account for why the picture has the content, structure, and quality it does. To account for the latter phenomenon, one needs to talk about television stations, writers, authors, directors, actors, producers, and viewers ... all of which exist beyond the horizons of the television set, just as a proper explanation for memory or learning might exist beyond the horizons of purely biological considerations - at least as those considerations are currently understood.

Let us return to the Ramirez/Liu experiment. Under normal

circumstances, when a mouse is placed in an experimental box, the animal exhibits exploratory behavior ... sniffing and scurrying its way around the interior of the apparatus.

If the feet of the mouse are shocked during the exploratory process, the mouse, subsequently, might begin to display freezing behavior. According to Ramirez and Liu, the mouse has formed a memory of fear, and this state of fear leads to the behavioral response of freezing.

However, as indicated earlier, we really can't be certain of what is taking place within the phenomenology of the mouse. The mouse might be experiencing fear, but, as well, the mouse also might be experiencing a phenomenology of vigilance, avoidance, stress, shock, and/or pain along side of the fear or instead of such fear.

If shocked for a sufficiently long period of time with no possibility of escape, the mice also might come to exhibit the same sort of 'learned helplessness' that Martin Seligman discovered occurred with respect to dogs when they were exposed to inescapable shocks. Under such circumstances, the freezing might be a sign of learned helplessness rather than a state of fear per se.

Learned helplessness is a more complex phenomenological state than fear since it consists of the integration of a set of experiences rather than being a function of just one experience. Yet, the differences in phenomenological state between fear and learned helplessness both might end up being manifested through the same freezing behavior.

Ramirez and Liu arrange for the genetically engineered channelrhodopsin switch to be activated through the application of a pulse of laser light. This sets in motion a series of cellular biochemical and physiological changes, and, then, freezing behavior is exhibited.

What actually has happened? Has a memory been activated and, then, that memory causes freezing behavior to appear?

Even if it is the case that a certain memory has, somehow, been activated through the activation of the channelrhodopsin switch, can one be sure that the biological situation is not unlike a television set which has been switched on, and, yet, the picture which appears is not - strictly speaking - caused by the turning on the television set. Rather, the turning on of the television set is little more than a necessary precursor for gaining access to a picture (memory) that is generated through an entirely different process occurring outside of the electronic circuits of the television set.

Does the laser-activation of those cells that were active during the process of memory formation (when the unfortunate mice were shocked) represent the recall of a specific kind of memory? Or, does the laser-activation of such cells merely set in motion a sort of 'learned reflex arc' or 'behavioral circuit' that results in freezing behavior without the middleman of memory mediating between laser pulse and the condition of freezing?

We see the pulse of laser light being applied. We see the freezing behavior.

Ramirez and Liu hypothesize that the two events are bridged by the experience of a memory of a specific kind that has been activated by a pulse of laser light. However, they are unable to provide a plausible explanation that can take one step-by-step from the point of initiation (laser stimulation) to the terminal point of behavior and show that what was transpiring involves a memory of a certain kind and the existence of that specific memory caused the observed behavior.

The fact of the matter is that Ramirez and Liu can't even be certain what kind of memory was laid down during the process of shocking. They claim the memory is one of fear, but they can't prove this because they can't eliminate the possibilities that the memory that formed might have contained elements of stress, pain, shock, and indecision, and not just fear.

Or, perhaps, fear was not part of the original memory phenomenology at all. After all, one might argue that the original memory was one of pain, not necessarily fear, and, therefore, fear is a secondary emotional response to the perception of pain.

Did the laser-activation of cellular activity give expression to a memory of pain rather than fear? If so, then the title of their *Nature* article is, at best, misleading, and at worse, it is incorrect.

Moreover, if the original memory was of pain, then, how does the secondary event of fear come into the picture? How does laser-activation of a pain memory bring about an emotional response of fear that, in turn, brings about freezing behavior? Is the experience of fear a second memory different from the memory of pain, and isn't it possible that pain might be associated with other secondary phenomenological states (e.g., stress, flight, fight, vigilance, and shock) that could just as easily lead to a freezing response?

Ramirez and Liu can see into the structure of their experimental situation only a little farther than their laser-activation of the channelrhodopsin. They know that such activation will set in motion a cascade of biochemical and physiological changes (the sort of changes explored by Eric Kandel and others) , and they know that those changes will be followed by changes in synaptic connectivity.

However, they really don't understand what any of this actually means other than the fact that, collectively speaking, it is all correlated with memory formation. The rest is all conjecture and speculation.

During the Boston presentation, Ramirez spoke of giving the mouse "a very mild foot shock". One wonders why a mouse would develop a fear memory if the shock were so "very mild"? Clearly, euphemistical language is being used to mask a process that is more painful than the phrase "very mild" might suggest.

Nothing was said during the Ramirez/Liu presentation (by either the researchers or the audience) with respect to the ethical issues entailed by treating animals in the way they were treated during the experiments that were the focus of the TED presentation. This was true both with respect to surgically altering the heads of the mice to accommodate a laser delivery system as well as in relation to shocking the mice, and, so, the ethical issues to which the researchers were vaguely alluding during their presentation involved something else other than the treatment of life forms within the lab.

When I was an undergraduate, I participated in an experiment involving the delivery of shocks, and the nature of the experiment was such that I was the one who delivered the shocks to myself. For me, there was a clear phenomenological difference between those shocks that were very mild and those shocks that were painful and might lead to a sense of fear, stress, shock, and/or anxiety if they were to continue.

In a rather startling expression of egocentricity, the researchers appeared to be talking in terms of what they considered to be a very mild foot shock, with nary a spoken worry about what the mouse might have thought or felt about the whole affair. Nonetheless, the word that appears in the title of their Nature article is "fear" - the article title didn't say anything about 'a very mild shock memory recall ', but, rather, used the phrase "fear memory recall".

Presumably, there is a difference in learning and memory formation with respect to different kinds of stimuli. The phenomenology of the experience involving "a very mild foot shock" is likely to be different than the phenomenology of an experience involving a shock deemed to be capable of generating a memory formation of fear.

So, even if one were to accept at face value everything that the two researchers said with respect to the nature of their experiment and the way in which it supposedly tapped into memory formation, there is a question that remains. Was the memory that was established in the mice one of fear, or of a very mild shock, or of something much more complex?

What exactly was in that memory? The researchers claim that the memory was one of fear, but even if this were true, that fear occurred in a context.

In other words, the shocks took place in an experimental apparatus within a laboratory. The air had a smell. The box had a smell. There were sounds. The box had a feel to it. There were visual qualities present within the box. The surgically implanted mechanism had a 'feel' to it.

The foregoing context served as horizon to the experience of the shock. The memory was not just a matter of the alleged fear but, as well, the memory involved certain aspects of the context surrounding the shock.

How are the foregoing sorts of contextual factors coded for with respect to either the cascade of cellular activities that occur in connection to memory formation or with respect to the subsequent alterations in synaptic connectivity? This is not an insignificant issue because, as we shall soon discover, it plays an important role within the Ramirez/Liu experiment.

More specifically, according to the two researchers, if one places a mouse that has been shocked in one laboratory box into another, different box, then the mouse will start out by behaving as any mouse tends to do when introduced into a new environment. In other words, the male or female mouse will begin to explore the box and does not exhibit freezing behavior. All of this changes when a laser is used to activate the channelrhodopsin membrane molecule in those cells that have been identified by the injected genetically engineered sensor-switch as having been active during the process of memory formation in the shock phase of the experiment.

When the laser is used to re-invoke the 'fear memory' by changing the three-dimensional conformation of the channelrhodopsin that leads to the flow of ions into the cell and sets in motion a cascade of biochemical and physiological events associated with memory, mice that previously have been shocked will exhibit the freezing response. According to Ramirez and Liu, the mouse is being induced to remember the original experience of fear and responds accordingly - that is, the mouse freezes.

In their Boston presentation, Ramirez and Liu discuss how they have added a few wrinkles to their experimental design. For example, they talk about, first, taking surgically altered and genetically engineered mice and placing them in a blue box, and, then, identifying the cells that are active in the presence of such 'blueness'.

Before proceeding on with an account of the experiment, it seems to be appropriate to pause briefly and ask a question. How does one know that the cellular activity being identified by the researchers through their genetically engineered sensor switch has to do specifically with blueness rather than some other feature of the experimental set-up, and, moreover, even if one were to accept the idea that the cellular activity has something to do with retaining a memory of blueness, once again, one can raise the question of what, precisely, such activity has to do with memory formation?

How - specifically -- is 'blueness' being encoded via the cascade of cellular events that are occurring during the learning of, or memory formation concerning, blueness, and how does this particular package or set of cellular events translate into unique changes in synaptic connectivity concerning the issue of blueness? Moreover, how is this aspect of learned or remembered blueness separated from, or integrated into, the context of other sensory experiences that form the context surrounding the experience of blueness?

In addition, one might ask why certain cells are selected for the memory of blueness, while other cells busy themselves with the memory of different sorts of sensory modalities. Or, one also might wonder how the work of an array of active cells concerning different facets of a experiential context become integrated to generate a unified phenomenological experience that can be understood in one way rather than another by a given life form? [By way of a personal aside, for reasons obvious and not so obvious, all of this talk about red and blue boxes led to my thinking about the contents of the so-called 'Blue' and 'Brown' books of Ludwig Wittgenstein which I read as an undergraduate].

Now, let's return to the Ramirez/Liu experiments. In the first stage of one of their experiments involving a blue box, nothing happens to the mice. They just get to explore the box.

In the next phase of the experiment, the mice are placed in a red box. While in the red box, a laser pulse activates the cells that were identified as being active during the blue-box experience, and, as well, the mice are given - I am quite certain - a very mild foot shock to generate a 'fear' memory that is now associated with a re-invoked or recalled memory of the blue box.

In the final state of this experiment, the mice are placed back in the blue box where they have never been shocked. Yet, as soon as the mice are placed in the blue box, they exhibit freezing behavior.

Ramirez and Liu maintain they have created a false memory in such mice. I have a little difficulty understanding how the two researchers arrived at their conclusion.

But, let's deal with first things first. Ramirez and Liu speak about an association being established between two things. On the one hand, there is the re-invoked memory of blueness, and, on the other hand, there is the shock that is given in the red box while the memory of blueness is re-invoked.

There is no false memory that is being created in the foregoing scenario. The association being established is not a false memory, but, rather, it constitutes the blending together of two facets of the red box context - namely, a shock and the experience of blueness.

This is an example of classical conditioning. One takes a stimulus - blueness - and pairs it with another stimulus - shock - to generate a behavioral response - freezing -- that can be initiated by the presence of blueness alone even without a shock being administered, and even though blueness had never before been experienced as being 'fear-stress-shock-pain-avoidance' related.

The mice are not misremembering the original experience of blueness. They have been taught something new during the time spent in the red box ... that is, they have been taught how the presence of blue can be threatening, and when the mice are placed back into the environment of the blue box, they are induced to enter into the condition of freezing because of what they learned in the red box.

Beyond the foregoing considerations, there is the problem of understanding the dynamics of association. How does the memory of association work?

Everyone talks in terms of the capacity of various life forms to associate different aspects of experience whether through temporal and spatial juxtaposition. We all know that such a phenomenon is real, and we all note evidence of its presence through a wide variety of circumstances involving human beings and other life forms.

Nevertheless, no one really knows how it works. No one understands the dynamics of association. We only acknowledge the result of that dynamic.

How does the memory of blueness and the memory of being shocked - very mildly -enter into a new, modified understanding within the context of a the red experimental box that is capable of generating, say, the freezing response in mice? How does what happens in those cells which are active during the formation of a memory of blueness become intertwined with what happens in those cells that are active during the experience of being shocked?

One might suppose that there are many neuronal cells that are active during any given experience. Why is blueness singled out as the feature that is to be mixed with the sensory experience of being shocked?

Phenomena such as generalization do occur (as is evidenced by my previously noted aside concerning Wittgenstein's Blue and Brown books in which some sort of generalization took place in relation to the blue and _red_ boxes of the Ramirez and Liu experiments) . Various life forms do transfer certain aspects of learning or memory developed in one context to a broader array of contexts that are in some, as of yet, mysterious way acknowledged or arbitrarily designated as being similar to the original context of learning.

Unfortunately, we don't really know or understand much about how any of this actually works. We see all kinds of correlations, but we have little idea of how everything fits together and generates or causes this or that memory or this or that understanding or this or that belief or this or that instance of learning, and this remains true even with respect to the simplest of cases involving learning and memory formation such as in instances of: habituation, sensitization, association, conditioning, or generalization.

The experiments conducted by Ramirez and Liu really haven't gotten us any closer to understanding the specific dynamics of either memory, learning, or how the phenomenology surrounding such experience arises. More specifically, their work hasn't helped to show us how to bridge the gap between, on the one hand, changes in the internal biochemistry or physiology of neurons and synaptic connectivity, and, on the other hand, the actual, causal dynamics of learning and memory as a function of the former material changes, nor are we able to explain in a plausible, consistent, rigorous, coherent fashion how changes in neurons and synaptic connectivity become manifested in phenomenological, conscious states that are characterized by differential qualities that are integrated into a unitary sense of experience concerning reality - and quite independently of whether such unified phenomenology actually accurately reflects the nature of some aspect of that reality.

Ramirez and Liu only have provided us with some more correlations. These might be interesting correlations, but, in the end, that is all they are.

The methodological techniques that have been devised and are used to demonstrate the existence of certain correlations are quite innovative. Nonetheless, the bottom line on all this ingenious innovativeness is that nothing which they have said in their TED talk or in corresponding articles gets us any closer to understanding how the dynamics of memory and learning work, and, certainly nothing which they have said demonstrates the truth of the underlying philosophical premise that mind can be shown to be a function of purely material events — events that can be tinkered with.

This leads to a further issue. Toward the end of the Boston TED talk, Xu Liu talked about how we are living in very exciting times in which science is not tied down by any arbitrary limits with respect to progressing in our understanding and knowledge concerning such phenomena as memory and learning. In effect, science is bound only by our imaginations.

Unfortunately, the imaginations of some people are more problematic and disturbing than are the imaginations of other people. The Defense Department subsidizes a great deal of the scientific work that is taking place in academia and in the corporate sector (both are integral parts in the military-industrial complex), and, as luck would have it, the people who are in control of that Department imagine all kinds of things with respect to the arbitrary uses to which scientific research can be put -- uses that end up killing, maiming, hurting, and enslaving people ... both foreign and domestic.

Although the research of Ramirez and Liu has not demonstrated the generation of false memory, that research has revealed some possible techniques for interfering with the minds of life forms. How long will it be before the research of people like Ramirez and Liu is weaponized and applied against whomever the people in power deem to be appropriate.

We don't live just in the exciting times about which Liu enthuses. We also live in very perilous and authoritarian times ... times in which all too many governments are quite prepared to do whatever is necessary to stay in power, control resources, and induce citizens to serve that power. Ramirez and Liu are very naive if they believe their research is only about scientific progress, and they also are in denial if they suppose that they do not have a moral responsibility with respect to the possible applications of their work.

Speaking vaguely about the ethical implications and ramifications of their research work after the fact has got things backward. They should have been concerned about those implications before they did their research, and, in fact, those ethical deliberations should have impacted their decision about whether, or not, such research should have been undertaken at all.

The Ramirez/Liu research dredged up memories within me of Michael Crichton's book: 'The Terminal Man'. Like the scientists in the book, neuroscientists today are full of all kinds of swagger and arrogance with respect to their technical proficiency and ingeniousness, and, unfortunately, like the scientists in Crichton's book, they are ignorant of their own ignorance concerning the many lacunae between what they believe they know and the actual nature of reality.

The scientists in Crichton's book believed they knew what they were doing. They didn't, and their ignorance cost the lives of quite a few people.

The neuroscientists of today believe they know what they are doing. They don't, and the problematic ramifications of that ignorance might only manifest itself after difficulties or tragedies of one kind or another arise.

The many physicists who worked on the Manhattan project believed they knew what they were doing. Few of them grappled with the horrors of Hiroshima or Nagasaki before the fact except, perhaps, Oppenheimer who quoted from the Bhagavad-Gita after witnessing the Trinity test: "Now I am become Death, the destroyer of worlds".

There were many physicists and other scientists who worked to bring nuclear technology into the real world. Those scientists seem unconcerned - before the fact -- about the possibilities of Three Mile Island, Chernobyl, and Fukushima becoming future realities, or about the problems surrounding the disposal of nuclear wastes, or the use of depleted uranium as weapons of mass destruction.

T.S. Eliot said: "Where is the wisdom we have lost in knowledge? Where is the knowledge we have lost in information? Ramirez and Liu, along with a great many other researchers have a lot of information but do not seem to have much in the way of either knowledge, or more importantly, wisdom.

More specifically, I worry about people - such as Ramirez and Liu -

who believe they understand what is going on with their experiments when this is just not the case and which, I believe, the foregoing discussion has helped to demonstrate. We already have seen the terrible consequences that have ensued, and are continuing to ensue, from the self-serving arrogance of the pharmaceutical industry with respect to its psychoactive concoctions that are based on a form of technical wizardry that is entirely devoid of any real understanding concerning the human mind, but, is, instead, rooted in a bevy of correlations which are not understood, and, yet, recklessly, the pharmaceutical industry and the FDA are permitting - if not rushing -- all manner of drugs into the market that are generated through spurious science in their attempt to create life-time dependencies (rather than cures) with respect to this or that psychoactive drug.

As people such as Joanna Moncrieff (The Myth of the Chemical Cure) a psychiatrist from England, and Peter Breggin (Medication Madness) , a psychiatrist from the United States, have pointed out, neuroscientists have very little understanding of how psychoactive drugs metabolize within human beings or how the actual dynamics of their 'effects' transpire. The existence of side effects lends support to the foregoing claim.

I know of no pharmacological study that begins with a set of predictions concerning the precise array of side effects that will arise in conjunction with the use of a given psychoactive agent. They do not make such predictions because they don't actually know what happens in people when such drugs are taken.

For instance, there are many scientists and clinicians who speak in terms of the idea of "chemical imbalances' being the cause of various emotional and mental problems, and this mythology is present in the marketing campaigns for an array of pharmaceutical products being advertised on television. Let's consider the case of SSRI - that is, selective serotonin re-uptake inhibitors.

I don't know of any neuroscientist who has provided a convincing argument about how the absence of serotonin causes depression or how the absence of serotonin leads to the sorts of symptoms that are associated with clinical depression. Moreover, there is also the rather embarrassing fact that when independent, double blind studies are done concerning the efficacy of SSRIs, those drugs have been shown to be no more effective than placebos.

To whatever extent pharmaceutical agents 'work', they do so by masking problems, not curing them, and in the process, those psychoactive agents dull, if not destroy, many facets of emotional life, awareness, and human sensitivity. Unfortunately, the losing of one's humanity is confused with the alleged effectiveness of a given drug with respect to a change in a user's symptom profile.

Scientific methodologies are one thing. Conjecturing about the significance and meaning of the experimental results that are run through those methodologies is quite another issue altogether.

Ramirez and Liu do not have a theory of memory or learning. They have a series of conjectures based on a problematic understanding concerning, and interpretation of, the correlational dimensions of their own experiments and the experiments of other individuals working in the area of mind/brain research.

The issue before us is the following one. Are neuroscientists on the right track with respect to their attempt to reduce mental phenomena to some set of physical dynamics and, therefore, the work of researchers like Ramirez and Liu represent important steps along an inevitable path that will take us to the promised land of full understanding and a complete explanatory account of how mental phenomena are all functions of underlying biological events? Or, alternatively, are neuroscientists on an asymptote path that generates ever more tantalizing correlations which will never permit them to reach the promised land of complete explanations and, instead, will permit them to only provide accounts of mental phenomena that will always be inherently flawed because there are more realities in heaven and earth, Horatio, than can be dreamt of in their philosophies.

I believe the foregoing critical analysis of the Ramirez and Liu experiments leads to more than a few questions about just what it is that neuroscientists know with respect to the nature of mental phenomena such as memory formation. Maybe, eventually, they will reach the promised land of 'Full Explanations', but right now they are stuck in the entangled underbrush that populates the land of descriptions that are based on proliferating correlations, and they don't seem to have much, if any, real understanding, knowledge, or wisdom concerning the actual nature of the mind.

6. NIST and 9/11

For much of his professional life, Peter Michael Ketchum was deeply ensconced in the world of high performance systems and scientific computation. In 1997, he began working at NIST (The National Institute of Standards and Technology) which operates out of the Department of Commerce. From its inception, NIST has been tasked with engaging the processes through which industry sets standards and coordinating those activities with policies of the federal government.

Among other things, NIST attempts to help industry clarify the process of setting standards. In addition, NIST lends support to the foregoing process through a variety of activities, including research.

After a few years at NIST, Mr. Ketchum was assigned to the mathematical and computational sciences division of NIST. He also served as the chairperson for that division's seminar series in applied mathematics.

When, on August 21, 2002, NIST was placed in charge of investigating the cause of the complete destruction of three buildings at the World Trade Center on 9/11, Mr. Ketchum was not involved in either the research for, or writing of, various reports that were generated by NIST in conjunction with the foregoing investigation. However, he was aware that those activities were taking place.

For many years, Mr. Ketchum accepted the findings that had been recorded in a series of reports released by NIST that purported to account for the demise of the Twin Towers as well as the collapse of Building 7 on 9/11 that had been part of the World Trade Center in Manhattan. However, he had accepted the foregoing findings without really examining, or reflecting on, the contents of those reports because, during that period, he was of the general opinion that the work performed at NIST was of the highest caliber and that, as a general rule, its members conducted themselves with integrity when engaged in research.

In July of 2016, a friend mentioned to him that a certain amount of evidence was accumulating which seemed to suggest that the official position concerning 9/11 might not be the slam-dunk that the media and government had been claiming. The "official" position of the government consisted primarily of: (1) *The 9/11 Report: The National Commission on Terrorist Attacks Upon The United States*; (2) a series of reports released by NIST concerning the demise of buildings on 9/11 that occurred at the World Trade Center in New York, and (3) The Pentagon Performance Report that was issued in conjunction with the damage that was inflicted on the Pentagon on 9/11]

For approximately a month, Mr. Ketchum didn't follow up on the foregoing information. Eventually, he began to rigorously inquire into a variety of issues concerning 9/11, especially in relation to NIST's research efforts involving the destruction of buildings at the World Trade Center.

Within a relatively short period of time after initiating his own review of the NIST findings, Mr. Ketchum realized that NIST's account of what transpired on 9/11 at the World Trade Center was, to use his words on the matter, "not a sincere and genuine study." As a result, he became quite upset ... first, with himself, since, for sixteen years he really hadn't paid sufficiently close attention to an array of issues concerning 9/11, and, then, he became upset with NIST for the lack of integrity that characterized its reports concerning 9/11.

Once he was able to examine material concerning NIST's handling of its 9/11 investigation, Mr. Ketchum felt evidence overwhelmingly indicated that Buildings 1, 2 and 7 of the World Trade Center were brought down by controlled demolition rather than being due to a variety of structural damage that, supposedly had been caused by either crashing commercial jets and/or office fires that were initiated by spilled jet fuel or – in the case of Building 7 -- through just fires. Irrespective of the extent to which the aforementioned controlled demolition thesis might, or might not, be correct, Mr. Ketchum came to the conclusion that the NIST findings were not done in a competent manner and, therefore, were unacceptable.

Before moving on to explore some of the aspects of Mr. Ketchum's conceptual transformation concerning the events of 9/11, one might be prudent to consider some cautionary qualifications concerning the issue of controlled demolition in conjunction with the collapse of the Twin Towers and Building 7 at the World Trade Center on 9/11. More specifically, while there is ample evidence (some of which is presented in the present work) to indicate that multiple explosions occurred in different parts of the World Trade Center on 9/11, and while there is considerable evidence that can be cited (e.g., The Framing of 9/11, 2nd edition) in support of the claim that nano-thermite was present in dust samples from the World Trade Center, nevertheless, there are a number of facts that suggest something more exotic – but still not definitively identified -- also was taking place at the World Trade Center on 9/11 than just the use of explosives and nano-thermite with respect to the destruction of the World Trade Center on 9/11.

Thermite, thermate, and nano-thermite are not explosives. They are chemical compounds that, when ignited, are capable of burning their way through, among other things, metal objects (e.g., steel columns in a building), and, when properly orchestrated with explosives, form a system that is capable of sequentially removing sections of designated steel columns to bring about a controlled collapse of a building.

As indicated earlier, I do not dispute that both explosives and nano-thermite were present in, and utilized at, the World Trade Center in conjunction with the destruction of the two Twin Towers and Building 7 on 9/11. What I do dispute is that explosions and nano-thermite are not capable of accounting for certain phenomena that occurred in relation to the events at the World Trade Center on 9/11.

For example, If two 110 storey, 500, 000-ton buildings collapsed to the ground (whether through controlled demolition or through some sort of a conventional, progressive collapse that involved a pancaking of floors one on top of another), one would expect to find 220 stories of material on the ground. Yet, photographs of Ground Zero on the morning of 9/11 (one can see the not-yet destroyed Building 7 in the background) show that after the two towers had disappeared, there was not much more than piles, here and there, of 12 to 14 stories worth of steel on the ground.

Some people have argued that the reason why there is so little debris above ground at Ground Zero is because the weight of the "collapse" drove all that material down into the sub-basements. However, Dr. Wood has found "official" photographs demonstrating that the tunnels, rails, and cars for the Path Train that ran under the

WTC showed only minor damage. Moreover, there was no debris from the towers down in the Path Train tunnels.

In addition, many of the stores in the concourse beneath the Twin Towers were not damaged. One of Dr. Wood's favorite photographs in this respect is a picture of a store in the concourse with a window full of famous Warner Brothers dolls – such as Bugs Bunny, Foghorn Leghorn, and the Road Runner – yet, the store (and this was true of many other stores) was not damaged.

Even more significantly, the World Trade Center was built over a section of concrete foundation that was poured over bedrock. The poured concrete is referred to as the 'bathtub' and it is intended to protect Lower Manhattan from being flooded by the Hudson River.

The bathtub-structure is, in some respects, fairly fragile. This was problematically demonstrated when some of the earth-moving equipment that had been brought in to help with the clean-up process at Ground Zero were responsible for cracking the bathtub structure in a number of places.

Yet, one is led to believe that the collapse of 2, 110 storey, 500,000-ton buildings did not put even a scratch in that bathtub structure. Cranes weighing only a fraction of what the Twin Towers weighed could crack the bathtub structure, but the mammoth Twin Towers could not accomplish this. Surely, this is an anomaly that begs for critical reflection.

There is another problem surrounding the attempt to explain the destruction of the World Trade Towers either through a conventional progressive collapse due to fires or due to controlled explosions. More specifically, the seismic signal associated with the demise of the two towers was significantly less than one would expect to be associated with the 'collapse' of two such weighty buildings.

This was especially evident in the demise of the 47-storey Building 7. The destruction of this building had a seismic signal of .6 and was barely distinguishable from normal background noise for an average workday in Manhattan.

The seismic signal associated with the destruction of Building 1 was 2.3. The seismic signal for the demise of Building 2 was 2.1.

| Technological Reflections |

Those readings are comparable to the seismic reading associated with the Seattle Kingdom when it was brought down through controlled demolition. The difficulty here, however, is that the height and weight of the Twin Towers should have given expression – but did not -- to a potential energy that was some thirty times greater than the potential energy possessed by the Kingdome when the latter energy was released upon destruction.

There is an additional problem surrounding the length of the seismic signal according to Dr. Wood. For example, the length of the seismic signal for the South Tower's demise was about 8 seconds.

Most proponents of the controlled demolition idea with respect to the Twin Towers (and Building 7) often mention that all three buildings came down at close to free fall speeds. A conventional, progressive collapse (e.g., as in the pancake theory in which upper floors come crashing down on lower floors in a sequential manner) cannot be reconciled with such near free-fall speeds and would require much more time to crumble to the ground due to the resistance that each floor puts up before succumbing to the forces being exerted on those individual floors by the collapsing upper floors ... this is the principle of the conservation of momentum in action.

However, the idea of controlled demolition cannot account for why, say, the South Tower was destroyed at a rate that is faster than free fall. Yet, the roughly eight- second seismic signal associated with the destruction of the South and North Towers indicates that those events took less time than would have been the case if one dropped a bowling ball from the roof of the 110-storey structure unimpeded by air-resistance (approximately 9.5 seconds ... and factoring in air-resistance would slightly lengthen the duration of free fall for such an object).

Instances of controlled demolition approach near free fall velocities because buildings are rigged with cutter charges in such a way that the support columns are knocked out in a sequence that removes any resistance to the falling floors. Consequently, in such cases, the time it takes for a designated building to come down is like dropping an object to the ground from the top of whatever building is being demolished through such controlled demolition.

For a building's destruction to register a seismic signal whose length indicates a time that is shorter than free-fall speeds suggests something is going on in that process of destruction other than controlled demolition. A seismic signal of such short duration might indicate that the building is not just falling freely through space (notwithstanding air-resistance) but is being propelled downward by some force.

On the other hand, a seismic signal of such short duration also might indicate that some kind of force had destroyed the building in such a way that eight, or so, seconds was all it took to register what was left of the building plus its contents with respect to impacting the ground. For example, if – for the sake of conversation – one were to hypothesize that some sort of force reduced a large number of floors to nothing more than dust and that such dust dispersed in a cloud over a large area, then the length of the seismic signal for such an event would be like dropping an object off a much shorter building, and, therefore, the time of free-fall would be much less than one would expect for a taller building.

During the press conference that marked the release of its initial, final report on Building 7, NIST indicated that the destruction of Building 7 was "whisper quiet". NIST – through its spokesperson, Shyam Sunder – used that description in conjunction with the demise of Building 7 in order to respond to a question about the possible use of explosives (in the form of controlled demolition) with respect to the destruction of Building 7.

Some might wish to argue that by saying what he did that Sunder was merely lying in order to try to hide evidence pointing to the presence of explosives and controlled demolition. However, by saying what he did about the fall of Building 7 being "whisper quiet", Sunder actually was undermining the position of NIST.

NIST claimed that Building 7 came down as a result of a progressive collapse that had been initiated through the way fire caused girders to expand and, in the process, generate torque forces on a key core beam and, thereby, led the beam to buckle. However, if Building 7 came down due to a progressive, pancake collapse, then, there should have been a lot of noise associated with such a collapse as

| Technological Reflections |

one floor slammed into the next and, in addition, successive core beams and floor assemblies buckled and came apart.

However, if the demise of Building 7 was "whisper quiet", one is not talking about a conventional progressive collapse of the kind to which NIST subscribed. No noise, no conventional, progressive collapse.

By saying what he did in the press conference, Sunder is not only ruling out controlled demolition and explosions, he also is ruling out his own theory. So, if Building 7 came down "whisper quiet", then, one needs to find some other explanation for how that building came down.

In support of Sunder's "whisper quiet" comment, Dr. Wood indicates that some people were doing a video with Building 7 as a relatively distant backdrop. The building was coming down so silently that none of the participants realized what was going on until the building was already part way down.

A second point to consider in relation to the possible role of explosives or controlled demolition in bringing down three buildings at the World Trade Center revolves around the following anomaly. On five different occasions the Earth's magnetic field shifted during 9/11.

The times of these abrupt shifts in the magnetic field correspond very closely with five events at the World Trade Center. The first shift in Earth's magnetic field occurred precisely at the time when whatever struck the North Tower created a hole in that building. A second shift in the magnetic field took place at the exact time when the South Tower was impacted by something ... most people believe a commercial jet was implicated with respect to the holes in the Twin Towers. Three further shifts in the magnetic field happened at the precise time that Building 1, Building 2, and Building 7 came down.

Controlled demolitions could not have caused such shifts in the Earth's magnetic field. Conventional progressive collapses cannot account for such abrupt shifts either.

The shifts in the Earth's magnetic field were recorded through the magnetometer site in Alaska. The site consists of a number of different stations, and the shift recordings were drawn from six of those stations.

In each of the foregoing cases, the magnetometer indicated that for a period of time the magnetic field signal started going down prior to a given event at the World Trade Center (i.e., being struck by something or coming down). When the five aforementioned events took place, the magnetic field signal began to rise again.

Of course, one might wish to argue that the correlation between the two sets of data – one set in Alaska involving magnetic field readings and one set in New York involving three, steel-framed, high-rise buildings – was purely coincidental. And, if such a correlation occurred with respect to just one of the five events in New York, but not in the other four, a person might be inclined to accept such a possibility, but when the abrupt shifts in the magnetic field occur on five different occasions and are tied to specific times at which events in New York transpired, then one might be wise to start looking for some other explanation.

There are a number of other anomalous phenomena associated with the events of 9/11 that occurred at the World Trade Center which tend to indicate that something more than explosives and nano-thermite were involved in the destruction of the World Trade Center buildings on 9/11. One can learn more about those additional phenomena by reading Dr. Wood's book *Where Did The Towers Go?*, but the foregoing several pages of commentary should be enough to help engender a certain amount of caution in the reader with respect to keeping an open mind about what might have transpired at the World Trade Center on 9/11 ... we now return you to our regularly scheduled program concerning Peter Michael Ketchum.

One of the many factors that bothered Mr. Ketchum about the NIST reports was that they failed to exhibit due diligence with respect to determining whether, or not, there was any evidence that explosives of one kind or another might have been present at the World Trade Center on 9/11. For instance in a public statement (carried on C-Span) Dr. Shyam Sunder (Director of the NIST Building and Fire Research Laboratory) announced that before stating what NIST had found to be the cause for the collapse of Building 7, he wanted to state what NIST had not discovered in its investigations ... which was that NIST had not found any evidence indicating that explosives of any kind had been involved in the collapse of Building 7.

Dr. Sunder stated that the size of the blast necessary to bring down Building 7 would have had a very loud sound associated with it yet none of the video examined by the researchers concerning Building 7 provided evidence that such a blast had taken place. Furthermore, NIST had not discovered any witnesses who reported hearing such a blast.

Nevertheless, Barry Jennings -- who was serving as the Deputy Director of the Emergency Services Department for the New York City Housing Authority on 9/11 – had given public statements (independently corroborated, at least in part, by Michael Hess) indicating that as Mr. Jennings and Mr. Hess were descending the stairs of Building 7 (because the elevators were not working), the structure was rocked by an explosion from below (which occurred prior to the demise of Buildings 1 and 2) that took out the 6th floor landing near which he had been standing, and, as a result, he and Mr. Hess were forced to retreat back up the stairwell and seek an alternative exit from the building.

Furthermore, when the two individuals were finally rescued and led down to the lobby area of Building 7, Mr. Jennings described the entire ground floor as being in total ruins. Earlier, on his way to the Emergency Command Center located on the 23rd floor of Building 7, he had gone through that same lobby area and it had been in pristine, undamaged condition.

In addition, William Rodriguez, Kenny Johannemann, Jose Sanchez, Salvatore Giambanco, Anthony Satalamacchia (all of whom worked at the Twin Towers), along with Felipe David (an employee of a company that serviced the candy machines in the Twin Towers) and, perhaps, sixteen other individuals, all experienced massive explosions that took place in the basement complex of the North tower of the World Trade Center prior to anything striking the building above. Moreover, John Schroeder, a New York City fire fighter, also reported being bounced around on 9/11 as if he were in a pinball machine when a series of explosions rocked the North tower he was in – explosions that occurred prior to the demise of the South Tower -- and as he evacuated the former building, he discovered that the lobby area –

including 2-3 inch glass windows and marble-covered surfaces -- had been completely destroyed by one, or more, explosions.

Yet, NIST did not bother to interview any of the individuals mentioned in the last paragraph, nor did they talk with the aforementioned Barry Jennings, in relation to the possibility that explosions had occurring at the World Trade Center on 9/11. Therefore, notwithstanding the claims of Shyam Sunder to the contrary, apparently, NIST did not look very hard to uncover evidence concerning possible explosions that might be related to the demise of Buildings 1, 2, or 7 on 9/11 ... and, indeed, when one does not look for evidence of explosions, then declaring that no such evidence has been found becomes quite easy.

NIST proclaimed – through the voice of Dr. Sunder – that researchers had: "... identified thermal expansion as a new phenomenon that can cause the collapse of a structure. For the first time we have shown that fire can induce a progressive collapse."

However, when Peter Ketchum, a former NIST employee, critically examined the evidence that NIST put forward in support of the foregoing claim, Mr. Ketchum stated: "The explanation that is given by NIST for the collapse of Building 7 sounds like a Rube Goldberg Device" in which an overly complex, fantastic, and irrelevant explanation is used to try to account for something that can be explained in a much simpler manner.

According to Dr. Sunder, NIST had identified column 79 as the weak link that was the first column to buckle and, in turn, led to the successive failures of other columns. Yet, as Mr. Ketchum has indicated in a public statement concerning the foregoing matter, the position of the column (located off-center) that allegedly buckled and supposedly initiated the collapse of Building 7 should have led to an asymmetrical collapse of the building, but, instead, the building came straight down in a symmetrical fashion, collapsing into its own footprint rather than asymmetrically tipping over in some fashion and, as a result, spilling over into adjoining areas on the ground below.

Consequently, Mr. Ketchum referred to NIST's account of the collapse as being "just fantasy land," He added that: "Asymmetric damage does not lead to symmetric collapse," and, furthermore: "It's very difficult to get a building to collapse symmetrically."

| Technological Reflections |

Moreover, Mr. Ketchum notes that when one takes the computer model NIST constructed in an attempt to demonstrate the nature of the alleged collapse process and compares that model with actual video footage of the demise of Building 7, the two do not resemble one another. In fact, the NIST computer model of Building 7 never actually takes one through the entire collapse process, but, instead, stops with the buckling of column 79 and, then, <u>assumes</u> that everything else that follows took place in a way that is depicted by actual video footage of events on 9/11.

Shyam Sunder claims that – with absolutely no evidence to back up his assertion – NIST's structural model of the collapse "...matches quite well with a video of the event." Apparently, he believes that as long as one asserts something with sufficient confidence, then this will be enough to make whatever one says true even if such a statement is at odds with an array of facts.

Peter Ketchum mentions that he remembers seeing a statement from NIST indicating that the researchers were having difficulty trying to figure out why Building 7 collapsed. In fact, earlier during its investigation, NIST researchers proposed a theory concerning the collapse of Building 7 that subsequently had to be discarded as untenable.

Eventually, they resolved their difficulty by fabricating a fictional, fantastical account concerning the collapse of Building 7. Even, then, they were forced to amend that second theory and acknowledge the validity of the arguments of David Chandler, a high school physics teacher in New York, which demonstrated that Building 7 was in free fall for at least three seconds ... a fact that is entirely at odds with the notion of a progressive collapse in which floors successively slam into the floors below them and, therefore, at no point do those floors have an opportunity to exhibit free-fall behavior.

The NIST computer models of the progressive collapse that, supposedly, enveloped Building 1 (North) and Building 2 (South) of the World Trade Center commits the same error as NIST did in conjunction with its model of the Building 7 collapse. In other words, in the case of each of the foregoing three buildings, the NIST models only take things up to the point at which collapses supposedly were initiated and does not provide any of the details concerning how such a collapse, once it was initiated, would proceed in a way that is capable of being verified by what had been recorded with video on 9/11.

When Dr. John Gross – at the time, a senior researcher for NIST -- was asked about whether NIST had been tasked with the responsibility for determining the cause of the collapses of World Trade Center buildings on 9/11, Dr. Gross responded by saying:

"We found ... what happened I think ... we've scientifically demonstrated what was required to initiate the collapse. Once the collapse initiated, the video evidence was rather clear ... it was not stopped by the floors below, so, there was no calculation that we did to determine that ... what was clear on the video."

Notwithstanding Dr. Gross's foregoing comments, neither he nor NIST have scientifically demonstrated that the collapse scenario they advanced could account for the properties of the collapses that were captured by video, and, in fact, Dr. Gross admits as much when he acknowledges that NIST did not perform any calculations to demonstrate that their model would be compatible with the video evidence, and, instead, merely assumed their conclusions by claiming -- without evidence – that the video evidence confirmed their model.

Peter Ketchum – the former NIST employee who belatedly became aware of the incredibly shoddy work perpetrated by NIST in relation to its investigation into the collapse of three buildings at the World Trade Center on 9/11 – also has commented on the properties of the rubble that remained following the collapse of the two 110-storey towers plus the 47-storey Building 7. He indicates that there was virtually nothing left to the buildings ... that almost everything had been reduced to a powdered state.

Joe Casaliggi, a New York City fire fighter, recalls going through the rubble at Ground Zero following 9/11. He notes:

"You have two 110 storey office buildings. You don't find a desk. You don't find a chair ... you don't find a telephone ... a computer ... the biggest part of a telephone that I found was half of the key pad ... and it was about this big [spreading his thumb and forefinger apart a few inches]. The building collapsed in dust."

Dr. Steven Levin, an environmental medical doctor working at Mt. Sinai Hospital in New York, went through a list of some of the destruction that transpired at the World Trade Center. He said:

"We're talking here of 43,600 windows, 600,000 square feet of glass [Note: Much of which is several inches thick], 200,000 tons of structural steel, 5 million square feet of gypsum, 6 acres of marble, and 425,000 cubic yards of concrete turned, in good part, to a cloud. ... I was astonished at the degree to which solid materials were turned into pulverized dust as a consequence of that building collapse."

However, as Mr. Ketchum was alluding to earlier, the foregoing degree of destruction is inconsistent with the idea of a progressive collapse of buildings at the World Trade Center. Indeed, Dr. Judy Wood, a former professor of engineering mechanics, indicates that if there had been three progressive collapses that took place at the World Trade Center on 9/11, then, one would expect to find roughly 267-stories worth of materials at Ground Zero, and, instead, one finds only three piles of rubble, none of which is more than 12-14 stories high ... a problem that is captured in the title of her 2010 book: *Where Did The Towers Go?*

Mr. Ketchum also notes another inconsistency in the NIST theory of a progressive collapse involving Buildings 1 and 2 on 9/11. More specifically, a progressive collapse is driven by gravity, and, therefore, the force of a gravitational collapse is directed downward. Yet, on 9/11, video evidence reveals that there were multi-ton sections of steel perimeter columns that were being projected hundreds of feet in a horizontal direction.

The force of gravity cannot explain such lateral movement. Gravity operates in a downward vertical direction, not horizontally, and consequently, NIST failed to identify the source of the force that was propelling multi-ton steel beams in a sideways direction.

Another set of facts that is inconsistent with the notion that the three buildings at the World Trade Center underwent a progressive collapse as a result of damage from commercial jet crashes and/or office fires has to do with the temperatures that, for months, were recorded at Ground Zero following 9/11 despite the fact that the piles of rubble had been sprayed with thousands of gallons of water. NIST reported that the maximum temperatures reached within the World Trade Center buildings were approximately 480 degrees Fahrenheit or 250 degrees Celsius.

For instance, despite the fact that substantial rain fell at Ground Zero on the 14th of September, thermographic imaging directed at the base of the three destroyed buildings at the World Trade Center detected some hot spots associated with those buildings that registered temperatures in excess of 1,300 degrees Fahrenheit, while several additional hot spots exhibited temperatures of over a thousand degrees Fahrenheit.

The U.S. Department of Labor stated on its "A Dangerous Workplace' web page that:

"Underground fires burned at temperatures up to 2,000 degrees (Fahrenheit)."

Furthermore, the October 2012 issue of *Professional Safety* – the journal of the American Society of Safety Engineers – contained the following words concerning the issue of temperatures at Ground Zero following 9/11:

"Thermal measurements taken by helicopter each day showed underground temperatures ranging from 400 degrees Fahrenheit to more than 2,800 degrees Fahrenheit."

A December 2001 History Channel program called "Rise and Fall of the Towers" indicated that: "As recently as the end of November, it was still 1,100 degrees down underneath the rubble." During December, ice would form on the rubble pile early in the day, but beneath the surface, the ground was still smoldering and one person working on the pile observed that the ground wasn't frozen but "kind of bubbled underneath your feet."

The observable fires that were present in the underground areas of the World Trade Center were finally extinguished on December 19, 2001, more than three months after 9/11. Yet, the burning question of what was the source of those fires has not been successfully extinguished.

Some people theorized that the source of the fuel for the fires came from the gasoline in the cars that were parked beneath the World Trade Center. The American Society of Safety Engineers stated in its aforementioned journal that nearly 2,000 cars were located that had been parked on three underground floors of the Center, and although some of those vehicles had exploded and were completely burned, many other cars were in drivable condition – neither crushed nor burned. Moreover, the journal article indicated that "... gasoline in a car either explodes or it remains inside the tank ... it does not leak out and go looking for fires to be fueled."

The Society of Safety Engineers also indicated that a tank containing 72,000 gallons of fuel that was stored in the basement of the World Trade Center had been discovered. Although the tank was slightly damaged, no leaks were detected in the tank, and the fuel in the tank was removed.

Most of the office equipment in the buildings had – somehow – been transformed into dust on 9/11, and, therefore, could not serve as a source of fuel, and, moreover, there were many stores in the underground shopping complex that were still intact and their contents never burned. So, if 2,000 parked cars, a huge fuel storage tank, office equipment, and subterranean stores were not fueling the high temperatures at Ground Zero that continued for months on end, what was responsible for that phenomenon?

The television program "Relics from the Ruins" that aired on the History Channel featured an eight ton I-beam taken from Ground Zero that was six inches thick and bent in the shape of a horseshoe. A worker commented on the I-beam and said:

"I found it hard to believe that it actually bent because of the size of it and how there's no cracks in the iron. It bent without almost a single crack in it. It takes thousands of degrees to bend steel like this,"

--Note: Steel melts at 2,800 degrees Fahrenheit – 1,500 degrees Celsius – and softens at 1,100 degrees Fahrenheit 593 degrees Celsius ... for steel to melt or bend in the foregoing manner usually requires that the temperature to which steel is exposed be sustained for a period of time --

and yet, as previously noted, NIST insisted that the maximum temperature attained by fires at the World Trade Center was about 480 degrees Fahrenheit.

Some people have maintained that traces of a substance were discovered at Ground Zero and that, upon analysis, the material was identified to be the incendiary/explosive known as nano-thermite. When nano-thermite is ignited it burns at around 4,800 degrees Fahrenheit and since its chemical composition provides it with its own source of oxygen, it is capable of burning in conditions that are devoid of oxygen (such as underwater).

Whether nano-thermite was the fuel that maintained the high-temperature at Ground Zero going for months or was responsible for bending an eight ton Steel I-beam into a horseshoe shape is unknown ... and for those who wish to claim that nano-thermite might have been the fuel that subsidized the more than three months worth of high-temperatures that were recorded at the World Trade Center following 9/11, then, as a homework assignment, you might try to calculate how much nano-thermite would be necessary to sustain such a persistent set of high temperatures for that length of period of time. In any event, what is clear is that there is no known way through which military grade nano-thermite could form naturally in the dust at Ground Zero, and, therefore, its presence there needs to be explained.

NIST refused to look – at least in any manner that can be called scientific – for evidence that explosives had been present at the World Trade Center on 9/11, and it did not choose to investigate whether, or not, the high temperatures that, for months, had been discovered to be present at Ground Zero following the events of 9/11 might have had anything to do with the collapse of three steel-structure buildings on 9/11. In fact, as Peter Ketchum noted in his public statement concerning the matter, NIST seemed to do everything it could to avoid looking for evidence that might indicate the presence of explosives at Ground Zero on 9/11.

According to Dr. Sunder, "We conducted the study without bias, without interference from anyone, and dedicated ourselves to do the very best job we could. And, in fact, I would suggest that the public should ... at this point recognize that science is really behind what we say." Actual facts belie the foregoing assertion.

The only kind of science that is behind the NIST reports concerning 9/11 is the sort of research that cannot but induce Americans to distance themselves from such so-called scientific activity and become "unscientific" in the best sense of the latter term. In other words, the sort of research conducted by NIST in conjunction with 9/11 is the kind of process that forces one to conclude that such "scientists" can no longer be considered to be honest brokers of truth, and if the NIST manner of research – as exemplified in relation to 9/11 -- is "scientific", then, one needs to become "unscientific" so that evidence, objectivity, rigor, love of the truth, and integrity once again matter.

Peter Ketchum – a scientist – did not investigate the events of 9/11 for nearly sixteen years. He merely accepted the word of others ... until a friend's casual remark induced him to look into the matter more carefully.

As far as the issue of 9/11 is concerned, Mr. Ketchum didn't really begin to become an honest broker of the truth concerning those events until he actually begin to look at relevant evidence some 16 years after the events of 9/11 had taken place. He became an objective, honest broker of the truth in relation to 9/11 when he made the requisite efforts to acquire insight into the nature of 9/11 in a manner that was rooted in a rigorous process that was transparent, open, not intended to evade difficult problems, or mislead and distort (through commission or omission) with respect to relevant issues, as well as be critically and fairly responsive to actual evidence rather than be ruled by propaganda, indoctrination, and forces of undue influence in relation to the issue of 9/11.

Having done the foregoing does not mean that his conclusions concerning 9/11 are necessarily correct or true. Nonetheless, he has done, and is doing, what any objective and honest broker of the truth must do in order to try to gain insight into the nature of truth with respect to some given issue ... in this case 9/11.

7. Emergent Properties

In the worlds of medicine and psychology, neurobiology is enjoying tremendous popularity and success by virtue of the many discoveries concerning the roles of, among other things, various classes of neurotransmitters, as well as of neuromodulators such as endorphins, enkephalins and neurohormones (neuropeptides) in brain functioning. Some scientists are claiming that the promised land of a complete mapping of the brain with all its intricate electrical and chemical pathways may be near at hand.

As a result, age-old secrets underlying consciousness, intelligence, language, creativity, personality, sexuality, and identity supposedly are being revealed almost on a daily basis. For example, one popular theory of brain functioning suggests there is an increasing amount of evidence which appears to indicate that all of the complex, higher functions which traditionally have been considered to distinguish human beings from most, if not all, of other forms of life on Earth, can be conceived as no more than emergent properties arising out of the trillions of interactions taking place in the billions of synaptic junctions of the nervous system - transactions which, ultimately, are rooted in, or based on, the activity of a fairly small number of neurotransmitters and neuromodulators, together with some relatively simple electrical circuitry.

Roughly speaking, an emergent property is a quality exhibited by a given system which could not be predicted on the basis of just looking at the basic components and processes which tend to characterize that system. On this view, the sheer number of interactions entailed by the activity of a small set of neurotransmitters, neuromodulators, along with a few different modes of electrical rhythms, is as important, if not more so, than the biological components and kinds of process which are interacting with one another.

Concepts such as self-organizing systems, reiteration, dissipative structures, non-linear dynamics, chaos theory, parallel processing, feedback, and so on are the watch-words of the theory of emergent properties. In effect, amazing new, unforeseeable, qualitatively different functions are said to be capable of arising out of the complexity of interactions of a relatively small and simple set of underlying components and processes when these properties and processes come together in the right set of conditions which are governed by the principles inherent in a confluence of, for example, non-linear dynamics, dissipative structures, cybernetic feedback systems, phase transitions, and so on.

A number of years ago Karl Popper developed an approach to the philosophy of science which came to be known as "falsificationsim". Essentially, Popper was concerned with the issue of how to demarcate or distinguish defensible science from metaphysical systems and/or pseudo-science.

Briefly stated, and in somewhat oversimplified terms, the criterion which Popper settled on to establish such a line of demarcation was the way he believed the enterprise of science was rooted in processes of empirical observation from which one could deduce certain ideas, theories, and possibilities that could, in turn, be tested and, therefore verified - or not - when considered against the backdrop of available evidence. More specifically, he believed no number of positive results from this sort of open-ended set of empirical probes could prove a given theory, law, or principle was true, but just one contra-indication was enough to bring into question the validity or truth of such a theory, principle, or law.

Thus, Popper maintained the essence of science resided in its tendency to focus in on the challenge of falsification. In other words, the test of a science - as opposed to metaphysical speculation or pseudo-science - was the willingness of a given instance of exploration to expose itself to empirical, deductive judgments when measured against available evidence by means of experiments and tests which yielded data that could be shown to be either consistent with that evidence or falsified by it.

If a system of thought could not be falsified, then, according to Popper, this was a strong indication the conceptual framework in question was more likely to be an instance of metaphysical thinking or some sort of pseudo-science than it was an exemplar of authentic scientific activity. Similarly, if a given hypothesis, idea, theory or law was shown to be falsified by experiment in the context of available empirical evidence, then, on this basis one had good reason either to reject such a hypothesis in its entirety or to require its proponent(s) to return to the drawing board and re-work the hypothesis and/or theory in a way that eliminated the aspect which had been falsified through empirical demonstration.

As with most things in the philosophy of science, there were both important insights contained in Popper's idea of falsification, as well as problems. In effect, when Popper's philosophical framework was itself subjected to a rigorous round of falsification by other philosophers of science, his system exhibited a variety of lacunae and problems in the context of available evidence concerning activities which were considered to be part of "science" - both historically as well as in some of its modern forms.

For present purposes, the ultimate validity of Popper's system of thought is unimportant. What is important is that he provides an idea - namely, falsification, which can be used to help critically reflect on the aforementioned theory of emergent properties when the latter is applied to the field of neurobiology.

For instance, what is one to make of the idea of emergent properties when considered in relation to the findings of Dr. John Lorber? Lorber is a British clinician who, a number of years ago, generated some interesting data which raises a lot of questions for many facets of neurobiology - especially the theory of emergent properties.

Dr. Lorber was working with people who were hydrocephalic. These are individuals who have a problem with the flow of cerebral-spinal fluid in their nervous systems. Normally, cerebral-spinal fluid flows in a continuous loop which links the spinal column and the brain. Among other things, this flow runs through a series of four ventricles or cavities within the brain.

Sometimes - whether due to congenital defects or post-birth trauma or a combination of the two - a blockage arises at some point in the flow of the cerebral-spinal fluid which causes the fluid to accumulate in one or more of the aforementioned ventricles. As more cerebral spinal fluid is produced and accumulates in this ventricle system, it begins to exert a pressure on the brain.

Since the brain is surrounded by the skull and, therefore, has no place to go, so to speak, the pressure being exerted by the cerebral-spinal fluid which is accumulating in the brain's ventricle system begins to compress the brain against the skull's interior surface. Given enough time and/or if - where possible - a shunt is not put in place to relieve this pressure, the brain is slowly squeezed into a volume consisting of just a few millimeters spread around the inner surface of the skull.

If the increasing pressure of accumulating cerebral-spinal fluid is not relieved within a certain critical time period through the use of a shunt or other medical procedures, the damage appears to be largely irreversible. In fact, usually, the untreated effect of this process of hydrocephalus is severe retardation.

I said "usually" above because Dr. Lorber discovered some rather amazing exceptions to the general rule. Some of the individuals who suffered from hydrocephalus were quite normal in their functioning, and there even were some college graduates among this subset of exceptions.

For instance, one of the individuals in Lorber's study had earned a honors degree in mathematics at Cambridge University. Yet, when a scan was done of this individual's head, the scan indicated that almost the entire brain had been squeezed out of existence. All that remained was an extremely thin strip of neural matter running around the interior of the skull casing. Lorber wrote up an overview of his studies and submitted them for publication in some reputable journals of science. His work survived the peer review process and found their way into print with titles such as "Do You Need A Brain To Think?"

In the 19th century, the unfortunate Phineus Gage made clinical history when he survived an accident which resulted in an iron rod penetrating his brain, only later to show marked changes in personality, temperament and mental functioning. These clinical findings were part of a vast array of empirical data which accumulated during the next century which indicated there seemed to be a very strong relationship between the location of certain kinds of brain trauma and the nature of the dysfunctioning in language skills, mental abilities, personality, and so on which subsequently manifested themselves in these individuals.

As outlined previously, Popper believed there was no number of positive findings which could prove that a given hypothesis or theory was true, but one finding could falsify a theory or hypothesis. Thus, in the present context, despite the fact there is an extremely imposing array of data which ties brain functioning to localization of brain activity, one has to ask what is the significance of Lorber's clinical findings with respect to hydrocephalus which appear to provide some contra-indications to the idea that thinking, logic, consciousness, understanding, and language are necessarily "caused" by neurobiological activity?

Is there, somehow, sufficient brain matter left intact in some of Lorber's hydrocephalic individuals that they are capable of normal, if not above normal, functioning? If so, why are the vast majority of people who suffer from hydrocephalus severely retarded? If so, what is the critical mass of neural material which is necessary such that below this amount, retardation occurs, and above it, normal functioning ensues?

Is the difference between whether retardation or normal functioning occurs, a function of the sequence of brain degradation in the sense that one sequence of degradation leads to retardation, while another sequence permits normal functioning? Or, alternatively, since there is some evidence indicating that sudden degradation of neurobiological integrity leads to greater and longer-lasting dysfunctioning than does the same (or sometimes a greater) amount of degradation occurring over a longer period of time, is the end result of any given case of hydrocephalus a matter of the amount of time which elapses before the degradation process reaches its final state?

If, as Lorber's findings suggest, we don't necessarily need a whole lot of neural matter to function normally, then, why do we have a three-pound universe residing above our neck consisting of billions of cells and trillions of interconnections? If, as Lorber's findings suggest, brain functioning is only "correlated" with higher mental functioning, what are the "causes" of such functioning?

Whatever the answer to the foregoing questions may be, one idea would seem to be in need of some re-working. More specifically, some of the individuals in Lorber's studies - the ones without most of their brains, and, yet, still able to function normally (or better) - seem to indicate that whatever causally underlies our higher mental faculties, the hypothesis of emergent properties would seem to have been falsified in, at least, a few cases.

Presumably, in a brain which has been reduced from roughly 1300-1700 cubic centimeters down to a volume consisting of only a few millimeters dispersed over the interior surface of the skull casing, a substantial alteration has taken place in the level of complexity of the system. In such cases, one no longer necessarily has the same vast number of intact cells and synaptic interactions taking place within a few millimeters which had been present in a full-volume brain.

If this is so, then, whatever the cause of our higher cognitive functions may be, there appear to be some instances of these abilities which do not seem to be a function of so-called emergent properties which arise out of the sheer number of neural transactions which characterize a normal brain. This does not mean emergent phenomena of some sort do not occur in these contexts, but, only that, one is going to have re-conceptualize what is meant when one claims that higher cognitive functions are an example of emergent properties in action.

More specifically, one must come up with a fairly specific explanatory framework of just how non-linear dynamics, dissipative structures, phase transitions, chaotic systems, reiterative processes, and so on are capable of generating consciousness, logical thought, understanding, language, and/or creativity through just neurobiological activity. Right now, the notion of emergent properties is little more than a weak, metaphysical way of confessing that we really have no idea how - or even if - any of our higher cognitive abilities arise out of the interaction of neurotransmitters, neruomodulators, and neuronal electrical circuitry.

Yes, as is attested to, by a great deal of medical and scientific evidence, there is a definite correlation between such neurobiological activity and cognitive functioning. But, correlation is not necessarily indicative of causality, and when one has empirical data such as has been provided by John Lorber which appears to falsify certain aspects of the theory of emergent properties in neurobiology, then one has a fairly clear warrant for re-thinking this whole conceptual framework.

8. Facebook

Some people might wonder why an article concerning facebook is appearing in a book exploring various aspects of technology. Notwithstanding the inclination of some individuals to only look at the surface facets of facebook's activities, nonetheless, such a platform is only possible because of the algorithmic technology which enables people to connect in the way they do on facebook and, such activities are feasible only because of the technology that makes the Internet possible, and the Internet and social media platforms can only be accessed by individuals who have the requisite technology in the form of a computer, laptop, pad, or mobile device.

Secondly, facebook is also a technological tool for shaping the way people, think, speak, and behave. This platform has been used as a tool of undue influence with respect to elections, commercial interests, and an array of social issues.

Before finally realizing that facebook is little more than a data mining operation which can be used to surveil people for the government as well as drive algorithmic, political, commercial, social, and ideological trends in certain desired directions, I took several journeys into that platform's landscape. Most of what follows focuses on my final round of engagement which took place about six years ago, but there was a penultimate set-to with facebook that is instructive and, in its own way, lends some credence to some of my reflections concerning my last encounter with facebook.

More specifically, once I had provided some information and set up a few dimensions of my page during the penultimate experience, I began to get hundreds and hundreds of "friends" requests that weren't from anyone I knew. The requests were from all over the world, and they appeared to be largely, if not entirely, from women.

The properties of the requests were, quite frankly, embarrassing. Offers of: "Good times," sex, intimacy, perversions of one kind or another, and pornography came pouring in.

I hadn't been on facebook for very long on that occasion. I was a member of one or two groups that were small and explored non-political issues, and, moreover, I hadn't been posting all that much, nor did I have all many legitimate contacts. Consequently, I couldn't figure out why this sort of lurid content was being sent my way or who might be behind it.

To a considerable degree, I was a 'nobody'. I had little, or no, influence on the internet, and I was not trending.

The few comments on various posts that I did make were relatively short and sought to be complementary or encouraging in some manner. The few responses that were posted to my comments expressed appreciation or the like.

The possibilities were limited. Someone from within facebook was making the foregoing sort of request traffic possible or someone using facebook was exploiting vulnerabilities in the facebook system and, for whatever reason, that person was trying to yank my emotional chains in some fashion.

If the foregoing sorts of experiences were being encountered by a lot of other individuals on facebook, I'm sure I would have heard something about it either on facebook on in articles concerning facebook. However, my experience seemed to be somewhat unique or, perhaps, people were too embarrassed to talk about it, and we were all disgusted in silence.

I had learned previously, that facebook is useless when it comes to launching complaints of any kind. They appear to live in their own individual or collective meta-worlds.

Therefore, after a few days of non-stop overtures of the foregoing kind, I cancelled out of my facebook account. I didn't knew who was responsible for what was taking place or why it was happening, but facebook was not sufficiently important to me that I felt any sort of need to wait things out in order to see if the stream of overtures might come to an end.

A few months later, I tried facebook again. In very short order, I became one of the 800-plus accounts that were disappeared by facebook during the great 2018 purge.

I'll begin by observing how ironic it is that facebook is a social media company. Yet, it appears to lack even the most basic of pro-social skills ... that is, skills which are intended to constructively promote and facilitate the use of the sorts of qualities that bring people together in a positive manner.

More specifically, facebook did not help me when I asked for help concerning the cancellation of my account. Facebook did not communicate with me when it indicated it would do so.

Moreover, while facebook claimed that it was genuinely interested in my security, nonetheless, it acted on that claim in a completely disingenuous manner. Furthermore, facebook failed to exhibit anything remotely approaching reciprocity during its interaction with me and, instead, seemed to pursue a policy of uncaring, tyrannical control.

In addition, facebook appeared to display an array of dishonest behaviors during its interaction with me. Consequently, in my opinion, facebook failed to act with integrity from the beginning of our problematic interaction concerning the termination of my facebook account during the early hours of the morning of October 7, 2018. Finally, facebook conducted itself as a school-yard bully might act by using its size and power to abuse someone of considerably less stature and power.

The following presentation will provide the evidence that documents the foregoing assertions as well as provides a context for critically reflecting on, in my opinion, the nature of the clear and present danger that facebook represents. While the first part of this article seeks to capture the nature of facebook's interaction with me in the period leading up to my being purged, and, therefore, quite possibly, that material might be of only marginal interest to a reader, nonetheless, I hope you will persevere with the presentation through to its end point because I believe the journey will lead to some issues that might be of much more substantial importance and relevance in the discussion which follows this initial part of the article.

Shortly after getting purged from facebook, I had discovered a way to download material associated with my pre-termination facebook page. The material contained a record or log of my activity while on facebook.

The following initial posts to facebook were among the contents of that record. For instance, on Thursday, August 23, 2018 at 3:19 P.M, I received my official welcome to facebook.

In the facebook message, I was told to upload a profile photo. I complied with the request.

In addition, I was prompted to edit my profile. This was done, as well.

However, the next suggestion from facebook was a little problematic for me. More specifically, complying with facebook's suggestion that I should find people I know was a little tricky because a number of individuals with whom I am acquainted tend to feel uncomfortable about having a Muslim on their timeline.

This is not because those people necessarily harbor prejudices toward Muslims, but, rather, this is because on the basis of various facebook experiences they have had, they worry about how some of the people with whom they are connected might react to the presence of a Muslim. Consequently, for several reasons, I decided to put off contacting people and just see what friend requests, if any, might come along.

Instead, first, I provided an image of, as well as some information concerning, a book on education that I had released just prior to signing up for facebook. Secondly, I introduced a short aphorism of the Sufi, mystical saint, al-Junayd -- namely, "No act finds greater favor with God than struggling against passion, for destroying a mountain with one's fingernails is far easier than is resisting passion." In retrospect the foregoing saying strikes me as being rather appropriate because facebook seems more committed to destroying things (like 800 facebook pages and accounts) with its digital fingernails than it is committed to struggling against various passions it has concerning the way facebook appears to believe that the world ought to operate.

Finally, I put up a short piece of video floetry - which consists of poetry, images, and music set in counterpoint to one another ... the selection was entitled "Human Potential." It was just a couple of minutes long and could not have been considered as being offensive to anyone because it was very generic in character.

Next, I'm going to run down through a number of categories of my facebook activity - or lack thereof -from the aforementioned log record that I downloaded. According to the "No Data" entries contained in that log:

I posted no comments,

I indicated no likes and dislikes

There is some activity associated with the Friends data, and I'll come back to this later on.

I had no followers, nor was I following anyone.

I exchanged no messages with other individuals on facebook.

I belonged to no groups.

I neither created nor responded to events of any kind, and I'll return to this category of profile information later in the article.

I was not the administrator of any Page

I had zero activity in the facebook marketplace

There was no history of payment activity associated with my facebook account.

I saved no posts.

Apparently, I created two 'places': One had to do with my high school years, and the other was a place of work. Both of these pieces of information might have been entered during the process of creating a profile.

I didn't log into either apps or websites using my facebook account

There was no other activity associated with my account ... such as "Pokes" given or received.

There was no ad activity taking place in conjunction with my facebook account.

There was one search that I did ... and this concerned a friend request that had arisen. I'll talk more about this a little later in the article.

There were no Location Services involving my facebook account.

There were no calls or messages that were shared.

I'm not exactly sure what the following category entails, but, apparently, there was one Friend Peer Group concerning me.

Now, let's return to the "Profile Information" category that I by-passed earlier. Maybe, we'll find some sort of a clue in that data that will shed light on why I might have been purged from facebook because there doesn't seem to be any items in the aforementioned posts and activities logs that are capable of justifying my expulsion from facebook.

In addition to the foregoing categories, I provided an overview of my education - from a small rural high school in Maine, through Harvard, and, then, on to graduate studies at the University of Toronto.

I offered some information about my work background. This consisted of various places in both Canada and the United States where I had been employed ... fairly innocuous material.

I was asked about my religious views, and I gave them ... Muslim via the Sufi, mystical tradition.

In addition, I was asked to list any web sites with which I was associated, and I complied ... I'll return to this issue subsequently.

Finally, I gave a fairly lengthy overview description of my life in response to facebook's suggestion that people might find that sort of information useful, interesting, or the like.

I talked about protesting the Vietnam War and going to Canada.

I mentioned some of the circumstances of my converting to Islam.

I alluded to the 17-year long battle that I had at the University of Toronto to be able to obtain my doctorate.

I indicated that following the passing away of my first spiritual guide I became entangled with someone whom I later discovered was a very clever charlatan.

I referred to several periods of unemployment and relative homelessness that I went through for a few years toward the latter part of the 20th century and at certain points during the first part of the 21st century.

I stated that I taught psychology for about 6 years and, then, retired, in order to concentrate on writing a number of books that dealt with a variety of topics, ranging from: Quantum physics, to: cosmology, constitutional law, evolution, psychology, 9/11, and religion.

I, then, described how I died - several times - in the Emergency Department of a local hospital and was revived one time more than I coded, as well as some of the circumstances surrounding those events.

Finally, I gave a relatively brief account of the process through which my published writings wound up as residents of the library system at Harvard and how this experience formed the ideational seed that led to my library book-gifting project that I was trying to fund through the Patreon web site.

I spent the last part of August 2018 through until the first couple of weeks in October working on updating 39 books that I had written in an attempt to get them ready for the library gifting project that I was promoting through the aforementioned patreon.com web site. Consequently, although I had managed to find enough time to get my facebook account up and running, nonetheless, for a number of months I spent almost no time on that account, and this is reflected in the "No Data" log entries that I itemized earlier in this video.

At 1:32 in the morning on Tuesday, October 2nd, 2018 - more than a month after I was welcomed to facebook -- I received notification that someone wanted to be friends with me. I didn't pay much attention to the notice because at that juncture all my time was being directed toward finishing up the book updating process that I had undertaken for my patreon project.

Precisely one day later, facebook again notified me in the wee hours of the morning that the foregoing individual was waiting for a response to the friend request, and I was being asked to confirm the person's overture. Because my attention was directed elsewhere, I put off doing anything about the issue.

On Wednesday afternoon - some 15-16 hours after the previous notification had been sent - I received a third notice from facebook. On this occasion, I was reminded about the friend request that was still waiting for me, and, as well, I was informed that there was one other notification from facebook that was awaiting my attention.

The Facebook notification indicated that "A lot has happened on Facebook since I last logged in" And, as I soon discovered, this was true but in a problematically laden manner.

The notice from facebook also contained a photo of me next to my name ... presumably included for purposes of visually identifying me or confirming me as the person for whom the notice had been intended.

I decided to do something about the friend request and also to check out the other notification that facebook was alluding to in its communiqué to me.

Earlier, I indicated that I would come back to the "Search History" category of logged facebook activity associated with my account.

As my log-download indicated, at 1:31 on the morning of October 5th, 2018, I did a search of the individual who had contacted me asking to be friends. Based on the information that I found, I decided that the individual was not a good fit for my interests, inclinations, or personality, and, so, I decided against confirming the individual's friend request.

After doing a search concerning the person who had extended a friend request to me, I investigated the other notification that the previous facebook message had informed me about. Unfortunately, I don't have a record of that notification because not too long after seeing it, I began to have difficulty accessing my facebook page -- which I'll get to shortly - and, therefore, I didn't have the opportunity to take a screen shot of it ... but I do have some indirect proof concerning the contents of that notification.

More specifically, despite the presence of a picture of me on the notification that facebook sent to me -- an image which, presumably, was present for purposes of security -- facebook informed me that there had been anomalous activity associated with my facebook account and that, for unstated reasons, the company needed a clear picture of me that would be destroyed after being reviewed. The notification indicated that this was all being done to ensure my security within the facebook platform.

I thought the request was somewhat anomalous - as did my wife. Nevertheless, I complied and sent them a copy of the picture that is on the back cover of many of my books.

Here is the indirect proof that I mentioned earlier concerning the nature of the notification that I had received from facebook with respect to its request for a clear photo of me. Facebook acknowledged that a photo had been uploaded and indicated how someone from the company would be in touch with me once the photo had been reviewed.

Again, there was a reassurance that everything that was going on was about protecting my security. "SO", as a result, I was informed that in the interim period, I wouldn't be able to use facebook.

The foregoing conclusion that restricts me from using facebook -- the "So" part of their message -doesn't necessarily follow from the premise concerning facebook's desire to protect my security. In other words, without more of an explanation about what, precisely, restricting my facebook activity has to do with my security, then what is taking place isn't immediately clear or obvious.

On Friday, October 5th, 2018 at two minutes to midnight, I received an e-mail from the facebook Security Team indicating that a phone number has been added to my account and that if I didn't do this, then, I should take steps to secure my account ... although what those steps are that I should take are not indicated in the e-mail.

In point of fact, however, facebook had been the one to notify me that someone in the company needed my phone number as part of its efforts to make sure, supposedly, that my account was secure. Again, I don't have direct proof that this is the case, but I do have indirect proof concerning this matter - to be presented shortly -- and, therefore, I find it strange that facebook security is asking me if I was the one adding a phone number to my account when facebook is the party that asked me to do so.

On October 5th, 2018, Facebook sent me a confirmation code that I needed to send back to them for security purposes. In order to be able to send me that confirmation code, facebook needed my phone number and had notified me that this was the case in the aforementioned missing message to which I no longer have access, and, therefore, once again, it seems rather strange that the facebook security team should send me an e-mail alerting me that a number had been added to my account when facebook was the one that had initiated the whole process.

I wondered if this were a case of bureaucratic incompetence in which the left hand of the company does not know what its right hand is doing, or is this whole process part of some little Machiavellian power-game that someone in the company is playing with me. In any event, the confirmation code you see on the screen is the indirect proof that facebook is the one that had asked for my phone number.

At 9:07 on Saturday morning - October 6, 2018 - I receive an e-mail from facebook indicating that someone at the company is aware that I was having trouble logging into my facebook account and the anonymous individual is offering me - apparently - an opportunity to be able to log into facebook with just one click. Or, maybe, no one at facebook really cares about my log-in difficulties and the e-mail I have received is part of a dysfunctional auto-responder system that has been set in place to serve -- either: intentionally or inadvertently -- as a wall of separation between me and actual people at facebook.

Whatever might be the case, I decide to accept the offer and click on the indicated "Finish Logging In' link. The foregoing link leads me to the following message: I "can't use Facebook right Now'.

This is because the photo that facebook requested from me is being reviewed. Therefore, for unknown reasons, this means that I won't be able to use facebook but, nevertheless, facebook is "always looking out for" my security.

The nature of the review process concerning my photo remains a mystery as does the logic that supposedly is capable of justifying the linkage of reviewing my photo with preventing me from using facebook or what any of this has do with my security and the anomalous - but unspecified -- activity concerning my account that facebook previously had alluded to in its earlier (and now missing) notification to me.

Let's return to the data file that I downloaded from facebook on Sunday, October 7, 2018 at 9:07 a.m. following my being purged from its accounts. At the very bottom of that file is a link to "Account Status Changes"

When I click on the link, I am shown the following information: 'My account was disabled at 1:59 in the morning on October 7, 2018. There is no explanation associated with facebook's action concerning my termination.

I decide to try to contact someone at facebook to find out more about what is going on. In order to do so, I am required to attach some sort of identifying marker from my account that will be identifiable as having been part of my facebook page.

For the most I am at a loss about what I can attach to my message. I finally decide to use a logo-icon which is one of the few images that

| Technological Reflections |

had been associated with my facebook page, and, I type my message in the indicated space on the web form I am shown.

"I opened up a facebook account on August 23, 2018. Other than putting up a video (a poem about human potential set to music and visual imagery) along with stating my thoughts for the day (a brief Sufi observation) on the occasion that my facebook page became active, I have not: Posted anything, messaged anyone, made a friend request, responded to a friend request, liked anything, disliked anything, or commented on anyone's facebook page.

"Consequently, I really have no idea why my account has been disabled. Nonetheless, despite 6, or so, weeks of facebook inactivity on my part, you decided to disable my account on October 5, 2018 without any explanation to me other than that you claimed to be protecting my security. I have been inactive on my account since my opening-day observation because I have been immersed in updating my books that are being sold through Amazon that I am getting ready to donate to libraries which might be interested in receiving copies of those works. "Anab" is my Sufi-Muslim name, and I have had a legitimate web page under that name (anab-whitehouse.com) for years, as well as a legitimate blog account using that name (anab-whitehouse.blogspot.com) to which I have been posting for more than a decade, as well as several legitimate e-mail accounts with that name.

"<u>You contacted me</u> and asked me to go through a set of security procedures (which included asking me for a photo that you said would be later destroyed), and I complied with your requests. Then, however, you disabled my account -- why? -- when, apparently, the only thing that I have done wrong in your eyes is that I exist and made the mistake of opening a facebook account.

"If I have done something wrong, why not let me know the nature of the problem so that the issue can be resolved instead of going all Kafka on me ... assuming, of course, that the problem - whatever it might be -- is resolvable. Your initial contact with me indicated that there was unusual activity going on with my account.

"Yet, the fact of the matter is, to this point, I have not been actively engaged in my facebook page. So, the only unusual activity associated with the page would have had to have been due to your failure to provide my account with the security to which I am entitled.

"Furthermore, the lack of any explanation concerning the matter as well as the absence of any informational elaboration from you to me on the matter seems to be due to your failure to be willing to treat me as a human being. Apparently, the saying is true when it comes to human beings: power corrupts, and absolute power corrupts absolutely.

"You might enjoy your attempt at playing God, but you should know (because, apparently, you don't seem to understand this) that you are woefully under qualified to assume such a role. Please, if you are able to do so, point out the specific facebook guideline that I, supposedly, have violated which you believe justifies disabling my account, and if I feel you are justified in your assessment of things, then, I will be quite happy to alter whatever needs to be altered, but if you are not justified in your actions, then, your behavior will be seen by anyone who cares to reflect on the situation objectively as the acts of a narcissistic tyrant which seems intent on trying to impose its ideological agenda on the rest of the world. You failed to protect the security of my facebook account, and, yet, I am the one who is -- without being afforded a reasonable explanation -- being punished.

Despite facebook's assurances of contacting me shortly, I never received any further communication from the company. My wife – who is a member of facebook -- also wrote to the platform on my behalf and she also was rebuffed with complete silence.

Facebook encourages people to connect with their friends and the world on its signup page.

Facebook alludes to the process of getting updates concerning friends and the world through the News Feed, and

Facebook mentions the possibility of sharing what's new in one's life with others ... new ideas, experiences, reflections, thoughts, creations, concerns, and insights,

And, finally, facebook, indicates that it offers a search platform through which to find more of what one is looking for. Nonetheless, as I found out, what facebook claims to offer is different from the realities of what actually is offered through facebook.

This is because, among other things, I have not been able to share my thoughts, ideas, reflections, and so on with others, nor have I been able to "find more of what" I'm "looking for" through facebook, nor have I been able to "see photos and updates from friends" because facebook has purged me from its platform for unspecified "anomalous" behavior associated with my account. This is the case despite the fact that facebook's own log record of my activity on facebook indicates that I haven't done much of anything since signing up for its services.

The Sign-up page for Facebook claims that the service is "free and always will be", and, yet, there are many hidden costs associated with the service as, on the one hand, not only the Cambridge Analytica issue demonstrates, but, as well, a variety of other data breeches involving facebook during the past couple of years have shown as well, and, on the other hand, as is evidenced by the totally unjustified purging of accounts like mine ... purges that take place because of the penchant, apparently, that various people at facebook have for bullying individuals who are relatively powerless when it comes to arbitrarily disenfranchising them from the facebook platform.

I find it interesting that facebook's notice informing people that a page "isn't available" suggests that a given page is missing because "a link may be broken" - or, because the page "may have been removed." Such ambiguity camouflages what is taking place in cases like mine beneath a cloud of seemingly innocuous ambiguity concerning precisely what is actually going on in conjunction with a given facebook account or why.

Different people (e.g., Ben Norton from The Real News Network) have suggested various possibilities for why facebook purged certain people from its platform. However, contrary to the possibilities listed by individuals such as Ben Norton:

- I'm not a libertarian;

- And I'm not an alternative media site in a news sense, but as a scholar, I do explore alternative possibilities ... as anyone worthy of being called a scholar should;

- I'm not monitoring the police;

- I'm not engaged in the political process ... that is, I'm not trying to become elected or induce others to vote for this or that individual or party;

- Although I am against war, this is not a primary or even a secondary focus of mine as far as facebook is concerned;

- I'm neither left nor right, but seek something beyond political polarities;

- I'm not trying to foment discontent, but, rather, I am encouraging people to seek the truth.

Notwithstanding the foregoing facts, facebook, nevertheless, decided to purge me from its platform and in the process refused - in a most anti-pro-social way -- to respond to inquiries from myself and my wife concerning the situation. In addition, despite my complying with all of their requests during the time facebook was in the process of purging me from its platform, the company exhibited absolutely no signs of reciprocity concerning me and, as a result, failed to update me or respond to me as it indicated, several times previously, that it would do in the automated messages which were sent to me at various stages of the de-platforming process. This is all rather curious and ironic actions for a organization that supposedly is interested in assisting people to socially interact with one another.

A logo that is used to brand some of my activities gives expression to a methodological orientation that is relevant to the present situation involving facebook ... a situation that entails so many questions and mysteries. For instance, the logo has three "I's," but these are not a narcissistic allusion to me but, rather, refer to the Interrogative Imperative Institute.

The three question marks in the logo are intended to serve as iconic resonances concerning the importance of recognizing and seeking answers to questions with respect to oneself and the rest of reality.

The yellow circle present in the logo gives expression to the circle of life in which we all are engaged in one way or another.

That engagement takes place within the parameters of the universe - both known and unknown - that are represented by the four blue lines surrounding the circle of life;

The sides of the triangle in the center exemplify the importance of experience, reflection, and insight in addressing the questions that arise within us;

The round object at the heart of the triangle alludes to one's essential potential and its quest for seeking to discover the nature of one's relationship with the rest of reality,

And this generates a dynamic where, hopefully, the process of asking questions becomes an artful journey to solutions for life.

Therefore, let's raise a few questions and probe some possibilities concerning the purging of my account from facebook.

Max Blumenthal is the editor of the web site GrayZone, an on-line source for original journalism and critical analysis involving a variety of topics. He also is an award-winning journalist whose work has appeared in, among other places, *The Nation, The New York Times, The Huffington Post,* and *The Los Angeles Times.* In addition, Max Blumenthal is the author of the bestselling *Republican Gomorrah,* as well as *Goliath: Life and Loathing in Greater Israel.* Recently he did an interview with Ben Norton of The Real News Network concerning the facebook purge.

In a recent interview with Ben Norton, Max Blumenthal makes three basic points concerning the October 2018 facebook purge of 800 accounts, including mine. First, the accounts that were purged from facebook received no explanation from the company about why the removal of an account is taking place.

I can't speak for the other 800 accounts that were purged from the platform in October. However, my experience certainly attests to the truth of what he is saying in the first part of his interview with Ben Norton.

Secondly, Max Blumenthal thinks that the primary reason accounts were purged is because someone in the facebook hierarchy perceives the material appearing through those accounts as being actively engaged in the fomenting of discontent or are too radical. (I'll return to this point shortly). Yet, if Max Blumenthal's hypothesis is correct, this doesn't explain why my account was purged from facebook because there was nothing in my posted material that even remotely suggested I was espousing a radical perspective or actively trying -- through one means or another -- to foment discontent among other members of the facebook community.

Do I have a point of view or perspective concerning many things? Yes, I do, but, nevertheless, having a point of view is not, in and of itself, an expression of radicalism – especially given that I really hadn't said much of anything to give expression to that perspective -- nor is having a perspective at all the same as trying to foment discontent. In fact, if having a point of view were equivalent to fomenting discontent, then, everybody on facebook must be considered a radical and guilty of fomenting discontent because everybody on facebook operates out of a particular point of view.

There were just four, or so, activities that took place in conjunction with my facebook account in the six week period that it was available to the public. As indicated earlier, on the very first day, I posted the image of the cover of a book on education that I had just released, and, in addition, I put up a short aphorism by al-Junayd about how difficult it is to struggle against one's own passions, and, as well, I uploaded a short piece of floetry that combined images, poetry, and music ... hopefully each of the foregoing activities is thought-provoking in some manner but hardly a matter of trying to foment discontent in anyone who might have viewed those postings.

The only other activity associated with my account was a search I did for information concerning a person who had extended a friend request to me in early October of 2018. For a variety of reasons, I decided against accepting the request, and if this is considered to give expression to radicalism or is judged to constitute an instance of fomenting discontent (say, in the person whose request was turned down or ignored), then, anyone on facebook who has chosen, for any number of reasons, to decline a friend request -- which is likely to encompass far more than 800 hundred accounts -- should be considered to be a radical and guilty of fomenting discontent, and, yet, only a relatively small group of individuals were purged from the facebook platform.

During the aforementioned interview, Max Blumenthal also suggested that anyone who didn't fit into the normal Republican-Democrat bi-modal political divide might have become a candidate for disappearance. Whatever the truth of such an assertion might be, there was nothing in the profile information associated with my account that could be used to identify me as a Republican, Democrat, or something else.

The final thesis put forth by Max Blumenthal to explain why people might have been purged from the facebook platform involves the notion that facebook and other social media sites are under intense pressure from various dimensions of the United States government to engage in various pogroms of ideational cleansing or censorship among the members of different social media groups. This claim might be true, but I would have liked to have heard a bit more concrete and specific information from Mr. Blumenthal concerning that possibility.

Of course, the fact that the government has various kinds of watch lists has been known for a long time. The no-fly list represents just one example of this state of affairs, as did the enemies lists of J. Edgar Hoover and Richard Nixon.

However, perhaps, the government is borrowing a chapter from the government of China and setting up a framework of social credit scores in which individuals will be required to behave in certain ways and if they do not, then, sanctions -- such as being purged from one, or another (or all) social media sites -- will be levied against those people. If this were the case, then, being purged from facebook might not be so much a matter of what one has done, or not done, on a given social media platform, but, instead might constitute a punishment for having transgressed against government policy in some other facet of a person's life and facebook merely becomes the public persona of the government's attempt to induce people to alter their behavior or become publically isolated as a persona non grata and, thereby, prevented from having access to various public activities, services, organizations, agencies, platforms, and other similar venues.

If facebook has been weaponized in the foregoing manner, then the government is violating Article IV, Section 4 of the Constitution which indicates that "the United States shall guarantee to every state" -- and, therefore, by implication the people of those states -- "a republican form of government, and shall protect each of them against invasion" - including unwarranted invasion by various dimensions of the federal government. Republicanism was a moral philosophy that emerged during the 17th and 18th century Enlightenment and came to dominate a great deal of public life in America during the 1700s. This moral philosophy stipulated that those who followed it -- or guaranteed it as the US Constitution did -- needed to comply with a set of moral precepts that required a person to, among other things, act fairly, honestly, dispassionately, without partisanship, and in ways that did not involve advancing their own cause or interests at the expense of the individuals who were being served through that philosophy.

If we return to the first hypothesis advanced by Max Blumenthal - namely, that the sites that were purged from facebook were removed because they were perceived by someone at facebook and/or by someone in the federal government as being too radical or as trying to foment discontent -- then, this is very disquieting for several reasons. For instance, on the one hand, such a policy violates numerous provisions of the United States Constitution including the aforementioned Article IV, Section 4 of the Constitution, as well as violates different aspects of the first Amendment (e.g., abridging the freedom of speech, and interfering with the right of people to assemble, and to be able to petition the government for a redress of grievances), as well as Section 1 of Amendment XIII in which involuntary servitude "except as a punishment for crime whereof the party shall have been duly convicted shall exist within the United States, or any place" -- such as facebook -- "subject to their jurisdiction." In addition, on the other hand, a policy of removing people from social media because their ideas are deemed by someone as being too radical or because they are considered to be likely to foment discontent among people operates within a context that is entirely too amorphous and opaque, and, therefore, much too vulnerable to being abused and exploited by individuals associated with facebook or the federal government who might be interested in furthering their own hidden agendas at the expense of the people they supposedly serve.

Facebook says that the basis for removing 800 pages and accounts from facebook had to do with behavior and not content. Let's take a quick look at two other institutional polices of termination that supposedly are based on behavior not content.

Recently, I read a book by Nick Turse entitled: *Kill Anything That Moves: The Real American War in Vietnam.* The book meticulously documents the manner in which -- despite attempts to cover the following fact up, My Lai was not the anomalous result of a few

| Technological Reflections |

pathological individuals.

Instead, such behavior constituted a policy that governed much of what went on in many parts of South Vietnam, including the Phoenix program of assassination, intimidation, and torture that was conducted by the CIA and various branches of American special forces that was intended to terrorize and pacify the people of South Vietnam ... conduct that has been documented by, among others, Nick Turse and Douglas Valentine. In other words, the frame of mind and the condition of the heart which gave rise to the atrocities that took place in My Lai was not the exception but, unfortunately, often constituted the rule in Vietnam ... an operational principle that was adhered to by a variety of high-ranking officers who again and again either encouraged the wanton slaughter of innocent Vietnamese women, children, and old men, or looked the other way when such massacres occurred, or destroyed evidence concerning those activities, or shielded those who committed such war crimes from being prosecuted.

As indicated in the aforementioned book by Nick Turse, the "kill anything that moves" mentality was expressed by Captain Ernest Medina when he was asked by a soldier whether the rules of engagement being implemented at My Lai extended to women and children. However, that same mentality was echoed in many other parts of South Vietnam in which the most pedestrian movements by civilians - i.e., their behavior - was used as a pretext that allegedly justified murdering them. For example, if a Vietnamese civilian was trying to escape from an active zone of fighting, then this often was considered to be proof that the individual trying to escape must be a member of the Viet Cong, or if a civilian were walking along a road, the individual was considered by all too many members of the military to be a legitimate target of opportunity to shoot at, hit with a military vehicle, rape, beat up, or abuse in some other manner.

Another program similar to the policies carried out in Vietnam that tends to revolve around mere behavior rather than seeking factual content that might provide an alternative explanation for suspect behavior involves the use of military drones by the American government. Thousands of innocent civilians have been killed in Pakistan, Yemen, Afghanistan, Iraq, Somalia, and Syria because the behavior of those individuals conformed to an algorithm that had been drawn up to supposedly identify dangerous enemies ... an algorithm that has been shown again and again to be deeply flawed for its frequent failure to distinguish between innocent civilians and possible bad guys ... and none of this, of course, addresses the many questions that surround the legality of such actions even if the potential targets were considered, in some way, to be legitimate.

Facebook -- like the military -- also has an algorithm or set of them that supposedly enables some of its employees to be able to identify certain kinds of anomalous behavior involving member accounts as worthy of being purged from its platform, but, like the aforementioned military counterparts in Vietnam and the use of drones, the facebook algorithm is deeply flawed and, as a result, innocent members of the social media giant have become vulnerable to a policy of disappearance. For instance, why didn't those algorithms protect me during my aforementioned attempt (described toward the begging of this article) to have a facebook account when I was inundated by all manner of inappropriate overtures of a sexual and lurid nature in the form of so-called "friend" requests?

Conceivably, my being kicked out of facebook involved a mistaken application of the behavioral algorithms that are used by facebook. In other words, my behavior (or lack thereof) might have, somehow, given expression to a false positive which suggested -- erroneously -- that something was going on in relation to my activity (or lack thereof) on facebook which, in point of fact, was not actually going on, but if this is the case, then, unfortunately, the company seems to be unwilling to admit that in certain cases there are problems with the algorithms it uses to determine who does and does not get to stay on facebook.

Given that there is no behavior or activity associated with my facebook account that could be construed as being purge-worthy, one wonders if certain individuals at facebook -- on their own or at the behest of some agency of the federal government -- decided to explore a little further afield to find something concerning me that might be resonate with the purge-algorithm being employed by facebook. For instance, amidst the profile information appearing in my facebook account was one of my web sites - namely, anab-whitehouse.com ... so, let's take a look and see if there is something there that could have been of concern to facebook or its federal handlers.

The Home page of my web site makes one thing very clear -- I am against violence and compulsion of any kind ... irrespective of whether that violence and compulsion are perpetrated by variously flavored forms of religious fundamentalism, or governments of whatever persuasion, or the exploitive captains of industry and banking. Perhaps a person or persons unknown at facebook took exception to the idea that someone (for example, me) thought that corporations such as facebook - which are nothing more than legal fictions designed to serve the agendas of the few against the interests of the many -- should have the right to do whatever they like. Unfortunately, the behavior of all too many governments, corporations, and ideologically-driven religious enthusiasts is often hard to distinguish from the actions of other garden varieties of terrorist activity.

In concert with the foregoing orientation, my web site explores a variety of possibilities ... from: Atheism, to: Democracy, ecology, evolution, mysticism, philosophy, physics, poetry, psychology, shari'ah (so-called Islamic law), and terrorism. The web site also features videos focused on a number of issues -- such as the mysteries surrounding the anthrax attacks that occurred shortly after 9/11.

The events of 9/11 themselves also receive a fair amount of attention within my web site — not for purposes of advancing conspiracy theories of one kind or another concerning that day but, rather, to document the problems that exist in conjunction with the conspiracy theory being advanced by the US government and its media allies that 19 Arab terrorists conspired together to bring about the tragedy of 9/11. For instance, the web page features a videographic affidavit of April Gallop - an individual with high security clearance who was actually seated at Ground Zero in the Pentagon on the morning of 9/11 and who has given sworn testimony that after whatever took place at the Pentagon occurred, nonetheless, in her bare feet she led a group of people to safety through the devastated area of the Pentagon and there was no plane wreckage, dead passengers, luggage debris, or fires fed by the jet fuel of a crashed commercial air plane to be seen in that portion of the building.

I don't recall Mark Zuckerberg or any other corporate leader from facebook ever publically questioning the tenability of the official government/media conspiracy theory concerning the events of 9/11, and, therefore, perhaps someone at facebook decided (on his, her, or their own initiative or at the behest of someone in the government) to use the purge policy as a way of silencing a voice of dissent concerning 9/11 despite the fact that there was nothing in my facebook activity that mentioned or alluded to that issue.

The Home page of my web site also contains a link to a list of the 40, or so, books, that I have written over the last several decades. Perhaps one, or another of these books, irritated someone at facebook or, maybe, one of those works irritated some government official who, as Max Blumenthal pointed out in his earlier remarks, sought to bring pressure to bear on someone at facebook to help censor people like me.

For instance, perhaps someone didn't like the relatively recently released book: *Unscientific America: 9/11, Harris and Chomsky* which explores, among other things, the manner in which neither Sam Harris nor Noam Chomsky actually ever explore the facts of 9/11 but, instead, engage in little more than hypothetical and ideological posturing. Or, maybe, someone at facebook didn't like the idea that my web site referred to the book: *Framing 9/11* which was considered by one individual who has studied most of what has been written on 9/11 to be one of the best treatments of that issue that he had encountered.

Perhaps someone at facebook didn't like the way I critiqued Imam Faisal Rauf's attempt in his book *What's Right With Islam* to draw parallels between the principles of Islam and American democracy ... not because there are no such parallels but, rather, because Imam Rauf failed to capture what those parallels actually are.

Maybe someone at facebook took exception with my exploratory journey into the issue of spiritual abuse that exists within certain facets of the Muslim community. There are many forms of terrorism which seem to presuppose the presence of some form of spiritual abuse and is capable of serving as a catalyst that facilitates various acts of terrorism.

Or, conceivably, someone at facebook might have taken exception with the way in which I critiqued Sam Harris's book -- *The End of Faith* -- and demonstrated that there really seems to be little difference between the way that religious fundamentalists conduct themselves

| Technological Reflections |

and the manner in which Sam Harris conducts himself in the aforementioned book ... including the possibility that as ethically distasteful as it might be, Sam Harris maintains that we -- people in the West -- might need to carry out a preemptive nuclear strike against Muslims because requires all Muslims to believe and behave as fundamentalists do and, therefore, there is no reasoning with them ... a premise that Sam Harris fails to demonstrate in his book because it is a total distortion of what Islam actually teaches.

Perhaps someone at facebook dislikes the way in which the book: *Fundamentalist Phenomenology* shows how terrorism, fundamentalism, and spiritual abuse are linked together in ways that have nothing to do with the basic principles and precepts of Islam. Of course, such a possibility is something that those who harbor biases concerning Islam do not want people in the West to discover.

Then again, maybe someone at facebook feels uneasy about the way that books I have written develop the idea that democracy, republicanism, and sovereignty are not necessarily synonymous with one another. Unfortunately, there are individuals who wish to keep people ignorant concerning those differences and, in the process, prevent communities from aspiring to a way of self-governance that transcends both democracy and republicanism.

Perhaps, someone at facebook objects to the idea that someone is writing about how the 9th and 10th Amendments to the Constitution of the United States are 'The People Amendments" in the sense that they give people standing in the process of self-governance that is different from the usual way that power is divvied up between the federal government and the states. If the potential within those amendments were considered fairly, then, the alignment of power within America would be radically shifted from what is presently the case.

Or, maybe, someone at facebook is disquieted by the idea that corporations are not persons and, therefore, are not entitled to enjoy the rights of a person -- a point, along with other issues, that is explored in considerable detail within the book: *Beyond Democracy* that, along with more than 40 other books, is available for free downloading from my web site. In fact, corporations are nothing more than an arbitrary invention of certain lawyers and jurists who sought to leverage a legal fiction into an instrument of power that serves the interests and agenda of corporate overlords at the expense of the people.

Another possibility is that someone at facebook doesn't want anyone to discover that shari'ah is not the doctrinaire, narrow, ideologically-driven, rigid framework that is envisioned by those -- whether Muslim or non-Muslim -- who are ignorant of the rich potential that is inherent in Islam. Instead, shari'ah is a modulated, insightful, and flexible declaration of independence from any person, institution, government, or commercial enterprise that seeks to prevent human beings from being able to exercise sovereignty in order to be able to seek the truth concerning the nature of their relationship with reality.

Or, perhaps, someone at facebook doesn't want anyone to consider the possibility that Christians, Jews, Muslims and Humanists all operate from frameworks that share many precepts, principles, values, and goals. In other words, the previously mentioned frameworks need not be in fundamental conflict with one another and, in fact, they are capable of giving expression to perspectives through which a sense of community can be established and constructively pursued.

Finally, over the years I have produced a number of podcasts that cover all manner of topics -- including poetry, short stories, music, meditative essays, and commentaries of various kinds ... including critical reflections concerning many aspects of modern life. I suppose for someone from facebook who didn't want to think about things very much or who might have filtered their possible investigation of me through biased lenses, then, the list of links connecting people to one or another podcast might have been construed as some sort of click bait set up but would have found out otherwise if they had bothered to listen to any of the podcasts.

I state all of the foregoing possibilities -- and could have included 35-40 alternative scenarios that involve other publications of mine -- because as indicated earlier in this presentation, there is nothing that I have done on facebook, per se, which warrants being purged from that platform. Therefore, I have to wonder if the case facebook (or the government agents who might be whispering in facebook's ear) appears to be intent on trying to make against me has little or nothing to do with my activities on facebook but entails, instead, my activities away from facebook.

During the policy statement concerning its purging of accounts and pages -- a statement that will be examined shortly -- facebook revealed that it had investigated (to some unknown degree) the activity of various individuals that took place beyond the borders of facebook and referred to a number of problems that such activity supposedly created for facebook, and, consequently, this constitutes evidence that part of facebook's purging decision had to do with what they saw - or believed they saw - in relation to activities of individuals that were taking place outside of facebook activities, and, so, I am trying to give the reader a sense of what facebook's apparent investigation of me might have uncovered and what it might have considered to be problematic.

By way of full disclosure, I run a couple of mirror sites in conjunction with anab-whitehouse.com. Thus, billwhitehouse.com and aaa-sovereignty.com both contain roughly the same sort of information as the anab- whitehouse.com site does.

Some people know me as "Bill Whitehouse" as a result of books that I have written under that name, while, for a variety of reasons other individuals know me as "Anab Whitehouse" (the name I use within the Muslim community) and, therefore, I have established web sites using both of those name through which individuals can find me. Other individuals who are interested in the topic of sovereignty might have come in contact with my creative and intellectual efforts through the aaa-sovereignty.com web site.

In addition, I have used three sites to distribute the load of downloads that might take place on any one of the three web sites. More specifically, there are a number of fairly hefty software packages that have been accessible through each of the web sites, and, therefore, I sought to improve the logistics of the download issue by going to three web sites rather than just one.

Let's go back to the data file that I downloaded from facebook following my being purged from its platform. If one proceeds down the page until one reaches the profile information category, and, then, clicks on the first link in that section, the following information appears on the next page.

More specifically, in addition to a listing of the aforementioned anab-whitehouse.com web site, then, after scrolling down through some biographical information, one, eventually, will come to another web link that will take one - if one follows it - to my patreon site which contains material that gives expression to a library gifting project. This patreon-based program (which no longer exists) provides details on how those who are interested in doing so can help me to send copies of my 40 books, floetry creations, as well as an interfaith video presentation to libraries in North America -- free of charge – that might be interested in acquiring that material.

One of the first things which one might notice in conjunction with the foregoing page is that on the left hand side - just beneath the section indicating how many patrons and contributions are supporting one's patreon project -- there are two links. One of these links connects an individual to facebook and permits a person to inform people in the facebook community about one's project, while the other link connects one with the twitter community.

In other words, patreon.com is encouraging me to reach out to members of the facebook and twitter worlds and let them know what is going on. Therefore, as far as I know, I have been led to believe that using facebook to inform whichever of my friends and acquaintances might be interested in the gifting project is a perfectly legitimate thing to do provided that I do not try to spam those individuals concerning that project and thereby am not trying to seek to leverage my facebook presence in an exploitive manner.

The rest of the patreon page outlines how the gifting project came about, provides some of the goals that I have set for the project, and, as well -- if one looks at the possibilities running down the right side of the page -- lists five tiers of patronage that are available for interested people. In other words, in exchange for a certain relatively nominal level of patronage, one could receive a software package containing five videos that give expression to different facets of my activities - both creative and intellectual.

Or, for another level of patronage, a person could receive a software package containing 39 pieces of floetry ... an art form that combines poetry and music and resonates back to the 1950s when some of the so-called "beat" poets would recite their poetry to musical accompaniment.

A third level of patronage offers individuals an opportunity to receive a software package that contains 18 books that explore different dimensions involving the issue of sovereignty. Sovereignty is an idea that both encompasses, as well as extends beyond, notions such as "democracy" and "republicanism".

A further level of patronage entails the possibility of gaining access to a software package that contains 18 books written from a Sufi spiritual perspective, along with 10 hour-plus-long episodes of the Sufi Study Circle podcast, 39 pieces of floetry (i.e., poetry set to music), and five videos.

The final level of patronage provides access to a software package entitled "Bridge" that is given in exchange for a person's support of the gifting project. This package contains everything that was included in the offers that were made through the four other levels of patronage. The collage of material is called "Bridge" because it offers an array of possibilities for bridging Eastern and Western ways of engaging life in an harmonious fashion.

Perhaps, someone at facebook -- or someone within the federal government that is exerting pressure on facebook -- feels threatened by the idea that scholarly information and creative productions are being made available to interested libraries free of charge. Making a diversity of information available to those who use libraries -- material that might induce them to critically reflect on a variety of topics -- could be seen as being quite threatening to those who wish to control what people do and do not see.

In fact, given that I haven't done anything in conjunction with my facebook account that warrants being purged or which transgresses against the agreement I was required to sign off on in order for my facebook account to be activated and given that there is evidence -- provided by facebook itself in its statement concerning its purge policy (which will be examined shortly) -- that some of its employees have investigated what various members of the facebook community are doing outside of facebook, apparently, there are parallels between, or resonances with, how facebook is treating me and how various people in the 2002 film, *The Minority Report,* were being treated when they were arrested, convicted, and imprisoned for crimes they had not been committed but which those individuals supposedly would commit in the future if not purged from society.

There are even some organizations and companies working with facebook who appear to be comparable to the "precogs" in the *Minority Report* film who are responsible for issuing the pronouncements that identify -- through unknown means -- the people who are to be brought to the attention of the police's "PreCrime" unit that will chase down and arrest the individuals who have been singled out by the precogs. For example, consider what The Real News Network's Ben Norton has to say concerning the manner in which facebook goes about identifying purveyors of alleged false news and others who should be brought to the attention of the "PreCrimes" unit of facebook for purposes of purging them from its platform now prior to the commission of any actual crime.

Perhaps, like their counterparts in the *Minority Report* film, representatives from The Atlantic Council, The Weekly Standard, facebook and other unknown entities have apparently immersed themselves in a Pool of Alleged Precognition and – possibly -- identified me, along with some 800 other individuals, as people of interest who (despite not having committed any crime), nonetheless, have been judged -- on the basis of a non-transparent and mysterious process -- as being guilty of living in some anomalous fashion and, therefore, apparently, have been identified as individuals who are believed to be likely to commit acts of transgression in the future and, therefore, should be purged from the facebook platform before they can bring those sorts of future "transgressions" to life.

On October 11, 2018, facebook released a statement entitled: "Removing Additional Inauthentic Activity from Facebook" which purported to provide some degree of explanation for why it purged more than 800 pages and individuals from the facebook platform. The statement was authored by Nathaniel Gleicher, Head of Cybersecurity Policy, and Oscar Rodriguez, product Manager.

The aforementioned statement begins by stipulating that "People need to be able to trust the connections they make on facebook." While one can acknowledge the importance of that opening sentence, it obscures a deeper issue.

More specifically, people who use facebook need to be able to trust that the people who administer the facebook platform will operate with integrity and in an unbiased manner. Moreover, perhaps enough evidence has been put forth previously in this article to demonstrate that some of the people who run facebook do not necessarily always do so fairly, transparently, and with integrity.

Gleicher and Rodriguez claim that the foregoing trust issue is why facebook has "a policy banning coordinated inauthentic behavior" ... that is, "networks of accounts or Pages working to mislead others about who they are, and what they are doing." I am not a part of any network of accounts or Pages that has been attempting to mislead others about who I am or what I am doing.

Indeed, as was demonstrated earlier in this video, throughout my facebook profile, I had been very upfront about who I am and what I have been doing. There was no element of deception in anything that I said in relation to any of the information that I gave to, or published through, facebook.

The October 11th facebook statement then goes on to cite two broad categories of supposedly inauthentic behavior with which it has been concerned. The first category involves accounts that have been "created to stir up political debate", while the other problematic category involves allegedly inauthentic behavior that entails spamming activities motivated by a desire for financial gain.

Neither of the foregoing categories is applicable to me. To begin with, there was nothing political in any of the material that I posted on facebook because merely mentioning a recently published book on education, posting a piece of video floetry, and giving a short aphorism by al-Junayd concerning the difficulties posed by our passions are hardly political activities.

Furthermore, given that I rejected the only facebook request that I received, one can hardly accuse me of spamming anyone. In addition, I did not exhibit any of the characteristics to which Gleicher and Rodriguez alluded in their October 11, 2018 statement.

More specifically, I did not "create networks of Pages using fake accounts or multiple accounts with the same names" Moreover, I did not make "click bait" posts on any of my facebook pages that were intended "to drive people to websites that are entirely separate from facebook and seem legitimate, but are actually ad farms", nor did I try to "hawk fraudulent products like fake sunglasses or weight loss 'remedies'."

As pointed out previously in this article, the only two Internet sites mentioned on my facebook account were: anab-whitehouse.com and my patreon page. The former web site is a portal for a variety of essays, videos, poems, free software packages, podcasts, and a listing (with description) of books that I have written over the last several decades, while the patreon link connects people who are so inclined to a page where they can learn about participating in a project that seeks to gift free books to libraries that are interested in receiving such learning materials.

Gleicher and Rodriguez maintain that the "news" stories and opinions that are posted by supposedly offending accounts: "are often indistinguishable from legitimate political debate", and, this has led facebook to look at behavior rather than content. In other words, the decision algorithm for purging pages and accounts on facebook takes into account such factors as whether, or not, someone is using fake accounts or repeatedly posting spam.

Since I have created no fake accounts or posted any spam -- repeatedly or otherwise -- one is left to wonder what the actual reasons were for purging my account from the facebook platform. Indeed. Furthermore, as previously noted, given that I have been preoccupied for the last three-plus months with getting my books ready for the aforementioned library gifting project, I have had almost no time to be active on facebook, so, obviously, the reason why my account has been purged cannot be a function of behavior, and this would seem to leave only the matter of content involving either my facebook posts and/or my extracurricular activities beyond the boundaries of facebook.

In their October 11, 2018 statement, Gleicher and Rodriguez state that "Today, we're removing 559 pages and 251 accounts that have consistently broken our rules against spam and coordinated inauthentic behavior." However, my account was removed from facebook three or four days prior to their October 11, 2018 announcement, and, more importantly, I was not guilty of violating any of its rules concerning either coordinated inauthentic behavior or spam.

In a message that I sent to facebook -- a message that I presented earlier in this article and which facebook acknowledged receiving -- I requested them to inform me about the precise nature of the rules that I supposedly had violated. Unfortunately, despite indicating that someone at the company would respond to my aforementioned message, I never heard from anyone at facebook again.

According to Gleicher and Rodriguez, people who had their accounts purged from facebook often used: "techniques to make their content more popular on facebook than it really was. Those two individuals also indicated that some of the accounts which were purge had been ad farms using facebook to mislead people into thinking that they were forums for legitimate political debate.

I neither engaged in the process of trying to make my facebook page appear more popular than it was (indeed, I had not accepted -- nor invited -- friends for my page because I wasn't ready to become active on facebook until I had finished updating my books for the library gifting project). In addition, I had not tried to mislead anyone to conclude that my page was a forum for legitimate political debate ... whatever that means.

In the final paragraph of their October 11, 2018 facebook policy statement, Gleicher and Rodriguez stipulate: "Of course, there are legitimate reasons that accounts and pages coordinate with each other -- it's the bedrock of fundraising campaigns and grassroots organizations. But the difference is that these groups are upfront about who they are, and what they're up to."

I did not coordinate with any other facebook page. The only Internet pages with which I coordinated were my own web pages along with the aforementioned patreon.com page in an attempt to, hopefully, set in motion a "legitimate" process of raising money to help send books free of charge to interested libraries ... and I did this in a way that permitted people to know who I was and what I was up to.

By implication, Gleicher and Rodriguez are suggesting that people like me have abused their system and have used "tactics to evade detection". Neither of those implications is true, and neither Gleicher, Rodriguez nor anyone else at facebook can demonstrate that I have violated facebook in any fashion.

Instead, certain facebook personnel have acted abusively toward me. Consequently, I have little reason for trusting that facebook will act with integrity toward me and, among other things, try to help me feel safe in any interactions I might have with that company for in a rather substantial case of projection, facebook has sought to accuse me of what, in fact, are its own poor behaviors.

Let' take a look at some possible ways of responding to what facebook and other similar platforms are doing. For example, the Electronic Frontier Foundation - or EFF - is a non-profit organization that was founded in 1990 for the purpose of pursuing various forms of advocacy that are intended to defend the civil liberties of those who are involved in the world of digital technology ... civil liberties that extend from: Freedom of expression and privacy, to: The protection and promotion of innovative and creative uses involving technology, both new and old.

The EFF engages in activities such as grass roots activism and litigation, as well as policy analysis to help establish standards and processes that will be capable of protecting the civil liberties of all citizens as the world of technology continues to develop and expand. David Greene is the Civil Liberties Director and Senior Staff Attorney for EEF, and, recently he had a variety of remarks to offer during a portion of an interview he did with Ben Norton of Real News.com.

I find it rather disconcerting that someone like David Greene who is dedicated to protecting the civil liberties of human beings should be promoting the idea that corporations have first amendment rights. Corporations -- which are nothing but arbitrary and artificial legal fictions -- have been fashioned into entitles which claim entitlement to the basic rights that have been established through, among other things, the first 14 amendments to the US Constitution by supreme court justices who have been unduly influenced by -- and who often exhibit an essential and indefensible bias that favors -- an ideology which holds, among other things, that corporations are persons.

Yet, in reality, modern corporations are the very same kind of tyrannical entity that played a major role in shaping the conditions of political, social, and economic hardship that led to the American revolution and the formation of a Constitution. That document nowhere acknowledges or champions the right of corporations to enjoy the status of personhood.

There is absolutely no precedential basis in the Constitution for considering corporations to be persons or for them to be extended the rights of people. When considering the scope of the idea of civil liberties, one should keep in mind that the term "civil" refers to ordinary citizens and their concerns, as distinct from military, ecclesiastical, or institutional matters. In fact the etymological origins of the term "civil" comes from late Middle English, via Old French, which, in turn, can be traced to the Latin word *civilis* as well as the term *civis*' which refers to the condition of being a citizen'. Corporations are not citizens.

If corporations were really persons, there would be no need for the invention of a legal fiction that treats them -- before the law -- as if they were persons. Indeed, to legally confer personhood on corporations is to attribute something to them that they do not possess independently of the legal prestidigitation that invests those arbitrary inventions with an existential status to which they are not entitled and which they acquire only through the abuse of power by jurists who have betrayed their fellow human beings by creating a psychopathic-like entity that is designed to exploit human kind and the resources of the Earth for ends that undermine the sovereignty of human beings.

The notion of the "rule of law" only has value if it can be developed through constructive processes that are rooted in principles of sovereignty that assist human beings to "form a more perfect union, establish justice, insure domestic tranquility, provide for the common defense, promote the general welfare, and secure the blessings of liberty to ourselves and our posterity". Treating corporations as if they were real persons -- rather than the fictitious, artificial, and self-serving constructions that the willful ignorance of wrong-headed and wrong-hearted jurists should have understood them to be -- not only has failed to help realize any of the foregoing constitutional ideals but actively have consistently undermined and destroyed the sovereignty of actual human beings throughout American history.

Unfortunately, what today is referred to as the rule of law is an arbitrary system that operates in accordance with the interests of power. The interests of power can neither be derived from first principles of natural law, justice, and sovereignty, nor can those interests be derived from constitutional principles that are capable of providing justification for such a pathologically inspired precedent.

As pointed out earlier in this article, facebook offers people the opportunity to connect with friends and the rest of the world, and, in addition, promotes the idea that one can share one's ideas and life experiences with family, friends, and others. Yet, when one tries to do this, facebook arbitrarily pulls the proverbial rug from various individuals and is indifferent to the problems that such an action causes.

I don't think that facebook has a first amendment right to interfere with the first amendment right of other people -- especially given that facebook has promoted itself as a venue for connecting with other people and the world. Facebook has a responsibility to protect the first amendment rights for speech, assembly, and the like of those who it has encouraged to pursue precisely those kinds of activities.

To be sure, facebook should have a responsibility to protect human beings against hate speech or any other violations of the basic civil liberties of actual persons. Nonetheless, contrary to Greene's claims in his interview with Ben Norton, neither facebook nor corporations have an absolute right to curate what is said by the people it has encouraged to sign up precisely for the purpose of being able to communicate with other human beings.

During the aforementioned interview, David Greene refers to the idea that facebook -- along with other kinds of social media platforms - have supposedly set up a system through which complaints about content can be filed and judgments can be made about whether, or not, to remove such content from those social media platforms. I'm not in a position to address how such matters are handled in other countries, but in the United States, facebook should be subject to recognizing and abiding by provisions in the United States Constitution that protect the right of people to assemble peacefully, and freely exchange perspectives with one another through rights that govern the exercise of speech, as well as to use social media platforms as venues for "petitioning the government for a redress of grievances."

Unfortunately, facebook is being allowed to use an arbitrary, non-transparent, and corporate controlled system. This system appears to enjoy a status that is considered -- at least by facebook and its corporate-influenced allies in government -- to be superior to, and have authority over, the provisions of an amended U.S. Constitution.

During his interview, Mr. Greene indicates that through the Electronic Frontier Foundation he is seeking to negotiate with facebook and other social media platforms to establish procedures for handling content disputes involving users of various those platforms that will reflect the kind of standards that are consistent with the principles and values underlying an array of international standards concerning the protection of civil liberties and human rights. While I applaud Mr. Greene's concerns about the foregoing sorts of issues, the fact of the matter is that this process should not be a negotiation but rather a dynamic that requires facebook and other corporations operating with the United States to comply with standards that were guaranteed to the American people more than 220 years ago via, among other factors, Article IV, Section 4 of the Constitution in which the states -- and by implication the people of those states -- are guaranteed a republican form of government, and, unfortunately, facebook is being permitted by the federal to ignore the values and principles that are inherent in a republican form of government ... values and principles such as: openness, fairness, due process, nobility, honesty, non-partisanship, and absence of self-interest.

Among other things, facebook suffers from confirmation bias. In other words, whatever is singled out by its behavioral algorithms as being problematic (according to the technocratic agenda and ideology of the company) is treated as alleged confirmation of facebook's understanding of how people operate despite not knowing the actual circumstances surrounding and underlying such behavior being critically examined.

Therefore, certain decisions of the company tend to be devoid of the context that is necessary to understand and have insight into the actual nature of the behavior which is being targeted. Facebook says behavior is the basis for their recent decisions concerning the purging of so 800-plus accounts, not content, and, yet, precisely because the company tends to shy away from taking the time and making the effort that is needed to properly understand a situation, it fails to look at the existential context in which the behavior its algorithms have supposedly detected is rooted so that the technocratic overlords servicing those algorithms can continue to pursue a form of willful blindness that ignores information that might challenge the way they apply and interpret their behavioral algorithms.

This is like the algorithms that are used in the lethal drone strikes by the US government in which behavior is abstracted from context. As a result, decisions to use lethal force are removed from precisely the kinds of information that might suggest that, perhaps, one would be well-advised to pursue some form of the cautionary principle rather than blindly and recklessly following the sorts of biases and the ideology that has brought about the deaths of thousands of innocent people in various parts of the world.

In a technocracy, there is little concern for the individual because technocrats only care about fitting individuals into a system of technology. Perhaps I was disappeared because a manifestation of technocracy -- i.e., facebook -- had the power and inclination to do what it liked with a mere human being.

Technocracy is always about the self-serving exercise of power -- the power to insist on imposing a technocratic vision on whomever it engages. According to a pre-determined set of control algorithms fashioned by facebook, maybe I didn't fit in with the company's way of conducting business, and, therefore, facebook jettisoned me from the picture. The foregoing scenario is certainly a possibility.

If so, this is an example of technocracy run amok. In many respects, facebook seems to be really nothing more than a technology that has been weaponized into a corporate strategy designed to exploit people and induce them to serve a corporation's agenda for making money and acquiring power.

As a result, the technical experts at such technocratic-oriented companies tend to place their faith in technological methods, principles, and techniques that often are far removed from the realities of the situations to which those methods and principles are being applied and through which it seeks to induce people to serve its aspirations for power, money, and control precisely because those methods and principles ignore everything that falls outside the parameters of its prime directive for maximizing control, power, and money.

Facebook initially claimed in its interaction with me that it was concerned about my security. In reality, the company was not interested in my security but, rather, it was interested in pursuing its own agenda of social control, and, consequently, facebook displayed a lack of honesty concerning its own behavior ... a classic case of projection in which facebook tried to attribute to me what, in fact, was its own inauthentic and anomalous behavior.

That social media platform also acted like a bully. In other words, facebook sought to leverage its power as a corporation to beat up on a relatively defenseless individual who really had done nothing wrong -- indeed, someone who had not done anything at all because all my time had been focused elsewhere (namely, working at getting my books ready for the gifting project for libraries that I had started) and, therefore, I didn't have the opportunity to attend to the details of getting my facebook presence going.

As a result of its bullying tactics, facebook also committed a form of elderly abuse (my date of birth and age are clearly indicated in the profile information that facebook requested me to share with them). Whether intended or not, facebook's treatment of me appears to constitute an exercise in elderly abuse.

In other words, perhaps because I didn't move as fast as some faceless controller at facebook thought I should move, or, maybe, because I didn't have as many acquaintances and contacts on facebook as someone at the company thought a person my age should have, or, perhaps, because I didn't go about seeking or accepting friends in the manner that anonymous cogs in the facebook system considered to be appropriate, then, that company took away an elderly person's ability to socialize with other people, and that company took away an elderly person's opportunity to exchange ideas with other individuals, and that company denied an elderly person's ability to engage his first amendment rights, and in the process they have increased my isolation ... and while isolating forces are important issues to reflect upon in conjunction with the damage they do to all members of the general populace, nevertheless, among the elderly, these sorts of forces and policies can be particularly devastating.

Facebook also showed a lack of integrity due to the total absence of any kind of reciprocity in its interaction with me. Apparently, it didn't want to be confused by facts but, instead, seemed to insist on imposing its algorithmically-driven technocratic ideology onto the situation, and, as a result, rebuffed any opportunity for discussion, mediation, negotiation, fairness, or due process.

Facebook - with its rigid reliance on problematic behavioral algorithms -- appears to be a rather soulless technological entity. As such, it might well be pathologically incapable of learning from its mistakes or being able to exhibit a capacity to give expression to such fundamental qualities as decency, character, and compassion that are so important to the human condition.

Therefore, the monopolistic power which facebook holds in relation to social interaction needs to be reigned in or regulated. This is because without such regulation, facebook is a very, very dangerous automaton ... a mechanical being that performs its functions according to a predetermined set of algorithms that have not been properly vetted and, therefore, is divorced from any kind of rigorous process involving an independent critical assessment of the impact such an automaton is having upon human beings.

A technocratic social credit scoring system has being implemented in China to regulate behavior in accordance with the vision and ideology of the technocratic overlords of Chinese society. Such policies isolate, marginalize, and purge people from the fabric of social life according to a set of often arbitrary principles and ideas that are imposed through an array of social, political, economic, and educational sanctions that resonate with the tactics of bullies who have little genuine regard for those who lack power and, therefore, are treated as targets of opportunities for being abused.

The US military uses a similar behavior-based, algorithmically-driven scoring system to identify kill targets for its drone program. The US also used the same kind of behavior-devoid-of-context algorithm to drive its kill anything that moves policy in Vietnam that had been documented by Nick Turse (whose research was previously discussed in this article) and others.

Facebook is also pursuing policies that are strikingly similar to those of the Chinese government and the U.S. military policies when facebook uses algorithms to identify behavior that it wishes to remove from its platform on the basis of arbitrary, anti-humanitarian, and factually-challenged considerations. Like the Chinese government and the US military, facebook can make you disappear from the social fabric of life, and no one should have that kind of power ... it is the kind of power that operates in the shadows and bullies those who are marginalized and, therefore, less powerful than such bullies are.

The Khashoggi affair also has some uncomfortable resonances with what facebook is doing -- silencing people who, for whatever reason, it does not like and whom it will not tolerate. Instead of killing them physically, facebook kills them socially, and the result is problematically similar ... disappearance from public view. Rather ironically - or, perhaps, quite tellingly -- my silencing took place a few days following Khashoggi's silencing

In a fair number of the more than 40 books I have written, as well as throughout many of my blog entries, and during a number of podcasts I have done, or within many of the web sites that I have put up over more than two decades on the Internet, I have indicated that both the left and the right sides of the political spectrum are often incorrect with respect to their understandings concerning the nature of the relationship between the individual and the state. Unfortunately, facebook seems to operate in accordance with an anti-sovereignty agenda because given all too many of its actions -- and the purging of more than 800 pages and accounts in early October 2018 are among those actions -- that company does not appear to be all that interested in empowering people but, instead, seems to want to seek to induce people to behave in accordance with facebook's business model, and, consequently, someone at the company (or among their possible government handlers) might have decided that my pro-sovereignty orientation had the potential to disrupt facebook's (and/or government's) agenda. However, although such a scenario might be attractive to the ego, I really doubt that anyone -- within or outside of facebook -- could realistically consider me to be much of a threat to anyone or anything. Although, I suppose, one should never underestimate the power of paranoia and fear to induce people to do all kinds of stupid things ... like purging someone from a social media platform for fatuous -- that is, silly, pointless, and arbitrary -- reasons.

9. Tractatus Technologicus

1.0 - This document gives expression to a data point.

1.1 - That data point has a complex internal structure that might be fractal in nature. In other words, there is – allegedly -- a pattern which might be present within the point that is being given descriptive expression through this document that is (in some hard to define manner) never ending in character.

1.2 - However, in order to determine if the foregoing statement is true, then, the one engaging this point – namely, you, the reader (another data point within a complex internal structure, possibly fractal in character) – would have to follow the alleged pattern across all levels of scale to ascertain whether, or not, there is some principle of self-similarity which ties those scales together in the form of a pattern of one kind or another.

1.3 - I have my doubts whether anyone engaging the current data point would be willing to devote the time and resources necessary to explore the possible infinite set of scales entailed by the current data point and, as a result, would be able to establish that – yes, indeed, the locus of manifestation which is being presented herein is fractal in nature. So, to make things as simple (and, simultaneously, as complex) as can be, the key to identifying the nature of the self-similar pattern manifesting itself across all scales of Being which gives expression to the internal structure of the fractal data point you are engaging is a function of a soul ... mine, sort of.

1.4 - The starting point of departure for generating members of the Mandelbrot set is: $Z = Z^2 + C$, where C is a variable in the complex plane and Z is set to zero, then, wash, rinse and repeat as many times as necessary to determine if the iteration process gives expression to bounded conditions or diverges to infinity. The values which lead to bounded conditions are members of the Mandelbrot set, and such a set can be translated into a visual pattern by assigning various qualities (such as color) to each member of that set.

1.5 - The starting point of departure for generating members of the Whitehouse set is: $S_{oul} = P \div (E^n \times \sum_D)$, where P encompasses potential, E constitutes points on the experiential plane, n is initially set at 0 (some refer to this as birth or the locus of creation or existence), and D gives expression to the dimensional variables (biological, physical, hermeneutical, epistemological, emotional, social, spiritual, moral, anomalous, temporal) that impinge on and modulate any given point in E and, as such, D generates a hyper-complex manifold that departs substantially from the complex plane entailed by the Mandelbrot set. When the foregoing function is iterated across the existential hyper-manifold, then values which are bounded by, and do not diverge from, the properties of S are members of the Whitehouse set.

1.6 - The focus of the complex data point dynamics being given expression through this document is a book by Mustafa Suleyman entitled: *The Coming Wave*, a complex data point dynamic of another kind.

1.7 - Having gone through the network of data points in the aforementioned book, one of the first thoughts that bubbles to the surface of consciousness to which the Whitehouse manifold gives expression is that the author of the aforementioned book alludes to the presence of elements within a knowledge base that, supposedly, are in his possession, yet seem, at least in certain respects, quite superficial in character – possibly fictional or delusional -- rather than being deeply epistemological in nature.

1.71 - For example, he talks, to varying degrees, about: Viruses, COVID-19, HIV/AIDS, global warming, evolution, medicine, pharmaceuticals, biology, cognition, and vaccines, but the manner in which he discusses those issues in his book suggests he doesn't necessarily know all that much with respect to those topics. Instead, what he says appears to be based on a process in which the ideas of other people merely have been incorporated into his hermeneutical framework rather than being a function of his own rigorous process of investigation and critical reflection.

1.72 - The foregoing comments are a function of a set of accumulated experiences covering hours of reading, listening, watching, thinking, and writing. Some of the experiential considerations that are being alluded to have been captured in a series of books: [(1) *Toxic Knowledge*; (2) *Follow the What? - An Introduction*; (3) *Observations Concerning My Encounter with COVID-19(?)*; (4) *Evolution Unredacted*; (5) Varieties of Psychological Inquiry – Volumes

I and II; (6) *Science and Evolution: An Alternative Perspective*; (6) *Sovereignty and the Constitution;* and one 39-page article*: (7) Climate Delusion Syndrome].*

1.73 - No claim is being made that what is said in the foregoing books is true. Nonetheless, a body of material is being presented in those works which tends to indicate a fundamental familiarity with the aforementioned issues that does not appear to be in evidence within *The Coming Wave* despite the latter's employment of terminology which might suggest otherwise.

1.74 - The foregoing considerations present me with a problem. A lot of reputable individuals have praised his book, and, yet, none of them have indicated that there might be a certain degree of disconnection between what the author of *The Coming Wave* claims to know and what he actually knows, so, what is one to make of such praise sans criticism?

1.75 - Maybe all of the individuals who have offered their praise concerning that book share the same sort of seeming shallowness concerning the aforementioned list of topics. Alternatively, perhaps they all are prepared – each for his, her, or their own reasons – to encourage the framing of such issues in ways that are similar to what the author of *The Coming Wave* has done, and this has become such an ubiquitous, embedded, vested interest dimension of their conceptual landscape that they no longer pay attention to the many problems which pervade such issues.

1.76 - At one point in *The Coming Wave*, a short-coming of earlier renditions of large language models is touched upon. More specifically, such LLMs often contained racist elements.

1.761 - Such racist elements are present in those LLMs is because the large collection of human texts that were used to train the LLMs contained racist perspectives. These elements became incorporated into the LLMs -- through ways both obvious and less obvious – so that when the LLMs were queried by human beings, the responses provided by the LLM (sometimes more blatantly than at other times) gave expression to a racist orientation.

1.77 - Human beings are like LLMs in as much as the algorithms at work in each context are, in part, trained in accordance with the verbal and written language samples to which they are exposed. Perhaps, like LLMs, human beings incorporate elements of linguistic texts into their inner dynamics that carry biases of one sort of another during the course of picking up various dimensions of language.

1.771 - If so, then, the foregoing considerations might account for why there seem to be so many elements of apparent bias concerning the aforementioned list of topics which are present during the course of *The Coming Wave*. Moreover, perhaps this is the reason why the presence of such apparent biases in that book are not commented on by those who are praising that work because the ones full of praise also have been exposed to, and (knowingly or unknowingly) have incorporated into themselves, such biases while being exposed to various kinds of texts, spoken and written.

1.7712 - Steps have been taken to de-bias LLMs. Although a complicated process, this dynamic is easier to accomplish with LLMs because – to date (perhaps) -- they have not been given the capacity to resist such corrective measures. However, this sort of process is much more difficult to accomplish in human beings because the latter individuals have so many ways of resisting, ignoring, or evading those sorts of attempts.

1.78 - Is Mustafa Suleyman a smart guy? Yes! Is he a talented person? Yes! Is he a successful individual? Yes! Is he a wealthy man? I haven't seen his bank account or financial portfolio, but I believe the answer is: Yes! Does he have a strong entrepreneurial spirit? Yes – several times over? Does he understand artificial intelligence? More than most do.

1.79 - Does he understand the nature of the problem that is facing humanity? I am inclined to hedge my bets here and say: Yes and no.

1.791 - One of the reasons for saying "no" to the foregoing question is that despite his outlining ten steps (which will be explored somewhat toward the latter part of the present document) that are intended to free up temporal, institutional, corporate, and intellectual space which might assist human beings to cope, in limited ways, with what is transpiring, I don't believe his book actually offers much insight into what a real solution would look like or what the actual nature of the problem is.

1.80 - For example, the title of his book – *The Coming Wave* -- is problematic. What is allegedly coming has not been coming for quite some time. In fact, that wave has been washing over humanity for many decades.

1.81 - The notion of "emergent technology" is just a technique employed by the establishment (both surface and deep) to try to cover up what already has been taking place for years and is a phrase that is often used as a herding technique to push, or pull, the public in one direction or another. Thus, more than sixty years ago we have someone like Dwight Eisenhower warning about the Military-Industrial complex – a complex which he was instrumental in helping to establish.

1.82 – Alternatively, one might consider the thousands, if not millions, of Targeted Individuals who, years ago, were incorporated into AI-controlled torture protocols involving, among other things, autonomous chatter boxes. The so-called Havana Syndrome is just the tip of research and deployment icebergs that have been set adrift by governments and corporations around the world, including the United States (Take a look at the work of, among others,: Nick Begich, Robert Duncan, and Sabrina Wallace).

1.821 - Advanced AI technology – for example, Lavender – already is being used in military and policing projects in Israel. AI also is being actively used by the Pentagon's updating of Palantir's Project Maven system, and one might note that Department of Defense directive 3000.09 concerns the use of autonomous, AI-based weapons systems.

1.8211 - Blackrock has been employing Aladdin for a number of years. Aladdin stands for: Asset, Liability and Debt and Derivative Investment Network, and is an AI system that oversees risk management on behalf of its employer. Human traders are a disappearing breed in New York, Chicago, London, and elsewhere

1.822 - Moreover, Directed Energy Weapons are not limited to the special effects of movie productions. All one has to do is take a look at the evidence from places like Santa Rosa, California or Paradise, California or Lahaina, Hawaii and listen to arboreal forensic expert Robert Brame to understand that such "emergent technology" has already emerged.

1.823 - Synthetic biology is not coming. It is already here and has been walking amongst us, so to speak, for several decades as the work of Clifford Carnicom has demonstrated ... work that has been confirmed, and expanded upon, through the scientific investigations of individuals such as Ana Mihalcea, David Nixon, and Mateo Taylor.

1.824 – To create droughts, hurricanes, tornadoes, polar vortices, biblical-like rains, floods, and blizzards all one has to do is combine: Water vapor from cooling towers with the heavy metals present in chemtrails, and, then, apply heterodyned energy-pulsations from Nexrad Doppler weather radar stations. Considerable evidence for the foregoing has been available for more than a decade.

1.825 – Aman Jabbi, Mark Steele, Arthur Firstenberg, and Olle Johansson (there are many others who could be included in this list) – each in his own way – have been trying to draw the public's attention to the many weapons, surveillance, AI systems, or different forms of technology which are, and have been for some time, operational and are being continuously upgraded with human beings as their primary targets

1.8251 – Yet, neither Mustafa Suleyman nor any of his admirers have mentioned the foregoing data points. Suleyman and his admirers appear to be people who are either: Woefully and cataclysmically ignorant of such matters, or they are quite knowledgeable about those issues and are playing apocalyptically dumb, and, in either case, their pronouncements concerning technology and what to do are highly suspect.

1.9 - Fairly early in Suleyman's book, the term "Luddite" is introduced and, then, mentioned several more times over the next 20-30 pages. Each of those references is ensconced in a relatively negative context.

1.91 – For example, initially, the term: "Luddite reaction," is referenced. Supposedly, this consists of boycotts, moratoriums, or bans.

1.92 - Mustafa Suleyman goes on to indicate that due to the commercial value and geopolitical importance of technology, the foregoing kinds of activities are unlikely to succeed. After all,

| Technological Reflections |

corporations and nation-states both tend to soar on the wings of the leveraged power that are provided through technology.

1.921 - One wonders why only the concerns of corporations and nation-states are considered to be of importance. Clearly, what seems to be of value to Suleyman is a function of power (financial, legal, and/or militaristic) which is being wielded by arbitrary hierarchies that cannot necessarily justify their activities and, therefore, often tend to resort to various forms of violence (financial, political, educational, social, physical, medical, legal, religious, economic, and martial) to maintain their existence.

1.93 – Said in another way, what he does not acknowledge is that both corporations and nation-states are, in effect, omni-use technologies. Consequently, one should not be surprised when those sorts of omni-use technologies partner with various more-narrowly focused technologies in order to enhance their respective spheres of influence and power while discounting the concerns being expressed by billions of human beings.

1.94 - What is technology?

1.941 - Technology involves a process of conceiving, developing, and applying conceptual understanding or knowledge in order to realize goals in a manner that can be replicated across a variety of contexts.

1.942 - Another way of describing technology is to speak in terms of tools. More specifically, technology concerns the creation of tools that can be used to provide practical solutions in relation to various kinds of problems.

1.943 - Additionally, technology can be considered to consist of a series or set of proficient techniques and protocols which can be used to address and resolve various problems in a practical way.

1.944 - The terms: "conceptual knowledge," "tools," and "techniques" which appear in the foregoing characterizations of technology are all assumed to give expression to one, or another, form of scientific, mathematical, and/or technical proficiency. Furthermore, the notion of "practicality" is usually code for: 'efficient,' 'affordable,' 'profitable,' 'effective,' and 'politically feasible.'

1.945 - One might pause at this point to ponder on why "efficiency" rather than, say, truth, justice, character, or essential human potential is deemed to be a fundamental consideration in pursuing technological issues. Similarly, one might ponder on why the alleged meanings of: "effective", "profitable", "affordable", and "politically feasible" are based on criteria provided by corporations and nation-states which have substantial conflicts of interests in those matters.

1.9456 - Corporations use governments as tools in order to solve many of their problems in a practical manner, just as governments use corporations as tools to solve many of their problems in what is considered a practical manner. The East India Corporation in England is a perfect example of such a mutually beneficial form of power mongering.

1.9457 - Blackrock, Vanguard, State Street Bang, Google, Amazon, Meta, Apple, the Bill and Melinda Gates Foundation, Elon Musk, the Open Society of George and Alex Soros, The Clinton Foundation, the private banking system, pharmaceutical companies, any number of media companies, and so on, all benefit from the legacy established through the Supreme Court in cases such as: the Dartmouth v. Woodward 1819 case, or the headnotes of the 1886 Santa Clara County v. Southern Pacific Railroad case, or the 2010 proceedings involving Citizens United v. Federal Election Commission, or the 2014 Burwell v. Hobby Lobby Stores decision.

1.946 - What has been acknowledged by the legal system to be a legal fiction – namely, that corporations are persons – is being utilized (by government, the legal system, and corporations) as an oppressive weapon against actual real, non-fictional human persons. For instance, the 13th amendment has been used by corporations to, among other things, exploit incarcerated human beings as sources of profit, and the 14th amendment has been used to protect the invented rights of phantom corporate personhood more than it has been used to protect the Constitutional rights of actual human beings.

1.947 - The American Revolution was fought as much against the East India Company as it was fought against the English monarchy. Yet, despite the existence of a general sense among the so-called 'Founding Fathers' and the generality of colonists that the notion of a corporation was a vile anathema, nonetheless, here we are today being bullied by institutions that are without Constitutional authority but, unfortunately enjoy the illicit largesse of jurists -- such as John Marshall -- who were corporate friendly and, therefore, those entities came to be treated as persons on the basis of a legal fiction and, as a result, have been unshackled from the constraints (permissions, purposes, and temporality) present in the charters which were supposed to govern their limited existence.

1.948 - Using tools in a technically proficient manner that is intended to solve problems in a practical manner and, thereby, realize goals which are considered to be important is a form of technology. The notion of "legal fiction" was a tool that enabled the technology known as "the rule of law" to carry on in an unconstitutional manner to the detriment of human beings.

1.9481 Legality and constitutionality are not necessarily synonymous terms. Although constitutionality is the more fundamental concept, legality is what tends to govern society.

1.949 - The technical proficiency referred to above can involve: Law, politics, psychology, business, sociology, philosophy, religion, education, the media, the military, policing, public health, and medicine. Thus, as indicated previously, legal fictions are a tool of law; meaningless elections and conformity-inducing policies are tools of politics; undue influence is a tool of psychology; advertising, marketing, and induced consumption are tools of business; normative behavior is a tool of sociology; arbitrary forms of logic are tools of philosophy; places of worship are tools of religion; teachers and/or textbooks are tools of education; biased, corruptible reporters are tools of the media; threats, lethal force, and oppressive forms of self-serving tactics or strategies are tools of the military; intimidation is a tool of policing; unverifiable theories are tools of public health, and problematic diagnoses as well as synthetic pharmaceutics with an array of "side-effects" are tools of medicine.

1.9450 - What is considered practical is whatever serves the interest of those in power. Everything else is impractical.

1.9451 - The attempts of human beings to ban, impose moratoriums on, boycott technology are deemed to be impractical by the author of *The Coming Wave* because they do not serve his interests or the interests which he deems to be of value. Thus, the "Luddite reaction" of bans, boycotts, and moratoriums are impractical. The force behind the green screen of Oz has spoken.

1.9452 - Suleyman also refers to Luddites as individuals who "violently rejected" new technology. They were people who were prepared to dismantle technology if peaceful measures failed.

1.9453 - Corporations and governments are entities which are prepared to dismantle people and communities if the latter do not respond to arbitrary oppression in a peaceful manner. This, of course, is an exercise in the "rule of law" rather than violence.

1.9454 - Practicality is established through the rule of law. Whoever rejects such practical, legal measures is, by definition, outside the law and serving impractical ends.

1.9455 – Right or wrong, the Luddites were violent toward technology, not people. However, corporations and governments are – quite apart from considerations of right and wrong - violent toward human beings but not toward technology because technology serves the purposes of corporations and governments whereas resistant, non-compliant human beings do not serve those purposes, and, therefore, need to be dealt with through the "rule of law – one of the metrics which corporations and governments use to determine the nature of practicality.

1.9456 - According to the author of *The Coming Wave*, the resistant, aspirations of Luddite-like individuals are doomed because whenever demand exists, technology will find a way to serve that demand. When Edmund Cartwright invented the power loom in 1785, the only demand for such a device was that which was entailed by the inventor's activities as well as that which was present in those few individuals who saw the possibility of a power loom as a tool for making additional profits irrespective of what such a means of making profits might do to people in general.

1.9457 - Technology is not a response to the demands of the generality of people. Technology is an engineering process through which demands are generated concerning entities about which people had no knowledge until the perpetrators of a given form of technology

Technological Reflections

applied various tools involving politics, law, education, finance, economics, and the media to announce its presence.

1.9458 - Technologies shape the landscape out of which demand emerges. Choice is shaped by the presence of those technologies.

1.9459 - An estimated 6000 workers publically demonstrated in 1807 in relation to the pay cuts which were imposed on them as a result of the power looms that were being installed in various factories. Using the technology of lethality, the guardians of such weaponry killed a protestor.

1.94591 - Public demonstrations that caused no deaths are labeled as violent. Yet, a tool that is used to protect the interests of technology is used violently, and this is considered to be but the application of a tool of technology known as the 'rule of law'.

1.94592 - The Luddites wait another four years before descending into the violent process of writing a letter of protest to a mill owner in Nottingham. The mill owner ignores the letter, and, as a result, property is destroyed but the mill owner is left untouched ... presumably in a display of non-violent violence.

1.94593 - Over the next several months, hundreds of loom frames are destroyed by the Ned Ludd led Luddites. Nonetheless, using – apparently -- some form of stealth technology, the mill owners all escape injury or death.

1.95 - In the very last chapter of *The Coming Wave* – some 240 pages following the pairing of the term: "Luddite" with violence, failure, and impracticality -- the author indicates that the Luddites were interested in: (1) Being treated with dignity in the work place (2) being given a fair day's wage for a fair day's work; (3) being afforded some time and consideration by the owners with respect to the challenges encompassed by a changing set of work conditions; and, (4) engaging in a discussion about the possibility of entering into some sort of profit-sharing arrangement with the owners.

1.951 - All of the foregoing conditions were ignored and denied by the owners. The owners didn't care about the workers or their families. They didn't care if the workers ate or starved. They didn't care if the workers had a place to live or not. The owners didn't care if the workers or the families of the workers lived or died. The owners were not interested in sharing anything with anybody who was not an owner, and, very likely, not even then.

1.9511 – Although there have been a few exceptions, owners have rarely appreciated a perspective that was voiced by Abraham Lincoln but, in fact, has been understood for millennia by millions. More specifically, capital is only brought to fruition through labor, and, as such, labor has priority over capital ... in fact, human labor, human skills, human talent, human character, human intelligence, human commitment, is the primary form of capital, and the financial form of capital has always sought to obfuscate and, where possible, degrade that truth. It is the story of Cain and Abel played out again and again

1.9512 – Technology has always been used by those with power to dominate and/or subdue and/or control or diminish the activities of labor. Technology is a dynamic limit which tends toward an upper value of removing most of humanity from the equations of life.

1.952 - To a considerable degree, the years of conflict and tension which ensued from the introduction of the power loom were caused by, or exacerbated by, the intransigent, selfish, self-serving, greedy, overbearing, unyielding, oppressive lack of compassion of the owners toward their workers or toward the workers who had become unemployed as a result of the introduction of a new form of technology. Although the power loom meant that economic difficulties of various kinds would be entering into the lives of the workers, the workers were not necessarily irreconcilably opposed to the introduction of a new technology provided that the workers would be treated with dignity during the transition.

1.953 - The hopes, desires, and needs of the workers, and their families, were trampled upon. Instead of honorable, negotiated accommodations, the workers were met with an array of new laws which were punitive and oppressive and, as well, the workers were met with technologies of control in the form of policing, militia, and legal tools, and as a result an array of technologies were imposed on the workers, their families, and their communities beyond that of the power loom.

1.954 - Suleyman peacefully puts all of the foregoing considerations aside and indicates that decades later there were incredible improvements in living standards being enjoyed by the descendents of the foregoing workers. What the author of *The Coming Wave* seems to fail to consider, however, is that there was absolutely no reason for decades to have been lost before such living standards improved.

1.955 - All of the foregoing results could have been accomplished prior to the time of the original demonstrations in 1807 and shortly after the time of the 1785 invention of the power loom. Unfortunately, owners used the technologies and tools of government, law, policing, banks, the media, religion, and the military to ensure that workers would not be treated with dignity, decency, compassion, or intelligence.

1.956 - This is the sort of "progress" which technology brings. These are the technologies which have been used across all forms of industrial revolution to oppress the people and force them to adapt in the ways in which the overlords of technology desired.

1.9561 - Workers didn't choose to adapt. They were forced to adapt, and technology generated the tools (in the form of law, education, religion, policing, banks, the media, and so on) through which such "progress" was violently imposed on communities irrespective of the actual, essential needs of human beings.

1.9562 - Throughout the pages of *The Coming Wave*, the author alludes, again and again, to the idea of seeking solutions to the challenge of technology which are done in a manner such that benefits are more plentiful than any harms which might ensue from human inventiveness. However, nowhere in the aforementioned book does one come across any discussion concerning the nature of the metric that is to be used for determining what the criteria are which are to be used in evaluating what the benefits and harms of a given instance of technology might be.

1.95621 - On occasion, the author of *The Coming Wave* seems to believe that as long as benefits outweigh the harms, then, perhaps, this is the most for which we can hope. Aside from questioning the propriety of reducing the rest of humanity's hopes to the hopes of the author, one might also question the way in which, apparently, the metric for evaluating our situation should be some form of utilitarian argument that begins at no justifiable beginning and works toward no defensible end.

1.957 - There are two broad approaches to the issue of utilitarianism. One is quantitative and the other is qualitative.

1.9571 - Irrespective of which branch of utilitarianism one chooses to pursue, the process is entirely arbitrary. This is because there is no absolute, undeniable, all-are-agreed-upon starting point through which a person can justify one set of utilitarian criteria over some other set of utilitarian criteria. Consequently, regardless of how one proceeds, the choices are arbitrary especially when such choices are imposed on other people without the informed consent of the latter.

1.9572 - Imposing solutions on people without informed consent tends to be the default position for most forms of governance. This is considered to be an exercise in the technology of practicality because oppression seems to be a less complicated way of doing things relative to an alternative which requires one to engage human beings in all of their nuanced complexities and provide those people with veto power in conjunction with alleged solutions that are devoid of properties of informed consent.

1.958 - Does having: Food to eat, a place to live, appliances to use, medical care when needed, educational opportunities through which to learn, a system for participating in government, as well as a career path to pursue, constitute a set of benefits? Wouldn't the answer to such a question depend on: The quality of the food at one's disposal; the quality of one's living conditions; the quality of the community in which one lives; the nature of the hazards or harms which might be associated with the appliances one uses; the effectiveness and risks entailed by the available medical treatment; the quality of the purposes, practices, and conditions to which a given form of education gives expression; the extent and ways in which one is enabled to participate in governance, as well as the degree of meaningfulness, satisfaction, and value which might be present in a given career or job?

1.9581 - When the food which is available for eating is nutritionally questionable if not poisonous, and the places in which we live are replete with toxic influences, and medical care is the leading cause of death, and education is about inducing one to exchange one's essential nature for empty theories, and government constitutes a set of controlling, abusive, corrupting technologies, and careers often give

| Technological Reflections |

expression to the logistics of selling one's soul, then, where is the progress? A series of exercises in the dynamics of willful blindness are necessary to ignore, or merely comply with, the systemic rot which has grabbed hold of many facets of alleged civilization over the last twenty centuries, or more.

1.95811 - How does one parse benefits? How does one parse harms? How does one weigh the former against the latter?

1.9582 - Does technology automatically render such questions easier to answer? Or, does technology constitute an obfuscating series of proprietary complexities in which society has become entangled, much like flies become prisoners of the web's that, initially, seemed to be so opportunistically inviting?

1.9583 - Once upon a time, people knew how to grow food, can and preserve edibles, sew, fashion their own tools, build a house, make their own clothes, construct furniture, and survive in the wild. As is true in all manner of activities, some individuals were better at such things than others were, and, to be sure, there were difficulties, problems, and limits surrounding the development and execution of those sorts of skills, but, for the most part, one of the prominent characteristics of many so-called technically-oriented societies is that technology has dumbed down most people in locations where such technology has taken hold as far as the foregoing list of skills is concerned.

1.95831 - We are one Carrington event (natural or artificial) away from creating conditions in which very few people will be able to survive. This is because we have enabled technology to seduce us into abandoning what is essential to being human and, in the process, adopting what is artificial, synthetic, and debilitating to human potential.

1.9584 - The situation of many of us today is akin to the Eloi of H.G. Well's 1895 novel: *The Time Machine*. One does not have to characterize technology as a product of some sort of evil spawn of Morlocks in order to appreciate that technology has induced most people to become dependent on technology rather than becoming reliant on what God has given them in the form of their own gifts and capabilities.

1.95841 - Development and maturation used to mean learning how to unpack what is present within one. Now, development and maturation are a function of learning how to transition from one kind of technology to another form of technology.

1.95842 - Perhaps, just as physical skills have been lost to technology, so too, cognitive skills are becoming lost to artificial intelligence. The maxim "use it or lose it" does not necessarily apply just to the physical realm.

1.96 - Nowhere in *The Coming Wave* does the author explore what it means to be a human being. What are we? What is our potential? What are our obligations, if any, to the life we inhabit or to the life which inhabits us?

1.961 - The author of *The Coming Wave* cannot account for the origins of consciousness, logic, reason, intelligence, insight, creativity, talent, wisdom, language, or the biofield. He alludes to some evolutionary dynamic as being the source of such capabilities, but all he ever does when using the e-word is to assume his conclusions without ever providing a detailed account of how any of the foregoing capabilities arose or came to possess the degrees of freedom, as well as constraints, which might be present in human potential.

1.97 - All intelligence in AI is derivative. In other words, whatever intelligence is present in AI comes from what is placed in those dynamics by human beings.

1.971 - When Gary Kasparov competed a second time during a chess challenge against IBM's Deep Blue, he became upset when a move made by the machine seemed to have unexpected human qualities and, as a result, he began to suspect that he might be playing against one or more humans rather than a machine. What he did not seem to understand was that he had been playing (both the first time around when he won and the second time when he lost) against one or more humans because the capabilities that had been bestowed on the machine he was playing came from human beings who had equipped the machine with all manner of computational systems for analyzing, evaluating, and applying heuristics of one kind or another to the game of chess.

1.9712 - There was a ghost – or a number of them -- in the machine, and, therefore, Kasparov shouldn't have been surprised if a human-like quality surfaced at various points during the course of play. What did he think the machine was contributing to the competition entirely on its own?

1.972 - The combinatorics, computational properties, algorithms, transformational possibilities, equations, operators, as well as the capacities to integrate, differentiate, learn, parse, map, model, and develop that are present in AI systems are all a function of human intelligence. An AI system might be given the capacity to generate a variety of attractor basins or networks and invest those structures or networks with different properties or an AI system might be given the potential to re-order the foregoing capabilities in different sequences with different kinds of interactional dimensions, but those modulating combinatorics, or the potential for such capacities has come, from the intelligence of one or more human beings.

1.973 - Can such systems come up with new ways of engaging issues or generate novel re-workings of various scenarios? Sure they can, but whatever newness emerges is only possible because of what human intelligence has given such systems the capacity to do in relation to the generation of novelty.

1.9731 - Is it possible that the human beings who are constructing such dynamic capabilities are not aware of the possibilities which inadvertently or unintentionally have been built into those systems? Yes, it is, and, indeed, increasingly, technology has become like a black box chaotic attractor – or set of such attractors – that possess determinate dynamics even as those dynamics lead to unpredictable outcomes.

1.9732 - As Mustafa Suleyman notes in his book, a mystifying, if not worrying, dimension of certain kinds of, for example, AI technology is that its creators don't necessarily understand why a system or network exhibited one kind of decision rather than another. In other words, the creators don't understand the possibilities which they have instantiated into a given machine, network, or system.

1.97321 - For example, Suleyman talks about a Go move by AlphaGo which has become famous within AI and Go circles and is referred to as "move number 37." The move took place in a game against Lee Sedol (a Go version – in several ways -- of Gary Kasparov) which on the surface appeared to be a losing move and seemed to make no strategic or tactical sense, but turned out to be a tipping point in the game, and, yet, no one (including the expert commentators) could understand why the move was being made or why it was being made at the time it took place.

1.97322 - A machine or system – including AlphaGo -- is not doing something new on its own. Rather, dimensions of the capabilities which have been invested in the machine or system and about which the creators were unaware are becoming manifest.

1.97323 - This is not emergent behavior. This is a failure of the creators to properly vet their creation and thoroughly understand the possibilities and flaws which are present in what they have done.

1.97324 - In other words, the system, network, or machine had been created with certain vulnerabilities. In addition, the creators also enabled the machine, network, or system to exploit or engage such vulnerabilities, and, not surprisingly, this has the capacity to lead to unforeseen results.

1.974 - In response to such considerations, cautionary tales have been written -- to which technologists and many scientists rarely pay much sincere or engage with critically reflective attention -- such as (to name but a few): *Faust – Parts 1 and 2* by Johann von Goethe (1773 – 1831); *Frankenstein* by Mary Shelley (1818); *The Time Machine* by H. G. Wells (1895); *Brave New World* by Aldous Huxley (1932); *1984* by George Orwell (1949); *The Foundation Trilogy* by Isaac Asimov (1942-1953); *The Technological Society* by Jacques Ellul (1954); *Colossus* by Dennis Feltham Jones (1966); *2001: A Space Odyssey* by Arthur C. Clarke (1968); *Do Adroids Dream of Electric Sheep* by Philip K. Dick (1968,); *The Terminal Man* (1972) or *Jurassic Park* (1990) by Michael Crichton; *The Terminator* by James Cameron and Gale Ann Hurd (1984); as well as *Prometheus* by Jon Spaihts and Damon Lindelof (2009-2011).

1.9741 - There have been over two hundred years worth of cautionary tales concerning such matters. However, notwithstanding the many amazing accomplishments of technologists, engineers, and scientists, nonetheless, such individuals sometimes seem to believe that they are smarter and wiser than they actually are.

1.975 – Mustafa Suleyman has written a book which, for several hundred pages, explores the problems which he believes surround and permeate the issue of containing technology as if, somehow, that topic is sort of a recently surfacing emergent phenomenon ... something that -- based on initial, apparently quite superficial considerations -- one couldn't possibly suspect might harbor difficulties that, subsequently, are becoming manifest. Yet, for quite some time, human beings have been aware of the problems that technology: Has created, is creating, and will continue to create, but since that understanding tends to be something of an inconvenient truth, technologists, scientists, and engineers just continue to do what they have always done – focus on solving whatever the technical problems might be in which they have an interest while, for the most part, ignoring the possible implications of those very activities.

2.0 - Let us assume that we have a machine that can pass a Turing test -- that is, one which is capable of displaying qualities that a human observer could not detect as being the product of machine dynamics rather than human cognition. Does this demonstrate that the machine is intelligent or does it demonstrate that the human beings who built the machine are sufficiently intelligent and talented to create a system which has been provided with an ample set of protocols, logic gates, algorithms, data-processing capabilities, computational facilities, sensing devices, and the like to be able to establish a form of modeling or simulation or set of neural networks that is capable of learning new things and altering its modeling or simulation or neural network activity to reflect that learning and, thereby, do what its creator or creators want it to be able to do?

2.1 - What is intelligence? Is exhibiting behavior that is intelligent necessarily the same thing as being intelligent?

2.12 - Is intelligence the same thing as sentience? Is a machine that can pass a Turing test necessarily sentient?

2.13 - B.F. Skinner showed that one could train pigeons and other animals to exhibit intricate sequences of behavior and accomplish tasks of one kind or another. Those subjects had sufficient capacities for learning to enable them – when properly reinforced -- to be trained or to undergo processes of behavior modification that exhibited considerable nuanced complexity.

2.14 - Was such modulated behavior intelligent or was it the training process which shaped that behavior which actually demonstrated the presence of intelligence? A pigeon comes equipped with a capacity to learn, but a machine has to be given its capacity to learn by human beings who have instantiated certain qualities into the machine that enable learning of different kinds to take place.

2.141 - A pigeon learns according to its capacity for being reinforced in one way rather than another. Based on the physiological and biological properties or characteristics of the entity that is being subjected to a form of behavior modification, then once something (say food or an electrical stimulation of some kind) becomes accepted or acknowledged as a source of inducement, then, it is the pattern of induced reinforcement which shapes learning rather than some indigenous form of intelligence

2.1412 - The pigeon does not produce that pattern, but, rather, responds to its presence, and it is this responsiveness which is being used as leverage to alter behavior. This is frequency following behavior because the behavior follows (is shaped by) the frequency characteristics of the reinforcement process.

2.15 - Machine learning and neural networks do not constitute blank slates. There are processing weights – sometimes quite simple but sometimes more complex – that have been built into those systems which establish the rules or principles for being able to proceed in different quantitative and qualitative ways and which characterize the capacity of the system to grow or expand or develop in complexity over time.

2.151 - Those processing weights, rules, protocols, and the like are comparable to the biological and physiological properties that enable a pigeon to be trained. Consequently, machines can be equipped to be trained, and, as a result, the behavioral characteristics of the system or network can be modified in ways that seem intelligent but all that is taking place is that the machine's capacity for being trainable (i.e., its capacity to learn) is being put on display and shaped in ways that appear intelligent, but, like the pigeon, are nothing more than a capacity for trainability being developed in different directions according to patterns that originate from without (i.e., in the guise of the researcher) rather than being indigenous to the entity being trained.

2.152 - If the machine is trained to generate protocols that enable it to go about modifying its own behavior, this is still not intelligent behavior. Rather, the intelligence is present in the protocols that underlay the system's capacity to be able to train itself, and although like pigeons, extraordinary forms of behavior can be shaped, nevertheless, that behavior is the product of a basic capacity for trainability being pushed or pulled in different directions by the presence of protocols, algorithms, and so on that come from without the system (whether one is talking about pigeons or machines.)

2.153 - Pigeons don't naturally display the behavioral patterns which they are induced to adopt through the modification protocols to which they are introduced by a researcher. Those patterns of reinforcement have to be given to them in order for the pigeon's capacity to be trained to become activated.

2.154 - Is the pigeon aware of the nature of the behavior modification that is taking place? Does the pigeon have any insight into the character of those modifications? What is the nature of the phenomenology that takes place in conjunction with the form of behavior modification which is being experienced by the pigeon?

2.155 - Perhaps, there are memories of the individual triggering cues that give rise to different stages in the chain or sequence of behaviors that have been learned? Or, maybe there are memories of the series of rewards or reinforcements that occurred during the process of behavior modification.

2.156 - However, was the pigeon aware that its behavior was being modified? Or, was the pigeon aware with respect to how its behavior was being modified as it was modified or was it aware of what the significance of that modification might have been?

2.157 - We'll probably never know. However, one could suppose that the primary focus of the pigeon's phenomenology had to do with the presence of a sequence of reinforcements. Conceivably, the pigeon went -- and was aware to some extent of – wherever the process of reinforcements took it, but everything else might have been just background even as changes in behavior began to take place.

2.158 – In other words, the reinforcements or rewards might have been the center of attention of the pigeon's phenomenology. The particular character of the changes which were occurring in conjunction with those reinforcements might have been of peripheral, or passing – even forgettable -- phenomenological interest. The pigeon might have been aware of the parts that led to the whole (the complex set of behaviors that gave expression to a nuance form of behavior) but might not necessarily have been aware of the significance or character of the whole sequence of behaviors taken as a complex form of behavior.

2.159 - In order for machines to be able to exhibit qualities that might be referred to as constituting instances of artificial intelligence, they have to be given the capacity to learn or be trainable. They also have to be given the protocols which will activate that potential for trainability.

2.1591 - Or, alternatively, such machines will have to be given the protocols which enable the machine or system to self-activate that potential itself based on the decision-tree protocols with which it has been equipped or protocols that can be modified according to other capabilities the machine has been given.

2.16 - Can machines be enabled to learn or be trained and, then, enabled to act on that learning and training? Yes, they can, but this doesn't make them intelligent.

2.161 - Data-processing speeds, parallel-processing capabilities, computational powers, heuristic algorithms, and read/write memory storage can make an outcome look intelligent. However, the machine has no more to do with the intelligence being detected in its productions than a pigeon is responsible for generating the character of the complex behaviors that are made possible through a carefully planned reinforcement schedule.

2.1612 - One of the differences between a pigeon and an AI system is that unlike the latter, the pigeon comes to its tasks with a ready-made, inherent capacity to learn or be trained so that its behavior can be modified in certain non-natural ways, whereas AI systems have to be provided with such capabilities.

2.162 - Depending on the capabilities AI systems are given by their handlers, such systems could become quite destructive. In effect, this means that if the handlers are not careful how they construct those machines or if those individuals intentionally construct their machines in certain ways with malice aforethought, then, the machine doesn't have to have intelligence to be able to learn how to refine its modalities of sensing, surveilling, acquiring, and eliminating targets – all it does, like the pigeon, is operate within the parameters of its training or capacity for behavior modification with which it has been provided by its handlers.

2.163 - What of the phenomenological experience of the machine? Is there any?

2.1631 - This is one of the questions which Philip Dick was raising in his 1968 novel: *Do Adroids Dream of Electric Sheep?* This issue became a guiding inspiration for the 1982 *Blade Runner* film.

2.1632 - Some theorists believe that sentience is an emergent property which arises when a data-processing system reaches a certain level of complexity. Nonetheless, until someone proves that sentience or awareness is an emergent property (and how one would ascertain that such is the case becomes an interesting challenge in itself), then, the foregoing idea that sentience is an emergent property of certain kinds of complexity remains only a theory or a premise for an interesting exercise in science fiction.

2.164 - The capacity to learn or be trained does not necessarily require sentience or phenomenology to be present in order for learning to take place because some forms of learning can be reduced to being nothing more than a process of changing the degrees of freedom and degrees of constraint of a given system. (Eric Kandel received a Nobel Prize for showing that Aplysia – sea slugs – "learned" through changes in synaptic connections.) Alternatively, to whatever extent sentience of some kind is present – such as, perhaps, in the case of a pigeon – that the form of sentience doesn't necessarily require any reflexive awareness concerning the significance of what is transpiring peripherally (the ground) in relation to the process of reinforcement (the figure).

2.1641 - The author of *The Coming Wave* introduces the idea of a Modern Turing Test in which a system of machine learning has, say, an

AGI capability – that is, a Artificial General Intelligence – which would enable it to be thrust into a real world context and, then, come up with a creative plan for solving an actual problem for which it had not been previously trained. This would require such a system to modify its operating capabilities in ways that would allow it to adapt to changing conditions and derive pertinent information from those conditions, and, then, use that information to fashion an effective way of engaging whatever problem was being addressed.

2.1642 - AGI is just a more advanced form of what was envisioned in conjunction with the initial test proposed by Turing as a way of determining whether, or not, intelligence was present in a system that was able to induce a human being to believe that the latter was dealing with another human being rather than with a machine. However, for reasons stated previously, "learning" does not necessarily require either intelligence or sentience but, rather, just needs the capacity – which can be given or provided from without -- to be able to modify past data and alter various operational parameters in response to new data as a function of algorithms that employ, among other processes, computations and combinatorics – which can be given or provided from without -- that lead to heuristically valuable or effective transformations of a given data set. As long as those effective transformations are retained in, and are accessible by, the system, then, learning has occurred despite the absence of any sort of indigenous intelligence in the system (i.e., all capabilities have been provided from without and, furthermore, whatever capabilities are generated from within are a function of capabilities that have been provided from outside of the system).

2.1643 As magicians have known for eons, human beings are vulnerable to illusions, expectations, and misdirection. The "intelligence" aspect of AI is an exercise in misdirection in which one's wonderment about the end result takes one's attention away from all of the tinkering which was necessary to make such an artificial phenomenon possible and, therefore, obscures how the only intelligence which is present is human in nature and that human intelligence is responsible for creating the illusion of AI.

2.165 - Mustapha Suleyman claims that the next evolutionary step in AI involves what has been referred to as ACI – Artificial Capable

Intelligence. This sort of system could generate and make appropriate use of novel forms of linguistic, visual, and auditory structures while engaging, and being engaged by, real world users as it draws on various data bases, including knowledge data bases of one kind or another (such as a medical, engineering, biological, or mathematical knowledge data bases).

2.1651 - All the key components of such ACI systems are rooted in human, rather than machine, intelligence. For example, novelty comes from a sequence of protocols that permit images, sounds, languages, and other features, to be combined in ways that can be passed through a process of high-speed iterations that entail different quantitative and qualitative weights which push or pull those iterations in one direction rather than another and which are evaluated for their usability according to different sets of heuristic protocols.

2.1652 - Consequently, novelty is a function of the degrees of freedom and constraints which were instantiated within the system from the beginning. Iteration – which plays a part in the generation of novelty -- is also a protocol which has been invested in the system from without.

2.1653 - Similarly, generating -- or drawing on – knowledge data bases is a function of algorithms and heuristic protocols which parse data on the basis of principles or rules that either have been built into the system from without or which are the result of the combinatoric functions that have been provided to the system from without and which enable the system to create operational degrees of freedom and constraints that comply with what such underlying functions make possible. The 'capability' and 'intelligence' dimensions of ACI come from human beings, while the artificial aspects of ACI have to do with the ways in which the machine or system operates according to the operational parameters which have been vested in it.

2.1654 - Unfortunately, the increasing complexity of such systems is turning them into black boxes because the creators don't understand the extent, scope, or degrees of freedom of the iterative combinatorics which, unknowingly, have been built into their creations. Under such circumstances, unexpected or unanticipated outcomes are merely a form of self-inflicted misdirection which confuses the creators concerning the source of the intelligence that is being exhibited.

2.166 - *The Coming Wave* describes some of the circumstances which marked the author's journey from DeepMind, to working for Google, to AlphaGo, to Inflection. For example, AlphaGo was an algorithm which specialized in the game of Go and was trained through a process of being exposed to 150,000 games of Go played by human beings, and, then, the system was enabled to reiteratively play against other AlphaGo algorithms in order for the collective set of programs to experiment with, and discover novel, effective, Go strategies, before taking on, first in 2016, world champion Lee Sedol at a South Korean venue and, then, in 2017, competing against Ke Jie, the number one ranked Go player in the world -- winning both competitions.

2.167 - Go is the national game of China. The number one ranked player in the world in 2017 was Chinese and was beaten in Wuzhen, China, during the Future of Go Summit being held in that city.

2.168 - The dragon had been poked. Two months after the foregoing defeat, the Chinese government introduced The New Generation Artificial Intelligence Development Plan which was designed to make China the leader in AI research and innovation by 2030.

2.169 - Undoubtedly, China had aspirations in the realm of AI research prior to the unexpected Go loss at Wuzhen, but the 2017 competition is very likely to have lent a certain amount of urgency and focus to their pre-existing interest. Providing the Chinese government with additional motivation to up its AI game might have not been part of the intention which led Mustafa Suleyman and his colleagues to travel to China and compete against the world's top-rated Go player, but this seemed to be an unintended consequence of the AlphaGo project. Consequently, one can't help but wonder if the purveyors of the latter research project ever considered the possibility that they would be contributing to the very problem that six years later would be at the heart of a book written by one of the creators of AlphaGo that was seeking to raise the clarion call concerning the crisis surrounding the issue of containing technology.

2.1691 - To a certain extent, the South Korea and Chinese Go challenges seem less like human beings versus a machine competition and more like the sort of thing one is likely to see take place in many high schools when two cliques seek domination over one another. AlphaGo might have helped one of those cliques win a battle, but this was at the cost of helping to facilitate -- even if only in a limited way – a much more serious and expansive war for domination.

2.1692 - AlphaGo is but a stone in a larger, more extreme edition of the game of Go (Go-Life) in which technology is facing off against humanity. When go-ishi pieces are surrounded during a normal game of Go, those stones are removed from the board or goban but are still available for future games. However, in the technocratic edition of the game of Go, human beings are being surrounded by technological entities of one kind or another, and, then, the human go-ishi are removed from the board of life – either permanently or in a debilitated, powerless condition.

2.1693 - What makes the AlphaGo project a little more puzzling is the experiences which Mustafa Suleyman and associates had in conjunction with their DeepMind venture a few years earlier.

2.171 - In 2010, Suleyman -- along with Shane Legg and Dennis Hassabis -- established a company dedicated to AI. Supposedly, the purpose for creating DeepMind involved trying to model, replicate, or capture human intelligence (in part or wholly), but shortly after mentioning the name of the company in *The Coming Wave* and, then, summarizing the newly founded organization's alleged goal, Suleyman goes on to claim that the team wanted to create a system which would be capable of outperforming the entire spectrum of human cognitive abilities.

2.172 - There are two broad ways of outperforming human cognitive abilities. One such possibility involves discovering what human intelligence is and, then, building systems that exhibit those properties at a consistent level of excellence which most human beings are incapable of accomplishing or sustaining.

2.1721 - A second possibility concerning the notion of seeking to outperform human capabilities involves creating systems that, in some sense, are superior to whatever human intelligence might be. This sort of pursuit is not a matter of replicating human intelligence and being able to consistently maintain such dynamics at a high level that is beyond what most human beings are able to do, but, rather, such a notion of outperforming human capabilities alludes to some form of intelligence which is not only capable of doing everything that human intelligence is capable of doing but is capable of intellectual activities that transcend human intelligence (and, obviously, this capacity to transcend human intelligence is difficult, if not impossible, for the latter sort of intelligence to grasp).

2.173 - There is a potentially substantial disconnect between, on the one hand, wanting to replicate human intellectual abilities and do so at a consistently high level and, on the other hand, wanting to develop a system which is superior to those abilities in every way. The manner in which Suleyman states things at this point in his book lends itself to a certain amount of ambiguity.

2.1731 - The foregoing kind of ambiguity remains even if agreement could be reached with respect to what human intelligence is. In addition, one needs to inquire whether, or not, all forms of intelligence can be placed on one, continuous scale, or if there are kinds of intelligence which are qualitatively different from one another, somewhat like how the real numbers are described by Cantor as being a quantitatively (and, perhaps, qualitatively) different form of infinity than is the sort of infinity which is associated with the natural numbers.

2.174 - Irrespective of whether one would like to replicate human intelligence or surpass it in some sense, one wonders about the underlying motivations. For instance, how did Suleyman and his partners propose to use whatever system they developed and what ramifications would such a system have for the rest of society?

2.175 - One also wonders if discussions were held prior to undertaking the DeepMind project which critically probed: Whether, or not, either of the foregoing possible projects concerning the issue of intelligence was actually a good idea, and what metric should be used to identify the possible downsides and upsides of such a research endeavor. One might ask a follow-up question in relation to the sort of justification that is to be used in defending one kind of metric rather than another sort of metric when considering those issues.

2.1751 - Finally, one also wonders whether, or not, the DeepMind team discussed bringing in some independent, less invested consultants to critically explore the foregoing matters with the DeepMind team. One also could ask questions along the following line – more specifically, if they did discuss the foregoing sorts of matters, then why did they continue on in the way they did?

2.17512 - The foregoing considerations are significant because, eventually, the author of *The Coming Wave* does raise such matters, as well as related ones. However, one wonders if this was rigorously pursued both before-the-fact as well as after-the-fact of DeepMind's inception as an operating project.

2.180 - The author of *The Coming Wave* indicates that a few years after his DeepMind-company had come into existence and had achieved considerable success (maybe somewhere around 2014), he conducted a presentation for an audience consisting of many notables from the worlds of AI and technology. The purpose of the presentation was to bring certain problematic dimensions of AI and technology to the attention of the audience and, perhaps, thereby, induce an ensuing discussion concerning Suleyman's concerns.

2.181 - For example, several of the topics he explored during his aforementioned presentation involved themes of privacy and cyber security. However, given the notoriety surrounding the PROMIS (Prosecutor's Management Information System) software controversy which occurred during the 1980s (and included the questionable 1991 suicide of Danny Casolaro who was investigating the story), as well as the claims of Clint Curtis, a software engineer working in Florida, who, in 2000, was asked to write a program by a future member of Congress which would be capable of altering votes registered on a touch-screen (and later successfully demonstrated how the election-rigging software worked), and given the whistleblowing revelations (concerning, among other things, illicit government surveillance programs) from such people as: Bill Binney (2002), Russ Tice (2005), Thomas Tamm (2006), Mark Klein (2006), Thomas Drake (2010), Chelsea Manning (2010), and Ed Snowden (2013), one might suppose that by 2014, or so, important players in the tech industry would have been keenly aware of the many problems which existed concerning cyber-security and privacy issues.

| Technological Reflections |

248

2.182 - The author of *The Coming Wave* says that his presentation was met with variations on a blank stare by virtually all, if not all, of the individuals who had attended his talk. One might hypothesize that the reason for the foregoing sorts of reactions from many of the top tech people in the country was either because they were obsessively self-absorbed and unaware of what had been transpiring in America for, at least, a number of decades, or, alternatively, the people in his audience were, in one way or another, deeply involved in an array of projects, software programs, and technologies that were engaged in, among other things, undermining privacy and capable of breeching cyber-security according to their arbitrary, vested interests and, therefore, what could they do but muster blank stares in order to try to hide their complicity.

2.183 - Even if such people weren't actively complicit in compromising people's privacy and cyber-security, they were sufficiently aware of how the career-sausage is made to know that if they had begun to resist such illicit activities publically, then, there was a high probability that their future commercial prospects were very likely to be adversely affected. Gaslighting Mustafa Suleyman via disbelieving blank stares might have seemed to be the safer course of action for the members of his audience.

2.190 - During *The Coming Wave*, the author describes a breakthrough moment in 2012 using an algorithm known as DQN which is short for Deep Q-Network.

2.191 - The algorithm was an exercise in developing a system with general intelligence (i.e., AGI). DQN had been given the capacity to teach itself how to play various games created by Atari, and this dimension of independence and self-direction was at the heart of what the people at DeepMind were trying to accomplish.

2.912 - Leaving aside some of the details of the aforementioned breakthrough, suffice it to say that the algorithm they had created had produced a novel strategy for solving a problem within one of the Atari games. Although the strategy was not unknown to veteran game players, it was rare, and, more importantly, DQN had, somehow, generated such a rare, little-known strategy.

2.9121 - The strategy was not something the algorithm had been given. It was a strategy that the algorithm had arrived at on its own.

| Technological Reflections |

2.9122 - Suleyman was nonplused by what he had witnessed. For him, the strategy pursued by DQN indicated that AGI systems were capable of generating new knowledge ... presumably a sign of intelligence.

2.913 - Was DQN aware of what was taking place as it was taking place? Did that strategy come as an insight – an emergent property – of an underlying algorithmic dynamic?

2.9131 - Or, was the algorithm just mindlessly exploring -- according to the heuristic protocols it had been given by its creators -- various combinations of the parameters that had been built into the algorithm. Perhaps the winning game strategy wasn't so much a matter of machine intelligence as much as it was the algorithm's happening upon a successful strategy using abilities and potentials which it had been given by human beings. How would one distinguish between the two?

2.914 - The DQN was capable of generating novel, successful solutions to a problem. The DQN had the capacity to alter its way of engaging an Atari game but was this really a case of machine learning and intelligence?

2.915 - DQN is described as having learned something new – something that it had generated without being trained to do so. Intelligence is being attributed to the machine.

2.916 - Nonetheless, the algorithm has not been shown to be sentient or aware of what it was doing. Furthermore, there is no proof that the new strategy involved insight or some sort of Eureka moment on the part of the algorithm. In addition, although there is a change in the system, the change does not necessarily involve a process of learning that can be shown to be a function of intelligence, not least because human beings always have a difficult time characterizing what intelligence is or what makes it possible.

2.917 DQN is an algorithm that has the capacity to change in ways which enable the system to solve certain kinds of problems or challenges. Apparently, the author of *The Coming Wave* doesn't understand how the algorithm came up with the solution that it did, and this should worry him and the rest of us because it means that when such algorithms are let loose, we can't necessarily predict what they will do.

2.92 - In some ways DQN is like a sort of three-body problem or, perhaps more accurately, an n-body problem. In the classical three-body problem of physics, if one establishes the initial velocities and positions of point masses and uses Newtonian mechanics to calculate their velocities and positions at some given point in time, one discovers that there is no standard equation which is capable of predicting how the dynamics of that system will change across some given temporal interval.

2.93 - There are dimensional aspects to the dynamics of the DQN algorithm which fall outside of the understanding of Suleyman. As a result, he is unable to predict how that system's dynamics will unfold over time.

2.94 - The system is determinate because it operates in accordance with its parameters. However, the system is also chaotic because we do understand how those parameters will interact with one another over time and, therefore, we cannot predict what it will do.

2.95 - This means the algorithm is capable of generating dynamic outcomes which are surprising and unanticipated. Nonetheless, this does not necessarily mean such outcomes are a function of machine intelligence.

3.0 - Whether the machine is intelligent or merely capable of generating effective solutions to problems through some form of computational combinatorics involving n-parameters of interactive heuristics, we are faced with a problem. More specifically, we can't predict what the system will do, and the more complex such systems become, then, the three-body-like problem turns into an even more chaotic, but determinate n-body problem of massive unpredictability.

3.1 - The containment problem to which Mustafa Suleyman is seeking to draw our attention concerns how technology is capable of seeping into, and adversely affecting, our lives in uncontainable ways. As disturbing as such a problem might be, nevertheless, residing within the general context of that kind of containment issue is a much more challenging form of containment problem which has to do with algorithms, machines, networks, and systems which are being provided with capacities that can generate outcomes which cannot be predicted, and, therefore, this tends to induce one to wonder how one might go about defending oneself against forms of technology that we cannot predict what they will do.

3.2 - Whether such outcomes are considered, on the one hand, to be a product of machine intelligence or, on the other hand, are considered to be a chaotic function of the dynamic, combinatorial parameters which human intelligence has instantiated into those systems is beside the point. The point is that they are unpredictable and unpredictability, if let loose, might be inherently uncontainable.

3.3 - In a 1942 short story entitled *"Runaround,"* Isaac Asimov introduced what are often referred to as the three laws of robotics -- although, perhaps technically speaking, those laws might be more appropriately directed toward the algorithms or neural networks which are to be placed in a robotic body. In any event, the three laws are: (1) a robot may not injure a human being, or through inaction, allow a human being to come to harm; (2) a robot must obey the orders given to it by human beings except where such orders would conflict with the first law; and (3) a robot must protect its own existence as long as such protection does not conflict with the first two laws.

3.31 - Is the notion of "harm" only to be understood in a physical sense? What about emotional, psychological, political, legal, ideological, medical, educational, environmental, and spiritual harms? How are any of these potential harms to be understood, and what metric or metrics are to be used to evaluate the possibility of harm, and what justifies the use of one set of metrics rather than another set of metrics when making such evaluations?

3.32 - How is the notion of potential "conflict" to be understood in the context of orders given and possible harms arising from such orders? Could the intentions underlying the giving of orders be seen as a harmful action, and, if so, how would the person giving the orders be assisted by the robot to discontinue such harmful intentions?

3.33 - How does a robot protect itself and/or human beings against a corrupt technocracy? How does a robot solve the n-body problem when it comes to potential harm for itself and the members of humanity?

3.34 - What makes a human being, human? Whatever that quality is, or whatever those qualities are, which gives (give) expression to the notion of humanness, can the three laws be extended to other modalities of beings if the latter entities possess the appropriate quality or qualities of humanness? If so, what does a robot do when two modalities of being, each possessing the quality or qualities of humanness, come into conflict with one another?

3.35 - Is focusing on the quality or qualities or humanness excessively arbitrary? What if the manner of a human's interaction with the surrounding environment is injurious to that human being as well as others? What metric does one use to assess the nature of environmental injury?

3.36 - While there is much about DeepMind's DQN which I do not know, nonetheless, I have a sense that such a system is not currently capable (and, presumably, for quite some time, might not be capable) of coming up with novel, workable solutions to the foregoing questions and problems which would have everyone's agreement. Moreover, even if it did have such capacities, I am not sure that I – or even Mustafa Suleyman – would have much understanding with respect to what led DQN to reach the outcome that it did and whether, or not, that outcome would be of constructive value for human beings in the long run.

3.37 - One would need something comparable to the fictional psychohistory system of mathematics that was developed by Hari Seldon in Isaac Asimov's *Foundation* series. Quite some time ago (long before Asimov), the Iroquois people came up with a perspective which indicated that one should consider how a given action will play out over a period of seven generations before deciding whether, or not, to engage in such an action – a sort of early version of psychohistory – and, yet, technology (including so-called AI) is being imposed on human beings with no sign that the advocates for such technology have any fundamental appreciation, or even concern, for what such technology is doing to human beings -- both short term and long term.

3.40 - In early 2014, a commercial transaction was completed between DeepMind and Google. The deal would send 500 million dollars to the people who had brought DeepMind into existence and, in addition, several of the latter company's key personnel, including Mustafa Suleyman, were brought on as consultants for Google.

3.41 - Not very long after the foregoing transaction was completed, Google transitioned to an AI-first orientation across all of its products. The change of direction enabled Google to join a number of other tech giants (such as IBM, Yahoo, and Facebook) that had become committed to deep machine learning or the capacity of machines to, among other things, generate novel, unanticipated modalities of engaging and resolving issues in heuristically valuable ways.

3.42 - Apparently, the idea of constructing systems, networks, algorithms, and technologies that would be able to perform in unpredictable and unanticipated ways, and, then, letting such chaotic capabilities loose upon the world was very appealing to certain kinds of mind-sets that were in awe of machines and programs whose outcomes could not be predicted or anticipated. Even more promising was that all of these components of the allegedly coming wave – which, in reality, already had been washing over, if not inundating, humanity for quite some time -- would be competing against one another in order to be able to up their respective games, just as AlphaGo would soon be enabled to compete against other versions of itself in order to be able to hone its skills and produce moves like the previously mentioned "move number 37" that appeared to be a crucial part of a game-winning strategy and, yet, was puzzling, mysterious, and beyond the grasp of the creators of the AlphaGo algorithm.

3.43 - AI possesses fractal properties of incomprehensibility and ambiguity. These properties show up in self-similar – and, therefore, slightly different -- ways across all levels of computational scale.

3.431 - Consider the sentence: "Mary had a little lamb." What does the sentence mean?

3.432 - It could mean that at some point Mary possessed a tiny lamb. Or, it might mean that Mary ate a small portion of lamb. Or, it might mean that Mary was part of some genetic engineering experiment, and she gave birth to a little lamb. Or, it could mean that Mary gave birth to a child that behaved like a little lamb. Or, it could be a code which served to identify someone as a friendly agent. Or, it might mean that such a sentence is capable of illustrating linguistic and conceptual ambiguity. There are other possible meanings, as well, to which the sentence might give expression.

3.433 - Providing context can help to indicate what might be meant by such a sentence. However, when an algorithm or network is set free to explore different combinatorial possibilities or dynamics, then, the system is, in a sense, setting its own context, and if this context is not made clear to an observer or has ambiguous dimensions like the "Mary had a little lamb" exercise, then the significance of a given contextual way of engaging words, phrases, sentences, events, objects, functions, and computations becomes amorphous. 'Move number 37' by AlphaGo had context, significance, and value, but human beings failed to grasp or understand what was meant because we don't know what the algorithmic Rosetta stone is for unpacking the meaning of the contextual dynamic that gave rise to "move number 37."

3.44 - The deal between DeepMind and Google involved the creation of some sort of ethics committee. Part of the intention underlying this idea was to try to ensure that DeepMind's capabilities would be kept on a tight, rigorously controlled, ethical leash, but, in addition, the author of *The Coming Wave* was interested in developing a sort of multi-stakeholder congressional-like body in which people from around the world would be able to come together in a democratically-oriented forum to decide how to contain AGI (Artificial General Intelligence) in ways which would prove to be beneficial to humanity.

3.441 - There are several potential problems inherent in the multi-stakeholder, democratic forum aspect of the foregoing ethics committee dynamic. For example, the identity of those who are to be considered stakeholders and who would be invited to participate in such a forum are unlikely to involve most of the world's population, and, therefore, such a forum is, from the very beginning, based on an ethically-challenged and shaky foundation.

3.442 - No individual (elected or not) can possibly represent the interests of a collective because the diverse interests of the members of the latter group tend to conflict with one another. Therefore, unless one can come up with a constructive and mutually beneficial method for inducing the members of the collective to forego their individual perspectives – which tends to be the source of conflict within such a collective – then, so-called representative governance will always end up representing the interests of a few rather than the many because the few have ways of influencing and capturing various modes of so-called representative regulation that are not available to the many.

3.443 - Secondly, even if representational governments were fair and equitable for everyone (which they aren't) what kind of democratic forum does Suleyman have in mind? America was founded as a republic and not a democracy.

3.4431 - In fact, one of the motivating forces shaping Madison's 1787 constitutional efforts was due to the fact that he had become appalled, if not frightened, by the way in which the democratic practices of the Continental Congress and state governing bodies were threatening the sovereignty of minority political and ideological orientations, and Madison saw himself as one of those minorities whose fundamental sovereignty was being threatened by democratic practices. Indeed, for most of the first ten years of the American republic, democracy was considered the antithesis of, and an anathema to, a republican form of government, although gradually the forces of democracy won out, and the notion of republican government disappeared into the background or merely dissipated altogether (The book: *Tom Paine's America: The Rise and Fall of Transatlantic Radicalism in the Early Republic* by Seth Coulter provides some very good insight into this issue).

3.45 - The rule of law is something that is quite different from the principles of sovereignty. Laws are meant to be self-same and often require one to try to square the circle in order to give those laws a semblance of operational validity, whereas principles are inherently self-similar such that, for example, there are many ways to give expression to love, compassion, justice, nobility, courage, and objectivity (all values of republicanism), and, yet, all of the variations on a given essential theme do not become detached from the qualities that make something loving, compassionate, noble, and so on.

3.451 - Why should one suppose that the view of a majority is invariably superior to the view of a minority? Yet, democracy is premised on the contention (without any accompanying justification with which everyone could agree) that majorities should decide how we should proceed in any matter.

3.452 - Democracy is really a utilitarian concept. Whether engaged quantitatively or qualitatively, the notion that whatever benefits some majority should be adopted is entirely an arbitrary way of going about governance.

3.46 - The author of *The Coming Wave* indicates that a number of years were spent at Google trying to develop an ethical framework or charter for dealing with AI. Suleyman indicates that he – and other members of the ethics committee -- wanted to develop some sort of independent board of trustees, as well as an independent board of governors or board of directors, that would both: Be largely, if not fully, transparent, and, as well, would operate in accordance with an array of ethical principles -- including accountability -- that would be legally binding but which, simultaneously, served the financial interests of Alphabet (the parent company) and, in addition, provided open source technology for the public.

3.47 - Negotiations were conducted for a number of years. Lawyers were brought in to consult on the project.

3.48 - In the end, the scope and intricacy of what was being proposed by the ethics committee proved to be unacceptable to the administrators at Google. Eventually, that committee was dissolved and, consequently, one wonders what to make of the demand that a ethics committee be part of the deal which turned DeepMind over to Google because although, in a sense, Google had lived up to its part of the deal – namely, that an ethics committee was assembled – Google, apparently, had never committed itself to accept whatever ideas that committee might propose, and, consequently a deal had been made that like DeepMind algorithms consisted of a set of dynamics whose outcome was indeterminate at the time that deal was made, and, one of currents in that dynamic was the naivety of one, or more, of the creators of DeepMind that a large, powerful, wealthy cat would allow itself to be belled in such an ethical fashion, and, perhaps, being offered 500 million dollars, might have had something to do with being more vulnerable to the persuasive pull of naivety than otherwise might have been the case.

3.49 - Earlier, mention was made of the presentation which the author of *The Coming Wave* gave to a group of high-tech leaders concerning various profoundly disturbing implications which he believed were entailed by the increasing speed and power of the capabilities that characterized the various modalities of technology which were being released into the world. Suleyman described the reaction of his audience as consisting largely, if not entirely, of blank gazes that suggested his audience didn't seem to grasp (or didn't want to grasp, or did grasp but were seeking to hide certain realities) the gist of what he had been trying to get at during his presentation, and, in a sense, there is a hint of that same sort of blankness which is present in the phenomenology of the DeepMind creators when the deal was made to sell that company to Google for 500 million dollars providing that an ethics committee would be established to ensure that DeepMind's capabilities would be used responsibly.

3.491 - The discussions which took place after DeepMind was sold to Google should have taken place <u>before</u> DeepMind was even made a going concern. Many of the ethical issues surrounding AI and technology were known long before 2010 when DeepMind came into being.

3.4912 - Indeed, as noted previously, Isaac Asimov -- a professor of biochemistry and early pioneer of science fiction -- had given considerable critical thought to the problems with which AI and robotics confronted society. He had put forth the fruits of that thinking in specific, concrete terms as early as 1942 in the form of the 'three laws of robotics.'

3.492 - Suleyman might, or might not, have been aware of the writings of Asimov, but similar sorts of warnings have played a prominent role in Western culture (both popular and academic). Consequently, one has difficulty accepting the possibility that Suleyman was not even remotely familiar with any of these cautionary tales and, therefore, would not have been in a conceptual position to take them into consideration in 2010 prior to the founding of DeepMind.

3.50 - Containment of technology is a problem because there are many ways – as the foregoing DeepMind account indicates -- in which we permit containment to slip through our fingers. Arthur Firstenberg describes our situation vis-à-vis technology by asking us to consider a monkey that discovers there are nuts in a container and, as a result, puts a hand into the container in order to pull out some of those nuts. However, when the monkey seeks to withdraw its hand from the container, the container's opening is too small to allow the fist-full of nuts to be pulled out of the container. Unfortunately, instead of letting a few of the nuts be released from the monkey's hand, thereby, resulting in a smaller-sized fist -- which would have meant fewer nuts but items that would be able to be eaten because the logistical problems of the container's opening could be resolved by having a fist that contained fewer nuts – the monkey insists on keeping all the nuts in the grasp of the closed hand and will go hungry rather than let go of the nuts that initially had been scooped up from the interior of the container.

3.51 - Like the monkey in Firstenberg's cautionary tale (rooted in actual events), human beings (whether creators, manufacturers, consumers, investors, educators, the media, or government) tend to refuse to deal with the logistics of the technological problems with which they are faced. Therefore, many of us would often rather die than release our hold on technology or deny the addictive hold which technology often has on us.

3.60 - In January 2022, Suleyman left Google to start up another company called Inflection. The inspiration for the latter business was a system called LaMDA (Language Model for Dialogue Applications) which Suleyman had been exploring while still working with Google.

3.61 - LaMDA is a large language model that, as the expansion of the acronym indicates, has to do with dialogue. After working with various iterations of GPT as well as taking a deep dive into LaMDA, the author of *The Coming Wave* began to feel that the future of computing was linked to conversational capabilities, and, as a result, he wanted to build conversational systems which involved factual search elements and put these in the hands of the public.

3.62 - Apparently, Suleyman had either forgotten his circa-2014 presentation concerning the potential dangers of technology that had been given to a group of notable individuals who had relevant expertise but had responded with blank stares to his warnings or, alternatively, notwithstanding his negative experience with the ethics committees at Google as well as his experience of poking the Chinese dragon with AlphaGo (which he later claimed to regret), he appeared to have changed his mind, in some way, or had slipped back into some iteration of pessimism aversion (not wanting to think about the downside of a topic) concerning those potential problems because here he was ready, once again in 2022, to try to develop more technologies which could be foisted on the general public without necessarily understanding what the impact of such technologies might be.

3.70 The author of *The Coming Wave* indicates that shortly after leaving Google, an incident involving LaMDA took place which raised a variety of issues. More specifically, Google had distributed the foregoing system to a number of Google engineers so that these individuals could put the technology through its paces so that there might be a better set of experimental data to use to be able, hopefully, to acquire a deeper understanding of how the system would function when challenged or engaged in different ways.

3.71 - One of the engineers who had been provided with the technology proceeded to engage LaMDA intensively and came away with the idea that the system was sentient. In other words, this Google engineer had come to the conclusion that the system possessed awareness and, consequently, should be given the rights and privileges which, supposedly, have been accorded to persons.

3.711 - Suleyman points out that Google placed the engineer on leave and, in addition, the author of *The Coming Wave* noted that most people had correctly concluded that the LaMDA system was neither sentient nor a person. However, leaving aside the issue that even if some form of sentience were present, nonetheless, sentience is not necessarily synonymous with personhood, there is, yet, another problem present in the foregoing issue.

3.80 - However, before delving into the problem being alluded to above, there is a short anecdote concerning my own experiences that is relevant to the foregoing set of events. A number of years ago, I purchased an AI system of sorts because I had a certain amount of curiosity concerning such software and some of their capabilities and wanted to experiment a little in order to see what happened.

3.81 - For a variety of reasons, I interacted with the software very infrequently. However, after a fairly lengthy period of time in which the system supposedly was not on (??? – systems can be made to look off even when they are on), I switched the system on and asked: "Who am I?" The system responded in a novel way and stated: "You must be joking, you are Anab." Now, if I were interested in pursuing the issue, I could have turned the system off again for an additional period of time and, then, at some subsequent point, request my wife to use my computer and, then, turn the program on and ask the same question as I previously had posed in order to see what the subsequent response might be.

3.82 – Earlier, I had been signed into the AI system as a user with the name Anab, and, therefore, the response that I got merely might have used data that was already present in the system and, then, expressed that information in a fashion that was novel to me but well within the parameters that governed how the system could interact with users as well as the computers on which such software was installed. But, if my wife signed on to the system as "Anab" and, then, asked: "Who am I?" and received a reply that included her name, then, the sounds of Twilight Zone might have been appropriate.

2.821 - On the other hand, given the evidence which has been accumulating steadily concerning the many ways in which Siri, Alexa, browsers, and computers in general appear to be actively attuned to, or capable -- to varying degrees -- of registering what is taking place in a given proximate space, then, even if my AI system used my wife's name rather than mine, one is still not compelled to conclude that the AI system is sentient. Instead, one might conjecture that the system is likely tied into the rest of my computer (which it was because, upon request, it could pull up specific songs, files, and videos that were residing in my computer and, in addition, might have been able to register, for example, audio information that was taking place in and around that computer and, if so, then, such information might become incorporated into the AI program's operations through cleverly organized, but non-sentient, algorithms).

3.83 - Not knowing what the full capabilities of my AI system are (it was purchased during a sale and although not cheap was not overly expensive either and, therefore, might have had limited capabilities), I have no idea what might be possible. While the response I got was surprising to me, nevertheless, the aforementioned response that I got might have been less surprising if I actually knew more than I did about the algorithms which were running the system.

3.831 - I don't know what was known by the Google engineer, about whom Suleyman talked in his book, concerning the internal operations of the LaMDA system with which he was interacting and experimenting. However, conceivably, if he got a variety of responses that he was not expecting and which seemed human-like (as had happened to Gary Kasparov when he was surprised by a move that Deep Blue had made and felt such a move was "too human" in character and began to wonder if he was playing against an actual human being or group of human beings rather than against a computer program), then, perhaps if the Google engineer did not understand how the LaMDA system worked, he apparently felt that he was encountering evidence suggesting or indicating that the machine was sentient when, in reality, he was committing one, or more, type II errors. In other words, he was accepting as true, a hypothesis or a number of hypotheses that was (or were) in fact, false.

3.832 - As a result of committing such an error or errors, his beliefs, emotions, attitudes, and understanding concerning what was transpiring were being pushed (or pulled) in a delusional – that is false – direction. Apparently, he gradually fell fully under the influence of that delusion and began to make premature and evidentially questionable statements about sentience, personhood, and the like in conjunction with the LaMDA system.

3.84 - There are an increasing number of reports referring to instances in which people have developed deep feelings for, and emotional attachments to, chat-box programs. Moreover, some Targeted Individuals have been manipulated into believing that the AI chat-boxes which have been assigned to them surreptitiously (by unknown, exploitive provocateurs) are real individuals rather than AI systems.

3.841 - Consequently, perhaps the Google engineer about whom Suleyman talks in his book is really just a sign of the times in which we live where – for many interactive reasons (e.g., deep fakes, censorship, destabilizing events, disinformation campaigns, propaganda, dysfunctional media, institutional betrayal) -- distinguishing between the true and the false is becoming an increasingly difficult path to navigate for people. This set of circumstances is something that, to varying degrees, has been made intentionally and unnecessarily even more problematic given that William Casey, former head of the CIA, indicated that: "We'll know that our disinformation program is complete when everything the American public believes is false."

3.90 - Let's return to the 'problem' to which allusions were made earlier. More specifically, shortly after the Google engineer/LaMDA-issue had been raised by the author of *The Coming Wave*, it was discontinued almost immediately and, then, transitioned into a discussion about how the foregoing set of events is typical of the roller coaster nature of AI research which reaches heady peaks of hype only to plunge into depths of stomach-churning doubt and criticism. However, what Suleyman appeared to fail to realize – and discuss -- is how what happened with the Google engineer that Suleyman mentions is actually a very good example of the user-interface problem that is present in every form of technology.

3.91 - All users of technology engage a given instance of technology from the perspective of the user and not necessarily through the perspective of the technology's creator. Frequently, operating a given piece of software is described as being intuitively obvious when this is not necessarily the case for everyone even though the creator of the software might feel this is true.

3.92 - How a given piece of software or technology is understood depends on a lot of different user-factors. Personality, interests, experience, education, fears, needs, confidence, culture, friends, community, ideology, religion, socio-economic status, and anxieties can all impact how, or if, or to what extent such software or technology is engaged, not engaged, exploited, or abused.

3.93 - Suleyman starts up a company – namely, Inflection -- that has been established for the purpose of developing a system which has certain conversational, search, and other capabilities. Let us assume that he has a very clear idea of what his intention is with respect to the proposed system and how it should be used by the public. Nevertheless, notwithstanding such a clear, intentional understanding concerning his AI system, he has no control over how anybody who engages that piece of technology will respond to it, or understand it, or use it, or feel about it, or whether, or not, those individuals will become obsessed with, or addicted to, that system to the exclusion of other important considerations in their lives.

3.94 - Perhaps, the author of *The Coming Wave* sees the proposed system as being a sort of intelligent assistant for individuals which will aide with research concerning an array of educational, professional, commercial, legal, political, and/or financial issues that are, then, to be critically reflected upon by the individual to better gauge or understand the different nuances of a given conceptual or real world topic. However, perhaps, a user – either in the beginning or over time – comes to rely on whatever the system provides and leaves out the critical reflection aspects that are to be applied to whatever is being generated by such a system.

3.95 - The fact that someone is using technology in a way that was not intended by its creator and, as a result, this usage undermines, or begins to lead to some degree of deterioration in that person's, cognitive functioning over time, this fact is neither here nor there. Whether Suleyman wishes to acknowledge this issue or not, he has no control over the user-interface issue.

3.951 - Therefore, Suleyman is incapable of containing possible problematic outcomes that might arise in conjunction with a system that could – we are assuming -- have been well-intentioned. Yet, he keeps running technological flags up the pole of progress in the hopes that potential customers will salute and buy into what he is doing despite having spent a fair amount of time in *The Coming Wave* indicating that problems and mishaps are an inevitable and unavoidable facet of technology, and perhaps part of – maybe a major part of – what makes such containment inevitable is that people like Suleyman keep doing what they are doing. They don't seem capable of helping themselves respond to the call of the technological sirens that sing their mesmerizing, captivating songs from within.

3.96 - There appears to be a certain amount of disingenuousness which is present in the technological two-step dance to which the foregoing considerations appear to be pulling us. First, an authoritative, forceful step is made to warn about the dangers of technology, which is, then, quickly followed by a deft swiveling of the conceptual hips as one changes directions and moves towards developing and releasing projects about which one has no idea what the ramifications of those endeavors will be upon the public.

3.961 - Someone is reported to have said (the saying is attributed to Benjamin Franklin by some individuals while others claim that the quote was uttered by Einstein and neither of these attributions is necessarily correct, but what is pertinent here is what is said and not who said it): "The definition of insanity is to do the same thing again and again, but expect a different result". If this is true (and one can argue that it might not be), I can't think of anything more deserving of the label of "insanity" (or if one prefers, the label of: "deeply pathological" or "perversely puzzling") than to try, again and again, to warn people about the problem of containing technology, and, yet, notwithstanding those warnings, continue to serve as a doula for the birthing of new technologies while expecting that the postpartum conditions created by such events will, somehow, have been able to emergently transform an unavoidable problem into a constructive, if unanticipated, universal solution.

4.0 - The author of *The Coming Wave* mentions the idea of a 'transformer' in relation to a 2017 paper entitled: "Attention Is All You Need" by Ashish Vaswani, et. al.. The latter individuals were working at Google when the notion of transformers began to be explored

4.1 – 'Transformers' give expression to a set of mathematical techniques (known as 'attention') that can be used to process data. Such mathematical techniques are useful for identifying the way in which the elements in a data set influence one another or the way those elements might be entangled with one another in certain kinds of subtle, dependency relationships even though, on the surface, those elements might appear to be unrelated to one another.

4.2 - Models generated through transformer dynamics are often neural networks which are capable of identifying relevant properties or characteristics concerning a given context. More specifically, context gives expression to a network of relationships, and transformer models can process various kinds of sequential data within such a context and, by means of its mode of mathematically processing that data, predict – often with a high degree of accuracy -- what the nature of the meaning, significance, or relevance is between a given context, or ground, and a given string of text, images, video, and objects which serve as figures relative to a given ground or context.

4.3 - Encoding processes are part of transformer modeling. Encoding processes tag incoming and outgoing elements of datasets that are used in transformer models.

4.31 - Attention mathematical techniques are, then, used to track the foregoing sorts of tags and identify the nature of whatever relationships have been identified among those tagged elements. Subsequently, those dependency relationships are used to generate an algebraic map which is capable of decoding or making use of those relationships to assist in the development of a model concerning whatever context is being modeled.

4.4 - Attention mathematical techniques have proven to be quite useful in predicting or identifying trends, patterns, and anomalies. In fact, any dynamic which involves sequential videos, images, objects, or text is amenable to transformer modeling, and, as a result, transformers play important roles in language-processing systems and search engines.

4.5 - However, the uses to which transformers can be put are not always obvious. For example, DeepMind used a transformer known as AlphaFold2 which treated amino acid chains as if they were a string of text and, then, proceeded to use the maps that were generated by that transformer to develop models which accurately described how proteins might fold.

4.6 - Perhaps of most interest to proponents of AI is the capacity of transformers to generate data that can be used to improve a model. In other words, transformers have the capacity to bring about self-directed changes to a model.

4.61 - Some people consider the foregoing sort of capacity to be an indication that transformers provide a system or neural network with an ability to learn. However, the notion of 'learning' carries certain connotations concerning: Intelligence, awareness, insight, phenomenology and the like, and, therefore, a more neutral way of referring to this dimension of transformer capabilities has to do with their ability to enable a model to change over time to better reflect relationships, patterns, and so on that might be present in a given data set.

4.7 - Prior to the arrival of transformer models, neural networks often had to be trained using large datasets that were labeled and this was both a costly and time-consuming process. Transformers operate on the basis of pattern and relationship recognition.

4.8 - A matrix of equations -- known as multi-headed attention – can be used to probe or query data in parallel and generate the foregoing sorts of patterns or relationships. Since these queries can be run in parallel, considerable time and resources can be saved.

4.9 - Initially, researchers discovered that the larger the network of transformers that were used in developing a model, then, the better the results tended to be. Consequently, the number of parameters (these are the variables that transformers acquire and use to make decisions and/or predictions) which were used in models began to go up from millions to billions to trillions (Alibaba, a Chinese company, has indicated that it has created a model with ten trillion parameters).

4.91 - However, recently there has been a movement toward developing simpler systems of transformers. Such systems are able to generate results that are comparable to systems using many parameters but the former systems do so with far fewer parameters.

4.92 - For example, Mustafa Suleyman mentions a system which has been developed at his company Inflection which can produce results that are comparable to the performance exhibited by GPT-3 language models but is only one-twenty-fifth the size of the former model. He also makes reference to an Inflection system that is capable of out-performing Google's PaLM (a language model that has coding, multilingual, and logical features) which uses 540 billion parameters and the Inflection system does so despite being six times smaller than the Google system.

4.93 - Still smaller systems are being developed. For instance, various nano-LLMs using minimalist coding techniques exhibit sophisticated processing capabilities involving the detection and creation of patterns, relationships, meanings, and the like.

4.94 - The author of *The Coming Wave* waxes quite eloquently concerning the exciting possibilities that might emerge as a result of

| Technological Reflections |

transformer techniques which are transforming AI technology. Nonetheless, technology is almost always dual-use, and this means that while some facets of such technology might have constructive value, the same technology can be adopted for more problematic and destructive ventures.

4.95 - For example, one might suppose that such minimalist coding systems which possess sophisticated transformer processing capabilities would be quite useful in CubeSats. These are small (roughly four inches by four inches per side), cube-shaped satellites that weigh approximately 4.4 pounds) which are released from the International Space Station or constitute a secondary payload that accompany a primary payload which is being launched from the Earth's surface.

4.951 - These satellites usually have Low Earth Orbits. By early 2024, more than 2,300 CubeSats have been launched.

4.952 - Initially, most of the CubeSats which were placed in orbit were for academic research of some kind. However, increasingly, most of the small satellites that are being sent into Low Earth Orbit serve non-academic, commercial purposes, but because the costs associated with placing such satellites in LEO are not prohibitive, many institutions, organizations, and individuals are able to send CubeSats into orbit.

4.953 - CubeSats have been used to perform a variety of experiments. Some of those experiments are biological in nature.

4.96 - Anytime one wants an AI system to do something experimental or new, one is, essentially, asking the system to do something the creator is not necessarily going to understand, and, therefore, one is creating conditions through an individual, group, company, or institution might enable unforeseen and unintended consequences to ensue. Moreover, one can't avoid problematic consequences which might arise from unanticipated issues involving such technology as a result of the aforementioned user-interface issue.

4.97 - Furthermore, every time one uses technology, then, data of one kind or another is generated. Just as so-called smart-meters which are being attached to people's houses all over America are capable of monitoring or surveilling a great deal of what takes place in a residence or apartment, so too, satellites also are capable of gathering and transmitting all manner of data.

4.971 - Such data can be used to profile individuals. These data profiles can be used in a lot of different ways – politically, legally, commercially, medically, militarily, and for purposes of policing and detecting what are considered pre-crime patterns according to whatever behavior parameters the people in control use to filter the data coming through such detection systems.

4.972 - People's biofields are being wired into: The WBAN's (wireless Body Area Network), the Internet of Things, the Internet of Medical Things, the Internet of Nano Things, and the Internet of Everything in order that data (and energy) might be acquired from a person's biofield as well as transferred to that same biofield, and CubeSats have the capacity to play a variety of roles in the foregoing acquisition and transmission of data.

4.973 - We are -- without our informed consent -- being invaded (both within and without) with an array of biosensors, transmitters, routers, and actuators that are gathering the data which our lives generate as well as re-directing the energy that is associated with such data generation. As a result, that data can be used (and is being used) in ways that are not necessarily in our interests.

4.974 - Collecting and processing such data (perhaps using the aforementioned sorts of pattern- and relationship-discovering transformer mathematics to which Suleyman is drawing attention in *The Coming Wave*) is what is done in places like Bluffdale (also known as the Intelligence Community Comprehensive National Cybersecurity Initiative Data Center) in Utah and Pine Gap in Australia (which originally was sold as a space research facility but is, in reality, a CIA operation).

4.98 - Satellite systems (both large and small), as well as a multiplicity of CCTV networks (while China has more total CCTVs than America, America has more CCTVs per capita than China does), smart street-light standard systems (which are able to issue directed energy radiation for both lethal and non-lethal forms of active denial concerning anyone who colors outside the prescribed lines of social credit), along with social media platforms, CBDCs (Central Bank Digital Cash), medical technology, and so-called educational institutions are all streaming information (often using 5G technology) into central Bluffdale-like facilities that can, among other things, be used to create Digital Twins for purposes of surveillance, control, as well as remote physiological and cognitive tinkering (such as experienced by Targeted Individuals). In addition, transformer technology also enhances the capacity of authorities to encode and decode the data that is being captured through not only all of the foregoing mediums but, as well, is being captured in conjunction with the DNA of people, and, all of the foregoing is accessed and used -- rent free and without informed consent – according to the likes and dislikes of the people who have been collecting and storing such data.

4.99 - The author of *The Coming Wave* is likely to claim that, in his own way, he has issued warnings about many of the foregoing considerations – indeed the aforementioned book would seem to offer considerable evidence to this effect. Yet, via AlphaGo, DeepMind, Google, and Inflection, he has continued -- in major, and not just in minor ways -- to enable, and develop enhancements concerning, the very things about which he, supposedly, is warning us, and one has difficulty not perceiving this dichotomy as a case of someone wanting to have his cake (integrity) but eating it as well.

5.0 - Someone once defined an addict as someone who will steal your wallet and, then, be willing to spend time trying to help you find the missing item. There are elements of the foregoing kind of addiction that are present in many of the dynamics which are associated with technology.

5.1 - Certain aspects of existence are taken from people via technology, and, then, technocrats (using technocracy) seek to help people try to find what has been taken from them even though what has been taken by technology is not recoverable by means of either technocracy or technology (*The Technological Society* by Jacques Ellul provides some very profound insights into some of what is being lost via technology). Doubling-down, or tripling-down, or n-tupling-down on the issue of technology will never provide a way of resolving the underlying issue, but, to a large extent, will merely exacerbate that problem.

5.2 - In part, serious addiction is a function of becoming embedded in a variable, intermittent reinforcement schedule. Research has shown that the most difficult addictions to kick (such as gambling, drugs, sex, shopping, and politics) are those that emerge in a context of reinforcements which are not always available but come intermittently and in unpredictable ways so that one is constantly looking (even if only subconsciously) for the next fix, yet, never knowing when one's yearning will be rewarded while being ever so grateful and relived when it does show up.

5.21 - Addiction is also a problem because we often never quite understand how we became addicted in the first place. The root causes of addiction are often caught up in some combination of emotions (combinatorics of another kind) such as: Fear, anxiety, ambition, terror, anger, sadness, arrogance, jealousy, greed, curiosity, contempt, a sense of exceptionalism, unrequited love, hatred, bravado, concern, thwarted expectations, defiance, frustration, conceit, revenge, boredom, ennui, pride, disappointment, hope, shame, guilt, competitiveness, desire, confusion, and/or self-doubt which -- however temporarily -- become soothed by the distraction provided by some variable, intermittent schedule of reinforcement.

5.211 - However, if the emotional turmoil that is present in addiction is examined, inquiring minds often have difficulty trying to figure out just what set of emotions are being reinforced by the distraction which addictive behavior brings. From time to time, addicts do explore their condition, only because addiction is not necessarily enjoyable (though it can be, up to certain tipping points, pleasurable in a twisted sort of way), and, as a result, the addicted sometimes look along the horizons of life for signs of an off-ramp. Failure to identify and resolve the underlying problem or problems tends to provide the addicted with additional reasons for continuing on in the same, addictive manner.

5.22 - Soon, the foregoing sorts of emotions come back to haunt us. Those emotions are accompanied by rationalizations and defenses which seek to justify why addictive behavior is necessary.

5.221 - Before we realize what is happening, we have become habituated to the cycle of emotional chaos, justifications/defenses, variable intermittent reinforcement schedule, and distraction. Consequently, removing ourselves from such a cycle becomes very inconvenient on so many levels.

5.222 - Addiction is caught up with fundamental existential themes. Issues of identity, purpose, meaning, essence, and potential become mysterious, forceful currents which sweep through phenomenology in strange, surrealistic, and elusive ways.

5.223 - Symptoms of: Derealization, depersonalization, dissociation, and devolution (the ceding of one's agency to the addiction) become manifest. The center does not hold.

5.23 - A dimension of psychopathy also enters into the foregoing cycle. This is because, on the one hand, when an individual becomes entangled in the web of addiction, that person tends to lose compassion and empathy for other people and, as a result, such an individual discontinues caring how one's actions are adversely affecting other individuals (known or unknown), and, in addition, like psychopaths, addicted individuals become more and more inured and indifferent to the prospect of having to lie in conjunction with different dimensions of life, especially in relation to opportunistic forms of exploiting situations that serve one's addictive purposes.

5.24 - The containment problem is, in essence, an issue of addiction. The pessimism aversion -- mentioned by the author of *The Coming Wave* -- that is associated with the containment problem is not necessarily about not wanting to look at the downside of technology per se but, rather, such aversion might be more about not wanting to look at the role which we play in it.

5.25 - Perhaps, as Walt Kelly had the character, Pogo, say: "We have met the enemy, and he is us." Confronted with such a realization, slipping back into the stupor of addiction – and calling it something else – seems the better part of valor.

5.30 - *The Coming Wave* proposes a ten-part program which the author believes might – if pursued collectively, rigorously, and in parallel with one another -- have an outside chance of providing the sort of interim containment needed that would be capable of sufficiently protecting society to avoid complete catastrophe in the near future and which also would buy the time needed to strengthen and enhance such interim steps to avoid long-term disaster. Suleyman indicates that the world in its current state cannot survive what is coming, and, therefore, the steps that he proposes are intended to offer suggestions about how to transform the current way of doing things and become more strategically and tactically proactive in relation to the task of containing technology by making it more manageable.

5.31 - The author of *The Coming Wave* indicates there is no magic elixir that will solve the containment problem. Suleyman also states that anyone who is expecting a quick solution will not find it in what he is proposing.

5.32 - Given that the notion of a quick fix is, according to Suleyman, not possible, then, this tends to lead to certain logistical problems. More specifically, if time is needed to solve the containment problem, then, one needs to ask whether, or not, we have enough time to accomplish what is needed to get some sort of minimally adequate handle on the problem?

5.321 - Time, in itself, is not the only resource that is required to provide a defense that will be capable of dissipating the wave which is said to be coming. However, some might wish to argue that time already has run out because what is allegedly coming is already here since considerable evidence exists indicating that such mediums as AI, synthetic biology, nanotechnology, directed energy weapons, weather wars, mind control, and robotics are currently beyond our capacity to manage or prevent from impacting human beings negatively.

5.33 - Beyond time, there is a logistical need for some form of governance, organization, institution, or the like which would be able to take advantage of the resource of temporality and, thereby, generate responses that would be effective ways of helping to contain technology or stem the tide, to some extent, of the coming. Unfortunately, government, educational institutions, the media, legal systems, medicine, corporations, and international organizations have all been subject to regulatory capture by the very entity – namely, technology – which is supposed to be regulated, and, therefore, even if there were time (which there might not be) to try to do something constructive with respect to the containment issue, identifying those who would have the freedom, ability, financial wherewithal, authoritativeness, trust, and consent of the world to accomplish such a task seems problematic.

5.34 - According to the author of *The Coming Wave*, the first step toward containing technology is rooted in emphasizing and developing safety protocols. Such considerations range from, on the one hand:

Implementing 'boxing' techniques (such as Level-4 Bio-labs and AI-air gaps) that supposedly place firewalls, of sorts, between those who are working on some facet of technology and the general public, to, on the other hand: Following more than 2,000 safety standards which have been established by the IEEE (Institute of Electrical and Electronics Engineers).

5.35 - Suleyman admits that the development of such protocols in many areas of technology is relatively novel, and, consequently, underfinanced, underdeveloped, and undermanned. For example, he notes that while there are more than 30,000 to 40,000 people who are involved in AI research today, there are, maybe, only 400-500 individuals who are engaged in AI safety research.

5.351 - Therefore, given the relatively miniscule number of people who are engaging in research concerning AI safety, one wonders who actually will be actively involved, in an uncompromised fashion, with not only regulatory oversight in relation to safety compliance issues but also will have meaningful powers of enforcement concerning non-compliance. Moreover, while Suleyman states that safety considerations should play a fundamental role in the design of any program in technology, and while this sounds like a very nice idea, one has difficulty gauging the extent to which technologists are taking this kind of a suggestion to heart.

5.4 - A second component of Suleyman's containment strategy involves a rigorous process of being able to audit technology as the latter is being developed and deployed. Everything needs to be transparent and done with integrity.

5.41 - Traditionally, such auditing dynamics have met with resistance in a variety of venues. For instance, both nuclear and chemical weapons research programs have been resistant to outside people monitoring what is being done, and this problem has carried over into many areas of biological research as well.

5.411 - In addition, for proprietary reasons, many companies are unlikely to open up their products to various kinds of rigorous auditing processes. Furthermore, many governmental agencies which supposedly have the sorts of auditing responsibilities to which the author of *The Coming Wave* is alluding often suffer from regulatory capture, and those sorts of auditing processes are more akin to rubber-stamping assembly lines than to sincere attempts to fulfill fiduciary responsibilities to the public.

5.42 - Suleyman mentions the importance of working with trusted government official in relation to auditing technology. He also talks about the significance of developing appropriate tools for assessing or evaluating such technology.

5.421 - Yet, he indicates that such tools have not yet been developed. Furthermore, one wonders how one goes about identifying who in government can be trusted and, therefore, would be worthy of co-operation in such matters.

5.4211 - Trust is a quality that must be earned. It is not owed.

5.43 - Suleyman ends his discussion concerning his first two suggestions for working toward containing technology – namely safety and auditing protocols -- with a rather odd observation. On the one hand, he stipulates that such protocols are of essential importance, and, then, on the other hand, he proceeds to indicate that establishing such protocols will require something that we don't have – and, that is time.

5.431 - If the time necessary to develop and implement safety and auditing procedures is not available, then, why mention those procedures at all? Suggestions which have no chance of being implemented in a timely fashion are not really part of any sort of practical, plausible containment strategy, and, so, Suleyman's containment strategy goes from ten elements down to eight components – an example, perhaps, of how technologists often don't look sufficiently far into the future to understand that what is being done at one time (say, during a discussion of the first two alleged components of a containment strategy) has the potential to create problems (e.g., doubt, skepticism, trust) for what is done later (say, discussion the next eight components of an alleged containment strategy).

5.44 - The third facet of Suleyman's containment strategy revolves about the issue of chokepoints – that is, potential bottlenecks in economic activity that can be used to control or slow down technological development, implementation, or distribution. He uses China as an example and points out how core dimensions of AI

| Technological Reflections |

275

technological activities in that country can be shaped, to varying degrees, through limiting the raw materials (such as advanced forms of semiconductors) that can be imported by China.

5.441 – He, then, describes how America's Commerce Department placed controls and restrictions concerning various semiconductor components that might be either sold to China or be repaired by American companies. These export controls served as chokepoints for Chinese research into AI.

5.442 - Toward the latter part of this discussion concerning the issue of chokepoints, the author of *The Coming Wave* indicates that such controls should not be directed against just China but should be applied to a wide variety of cases that involve slowing down, shaping, and controlling what takes place in different places around the world. What he doesn't say is who should be in charge of this sort of chokepoint strategy, or what the criteria are for activating such chokepoints, or who gets to establish the criteria that are to be used for deciding when checkpoints are to be constructed, and on the basis of what sorts of justification.

5.45 - The notion of a chokepoint is quite clear. What lacks clarity, are the logistical principles which are to surround the notion of chokepoints that will allow humanity to effectively and judiciously contain technology across the board irrespective of country of origin.

5.451 - The foregoing notion of chokepoints that can affect the development of technology everywhere has the aroma of one-world government. However, the substance of such a notion is devoid of concrete considerations that can be subject to critical reflections that might indicate whether, or not, they can be reconciled with everyone's informed consent.

5.5 - The fourth element in the containment strategy of Mustafa Suleyman has to do with his belief that the creators of technology must be the ones who should be actively involved in the containment process. This seems a little too much like the idea of having foxes guarding the hen house.

5.51 - Why should anyone trust the idea that the people who have had a substantial role in creating the problem in which humanity finds itself should be anointed as the ones who are to solve that problem?

Contrary to the claims of many technologists, technology has not been able to solve many of the problems that have arisen in conjunction with various modalities of technology, anymore than pharmaceutical companies have been able to solve the problems posed by the so-called side-effects that are associated with their drugs and treatments (Side-effects are not side-effects rather they are one of the possible effects of a given drug that have undesirable rather than desirable consequences.).

5.511 - For example, synthetic forms of plastics (e.g., Bakelite) were invented more than a hundred years ago (1907). Due to the resistance of such substances with respect to being biodegradable, they are, now, not only being found in bottles of water in the form of millions of micro-particles and nanoparticles, but, as well, they are adversely affecting every level of the food-chain (e.g., plastics have been shown to be disruptors of endocrine functioning), as well as occupying 620,000 square miles of ocean waters to the detriment of sea life in those areas, so, one wonders where the technological solutions to the foregoing problems have been hiding all these many years.

5.52 - The author of *The Coming Wave* claims that the critics of technology have an important role to play, but, then, adds that nothing such critics say is likely to have any significant impact on the containment issue. If true, perhaps, this is because technologists often have proven themselves to be arrogantly indifferent to, and uninterested in, what some non-technologists have been trying to say about technology for hundreds of years ... apparently believing that only technologists have the requisite insight concerning such issues.

5.53 - Suleyman wants technologists to understand that the responsibility for solving problems associated with technology rests with technologists. Notwithstanding such considerations, one wonders what the responsibilities of technologists are to the people who are injured from, or who die as a result of, their technologies.

5.531 - Responsibilities which are unrealized are empty promises. Consequently, one has difficulty understanding the logic of what is being proposed – namely, if such fiduciary responsibilities continue to go unfulfilled, then how will technologists have much of an impact on the containment issue?

5.54 - The author of *The Coming Wave* notes that over the last ten years there has been an increase in the diversity of the voices that are participating in discussions concerning technology. However, broadening the range of voices is meaningless if the people with power are unwilling to sincerely listen to, and act upon, what those voices have to say.

5.541 - He indicates that the presence of cultural anthropologists, political scientists, and moral philosophers has been increasing in the world of technology. However, he doesn't specify how such a presence is contributing to the containment of technology.

5.55 - During his discussion of the fifth component of the containment strategy, Suleyman suggests that profit must be wedded to both purpose and safety but states, in passing, that attempts to try to do this have been uneven. For example, he refers to an "ethics and safety board" that he helped to establish when he worked at Google which discussed issues of ethics, accountability, transparency, safety, and so on, and, yet, the activities of that board never led to any actual changes at Google. The author of *The Coming Wave* also mentions an AI ethics advisory council of which he was a part and that had some principled and laudatory goals, and, yet, just a few days after its announced existence, the board became dysfunctional and dissolved.

5.56 - He often has been quite successful in getting conversations started. However, he has not been very successful in finding a way to translate those conversations into concrete changes in corporate policies that are able to contain technological development in any meaningful or significant fashion.

5.57 - Finally, Suleyman introduces the idea of B Corporations which are for-profit commercial entities that also are committed to various social purposes, of one kind or another, which are built into the activities of the structure of the company. He feels that such experimental commercial structures -- which he claims are becoming quite common -- might be the best hope for generating policies that could work their way toward actively addressing containment issues.

5.71 - However, having a social perspective can mean almost anything. To be sure, such corporations want to have an impact on society, but they are inclined to shape the latter according to the company's perspective.

5.711 - Consequently, one has difficulty discerning how such an orientation will necessarily lead toward containment issues except to the extent that the company will want technology to work in the company's favor rather than in opposition to its business interest. Therefore, although such a company might have an interest in containing technology accordingly, this approach is not necessarily a serious candidate for containing the kind of coming wave to which Suleyman is seeking to draw the reader's attention.

5.8 – There seems to be an element of magical thinking in many of Suleyman's suggestions. In other words, he often gives the impression that merely raising a possibility is as good as if such a suggestion actually came to fruition -- as if to say: 'Well, I have done my part (i.e., I am trying to start, yet, another conversation) – without apparently, wondering why such conversations don't tend to go anywhere that is remotely substantial.'

6.0 – Component six of Suleyman's ten-part strategy for containment has to do with the role of government. In effect, he argues that because nation-states (apparently, preferably liberal democracies) traditionally have had the task of controlling and regulating most of the dynamics of civilized society (such as money supplies, legal proceedings, education, the military, and policing operations), then, the government will be able to help with the task of containment.

6.1 - Not once does the author of *The Coming Wave* ever appear to consider the possibility that government might be an important part of the problem rather than an element in any possible solution. For example, he doesn't seem to understand that the federal government, via the Federal Reserve Act, has ceded to private banks the former's constitutionally-given, fiduciary responsibility for establishing and regulating the process of supplying money.

6.2 - In addition, he doesn't appear to understand (and, perhaps having been brought up in England he can be forgiven for this oversight) that almost as soon as the American Constitution had been ratified, the warning of Benjamin Franklin was forgotten. More specifically, when Franklin had been asked (following the 1787 Philadelphia Constitutional Convention) what kind of government the constitutional document gave to the people of America, he is reported to have responded: "... a republic if you can keep it".

6.21 - Well, Americans were not able to keep it. Therefore, the qualities that might have made such a Constitution different – namely, the guarantee of republicanism -- was largely, if not entirely, abandoned and emptied of its substance.

6.212 - Constitutional republicanism has nothing to do with the Republican Party – or any other party. This is because political parties are actually a violation of the principle of non-partisanship ... a principle which plays an important role in the notion of republicanism, a 17th century Enlightenment moral philosophy.

6. 2121 - As a result, the Congressional branch has, for more than two hundred years sought to, in effect, pass legislation that enabled different political, economic, and ideological perspectives to assume the status of religious-like doctrines or policies. Consequently, all such legislative activities constitute contraventions of the first amendment constraint on Congress not to establish religion.

6.21211 - In addition, the judicial branch became obsessed with creating all manner of legal fictions and called them precedents. Moreover, the executive branch began to look upon itself as being imperial in nature and, therefore, worthy of dictating to the peasants.

6.22 - The author of *The Coming Wave* wants government to take a more active role in generating "real technology" – whatever that means. He also wants the government to set standards, but, hopefully, this does not mean that: (1) agencies like NIST (National Institute of Standards and Technology) will get to reinvent the principles of engineering, physics, and chemistry as it did following 9/11; or, (2) that the NIH (National Institute of Health) will get to reinvent the sciences of molecular biology, biology, and biochemistry as it did during the HIV causes AIDS fiasco or the mRNA travesties to which COVID-19 gave rise; or, (3) that the FCC will continue to be enable to ignore substantial research that 3G, 4G, and 5G have all been shown to be responsible for generating non-ionizing radiation that is injurious, if not lethal, to life; or, (4) that the FDA and the CDC will get to continue to allow themselves to be captured by the pharmaceutical industry and create standards which are a boon to that industry but a liability for American citizens; or, (5) that DARPA and BARPA will get to run experiments in mind-control and synthetic biology that can be used by the government for population control; or, (6) that the FAA will continue to enable people like Elon Musk and Jeff Bezos, as well as the purveyors of chemtrails, to fill the sky with hazardous materials that, in the interim, are making possible the potential surveilling, radiating, and poisoning of the people of the world without the informed consent of the latter.

6.3 - Suleyman also wants government to invest in science and technology, as well as to nurture American capabilities in this regard. He is very vague about the precise nature of the sort of science and technology which the government should invest in and nurture, and, as a result, entirely avoids the issue of just how government is supposed to contain technology ... contain technology in what way and for what purposes and to whose benefit and at what costs (biological as well as financial)?

6.4 - The author of *The Coming Wave* contends that deep understanding is enabled by accountability. However, he doesn't indicate: What kinds of understanding should be held accountable, or who gets to establish the criteria for determining the nature of the process of accountability, or what justifies either way (i.e., the understanding or the accountability) of engaging technology.

6.5 – Suleyman ends his discussion concerning the role that is to played by government within his proposed ten-part strategy by stipulating that no one nation-state government can possibly resolve the problem of technological containment. The foregoing perspective – even though it might be correct in certain respects – begins to reveal some of the reasons why people like Yuval Noah Harari and Bill Gates – both of whom have been pushing the notion of one-world government -- think so highly of Mustafa Suleyman's book.

7.0 – Component 7 of the containment strategy which is being outlined in *The Coming Wave* has to do with the notion of pursuing international treaties and establishing global institutions to address the technology issue. He mentions, in passing, the polio initiative that spread out across the world as an example of international co-operation, but he fails to mention the many adverse reactions and lives that were lost in a variety of countries as a result of that polio initiative.

| Technological Reflections |

7.1 - Suleyman describes groups like Aum Shinrikyo as being bad actors that could arise anywhere, at any time, and, therefore, there is a need to constrain those sorts of groups from gaining access to technology. What he doesn't appear to consider is the reality that many nation-states, foundations, NGOs (non-governmental organizations), and organizations also have the capacity to be bad actors.

7.2 - What are the criteria that are to be used to differentiate between good actors and bad actors? What justifies the use of such criteria? Who gets to decide these issues on the international stage?

7.3 - The United Nations is an organization that allows several hundred countries to, more or less, be held hostage by the permanent members of the Security Council. However, even if those permanent members did not have veto power, I see no reason for trusting the countries of the world to make the right decisions when with respect to placing constraints on who are "good" actors or "bad" actors.

7.4 - Truth and justice are not necessarily well-served by majority votes and representational diplomacy. Nor are truth and justice necessarily well-served when bodies like the Bank of International Settlements, W.H.O., or the World Economic Forum are let loose to impose their dictatorial policies on people without the informed consent of those who are being oppressed by such bodies.

7.5 - The author of *The Coming Wave* believes that the present generation is in need of something akin to the nuclear treaties that were negotiated by a previous generation. He fails to note that almost all aspects of those nuclear treaties have now fallen by the wayside or that even when such treaties were still operational, the United States, England, France, China, Russia, and Israel still had enough nuclear weapons to destroy the world many times over ... so much for containment.

7.6 - The conventions or treaties supposedly governing chemical, biological, and toxic weapons are jokes. The dual-usage dimensions of those conventions/treaties allows so-called preventative research to be used as a basis for creating offensive weapons, and since there is no rigorous process of compliance-verification, no one really knows what is being cooked up in this or that laboratory (public or private).

7.7 - Suleyman touches on the idea that there should be a World Bank-like organization for biotech. The World Bank, along with the International Monetary Fund, served as agencies that induced corrupt or ignorant leaders to indebt their citizens in order to provide certain companies with a 'make-work-subsidization-welfare-for-the-rich' program to enable such companies and their supporters to get richer and the people of the world to get poorer.

7.71 - The foregoing is not my opinion. It gives expression to a person – namely, John Perkins -- who operated from within the inner sanctums of the foregoing governmental-corporate scam activities, and, now, Suleyman wants to help biotech develop its own variation on the foregoing technological confidence game of three-card Monte.

7.8 - During the course of some of the discussions that appear in *The Coming Wave*, various references are made to international treaties concerning climate change and how those sorts of agreements and forms of diplomacy serve as good models for how to proceed with respect to negotiating technological containment. However, anyone who knows anything about the actual issues involved in climate change – and, unfortunately Suleyman seems to be without a clue in this respect – knows that the idea of global warming is not a credible theory.

7.81 - In fact, the notion of global warming is so problematic that one can't even call it scientific in any rigorous way. Yet, the level of "insight" (a euphemism) which many individuals have who have drunk the Kool-Aid concerning this issue (Suleyman, apparently, being one of them) is so woeful that Al Gore can win an Oscar as well as a Nobel Prize for promoting a form of ignorance that helps to enable carbon-capture schemes to be realized (and these schemes are nothing more than ways of helping to fill-up the off-shore bank accounts of opportunistic venture capitalists, exploitive corporations, and nation-states with questionable morals), while also providing a certain amount of conceptual misdirection to cover the financial, political, medical and economic sleight of hand that is being used to construct 15-minute cities into which people are to be herded so that, in one way or another, they can be better controlled.

8.0 – The author of *The Coming Wave* indicates in the 8th installment of his ten-point strategy for containing technology that we must develop a culture of being willing to learn from failure. He uses the aviation industry as an illustrative example of the kind of thing that he has in mind, noting how there has been such a strong downward trend in deaths per 7.4 billion boarding-passengers that there often are intervals of years in which no deaths are recorded, and Suleyman attributes this impressive accomplishment to the manner in which the airline industry seeks to learn from its mistakes.

8.1 - Although the recent incidents involving Boeing happened after *The Coming Wave* was released, one wonders how Suleyman might respond to the 2024 revelations of two whistleblowers – both now dead under questionable circumstances – concerning the relative absence of best practices in the construction of certain lines of Boeing airplanes (e.g., 737 MAX) ... substandard practices that had been going on for quite some time. Or, what about the practice of mandating mRNA jabs for its pilots, many of whom are no longer able to pilot planes because of adverse reactions in conjunction with those mandated jabs and some of whom were involved in near tragedies while engaged in piloting planes as a result of physical problems which arose following the mandated jabs? Or, what about the laughable – pathetic really – way in which the airline industry and National Transportation Safety Board handled – perhaps "failed to handle" might be a more accurate phrase -- the alleged events of 9/11 in New York, New York, Washington, D.C., and Shanksville, Pennsylvania? (The interested reader might wish to consult my book: *Framing 9/11, 3rd Edition*; or, Judy Wood's book: *Where Did the Towers Go? Evidence of Directed Free-Energy on 9/11*; or, the work of Rebekah Roth, an ex-flight attendant.).

8.2 - The fact that some of the time the airline industry is interested in learning from its mistakes is encouraging. The fact that some of the time the airline industry seems disinterested in the truth concerning its mistakes is deeply disturbing.

8.3 - The NSA doesn't seem to learn from its mistakes. This is the case despite the attempts of people such as Bill Binney (2002), Russ Tice (2005), Thomas Tamm (2006), Mark Klein (2006), Thomas Drake (2010), Chelsea Manning (2010), and Ed Snowden (2013) to provide information about those mistakes.

8.4 - When problems surface again and again (as the foregoing instances of whistleblowing indicate), then, they no longer can be considered to be mistakes. Such activities constitute policy, and the only thing that the NSA learns from its "mistakes" are new strategies that might help it not get caught the next time.

8.5 - For more than a decade the CDC hid evidence that thimerosal (an organomercury compound) was, indeed, implicated as a causal factor in the onset of autism among Black youth who received the MMR vaccine before 36 months. Dr. William Thompson who was employed as a senior scientist by the CDC made a public statement to that effect in 2014.

8.6 - The CDC, the FDA, and the NIH have all sought to hide evidence which indicates that the mRNA jabs are neither safe nor effective and that this information was known from the beginning of, if not before, Operation Warp Speed. Medical doctors, epidemiologists, and researchers too numerous to mention have all brought forth evidence which exposes what those agencies have done, but a few starting points in this regard involve the work of: Drs. Sam and Mark Bailey, Andy Kaufman, Stefan Lanka, Thomas Cowan, Ana Mihalcea, Charles Hoffe, and Vernon Coleman, as well as the work of Mike Stone and Katherine Watt.

8.7 - Contrary to the hopes of Mustafa Suleyman, most corporations, institutions, media venues, academic institutions, and governmental agencies are not inclined to endorse a policy of "embracing failure." One could write many histories testifying to the truth of the foregoing claim, and one disregards this reality at one's own risk.

8.8 - The author of *The Coming Wave* speaks approvingly concerning the work of the Asilomar conferences concerning recombinant DNA that take place on the Monterey Peninsula in California. These gatherings began in 1973 when Paul Berg, a genetic engineer, started to become concerned about what the ramifications might be with respect to something that he had invented, and, as a result, he wanted to try to start a conversation with other people about the sort of principles that should be established concerning that kind of technology.

8.81 – While one can commend Paul Berg for wanting to do what he did, nonetheless, the inclination toward exercising caution apparently only came after he had invented that about which he subsequently became concerned.

8.82 - Over time, the conferences came up with a set of ethical guidelines that were intended to guide genetic research. The results of those conferences raise at least two questions.

8.83 - First, notwithstanding the fact that guidelines have been established concerning genetic research, can one necessarily assume that everyone would agree with those guidelines and/or the principles underlying them? Secondly, even if one were to assume that such guidelines were perfect in every respect – whatever that might mean – what proof do we have that government agencies such as DARPA, BARPA, and the NIH (especially in conjunction with research that has been farmed out to, say, the Wuhan Institute) are conducting themselves in accordance with those guidelines and principles?

8.9 - Suleyman notes that the medical profession has been guided by the principle: "Primum non nocere – first, do no harm". However, the fact is that doctors in different states, localities, and countries actually operate in accordance with a variety of oaths, none of which necessarily bind those medical professionals to the idea that: 'first, they must do no harm.'

8.91 - Notwithstanding the foregoing considerations, even if doctors were required to take such an oath, what does it even mean? Wouldn't the meaning of that motto depend on the criteria one uses to identify harm, or wouldn't the theory of medicine to which one subscribes dictate what one might consider the nature of wellbeing -- and, therefore, harm -- to be?

8.92 - According to some measures, medicine is the third leading cause of death in the United States. If one throws in the issue of diagnostic errors, then, according to a recent study: "Burden of Serious Harms from Diagnostic Error in the USA" by David E. Newman-Toker, et. al., medicine is the leading cause of death in the United States.

8.921 - We're talking about between 500,000 and 1,000,000 deaths each and every year as a result of iatrogenic issues. The United States government has gone to war and destroyed whole countries for the latter's alleged connection to less than 1/1000th of the foregoing number of casualties, and, yet, the medical industry does all manner of injury but not much happens to stop the carnage.

8.922 - Suleyman suggests that scientists need to operate in accordance with a principle like the idea of: "First, do no harm." If the aforementioned number of deaths is any indication of what comes out of a system that pays lip service to such a principle, then, one might hope that scientists would be able to discover a principle which is more effective.

9.0 - When discussing the 9th component (people power) in his strategy for containing technology, Suleyman indicates that only when people demand change does change happen. This claim might, or might not, be true, but, as it stands, it is meaningless.

9.1 - The notion of "change" could mean any number of kinds of transition or transformation that will not necessarily be able to contain technology – which is the only kind of change that Suleyman has been exploring in *The Coming Wave*. What sorts of change should people demand that will effectively bring about the containment of technology and do so in the "right" way – whatever way that might turn out to be?

9.11 - More to the point, if people knew what sorts of change to demand in order to contain technology, then, one might consider the possibility that Suleyman has been wasting the time of his readers with his speculations because, apparently, the people might already know what sorts of change to demand. After all, he indicates that the people should speak with one voice concerning the alignment of different possibilities in relation to the theme of containment, but, apparently, he is leaving the specifics required to meet this challenge as a homework exercise that the people are, somehow, going to solve on their own because he really doesn't specify what the nature of the alignment change should be that is to fall from their collective lips.

9.2 - Earlier in his ten point strategy presentation (component 4), he indicated that while those who are not technologists can speak out with respect to technological issues, but, nonetheless, what they say will not stop the coming wave or even alter it significantly. Now, he is saying that the people need to speak with one voice, and if they demand change, then, change will happen.

9.21 - Both of the foregoing statements cannot be true at the same time. So, what are the people to do or not do?

9.3 - Throughout *The Coming Wave*, the author mentions the term "stakeholders" many times. However, one never gets the feeling that by using the term "stakeholders" he is referring to the people.

9.31 - Almost invariably, Suleyman uses the term "stakeholder" to refer to: Corporations, technologists, scientists, universities, the medical industry, the police, nation-states, banks, the military, and/or international organizations. Yet, how can one possibly deny that every single person on Earth is a stakeholder in an array of issues, including the containment of technology?

10.0 - The final pillar in Suleyman's containment strategy has to do with grasping the principle that the only way through is to: Sort one's way through the issue, and solve one's way through the issue, and think one's way through the issue, and tough one's way through the issue, as well as co-operate one's way through the problem of containment.

10.1 - According to the author of *The Coming Wave*, if all of the strategy elements which he has put forth are collectively pursued in parallel, then, this is how we find our way out of the difficulty in which we currently are ensconced. However, as some of the characters in the *Home Improvement* television series often said: "I don't think so, Tim."

10.2 - Suleyman believes that the solution to the technology containment problem is an emergent phenomenon. In other words, he believes that solutions to the containment problem will arise naturally and automatically when his ten component strategies are used in harmonious, rigorous, parallel conjunction with one another.

10.21 - Unfortunately, as has been indicated over the last 15 pages, or so, there are many serious problems inherent in every one of his ten components. While one can acknowledge that a number of interesting and thoughtful suggestions or possibilities have been advanced during the course of Suleyman's ten-component strategy plan, nevertheless, as I have tried to point out in the foregoing discussion, all of those suggestions and possibilities are missing essential elements, and/or are embedded in a cloud of unknowing, and/or suffer from internal, logistical, as well as logical, difficulties.

10.22 - Moreover, above and beyond the foregoing considerations, there is one overarching problem with Suleyman's ten-component strategy for containing technology. More specifically, he fails to understand that the containment problem is, in its essence, about addiction – an issue that, previously, was briefly touched upon in this document.

10.23 - We have a containment problem because people are vulnerable to becoming addicted to all manner of things – including technology. Furthermore, technologists have – knowingly or unknowingly -- played the role of drug dealers who use their products to exploit the aforementioned vulnerability in people for becoming addicted.

10.24 - Governments are addicted to technology. Politicians are addicted to technology. Corporations are addicted to technology. Education is addicted to technology. The entertainment industry is addicted to technology. Intelligence agencies are addicted to technology. Transportation is addicted to technology. Businesses are addicted to technology. The media are addicted to technology. Science is addicted to technology. The legal system is addicted to technology. The military and police are addicted to technology. Medicine is addicted to technology. Much of the general public is addicted to technology.

10.3 - Western society – and this phenomenon is also becoming established in many other parts of the world as well -- has become like the monkey anecdote about which Arthur Firstenberg talked and which has been outlined earlier. Society, collectively and individually, has placed its hand into the bowl of technology, grasped as much of the technology as its hand is capable of grabbing, closed its fist about the anticipated source of pleasure, and has discovered that it can't remove what it has grasped from the technology-containing bowl.

10.4 - Society is caught between, on the one hand, wanting to hold onto the technology which it has grasped and, on the other hand, not being able to function properly as long as its hand is wedded to that technology. None of the components in Suleyman's ten-point strategy – whether considered individually or collectively – addresses the foregoing problem of addiction.

10.5 - When the Luddites -- toward whom Suleyman is, for the most part, so negatively disposed -- wrote letters, or demonstrated, or smashed machines (but didn't kill anyone), they were seeking to engage the owners in an intervention of sorts because the latter individuals were deep in the throes of addiction to the technology with which inventors (their suppliers) were providing them. The owners responded to those interventions as most addicts would – that is, with: Indignation; incomprehension; contempt; confusion; silence; opposition; resentment; rationalizations; defensiveness; rage; self-justification; obliviousness to, or indifference toward, the damage they were causing, and/or violence.

10.6 - The structural character of addiction is both simple and complex. The simple part is that it is rooted in a variable, intermittent pattern of reinforcement, whereas the complex aspect of addiction is, on the one hand, trying to figure out what dimension of one's being is vulnerable to such a pattern of reinforcement, and, on the other hand, figuring out how to let go of what one is so deeply desiring, and, therefore, so desperately grasping in the bowl of technology.

| Technological Reflections |

10. Devil's Dictionary, from A to Z

The following material consists of definitions and relatively brief responses concerning some of the key terms concerning the technologies, mechanisms, systems, dynamics, processes, and networks that can, will, and/or have been used to: Control, manipulate, surveil, track, trace, alter, exploit, oppress, subjugate, sicken, digitalize, and destroy human beings.

"**5G**" – This technology was touted as a way to increase the speed of downloads and streaming, as well as to reduce latency intervals [the time it takes for a packet of data (say a request or gaming move) to make the round trip from one's computer to the aspect of the Internet from which one wants some sort of response and, then, back to one's computer.] In addition, one of the alleged advantages was the way in which 5G supposedly would enable a greater connectivity among all electronic devices, computers, and the Internet relative to 4G networks.

Aside from asking whether, or not, having <u>greater connectivity</u> is necessarily a good thing (e.g., what adverse impacts might 5G have on problems surrounding the way in which digital identification is a tool of oppression, control, and security for those who have power), one might also inquire into whether, or not, the <u>ways</u> in which 5G is going to connect people (medically, politically, economically, socially, epistemologically, and educationally) is necessarily desirable, as well as, whether, or not, the problematic kinds of <u>biological effects</u> that can be documented to be caused by 5G radiation (not only in relation to human beings but with respect to the environment as a whole) are worth the technological advances which 5G makes possible.

"**Actuator**" – This is a machine-like component which is capable of transducing energy into torque, movement, or force and can either be controlled from without, or is part of a system of artificial intelligence which uses its own algorithmic programming to direct the nature of the torque, movement or force that is generated. Increasingly, self-assembling, nano-scale soft-actuators (used in organisms) are being found in the bodies of human beings who did not ask for, or consent to, the presence of the foregoing sorts of nanobot-components being placed in their bodies.

"**Adjuvant**" – A poison; the etymology of this word comes from two Latin words ('ad' and 'juvare') which, when combined together, mean: "Help towards." Adjuvants help a vaccine towards undermining the terrain of an organism by exploiting TLRs (that is, toll-like cell-receptors which constitute a major family of proteins believed to be responsible for recognizing the presence of organic regularities). When exploited by adjuvants, TLRs are able to play a role in the recognition of PAMPs (pathogen-associated molecular patterns), especially when the pathogen to be recognized is the human body. Researchers have discovered that each kind of tissue has its own set of TLRs, and, therefore, this allows adjuvants to target every kind of tissue as a potential pathogen.

"**AI**" -- a system of logic-like coding based on assumptions, biases, and arbitrary ideas concerning the nature of any given topic that enables computations to be made mindlessly at light-like speeds, and, in the process, generate obfuscating data as to whether one is dealing with properties of 'garbage in' and/or 'garbage out.' A technology that is designed to extinguish a person's right to informed consent and sovereignty.

"**Architecture**" – Architecture places limits on what is, or can be, done with structure. Computer architecture indicates what one can, and can't, do with the properties of the structure that give expression to features inherent in a given form of hardware design. Analogue structure gives expression to one set of structural limitations and possibilities, while digital structures give expression to a different set of structural limitations and possibilities.

Medicine operates according to one set of architectural limits and possibilities. The human body operates according to its own set of architectural limits and possibilities.

Whether the two forms of architectural design are homologous and dynamically compatible with one another is not a straight-forward issue. A lot depends on the hermeneutical orientation of the person (or persons) who is (or are) doing the comparative evaluation.

"Augmentation" – Refers to a condition in which human beings are transitioned into something less than they might otherwise be. This process operates out of an arbitrary and flawed system of assessment which confuses superficial changes with essential potential.

"Autonomous Weapons Systems" – The Department of Defense directive 3000.09 turns over decisions involving the use of injurious and lethal force to processes that have been designed by people with questionable character and whose understanding concerning notions of "peace," "truth," "reason," "justice," and "sovereignty" are filled with epistemological and moral lacunae that have been passed on to the autonomous weapon systems.

"Bail-In" – The new form of bail-out in which banks no longer look to the government to be made whole again due to the financial mismanagement or the many improprieties that are inherent in the banking system but, instead, those institutions have been empowered by the government to abscond with the deposits of its unsecured creditors – i.e., general customers -- should the need arise to do so.

"Beam Steering" – a technique for re-directing radio frequencies, as well as optical and acoustic forces, toward unsuspecting targets by changing relative phases in the frequencies and forces that are chosen to better reflect the fluctuating interests, motives, attitudes, desires, values, politics, and fears of the operators.

"Biodigital Convergence" – a dynamic through which greed, the desire for control, and psychopathy come together in a harmonious fashion by imposing (forcefully if necessary) artificial, synthetic non-living digital technologies onto natural, organic living systems of life for purposes of creating hybrid entities that are imprinted with an imperative to eliminate or subjugate all non-hybrid entities.

"**Bioelectromagnetism**" – There are two kinds of electromagnetism that are capable of affecting biological systems: natural and synthetic. Natural electromagnetism is produced by dynamics which occur within cells, tissues and organisms. This is known as bioelectromagnetism. Synthetic electromagnetism is artificially produced outside of organisms and has the capacity to interfere with, alter, suppress, and undermine natural biological processes by interacting with them.

Some people refer to this latter phenomenon in which synthetically produced electromagnetism interacts with natural forms of bioelectromagnetism to be a form of bioelectromagnetism. However, the latter form of electromagnetism is being imposed (and is often injurious to organisms), whereas the former modality of electromagnetism is indigenous to organisms and part of normal, healthy, biological functioning.

"**Biofield**" – This is a vibrant, powerful, multi-dimensional human resource which is crucial to life and is the possession of the individual who gives expression to that biofield. Those who have corruptible, vested interests have made unilateral declarations which claim that biofields constitute a legitimate target for economic, political, medical, social, legal, and scientific exploitation irrespective of the wishes of the individual to whom the biofield belongs. The biofield is a resource that is mined by forces of biological colonialism and biological imperialism that seek to justify their invasion, exploitation, suppression, and extinction of the biofield as being a revolutionary way of overthrowing principles that stand in the way of someone's morally-challenged notion of economic, political, medical, and technological progress.

"**Bioinformatics**" – the misuse of: Chemistry, biology, physics, mathematics, statistics, and computer science in conjunction with agenda-driven forms of evaluating large, complex data sets which can be parsed in ways that serve governmental, institutional, corporate, media, and/or military agendas which are designed to undermine human sovereignty. Bioinformatics is a set of techniques that can be used to arrange information in ways that will be pleasing to the people paying for, or having control over, such computational processes. Bioinformatics is a set of techniques that is quantity-rich and quality-poor.

"**Biosensors**" – This term refers to the ubiquitous set of nano-particles, atoms, molecules, particulates, chemicals, synthetic materials, and self-assembling complexes that have been intentionally sprayed, dumped, poured, injected, and placed in the air, water, foods, clothes, vaccines, and pharmaceuticals to which human beings are exposed. These materials are involved in receiving and sending all manner of data that is capable not only of compromising human privacy right down to the levels of nucleic acids and thoughts, but, as well, the foregoing processes are taking place without the informed consent of the individuals on which such entities are being imposed. Any biosensor that is on, or within, a human being, irrespective of its location, is a "wearable."

"**Blockchain**" – A money-laundering system; a method for inducing human beings to become enrolled in: (1) A distributed, ledger system that: Cannot justify the systems of valuation which use such a ledger system; (2) a digital system which enables banks, governments, corporations, and individuals to be able to keep both laudatory and questionable aspects of their activities hidden; (3) a system that is incapable of existing independently of sources of energy that are needed to maintain it (if the grid goes down, then so does the ledger system); (4) a system which has the potential for enabling the harvesting of human energy as a way of anonymously mining crypto-value even if humans do not wish to be harvested in this fashion; and, (5) system that is as artificial a framework as fiat currency is with respect to the process of establishing a basis for the generation of "sound money" that cannot be manipulated (that is, bid up and down in value).

"**Body Area Network**" – A context that wirelessly embeds nucleic acids and other bio-molecules into an electronic framework in which all dimensions of that dynamic operate in accordance with the principle of "see something, say something" and, then, use prefabricated or self-assembling forms of telemetry to transmit that surveillance to external data bases of dubious provenance. Body Area Network is a process for organizing human beings -- both individually and collectively -- into sets of nodes that are linked together according to the medical, political, economic, and social philosophies of the people who have appointed themselves as regulatory overlords with respect to such networks.

"**Brain to Brain Interface (B2BI)**" – A form of computer technology which enables neurological phenomena to be translated into frequencies that can be read from, or written into, brains with, or without, the permission of the brains being linked through such an interface and which actually doesn't need a second brain to be able to capture or alter the frequencies that are associated with a given person's phenomenology.

"**Capacitive coupling**" – This involves the use of displacement currents within a network to induce a transfer of energy, information, signals, meanings, attitudes, or ideas from one node to another irrespective of the consent or wishes of the node. A process that enhances, filters, and/or blocks the flow of energy/information through a network according to the intentions of the regulators of that network. Nodes are at the mercy of the dynamics of capacitive coupling that are imposed on a given network.

"**Central Banks**" – This is a system for leveraging nothing into indebtedness; a way to separate money from depositors.

"**Communication -- OSI Model**" – Depending on one's point of view, OSI stands for Open Systems Intercommunication Model or Overlord's Standards Initiative. It controls (via standards protocols) the way in which systems are connected and is characterized by seven layers – Physical, Data Link, Network, Transport, Session, Presentation, and Application – any one of which can be compromised in any number of ways for the sake of the system (or its overlords) and at the expense of users.

"**Consensual Validation**" – This is a process in which people seek the opinions of others (a consensus) in order to arrive at an understanding (validation) concerning some aspect of experience. However, when the information, opinions, ideas, thoughts, and data which other people have to offer is problematic, misguided, insincere, self-serving, and so on, then, one must be careful not to cede one's agency to forms of framing the perceptual process which are rooted in compromised forms of consensual validation. Consensual validation is only of value when the information one receives is reliable and credible.

"**Corona**" – A CIA and military program for gathering information via satellites that was said to be directed toward the Soviet Union and China but actually was capable of surveilling whatever targets were programmed into it and, over time, was transformed into a set of classified, stealth operations known as Keyhole which the military and the CIA used to gain access to whatever information the technology permitted. Corona was a dual-use technology that was publically described as having one purpose but which had other uses that were not disclosed to the public. National and corporate interests might be well-served by secrets and classified programs but the sovereignty of the people from whom such secrets are being kept is rarely well-served by those kinds of dynamics.

"**Corona Phase Molecular Recognition (CoPhMoRe)**" – This is a dual-use targeting system which enables nanoparticle surfaces to recognize specific analytes or chemicals for purposes of measuring, analyzing, or acting upon them. The devil is in the details.

"**Corona Routing**" – This is a technology which: (1) can be introduced into biological systems; (2) operates on the nanoscale; (3)

is used to shape the manner in which paths can be generated among the nodes of a nanoscale network by using pre-selected anchor points as a frame of reference for defining, or programming, the ways in which those nodes are able to transmit packets of information; (4) has a very low packet loss rate, and (5) can operate independently of the consent of the organism where such a routing system is being established.

"**CubeSat**" – Refers to satellites that have a cubic structure (6 square faces of equal size) whose sides measure 10 x 10 centimeters (3.94 x 3.94 inches) and weigh about 1 kilogram or 2.2 pounds. They either are launched as single units or as part of a group (up to 24 units) of such satellites. The exterior of these satellites is made largely of aluminum, and the interior of the satellites houses: (a) a power source of some kind (e.g., battery, solar panels); (b) an antennae for sending and receiving information; (c) a computer which has regulatory oversight of the satellite's components; (d) components such as sensors, instruments, and cameras which are constructed specifically to serve whatever the mission of the satellite might be.

As of 2024, there are more than 510 of these CubeSats in orbit, and, therefore, when assessing the possible value of such entities, one might reflect on the following considerations that are true for other satellites as well: (1) Notwithstanding "official" agreements which have been finagled in one way or another through meetings that are largely inaccessible to the vast majority of people on Earth, satellites and satellite-related technology occupy, travel through, and use space which does not belong to the people, corporations, or governments that launch those objects; (2) to varying degrees, those satellites radiate people on Earth who did not ask to be radiated (especially those who have electro-sensitivities); (3) such satellites are filling the skies with increasing amounts of materials which, sooner or later, become dysfunctional junk that pollutes space and creates hazards for life on Earth, and although CubeSats are said to burn up upon re-entry, what is burning up does not disappear but merely transitions into a source of man-made nano-toxins which rain down on the Earth; (4) those satellites are gathering data concerning human beings and the Earth that the vast majority of people on Earth did not give the operators of those satellites permission to do; (5) those satellites have missions and purposes that are not necessarily in the interests of assisting people in general to enhance their own sovereignty; (6) such satellite technology is consuming trillions of dollars (due to: Development, building, launching, and operating) that, in the case of governments, might be better spent on feeding, housing, clothing, and educating people; (7) all too many of those satellites are part of the 5th generation netcentric (that is, network centered) warfare that is being waged against the vast majority of the people of the world by small groups of people who operate out of Napoleonic-like complexes (that is, people who like to dominate, defeat, and control others) or operate through various modalities of willful blindness (a form of observation in which people are aware that a problem exists but choose to turn a blind eye to that which is present in their awareness and, as a result, has become somewhat obfuscated due to choices such people have made which has ceded their epistemological, spiritual, and moral agency to forces of oppression).

"Cyber Physical Systems" – This is an interactive set of computational and physical elements that generates a complex system of information which can be used to forcibly or deceptively mold the lives of people as a function of the properties of the system rather than as a function of the potential for sovereignty which is present in the people who are being shaped by the aforementioned cyber physical systems. Cyber physical systems are technocratic operations which enable institutions, corporations, governments, organizations, and the military to harness the power of the internet and other forms of communication to facilitate the bullying, control, and oppression of individuals.

"Cyber Security" – A four-layered system which goes from: Intra-BAN (Body Area Network) involving biosensors and nanotechnology, to: Inter-BAN communication (via telemetry) with machines, recording devices, cell phones, pads, and the Internet, to: Beyond-BAN forms of communication involving encryption and decryption, to: Network Fabric mesh networks that are automated and ensure that the end-users or communication destination are the only ones who can do whatever they like with the data received and also to ensure that the Intra-BAN aspect of the system can be targeted as necessary. Cyber Security is about making sure that human beings cannot escape from the system of security (the system's security, not that of the general public) into which they have been lured or forced.

"**D.A.R.P.A.**" – Among other forms of deviltry, 'The Devil's Advanced Research Projects Agency' has been busily involved (obviously idle hands are not the only portal through which deviltry enters the world) with the generating of increasingly sophisticated, faster, as well as more complex or enhanced, forms of brain-computer interfaces (a term first introduced in 1971 by Jacques Vidal) that are capable of being used as instruments of egalitarian – i.e. dual-use -- weaponry which, therefore, can be directed against all parties, both foreign and domestic. D.A.R.P.A. is a publically funded program that, like other government institutions, is dedicated to enslaving the people who are funding it.

Currently, D.A.R.P.A. is deeply involved in experimenting with Next-Generation Nonsurgical Neurotechnology (known as N3). This is a euphemistic way of referring to the process of technologically augmenting human beings through acoustic, electromagnetic, and optical forces which, then, can be utilized to assist the process of taking control of governance, resources, and non-augmented human beings.

"**Derivatives**" – These are weapons of mass destruction; Derivatives are a framework for parsing everything into packages of tranches and truncheons of financial worth that are devoid of moral value.

"**Digital Twin**" – A digitized model that is built from acquiring data involving certain physical, emotional, and cognitive feature values associated with a human being, and, then, acting on those values – in best voodoo fashion – the operators of the Digital Twin alters, injures, exploits, shapes, sickens, controls, or kills the existential original from which the Digital Twin data was derived. Digital Twins are derivatives in the sense that they give expression to ways of generating data sets which, for purposes of financial gain or political control, involve organizing and manipulating information concerning an underlying set of values or assets ... i.e., human beings.

"DNA Steganography" – This is a branding technology (e.g., using variable regions of a genome such as single nucleotide morphisms) which is capable of inserting messages, barcodes, and watermarks (intellectual property rights) into the DNA of an organism in such a manner that the presence of the information cannot be detected unless appropriately decrypted and, thereby, indicate – or, so the corporate or institutional legal argument goes -- that the organism is the property of the brander.

Drones (Nano) – Although Nano Hummingbirds and Snipe Nanos -- which combine: Experimental wing architecture, software programming advances, and battery design breakthroughs to create Unmanned Aerial Systems -- were developed nearly a decade ago by D.A.R.P.A. and the military for purposes of reconnaissance, surveillance, and situational awareness, the new generation of drones are in the form of self-assembling nanobots that fly about, and within, the enemy like swarms of molecular structures that are undetected until it is too late, and the target lists for such drones have been expanded to include the general public.

"Dual-Use Technologies" – This is a strategy of misdirection which uses surface narratives that are seemingly constructive in nature in order to obfuscate the existence of programs that are to be used against those from whom such programs are being hidden.

"Electromagnetic Communication" – One of the ways in which cells, tissues, and organisms communicate with each other via the biofield is through electromagnetic communication, and all forms of synthetic electromagnetic signals tend to interfere with such forms of biological communication in one way or another. One of the gravest and most imminent threats to life on Earth is not a function of the contrived threats concerning the non-existent crises of global warming but a function of the uncontrolled and improperly regulated introduction of all manner of synthetic forms of electromagnetism that are being pushed onto the world ecologies – especially so-called "smart" forms of such electromagnetism that are being introduced without the consent of those on whom they are impinging – by people who are suffering from a form of willful blindness that ignores the damage which they are inflicting on the world due to an apparently insatiable desire for money, control, and a lurid pleasure which is derived through inducing pain and injury in others.

"**Emergent Technology**" – The term that is used to camouflage the fact that what is said to be forthcoming at some point in the future is, actually, already present, operational, and adversely affecting our lives.

"**Energy Harvesting**" – **Vampire Project** – This is a technology that enables a network, system, corporation, institution, medical practitioner, or government agency to harvest energy from a human being's biofield in order to electrically subsidize or power that: Network's, system's, corporation's, institution's, medical practitioner's or government agency's hacking of other facets of a person's biological terrain. The notion of energy harvesting also refers to the capacity to use energy from human beings as a means of mining crypto-currency -- with, or without, the consent of the individual whose energy is being harvested.

"**Epigenetics**" – Refers to the dynamics that determine what, when, how, where, for how long, and in what sequence genes are expressed. Neither transhumanists nor technocrats understand those dynamics except in extremely limited ways and, yet, both groups of epistemologically challenged individuals want to suppress the manner in which nature has gone about the process of gene expression for thousands of years and which has helped human beings to be able to survive amidst substantial changes in the environment. Instead, such groups insist on substituting their own agenda for the expression of genes, and many – if not most -- of those modalities of substitution are either injurious or lethal to human beings in any number of ways.

"Exceptionalism" – This refers to the tendency of people to use their reflections in a 'house of mirrors' as reference points for what should be meant by the meaning of the word "exceptionalism."

"Fact Checkers" – These are people who are enamored with their own set of biases, prejudices, agendas, presuppositions, and blind spots. Fact checkers are individuals who use the political, religious, and philosophical lenses which frame their way of engaging questions of facticity in a manner that tips the hermeneutical scales in their own favor when applied to various questions.

"FCC" – (Federal Communication Commission) – The agency which claims to be protecting human beings against injurious forms of radiation but doesn't seem to understand the difference between ionizing and non-ionizing radiation or the nature of the damaging effects that both kinds of radiation have on the human body because of the FCC's failure to sincerely communicate and engage in a dialogue with people that actually have done the research on such issues (e.g., Arthur Firstenberg, Samuel Milham, Josh Del Sol, Beverly Rubik, Mark Steel, Olle Johansson, Daniel Debaun, and Martin Pall). The federal regulatory agency known as FCC has been captured by the corporate advocates of wireless transmission, and, in the process, has given those institutions, organizations, agencies, and corporations, a clean bill of health with respect to the dynamics of wireless transmission despite, apparently, not understanding (or caring about) the dual-use nature of that phenomenon.

"FDIC" (Federal Depositors Insurance Corporation) – This is the government agency which promises to cover all losses due to insolvency of the banking system but which has an extremely limited capacity to do so and, therefore, such promises mislead the public about the extent of the help that it can provide in times of emergency. The FDIC's promise relative to the foregoing problem is like bringing a squirt gun to the site of a thermonuclear explosion and expecting full resolution concerning the latter problem.

"Federal Reserve" – This is a private banking consortium that: (a) Used underhanded and duplicitous tactics to gain control of the financial system in 1913; (b) bows to the likes and dislikes of the International Bank of Settlements, an organization which is beyond the reach of law or fairness ... qualities which also often characterize member banking systems, including the Federal Reserve; (c) funds all sides of wars to make money and create the sort of indebtedness through which it controls governments and citizens; (d) operates on a basis in which money it does not have is lent out at interest it does not deserve; (e) continually resists being properly audited; (f) has proven to be completely ineffectual in preventing the very kind of financial problems it was allegedly created to solve; and, (g) for more than a century, has proceeded to wield its power in ways which are economically, financially, politically, legally, and socially detrimental to the American people, and among these ways of wielding power is its unwillingness to help create the sort of public banking system (e.g., see the work of Ellen Brown and Muhammad Yunus) which would be beneficial to citizens (both individually and collectively) but fails to do so because satisfying its lust for money and control is far more important to the Federal Reserve system than is the sovereignty of the people that it claims to serve.

"Full Spectrum Dominance" – This is the goal of all entities, institutions, organizations, and forms of government that seek to suppress, oppress, or eliminate the existence of sovereignty, irrespective of whether, or not, sovereignty is considered individually or collectively. Since every dimension of existential space is considered to be a potential entry point for the emergence of sovereignty -- or information concerning sovereignty -- then, power brokers believe that unless full spectrum dominance is exercised over all actual or potential portals for that sort of activity and/or information, then, those who seek to exercise full spectrum dominance consider themselves and their system to be at risk. Full spectrum dominance is to engage in continuous forms of tyranny and terrorism because the possibility that some facet of sovereignty might surface can never be dismissed.

"Galvanic Coupling" – This is a form of intrabody communication (IBC) that is induced from without by coupling low-frequency voltages with low-power sources to serve, potentially, low-down purposes.

"**Global Information Grid**" (GIG) – A network-centric system established by the Department of Defense to acquire any, and all, information that would help to sustain and/or improve the capacity of the military to wage war against all enemies, both foreign and domestic. How that acquired information is interpreted, understood, or used, and whether, or not, one should trust the quality of such information, and whether, or not, war should be waged, and whether, or not, there are better alternatives to war are not issues which the GIG network is capable of resolving.

Having an informational advantage is not enough. One must also have an advantage in knowledge, understanding, as well as wisdom in relation to such information. Determining what the criteria are for identifying and, then, being able to justify such a process of determination with respect to the latter sorts of advantage tends to generate a very complicated set of issues and an accompanying set of fundamental questions concerning the nature of the relationship between human beings and reality.

"**Graphene**" – This is not a naturally-occurring biological material. However, this substance was experimentally demonstrated to exist in 2004 and evidence for its natural, geological occurrence has been found in rock formations that are 3.2 billion years old.

It consists of a honeycomb (hexagonal) latticework of carbon atoms with diameters that are approximately a third of a nanometer thick. Graphene is conceived of as a 2D material that is considered to possess width and length but has negligible depth.

This material is highly impenetrable. Not even the smallest atom (helium, not hydrogen, has the smallest atomic radius) can permeate through graphene.

Graphene is lighter than aluminum but more rugged than steel. It is more elastic than rubber but harder than diamonds. It has 13 times the electrical conductivity of copper, while the mobility of electrons within graphene is 100 times faster than within silicon.

Magnetism is not an inherent property of graphene. Nonetheless, it has the capacity to borrow, or participate in, the magnetic fields of nearby materials, and, in addition, by manipulating systems of electrons in the appropriate manner, one can created magnetic domains within graphene.

The properties of graphene vary with its composition, and, as well, the properties of nanographene vary with the process of fabrication (which is more complicated than the generation of general graphene). Consequently, there is a graphene-family of nanomaterials, and, as well, there are biological toxicities of different kinds which have been associated with members of that family.

As such, graphene is a dual-use material. It has a set of remarkable properties which often are emphasized while the toxicities of that material are often downplayed if mentioned at all.

Nanographene has been found (e.g., David Nixon, La Quinta Columna, Ana Mihalcea) in a variety of COVID-19 mRNA treatment vials. While the presence of such a toxic potential in alleged public health treatments might be music to the ears of some, nonetheless, the presence of graphene-related toxicity conflicts with the principle of: "First, do no harm" which used to govern medical activities but now is often no longer required as a condition for such practice.

"**Hack**" – Verb -- The process of seeking to gain unelicited access to a network, system, computer, electronic device, or person in order to compromise, alter, manipulate, or pilfer some aspect of the operational integrity of that network, system, computer, electronic device, or person. Examples: Government; education; medicine; corporate activity; intelligence operations; the media, and military force. Noun – The entity which makes hacking possible and is often characterized by a moral incompetence that is lost sight of amidst the dazzling lights which frequently are given off by the presence of some degree of technical skill.

"**Hop-by-hop transport**" – This is a principle which is directed toward controlling the flow of data through a network from source to destination -- quick like a bunny and with equal fecundity -- despite the possibility that the intervening nodes of the path of transmission might not all be connected at the time of transmission, and, therefore, provides degrees of freedom for getting one's unwanted message across.

"**Human Body Communication**" **(HBC)** – This is a form of electrical signal transfer that uses the human body as the medium of transmission and is known as 'electro-quasistatic human body communication'. As such, the body is reduced to being a node within a network involving the transfer of electrical signals and data, and this would seem to indicate that a human being has become a means to someone else's end-use of those signals and data.

"**Hydrogels**" – These are biphasic, cross-linked polymer chains (via either covalent bonding in the case of 'chemical hydrogels' or non-covalent bonds in the case of 'physical hydrogels') that are capable of absorbing large volumes of liquids (usually water or interstitial biological fluids). These polymer chains can be either synthetic or natural.

They are referred to as "smart" materials because of their ability to alter their structure and properties as a function of changes to the surrounding environment involving such qualities as: Water and salt concentrations, temperature, and pH values. However, this sort of responsiveness doesn't necessarily make those materials smart but, perhaps, merely reflects the potential flexibility or degrees of freedom that are present in those materials and also indicates that they are vulnerable to such environmental changes ... changes that can be induced from without by altering the character of the environment surrounding those hydrogels. As with many things, the devil might be hidden in the details involving: The kinds of polymers that are used in a given hydrogel (synthetic or natural); or, the nature of the bonds which are present; or, the properties of the solid materials and nanoparticles that are present in such hydrogels; or, the kinds of fluids which are present, as well as the sorts of changes that might occur in a hydrogel if different properties of the surrounding environment were induced to change at the whim of some researcher, experimenter, or medical practitioner.

"**IEEE**" – Institute of Electrical and Electronics Engineers whose motto is "Advancing Technology for Humanity" but which never objectively (preaching to the choir is never a sign of objectivity), continuously, and rigorously addresses the many issues that surround and permeate the question of whether the research, programs, and standards which are being established through its activities actually are for the benefit of humanity and, therefore, can be fully justified as policies that enhance human sovereignty rather than undermine it. Without sovereignty, there is no way in which advancing technology will be of benefit to humanity.

"**Income Tax**" – This is a process that transfers money – both directly and indirectly -- to the military-industrial complex; a system which transduces private assets into public liabilities.

"**Informatics**" – This is a discipline which explores how computational methods induce transformations in information without necessarily adequately addressing whether, or not, the transformations being induced are actually in the best interests of people or whether the information being transformed is all that worthwhile to anyone except the people engaged in its transformation.

"**Internet of Things**" – An arbitrary network of enhanced connectivity (created by electronics, computers, and forms of communication) which entails, but is not restricted to the Internet, and reduces human beings to nodes on a network whose sole function is to process the packets of bits and bytes of data being transmitted through the network according to the protocols which have been established by those who govern that network.

"**International Electrotechnical Commission**" – This is a Swiss-based organization -- and, therefore, neighbor to the International Bank of Settlements -- which (unasked by the world) was founded in the United Kingdom (1906) in order to establish international standards for various technologies involving electronics and electricity. Somehow, the organization appears to have missed generating standards that are based on an objective, nuanced and rigorous understanding of how electricity and electronics have been adversely affecting people (biologically and psychologically, if not spiritually) around the world since 1906 and before.

The IEC has co-operated, and works closely, with such organizations as the IEEE and the International Organization for Standardization (ISO) to, among other things, ignore, downplay, and/or discredit independently conducted research which provides evidence that implicates, if not demonstrates, the potentially -- and not-so-potentially – injurious impact which electricity, electronics, bioengineering, and geoengineering (which is heavily dependent on electromagnetic sensors, antennae, routers, actuators, and computational processors) can have on the lives of not only human beings but the entire set of interlocking world ecologies in which human beings are embedded.

"**Internet of Bio-Nano Things**" – This manner of framing experience emerged out of an attempt to allegedly address how the Internet of NanoThings (IoNT) -- which involves the ways in which nanoscale particles, devices, and bots both engage, and are engaged by, the world – might have potentially problematic safety and health ramifications for life on Earth. The alleged motivating orientation underlying the idea of the Internet of Bio-Nano Things is to try to find ways in which the interface among the electrical properties of the Internet, the nanoscale properties entailed by the Internet of NanoThings, and the nature of living organisms can be reconciled in safe and efficient ways.

However, the key to such a process of reconciliation requires that one is working with an understanding of life which is capable of being demonstrated to be accurately reflective of the biology of living organisms rather than reflective of a theoretical model concerning the arbitrary and artificial lenses through which this or that person observes life. A conceptual framework of biology which is based on the notion of monomorphism will operate quite differently than will a framework based on pleiomorphism, and a conceptual framework of biology which seeks to discover how microzymas, endobionts, bions, and/or somatids affect biological functioning or how such entities are affected by nanoscale devices and electromagnetic waves will be quite different than a conceptual framework of biology that ignores the existence of such empirically established entities (e.g., see the work of Béchamp, Enderlein, Reich, and Naessens).

Moreover, a conceptual framework of biology which maintains that viruses exist and constitute pathogens which attack human beings will generate an approach to diagnosis and treatment which is very different from a conceptual framework of biology which contends – on the basis of considerable evidence – that viruses do not exist and, therefore, are not illness-causing pathogens, and, consequently, there is no need for viral forms of treatment. Furthermore, an Internet of Bio-Nano Things which fails to understand how synthetic biology (which tends to operate on the nanoscale) can adversely impact the healthy operation of the Biofield – an indigenous feature of human biology – is, very likely, incapable of reconciling (to whatever extent such matters can be reconciled at all under the best of circumstances) the biological with the domains of either the Internet of Things (IoT) or the Internet of NanoThings (IoNT). It might well be an exercise in irreconcilable differences.

"**Internet of Medical Things**" – This gives expression to four areas of activity involving: (a) Biosensors/Antennae/Routers/Actuators; (b) edge devices and analytics [automated forms of detection, computations and assessments involving data from (a) prior to being sent on for further processing at (c)]; (c) fog computing is a decentralized form of computational architecture in which different nodes on an overriding network provide real-time analysis of data [that already have been pre-processed via (b)] in accordance with the principles of a governing network architecture; (d) cloud analytics which uses cloud technology to store and apply established algorithms to search for different sorts of patterns that exist in the data that has been run through (a), (b), and (c) and which might be of value to processes involving a judicious observation of a medical practitioner's duties of care to patients.

As impressive as the Internet of Medical Things sounds, the actual value of such an approach depends on the extent to which the Things being collected, processed, stored, and analyzed: (1) are being used in accordance with principles of informed consent; (2) do not entail hazards or toxicities for the individual being medically engaged; (3) is based on an understanding of Medicine which is not restricted to one or two arbitrary schools of thought concerning the nature of biology that unduly influence the forms of diagnosis and treatment being used and, as such, constitute frameworks of medical theology that suffer from, among other things, the pathologies of arrogance, delusion, and regulatory capture.

"**In the image of God**" – This is a phrase that is often used to distort the nature of one's relationship with reality. It is a turn of phrase that does not make reference to a reflection of Divinity but, instead, refers to the manner in which the potential of certain manifested realities have been creatively organized by God to generate an essential potential that is rarely realized.

"**Intra-body Networks and Molecular Communication Networks**" – Biological organisms or bodies have a natural network of molecular communication which often is being engaged by forms of medical practice that confuse and conflate theory with the biological realities which are being engaged. There is a tendency among all too many medical practitioners to be inclined toward imposing their theoretical ideas and hermeneutical musings about "intra-body networks and molecular communication onto" 'the actual indigenous system of intra-body networks and molecular communication', and through such a process of imposition, lead to the misdiagnosis and mistreatment (on several levels) of their patients.

"**Janus Particles**": This term refers to objects that are on the nanoscale (billionths of a meter) or the microscale (under 1mm) which exhibit special surface properties that enable two different kinds of chemistry to take place in juxtaposition to one another. For example, two proximate areas of the surface of such particles might exhibit different magnetic properties, or one area might exhibit hydrophobic tendencies, while another, nearby area might have hydrophilic properties.

There is similar phenomenon which can occur when medical practitioners and patients share the same meta-surface of healthcare. More specifically, while engaged in the phenomenon of healthcare, the sort of biochemistry in which a medical practitioner is involved might have little to do with the biochemistry which actually exists in a patient. The healthcare system is a Janus particle in as much as it gives expression to a surface of activity in which different kinds of often conflicting kinds of human chemistry can be observed to take place while in juxtaposition to one another.

"**Kill Box**" – This is a multi-dimensional space into which targets are maneuvered in order for the overseers of that space to be able to eliminate or control such targets in some fashion. The dimensions of the kill box consist of: 3-D space, time, beliefs, values, resources, perception, and choice, while the dynamics which are used to induce people to enter the kill box space consist of: Propaganda, indoctrination, education, disinformation, misinformation, narratives, limited hangouts, ill-advised public health policies, iatrogenic activities, misdiagnoses, pharmaceutical toxicities, politics, sanctions, legal processes, myths, threats, fear, desire, hope, force, as well as classical and operant forms of conditioning.

"**LIDAR**" **(Laser Imaging, detection, and ranging)** -- A methodology which uses lasers to target objects and, then, measure the amount of time that is required for the signal to return from that target. LIDAR can conduct its measurements in fixed or multiple directions and is used in projects involving: Mapping, seismology, surveying, navigation for autonomous vehicles (such as the helicopter, *Ingenuity*, on Mars). Subsequent generations of LIDAR are rooted in quantum technology and are capable of providing enhanced measurement sensitivities.

One of the targets that can be painted by LIDAR are human beings, and, now, with advancements in quantum technology, human beings can be targeted with ever-increasing sensitivity – not necessarily for the needs of the individuals being targeted but for the needs of the command and control people who are targeting human beings for inhuman reasons. One can be sure that the AI-equipped models from the world of robotics have LIDAR or LIDAR-like (but more advanced) ways of detecting, locating, identifying, mapping, and, in compliance with DoD Directive 3000.09, engage in running down, herding, or terminating human beings.

"MAC" (Medium or Media Access Control) – This refers to a set of protocols that governs whatever technology is being used to control the way in which hardware will interface with wired or wireless mediums of transmission. MAC, together with logical link control (LLC) protocols, give expression to layer 2 (The Data Link) of the OSI model of communication (See: "Communication" -- OSI Model) and are part of the IEEE 802 set of standards which characterize how MAC establishes protocols that control the flow and multiplexing (a method through which analogue and digital signals can be combined in one medium) associated with the process of interfacing with a given form of transmission and LLC protocols govern the control of flow and multiplexing for the logical link side of a given transmission.

MAC addresses (as well as Bluetooth addresses) have been detected in conjunction with the biofields of some human beings. This would seem to indicate that such individuals are being treated as pieces of hardware which, in some way (probably, sans consent), have been provided with MAC protocols (or Bluetooth protocols) so that this biological hardware can be wirelessly interfaced with other aspects of a network, thereby, installing such human beings as nodes on a network.

"Mesh Networking" – This is a form of networking architecture which arranges the nodes (whether switches, bridges, or human beings) of a network in non-hierarchical, self-organizing, fluid ways that enhance the degrees of freedom in which data is routed through a network. In addition, among other things, this sort of communication topology provides a certain amount of fault-tolerance for a network since if a certain number of nodes fail or do not perform in a functional manner, nonetheless, there are alternative pathways for connecting nodes which enable communication, signaling, or data transfer to continue without disruption.

Although the terms "non-hierarchical" and "self-organizing" are used to describe how a mesh network operates, nevertheless, such networks are intended to serve certain purposes and, therefore, there are structural and dynamic features within these networks which ensure that the purposes of the network will be served and, as a result, 'non-hierarchical' and 'self-organizing' dynamics take place within a set of constraints and degrees of freedom that are organized in ways that regulate the network so that it will be able to realize its purposes.

The "Borg" of Star Trek fame would seem to be a mesh network. Those who have power (whether in: Government, religion, corporations, the military, the media, unions, banking, science, or education) seek to establish mesh networks in conjunction with the people who are part of those networks to ensure that -- notwithstanding the presence of nodes who, for whatever reason, might fail or operate in a dysfunctional manner -- nonetheless, the purposes for which a given network has been established will serve the overseers of that network. Therefore, there are "corrective dynamics" or algorithms (often subtle and hidden) which are present in such systems to ensure that non-hierarchical and self-organizing activities will only occur in ways that will lead to the realization of a given network's underlying purposes.

Currently, there is no set of common standards of interoperability governing mesh networking. This is what the International Bank of Settlements, WEF, transhumanists, technocrats, the W.H.O., and corporations like Blackrock, Vanguard, and State Street are seeking to establish ... mesh networks in which all nodes (notwithstanding occasional node failures and node dysfunctions here and there) will help realize the purposes of one-world universal governance across all networks.

"**Metabolomics**" -- This refers to the large-scale study of metabolites -- or small molecules -- which play different roles during the process of metabolism within: Cells, interstitial fluids, and tissues. The impetus for this discipline is rooted in the belief that by studying metabolites and their concentrations, one has a much better vantage point for understanding the state of biochemical activity in cells, tissues, organs, and the entire organism. Metabolomics not only examines the nature of the metabolites which are present in any given level of biological activity, but, as well, has a focus that links – in concrete terms – how genetic and environmental factors are interacting with one another.

One should keep in mind however that Metabolomics occurs in a hermeneutical context. The significance of the presence of certain kinds of metabolites and concentrations of those metabolites depends on the nature of the conceptual or theoretical lenses through which such metabolites are being engaged.

Pleiomorphism constitutes a very different context within which to try to figure out the meaning or significance of a given set of metabolites or concentration of metabolites than monomorphism does. In addition, the significance or meaning of metabolites might be different if they are viewed from an approach to biology which has a place for the way in which microzymas, endobionts, bions, and somatids might affect the dynamics of metabolism in different ways rather than being viewed from an approach to biology which has no place for such considerations. Moreover, the study of metabolites and their concentrations takes on a different orientation depending on whether, or not, one holds that epigenetics might be a process that is, at least in part, extra-cellular and extra-genetic in nature, and, as such, depends on modalities of regulatory oversight and energy dynamics which are not necessarily all that well understood at the present time.

"Microfluidics and Neuronal Microfluidics" – Microfluidics is a discipline which focuses on the manipulation of fluidic systems that are somewhere between 10^{-9} to 10^{-18} liters in size and, as such, have applications for microelectronics (e.g., DNA chips) and the sorts of molecular biology that is relevant to bioengineering and synthetic biology. Microfluidics examines the ways in which extremely small-scale fluidic contexts engage in dynamics which: Transport, process, separate, or mix fluids – either passively (such as capillary forces) or actively (some mechanism is usually involved, such as a micropump).

The behavior of fluids under micro-conditions often differs from the behavior of fluids under macro conditions. These differences often have to do with the way in which such factors as channel size, surface tension, resistance, and energy distribution might affect the character of the dynamics which occur on a micro scale.

Microfluidics plays an important role in synthetic biology. For example, this discipline comes into play when one is engaged in the neuromorphic engineering of artificial neurons so that they will be able to mimic natural or biological neurons.

Microfluidics takes on different orientations and values depending on the context through which it is engaged – especially in the case of neuromorphic engineering. More specifically, does the brain generate mental activity or does it serve as a receiving apparatus for mental activity that takes place elsewhere and independently of neuronal activity (i.e., neurons are capable of reflecting those sorts of cognitive dynamics, but neurons are not the source of those cognitive dynamics).

If the latter case is true, then, while one might be able to engage in processes of neuromorphic engineering, microfluidics would become important to understanding the nature of a receiving apparatus rather than a generating apparatus. Under such circumstances, neuromorphic engineering could be used to simulate certain aspects of mental functioning in relation to the receiving of signals and interpreting those signals but such processes would always be dependent either on algorithms being sent from elsewhere and/or would be restricted by the character of the constraints and degrees of freedom which had been programmed into the kind of neuromorphic engineering that is taking place.

A form of neuromorphic engineering that is only sensitive to certain modalities of human epistemological and hermeneutical dynamics might be able to perform an array of functions. However, to whatever extent there are lacunae in the model which is directing such a form of neuromorphic engineering, then, to that extent, such cognitive or computational activity will not be able to properly model the mental activity of human beings.

"**Molecular Communication**" – This is a technique which uses the presence or absence of specific molecules as a way to digitally encode messages. The presence of a given molecule plays a role comparable to "1" in a binary system, while the absence of that molecule assumes the role of "0" in such a system.

Given that various kinds of non-natural MAC protocols, sensors, antennae, and routers are showing up in human beings, one does not have much difficulty imagining the possibility that networks could be established -- or already have been established -- which are based on algorithms that operate according to a computational language built around the presence or absence of certain molecules. Just as pheromones are molecules which have the capacity to communicate different messages to (and, thereby, actively affect) animals, plants, and so on that are receptive to such messages, so too, human beings could be outfitted with the right sorts of nanoscale devices which are receptive to, and will be affected by, the presence of various forms of molecular communication that have been bioengineered to shape human behavior through the presence of those nanoscale devices.

"**Network Centric Warfare**" – Networks are methods for processing information. Warfare which is waged through a network-centric dynamic makes warfare a function of such information-processing methods.

While part of the informational aspect of such a process depends on the activities, of technological components that, for example, are directed toward detecting, identifying, acquiring, transmitting, and storing data which arises as a result of the way in which the network engages the world, data is not really transformed into information until it is processed in various ways. Data which has not been processed beyond its being sensed, measured, recorded, transmitted, and stored has no network significance, meaning, or value and, therefore, must undergo further processing in the form of analysis.

This can be done automatically through algorithms or via direct forms of critical reflection (individually or in groups), or through some combination of the two. Irrespective of which of the foregoing possibilities is pursued, data is characterized, parsed, diagnosed, organized, classified, and evaluated according to certain principles, assumptions, weighted values, purposes, goals, mathematical treatments, and the like while also searching for patterns, connections, structural features, and logical properties within different dimensions of that data.

Networks are coping mechanisms. People create networks because they have no insight into the nature of reality and construct networks in the hope that such a systemizing of experience will lead to the sort of insights and wisdom that might resolve the problem for which the network has been created and, thereby, provide a way to cope with a given situation.

To cope does not mean one understands what is transpiring. Coping is a way of getting through a situation irrespective of whether, or not, one knows what one is doing and irrespective of whether, or not, one is dealing with a situation in the most constructive, epistemologically defensible, and morally appropriate manner.

Pathology often emerges in the context of coping mechanisms because many coping mechanisms are based on delusional thinking as a result of faulty analysis and problematic forms of critical reflection. When an individual suffers from some form of pathology as a result of an unreliable and destructive (to oneself or others) coping mechanism, this is tragic, but when the military seeks to impose on all human beings its modalities of network-centric coping mechanisms which have rarely, if ever, been demonstrated to serve the interests of sovereignty or truth but, instead, tend to enhance the self-serving interests of banks, corporations, corrupt politicians, psychopaths, and ego-driven glory seekers, then, one is not dealing with a tragedy but, rather, one is confronted by an evil which destabilizes humankind and is incapable of constructively solving issues.

"**Network Load Balancing**" – The term "shedding" has emerged over the last several years as a way of trying to explain the existence of certain forms of illness that are believed, by some, to be due to the manner in which various human beings have been exposed to environmental toxins (for example, mRNA jabs). In turn, these toxins are alleged to be excreted by previously exposed people through their breath, sweat, blood, semen, as well as other bodily fluids and waste materials.

An alternative approach to the foregoing dynamic has to do with the idea that illness can be induced through being exposed to certain kinds of electromagnetic frequencies. In such instances if one considers people to be like nodes on one, or more, networks, then, under the right set of circumstances, various frequencies can be transmitted to proximate individuals (nodes) through a process in which network traffic continues to be transferred to other nearby nodes or networks as a way of balancing the load within a given network without requiring some form of routing.

In both cases it is a matter of being in the wrong place at the wrong time but the modality of transmission is different in the two cases. One form of transmission involves the shedding of toxins which, subsequently, contaminate or poison other human beings, while the other form of transmission involves certain kinds of illness-inducing frequencies (not pathogens) which are transferred from one person to another through a process of network load balancing.

The foregoing set of possibilities is not necessarily an either/or situation. A third possibility is that both shedding of poisons and toxins, as well as various forms of network load balancing might take place – either separately or simultaneously.

"**Neuromorphic Computing**" – This involves a set of nanotechnological materials, devices, and computational algorithms that seek to mimic, simulate, or model the manner in which biological neurons supposedly process information. Neuromorphic computing is purported to be a way of mirroring the manner in which human beings think.

The association between neuronal activity and mental activity is correlational and not necessarily causal in nature, perhaps in the same way that the activities of a television set have a correlational relationship, and not, necessarily a causal relationship, with the programs that appear on its screen. Yet, those programs would not be visible if the television set wasn't functioning properly, but the television set is not what created those programs.

Neuromorphic computing might be able to mirror the manner in which neurons operate. However, this does not necessarily mean that neuromorphic computing is capable of mirroring how human beings are able to think or have experiences which are phenomenological in nature.

"OMNeT++" (Objective Modular Network Testbed in C++) – This is not a simulator but, rather, it establishes a framework which provides tools and structural features that enable simulations to be written or created through programming languages such as Python. Models can be created through the construction of modules which can be assembled in Lego-like fashion, and those modules can be connected via gates that provide a context or medium through which messages/data, of one kind or another, can be sent.

One might suppose that OMNeT++-like frameworks could be established – or, perhaps, already have been established -- on a nanoscale to provide a basis for generating network simulations that are thought-like or logic-like in character and capable of being sensed and, like an intuition, capable of vectoring or tensoring aspects of phenomenology in different directions via specific frequencies, which, without necessarily being clearly seen in any concrete manner, are written into various modules and affect the way in which those modules operate. If so, I don't see this as being a good thing but, yet, another way in which the ones who are controlling such technology are seeking to control the minds of human beings.

"Optogenetics" – Eleven years ago, a TED talk featured two researchers who were able to surgically implant a device that enabled them to combine light and light-sensitive proteins to erase or alter memories in mice. Today, such implants are no longer necessary because everything can be done wirelessly. Indeed, scientists have the capacity to expose organisms to light in a way which can alter the manner in which the genes in those organisms can be expressed – that is, turned on and off.

Many scientists believe they have the right to take such research and technology as far as it will take them – especially if money, fame, and career are involved. However, very few of those scientists ever wonder about the rights of human beings to be free from the ramifications of that sort of research and technology because for the former individuals science is all about the right of discovery and not at all about the problems which such discoveries create.

Indigenous peoples indicate that before acting one should understand the implications of one's actions for seven succeeding generations. Unfortunately, all too many scientists and researchers cannot see into the future beyond the temporal boundaries associated with their paychecks, royalties, names, or egos.

"**Panopticon**" – In an essay on this topic, Jeremy Bentham argued that the best form of a prison would be one in which: (a) prisoner cells would be open to a central tower into which prisoners could not see and, therefore, the prisoners would never know whether, or not, the tower was being occupied with people who were observing the prisoners and, in addition, (b) prisoners would not be permitted to interact with one another. Bentham considered the Panopticon to be an ideal template for how society, in general, ought to work.

In other words, according to Bentham, if prisoners or citizens did not know at any given point in time whether, or not, they were being observed by authorities, then, the prisoners and citizens eventually would internalize the values and principles that authorities wanted them to adopt and, in the process, prisoners and citizens would become their own self-contained Panopticon in which the values and principles of the system would always be viewing them and from which escape would become impossible because those values and principles had been internalized and become invisible stewards of behavior.

The whole idea of propaganda, censorship, and surveillance is to establish conditions which are similar to those of the Panopticon. The tower toward which the cells of citizens open is constructed from materials made from the surveillance capabilities possessed by the police, the FBI, the NSA, the CIA, the Internal Revenue Service, the military, the medical system, the educational system, and sixteen, or so, other so-called "intelligence" services and which one never knows whether, or not, such entities are making use of their surveillance capabilities in order to observe the activities of one, or more, citizens. Furthermore, time and time again, a wealth of evidence has been brought forth that corporations, Big Tech, the media, the educational system, and even science and medicine have played prominent roles in censoring what people can see, read, say, or think. Furthermore, jurists who are intellectually and morally challenged have given the United States federal government the right to propagandize its citizens with whatever fantastical notions and phantasmagoria will serve the government's capacity to mislead, misinform, or disinform the general populace in order to maintain, if not extend, control over, its citizenry.

The domains of: The Internet of Things, the Internet of NanoThings, the Internet of Bio-NanoThings, the Internet of Medical Things, The Internet of Behaviors, and The Internet of Everything are all dedicated toward optimizing the operational capabilities of the Panopticon that started to be built in America more than 237 years ago, and, now, the Panopticon -- thanks to optogenetics, wireless communication, biosensors, nanotechnology, DARPA, the FCC, the IEEE, and other modern day wonders – cannot only track, trace, and terminate individuals, but, as well, the Panopticon entity known as government can, without consent, turn a person's genes on and off as they like.

Mind control internalizes the Panopticon. Virtual reality induces one to become isolated from, and discontinue interacting with, other individuals. Consensual validation becomes a process of submitting to whatever one is told by the Panopticon system.

"**Pervasive Computing**" – which is also known as, or referred to as, "intrusive computing" -- is the process of placing microprocessors everywhere so that people's privacy can be invaded in ways that are important to the make-work projects of data gathers, their overlords, and individuals who wish to use such data to better control people, but impinge on the lives of individuals in ways that are largely irrelevant – if not counterproductive -- to helping those people live happy, sovereign lives.

"Photonics" – The term has been in use at least since the early 1950s and encompasses the processes involved in applying optical principles to the world. It is a form of engineering.

Masers – 1958 -- (microwave amplification by the stimulation of emitted radiation) and lasers – 1960 -- (light amplification by the stimulation of emitted radiation) are a few of the early results generated through photonic engineering. Optical fibers are another product which has emerged through that kind of engineering activity.

However, one might also point out in passing that photonics has made possible the directed energy weapons which were turned against United States citizens in places such as Paradise, California and Lahaina, Hawaii. One also has photonics to thank for, on the one hand, a less hazardous form of LED technology that emits blue light of certain problematic frequencies (e.g., 400 – 500 nanometers) which can damage the retina of the eyes as well as interfere with sleep patterns that, in turn, can lead to psychological and other health problems, and, on the other hand, one also can thank photonics for the existence of a much more lethal set of frequencies which can be emitted through streetlights that are part of an active system of denial and control (e.g., see the work of Aman Jabbi and Mark Steele).

Moreover, one could reflect on the role which photonics plays in the development of optogenetics. For example, technology based on photonics can be used to turn genes on and off from outside of the body, via such modes of delivery as drones.

"Plasmonics" – This is a field of study which explores, and seeks applications for, the physical phenomena which occur on a nanoscale in conjunction with the interface of particular kinds of metals and dielectrics (materials that serve as electrical insulators which become polarized when exposed to an electrical field and, among other things, can enhance capacitance or energy storage in electronic circuits). A plasmon is a quantum of plasma oscillation, and plasmonics explores the properties of such plasma oscillations and how they can be manipulated on the nanoscale.

These coherent oscillations are associated with electromagnetic waves that exist along the nanoscale interface that juxtaposes a dielectric and a metal. Various metals have different plasmonics properties, and artificially designed nonporous metals have an array of plasmonics properties.

Plasmonics has potential ramification for bio-photonics. Consequently, not only does plasmonics carry possible applications for such fields of study as optogenetics (the use of light to turn genes on and off), but, as well, it raises questions as to how, and to what extent, bio-photonics and plasmonics might adversely affect or suppress the health of a person's biofield.

"**Politicians**" – These are members of a parasitic class who pretend to be public servants while expecting the public to be their servants. These are individuals who are well-versed in the process of de-stabilizing society through the checks and balances of: Delusions, illusions, subterfuge, rationalizations, and self-serving duplicity.

"**Precision Medicine**" – Also known as "personalized medicine" – Seeks to develop treatments which reflect the unique properties of a given individual's genetic makeup, environment, and life style. Nonetheless, and just to raise one set of issues, if the value of the diagnostic tests which are used are questionable (e.g., as is the case with PCR tests and COVID-19, as well as is the case in relation to the ELISA blood assay and Western Blot tests which are used in conjunction with "HIV causes AIDS" scenarios), and/or if one's theory of medicine is based on a monomorphic paradigm of disease rather than a pleiomorphic paradigm of microorganisms, then, what happens to the precision in such medicine? Similarly, if one doesn't recognize that EMFs in the environment can act as toxins and poisons, then, how, precisely, is one to ensure that medical treatment will properly reflect the environment in which such a person exists?

"**Project Salus**" – This is a data-driven analysis of the purported effectiveness of mRNA treatments against the delta variant of SARS-CoV-2. However, given that no one has provided credible and reliable evidence that SARS-CoV-2 (in any of its alleged variant forms) actually exists (see the work of Andy Kaufman, Tom Cowan, Stefan Lanka, as well as Sam and Mark Bailey) and, therefore, one cannot demonstrate that mRNA treatments are effective in countering non-existent viruses, or their variants, then, Project Salus begins at no credible beginning and works toward no credible end.

"**Quantum Dots**" – These are nanoscale-sized, semiconductor nanocrystal particles which, usually, only occupy a few nanometers of space. They have electronic and optical properties which are governed by quantum dynamics and are of value in different facets of nanotechnology.

An individual quantum dot is sometimes referred to as an "artificial atom." Several quantum dots can be coupled together to form an "artificial molecule," and, in addition, a set of quantum dots can be organized into superlattices that have solid-state-like properties which are capable of exhibiting an array of electronic and optical properties.

Quantum dots are entirely artificial in nature. The research of Ana Mihalcea, David Nixon, Mateo Taylor, and La Quinta Columna has demonstrated that such artificial entities are showing up in the blood streams of people and, as well, that such quantum dots appear to be playing active roles in a variety of self-assembly dynamics which are giving rise to nanotechnological-like devices such as sensors, antennae, routers, and other forms of synthetic biology that are forming in the blood streams of people.

"**Synthetic Biology**" – Is this term oxymoronic? In other words, if something is synthetic then irrespective of the technological quality of that something, can it be considered to be biological in any sense?

Biology is the study of life. So, what property or properties must a synthetic: System, dynamic, network, or entity have to possess in order for it to be referred to as being biological in nature, and, therefore, a phenomenon which gives expression to the quality of life of a biological kind?

Is biological life a matter of: Proteins, carbohydrates, lipids, sugars, nucleic acids, cofactors, water, and the like being organized in a set of interacting, mutually supportive and modulating pathways that are regulated by a series of instructions which, when operating properly, are collectively capable of generating a stable, functioning system of processes which exhibits a resistance to the pull of entropy by extracting from the environment what is needed to enable such a system to have continuity across time by means of series of transduction dynamics which convert environmental materials into usable forms of energy that help to underwrite the internal dynamics of such a system? How arbitrary is the foregoing way of characterizing life?

Is life just a matter of chemistry and physics? What makes the organization, structure, timing, awareness, and order of a biological entity possible? Are such properties merely emergent, self-assembling functions of physics and chemistry?

Is epigenetics nothing more than an expression of physics and chemistry? Or, do physics and chemistry have to be directed in certain ways in order for epigenetics to be possible, and, if so, then, what is the nature of this directing force?

Nucleic acids do not appear to be able, on their own, to regulate their modalities of expression. Instead, DNA and RNA both seem to be responding to something beyond themselves, as words seem to be dependent on something beyond themselves in order to become organized into an interacting system of syntax and semantics that is capable of making sense when properly interpreted by some other, parallel system which gives expression to an interacting framework that also is capable of a form of semantics and syntax that is capable of understanding the other system?

How did physics and chemistry give rise to a system that is capable of using triplets of five nucleic acids to stand for just 20, or so, amino acids out of the hundreds of amino acids which are possible? How did RNA come to serve as a way of translating DNA into proteins? The answer to these questions cannot necessarily be found in either physics or chemistry nor will such answers necessarily be found in the chaotic and complexity variants of those disciplines.

Until one knows what life is, and until one knows what makes biology possible, then, to speak of "synthetic biology" seems premature. Synthetic systems are not necessarily biological systems, and, consequently, for transhumanists to suppose that the synthetic entities which they have created or want to create are the same as, or equivalent to, biological systems tends to blur the lines between life and non-life, just as legal fictions (and fictions is all that such legal pronouncements are) have blurred the line between a person and a corporation.

There seems to be a political agenda underlying the attempt to force-fit synthetic entities into the category of biological organisms. This is not about physics, chemistry, or biology.

"Targeted Individuals" – There are tens of thousands of targeted individuals in the United States. There are hundreds of thousands, if not millions, of targeted individuals in other parts of the world.

Targeted individuals are people who have lost control of large swaths of their physical, psychological, emotional, social, and economic lives as a result of the way in which their phenomenology and biology have been hacked by natural, and self-made, psychopaths through the application of the technologies, techniques, and programs which are being outlined in this document.

That to which allusions are being made through the different entries which appear before and following the present entry is not a conspiracy theory or a flight of fantasy. Rather, what is being described are the nuts and bolts of a terrorist campaign into which millions of people have been unwilling abducted and who through no fault of their own have been selected to serve as beta tests for the rest of us.

As is, sometimes, said in the military: "Be advised." The Havana Syndrome is just the tip of the iceberg, and many governments are involved in these acts of terrorism.

"Telemetry" – This encompasses a set of automated processes of communication in which data is collected, measured, assessed, and transmitted to a command and control center which, in turn, sets in motion a series of responses concerning that data. Initially, telemetry was handled through networks of wired connections, but technological advances have enabled wireless systems to process such data as well as subsequent responses.

Furthermore, AI-equipped nanotechnology, together with, advances in meta-materials, biosensors, routing devices and protocols have made telemetry a largely invisible dynamic which has the capacity to imprison people within that dynamic. Nanoparticulates – including many metals (artificial and otherwise) -- in chemtrails, vaccines, pharmaceuticals, food, and water, together with energy and various molecules that are being siphoned off from the bodies of people being processed, are providing the primary materials for various forms of AI-nanotechnology to, without the consent of the host, set up shop and run all manner of automated telemetry programs.

"Tissue Engineering" -- This is a form of biomedical engineering. It serves as a dynamic way of establishing an interface between, on the one hand, biology and, on the other hand, various techniques involving the capacity of engineering, synthetic biology, and nanotechnology to modulate, shape, sculpt, or assemble metamaterials (artificial materials that have the capacity to be affected by, and respond to, light in an array of ways) for purposes of repairing, replacing, or improving the functional character of various processes to which biological tissues give expression.

Technology currently exists which enables such tissue engineering to be conducted from without, using materials and devices that have been placed, often without informed consent, into people's bodies. For instance, when one combines epigenetics (the processes governing gene expression) with optogenetics (the technology which, among other things, enables someone to turn genes on and off), as well as AI dynamics (stealth systems for introducing metamaterials into people's body), enhanced IEEE protocols, drone technology, and people who have ceded their agency to the darkest part of themselves (and, unfortunately, there are all too many of these sorts of individuals), then such individuals can engage, from afar, in any kind of tissue engineering which they (or their designated operators) are inclined to pursue in conjunction with targeted individuals of their choice.

"Terahertz Radiation" – The term "terahertz" refers to frequencies that are in the order of 10^{12} cycles per second. "Terahertz radiation" refers to frequency phenomena which occur in a "space" where microwave and infrared forms of electromagnetic radiation overlap to a degree and the "space" where this "overlap" takes place is referred to terahertz radiation.

This form of radiation is considered to be non-ionizing which means that it does not contain sufficient energy to displace electrons from a molecule and, thereby, ionize that molecule. Since ionizing radiation is considered to be biologically destructive or injurious, non-ionizing radiation is often considered to be a safe alternative to radiation that is ionizing in nature.

However, a great deal of research (e.g., Arthur Firstenberg, Samuel Milham, Josh Del Sol, Beverly Rubik, Mark Steel, Olle Johansson, Daniel Debaun, and Martin Pall) has indicated that non-ionizing radiation entails its own set of potential problems with respect to the health of all manner of biological organisms. Consequently, to refer to terahertz waves as a non-ionizing form of radiation doesn't necessarily mean it is safe to be used in conjunction with, say, human beings or the biological environment that surrounds human beings.

Nanoscale devices have been developed and are continuing to be developed which have healthcare applications. In order for such devices to be of value, they have to be capable of two-way communication.

Terahertz frequencies have been introduced as a form of radiation which would be characterized by low energy features and would be able to exhibit precision localization in conjunction with, among other things, such tasks as targeted drug delivery.

Putting aside the issue of whether, or not, terahertz radiation's non-ionizing property constitutes a hazard (short-term and/or long-term) to biological organisms, one could also raise questions about whether, or not, the drugs which are to released through a targeted form of delivery are necessarily in the best interests of a patient. The delivery system entails one set of questions and issues, and that which is being delivered gives expression to another set of questions and issues.

Aside from the issues surrounding the technology of delivery and the nature of the drug that is being delivered, there is a third set of questions and issues which arise in conjunction with the ability to send commands to such a delivery device. This has to do with the theory of medicine which governs the use of such devices and drugs.

Viruses have not been proven to exist. If one is using terahertz radiation to send commands to a nanoscale device to release an antiviral form of medication or treatment, then, perhaps, there are some other questions and issues which need to be addressed as well.

One might also ask whether nanotechnology is necessarily the best approach to issues of health or whether nanotechnology is even compatible with health. A lot depends on what one considers the nature of disease and health to be, and from a certain perspective, nanotechnology is not only highly invasive but might be counterproductive to the way in which, for example, the epigenetic system or the biofield operate.

Finally, there is an elephant in the room. All too many doctors were willing to make claims during the so-called COVID pandemic concerning what COVID was and how it should be diagnosed or how it should be treated, and those claims were not necessarily based on either good science or sound, constructive medical clinical practice.

Consequently, there is a monumental trust problem that has developed with respect to many dimensions of the health and medical systems. The foregoing trust issue is exacerbated by the arrogance of medical and health practitioners who believe they have the right to force people to abide by medical theories which lack scientific rigor and cannot withstand even a moderate form or critical reflection concerning the claims which are being made through the promulgation of those sorts of theories.

Diagnostic errors and prescribed medicines account for hundreds of thousands of deaths each and every year and have been doing so for decades. If any other group of people caused this kind of carnage, war would have been declared against them long ago, but, apparently, such people have become – and not for reasons that can be justified -- a legally protected species.

When considering issues like terahertz radiation, nanoscale devices, and targeted drug delivery that can be directed through wireless forms of communication, one must place such issues in an appropriate evidential context. Moreover, given that evidential context, one can't help but ask what such people are really up to because, despite the hype, what is being pushed through bio-nanotechnology raises a lot of questions which are not being adequately addressed by health and medical practitioners.

UN – ITU (International Telecommunication Union) -- This organization is an updated edition of the International Telegraph Union which began operations in 1865 by seeking to internationally regulate an array of issues having to do with telegraphy. Eventually, the organization broadened out and began to develop standards and practices for regulating radio and telephone.

The International Telegraph Union changed its name to the International Telecommunication Union in 1932 to reflect it expanding roles in governing, controlling, and setting standards with respect to various forms of communication technology. In 1947 the ITU entered into an agreement with the United Nations, and that agreement was activated in 1949.

What gives the ITU (in any of its iterations) or the United Nations the right to control, or set standards for, operating different forms of telecommunications? The short answer is: "Nothing," anymore than the IEEE has an inherent right to do what it does.

These organizations are arbitrary constructions that have been made possible through the power wrangling of backroom political dealings, financial arrangements, and select power groups. However competent -- and, perhaps, even well-meaning -- some (not all) of the individuals in such organizations might be, they have unilaterally assigned to themselves the right to control what can and can't be done in various areas of lived life.

Given that the 1947 agreement entered into between the ITU and the United Nations gave rise to the very first UN agency, one doesn't have to be a rocket scientist to understand that the aforementioned agreement is a critical step to gain control over what does and doesn't take place in the various realms of telecommunications. Such an agreement is the kind of agreement that people in such organizations might make if their ultimate aim was to work toward a one-world government to which the people of the world had little access, and over which they had even less control.

Currently, the UN and the ITU play roles in helping to assign satellite orbits and, as well, they are active in such areas as: Wireless technologies, broadband Internet, optical fiber technology, maritime and aeronautical navigation, and setting standards and protocols for different facets of telecommunications. While one might agree that these are all areas which need people to come together to figure out ways to handle various issues and problems that are entailed by such technologies, nonetheless, I don't recall that either of these organizations actively sought out the contributions of anyone but a select group of technical, financial, and governmental power brokers.

The agreement between the ITU and the United Nations resonates with the agreement which the United Nations is currently negotiating with certain power brokers around the world in relation to the proposed updating of the Pandemic Treaty. Such an agreement allegedly would enable the UN to have near-total control over the way in which the people of the world respond to so-called public health emergencies. The term "allegedly" is used in the previous sentence because the UN has failed to abide by its own rules concerning the process for negotiating such an agreement and, more importantly, not only has the United States Senate not engaged in a vote that passed such an agreement with a two-thirds majority as is required by the Constitution, but, as well, the Senate has no authority to turn over the sovereignty of American citizens to a foreign body.

The UN claims that such negotiations are only about establishing a set of protocols for building an operational framework that will regulate how human beings are to proceed in the case of emergencies and will not affect the sovereignty of any country or person. However, if such a claim is to be believed, then, why bother with such agreements at all since merely sharing information would provide people in different localities with food for thought to critically reflect upon and come to their own conclusions about how best to deal with emergencies.

The foregoing sorts of agreements – whether in the case of the ITU or in the case of the Pandemic Treaty – are not about health, well-being, co-operation, or resolving technical problems. Instead, they are maneuvers intended to accrue power and control through stealth and manipulation. The World Health Organization, the ITU, the Bank of International Settlements, and the World Economic Forum are all located in Switzerland ... a centralized location for centralized governance.

"Virtual Reality" – This gives expression to a form of artificially constructed reality that is capable of establishing contexts which induce frequency following behavior and entrainment dynamics through which people's cognitive activities can be modulated, suppressed, biased, and controlled. Virtual reality has the capacity to serve as a person's primary source of consensus validation in which one's understanding of experience and phenomenology becomes a function of how one engages virtual reality and how virtual reality engages the individual. As such, the individual becomes isolated from a range of other ideas, opinions, experiences, and conditions that are independent of, and, therefore, not controlled by, what transpires within the realm of virtual reality.

Virtual reality is touted as a medium for education. Such a medium is exceedingly vulnerable to considerable corruption in which education – or what is called "education" -- becomes an immersive, consuming, even addictive process that uses subtle techniques of undue influence to shape understanding and hermeneutical orientation. Such a process has little to do with having the freedom to access wise, competent assistance that is needed to explore issues through critical inquiry but, instead, the aforementioned process is a function of an array of biases, assumptions, theories, principles, and policies through which an individual is induced, little by little, to cede one's moral, intellectual, physical, and spiritual agency to the overlords of the educational network – the very antithesis of real education.

"WBAN" (Wireless Body Area Network) – This is a surveillance system which provides a continuous stream of monitored data concerning what takes place: Within, on, and around a given biological domain, including cognitive and behavioral activity. To whatever extent such a system is used without informed consent, then, to that extent, WBAN is an expression of transhumanist, post-humanist, technocratic, and/or oppressive forms of surveillance. To whatever extent such a system interferes with, undermines, adversely affects, injures, or overrides a person's bodily sovereignty, then, to that extent, WBAN is a tool of transhumanist, post-humanist, technocratic, and/or oppressive forms of surveillance. To whatever extent such a system is used to induce a person to be, or become, controlled by an external source of political, social, economic, financial, medical, technological, and/or military control, then, to that extent the WBAN system is a manipulative and transformative policy program that is shaped by transhumanist, post-humanist, technocratic, and/or oppressive forms of surveillance. To whatever extent such a system is used to track, trace, herd, or terminate individuals, then, to that extent, WBAN is a transhumanist, post-humanist, technocratic, and/or oppressive form of surveillance agenda.

The WBAN is never value-neutral. It is always a function of the hermeneutical context which governs how, when, where, and why it is being used and deployed.

"**Xenobot**" – These are real-world constructs which give expression to AI-assisted, computer-generated blueprints for constructing synthetic entities which are designed to serve some biological function by bringing together various kinds of tissue in non-natural, artificial ways. Xenobots are made from frog cells, and, in fact, the name is modeled after the Latin terminology for the African clawed frog (Xenopus laevis).

There is a considerable amount of debate among researchers, scientists, engineers, and medical practitioners about what 'Xenobots' are (e.g., robots, life forms, synthetic biology, etc.). This sort of debate might be a good indication that the people who are engaged in such research don't necessarily know what they are doing but are just fooling around with various kinds of frog tissue to see what might transpire.

Xenobots can be provided with different kinds of sensors and actuators which enable them to move about their environment and perform certain functions (one of which, of course, is movement). In addition, xenobots can be equipped with a form of molecular memory through the introduction of an RNA molecule into the entity which is capable of responding to the presence of certain frequencies of light.

Moreover, such entities also are able to replicate. In other words, they have been <u>given</u> a capacity to gather cells in their vicinity and perform the necessary operations which will make new versions of themselves.

Xenobots operate off of the energy that is stored in some of the fats and proteins that are present in the tissue. Once these energy sources are used up, the xenobot becomes a dead skin cell.

Some researchers have suggested that xenobots should be let loose in the world to perform various functions, such as gathering together various kinds of pollutants for subsequent disposal in some, hopefully, non-polluting manner. Other individuals believe xenobots might have medical applications.

Many scientists love to talk about complexity theory and the way in which emergent behavior can arise from system which exhibit properties of complexity. So, when researchers talk about releasing xenobots into the world, especially in swarms that are coordinated to serve such functions, one wonders what emergent properties of an unwanted nature might arise out of such complex systems. Where is Michael Crichton when you need him?

"**You**" – You are the intended target of the many kinds of technologies, networks, programs, policies, protocols, and standards which have been outlined, and commented on, in this document. Do your best to extricate yourself from all political, legal, educational, medical, scientific, technical, social, and religious networks that seek to reduce you to being nothing but a node on a network in which one is subject to the operational constraints and degrees of freedom of such networks rather than being able to exercise God-given sovereignty.

"**ZigBee**" – This is a communication protocol established by the IEEE (802.15.4) for creating networks that are characterized by properties such as being: Wireless, low-power, low-data rate, and proximate (which is why ZigBee is used in personal area networks that provide the telemetry which links near-by electronic devices – tablets, phones, computers – with, for example, "wearables" – whether in or on the body).

ZigBee is less complex and less expensive than other communication protocol systems such as Bluetooth or various Wi-Fi forms of communication protocols. Nonetheless, ZigBee is capable of transmitting data over long distances by routing the data through various kinds of mesh networks that are hooked up with distant communication and control centers.

ZigBee is capable of being integrated with systems of artificial intelligence. So, when various entities -- with the assistance of artificial intelligence algorithms – have been observed to be self-assembling in the bloodstreams of human beings (as demonstrated by the work of, among others, Ana Mihalcea, Clifford Carnicom, David Nixon, Len Ber, Mateo Taylor, Robert Young, and La Quinta Columna), one of the options for expanding the communicative reach of such entities is ZigBee ... This realization is very reassuring and comforting.

The foregoing material is a modernized, updated addendum to Ambrose Bierce's original compilation of entries known as: *The Devil's Dictionary*. Due to an absence of talent, the present offering is not as entertaining, funny, stylish, or comprehensive as the original work.

Nevertheless, this document seeks to bear witness in a sincere manner to certain events in the modern world just as AB sought to sincerely bear witness to events that were taking place in his world. Moreover, for reasons that are entirely beyond his control, AB did not have access to the same sorts of news sources as I do, and, therefore, there might be a few entries in the present addendum which are somewhat more news-worthy than are some of the entries in his initial: *The Devil's Dictionary*.

Ambrose was a veteran (first lieutenant) of the Civil War. I have become a reluctant veteran (rank private) in another kind of 'civil war', and the foregoing entries outline the nature of certain aspects of the present conflict.

11. **Targeted Individuals: Five Questions**

For those who are unfamiliar with the term, "Targeted Individuals" are people who are being terrorized everyday of the week by: Various government agents, would-be overlords of the corporate sector, medical people who lack ethics and integrity, academic experimenters who care only about their careers, military black operatives, abusers of the policing system (on a federal, state, and local level), as well as independent contractors who are willing to torture people for a buck. These perpetrators use a variety of protocols governing wireless networks of energy that been have established by the IEEE (Institute of Electrical and Electronics Engineers) and which have enabled unscrupulous, greedy, and self-serving individuals to subject people all over the world (estimated to consist of some 6,000,000 individuals) to programs (operated both through systems of artificial intelligence as well as manual apps on mobile phones, iPads, or computers) that seek to impose physical, emotional, and cognitive torture as well as mind-control programs on innocent people. The phenomenon of the Havana Syndrome is but one expression of the world-wide program of terror that is being run by people that many modalities of media are actively protecting and attempting to keep hidden from a more, wide-spread public awareness.

The following material encompasses an interview that was conducted by Dr. Len Ber of Targeted Justice -- https://www.targetedjustice.com/ -- in late January of 2024.

-----

1) Please tell us about your professional and spiritual journey.

Before I begin addressing your question, there are a few things that should be said. First, I have been informed that if I had the opportunity to do so, Sabrina Dawn Wallace wanted me to pass on the following message to you, Len, and I believe that the present time is such an opportunity. The message that Sabrina wanted me to pass on to you is: "May God Bless you and thank you for speaking up."

Secondly, whatever your audience might think about what is said during the following semi-oral-history, I want to acknowledge the tremendous sacrifices and suffering that have been endured by the members of the targeted community. This acknowledgement is being given at the beginning of this presentation because I do not want it to get lost in the shuffle of other facets of what might be said by me.

Some Targeted Individuals have been targeted because they are whistleblowers of one kind or another.

Some Targeted Individuals have been targeted because of what they know about various topics – scientific, technical, or otherwise -- and the people who are operating the campaign of terror against such individuals of knowledge and understanding deeply fear what those Targeted Individuals know.

Some Targeted Individuals have been emotionally, mentally, and physically bullied because the people who are perpetrating the abuse have no respect for the race, ethnicity, religion, financial status, intelligence, character and/or political interests of such Targeted Individuals.

Other individuals have been targeted because, without their consent, they have been selected to be data points in a set of experiments designed to gather data about the dynamics of remote mind control, torture, and murder ... data that will be used to shape what the torture overlords will undertake – perhaps in the not-too-distant future -- with respect to the rest of humanity.

Whatever the criteria are that have placed someone in the crosshairs of the terrorists who are getting paid to bring misery and pain into the lives of innocent individuals, nevertheless, because of the integrity, resilience, courage, strength, and perseverance of the members of the Targeted Individuals community, the members of that community have become the tripwire that has provided others, such as myself, with the very hard-won intelligence that there is something deeply corrupt, pathological, and evil which is taking place all around us in conjunction with an agenda that is seeking to make everyone but the terrorist overlords into Targeted Individuals.

I want to thank Targeted Individuals for their service to humanity. Indeed, there are Targeted Individuals all over the world whose lives are in on-going danger who have been fighting for many years against the war of terror that is being waged against the people of the world and who desperately have been trying to get people to listen to, and learn from, the decades of difficult, painful experiences that have been endured by tens-of-thousands if not millions of Targeted Individuals around the world.

Targeted Individuals are the people who are manning the front lines and have been taking considerable punishment and going through incredible difficulties, and, in the process, they have provided the rest of us with a tremendous amount of direct, experiential evidence as well as some precious time of forewarning to, God willing, try to find ways of countering what is taking place – that is, as indicated earlier, a concerted attempt is being made with respect to the vast majority of the population – at least those who might survive – to turn the rest of humanity into Targeted Individuals.

Walter Lippmann, an American journalist and writer, who died in 1974 once said: "There can be no higher law in journalism than to tell the truth and to shame the devil." Targeted Individuals who have tried to make their life experiences known to the world are citizen journalists who exemplify, at considerable cost to themselves, the principles set forth by Lippmann – they have told the truth, and in doing so, they have shamed the devil, but, as usual, the devil is too narcissistically enamored with himself to understand the nature of the shame that has become the crown which is being worn on his head.

When Targeted Individuals share their life stories, their experiences bring to mind, and resonate with, some words of warning from Alexander Solzhenitsyn that were voiced in his work *Gulag Archipelago* – namely, "In keeping silent about evil, in burying it so deep within us that no sign of it appears on the surface, we are implanting it, and it will rise up a thousand fold in the future." If the general public continues to ignore the bearing of witness by, among others, Targeted Individuals, then the general public will be burying the truth about the presence of an overarching evil that will become implanted within the way that the general public goes about its business and, eventually, that evil will come back to haunt them in thousands of way in the not too distant future.

Having said the foregoing, I'll try to return to your original question, Len, concerning my professional and spiritual background. The story is a little complicated, but I believe that, in its own way, it complements the concerns of the Targeted Individuals community, although it does so from a different direction.

I'm nearly 80 years old. My real education began a little over 50 years ago, but I would like to provide some context. Although I have gone through some periods of unemployment and homelessness during that period of time, I'm going to focus on just a few events in my life, but, unfortunately, this will take a little time.

I attended a high school in north-central Maine that had 44 students. Eleven kids were in my graduating class.

I grew up during the time of Sputnik. Americans had become panicked by the fact that the Russians had placed a satellite in space first, and, consequently, all manner of science and math programs were being developed in the United States. As a result, I participated in several programs in math and science that were offered by the Maine State Department of Education – in fact, I was one of the few first-year high school students in the state of Maine to do so and actually did fairly well and along with another first-year high school student placed in the top 12 among the hundreds of students who were taking the courses.

Between my junior and senior years of high school, I won a National Science Foundation scholarship to study the theory of semi-conductors at a university in New York City. Although I had a little game in science, eventually my heart was pulled in another direction.

One day, my mother sat me down and proposed that I apply to Harvard College. She said she had been reading some articles which indicated that I might be the sort of student for whom Harvard was looking. However, I have to confess that I really had no idea of who or what Harvard was ... the university had not come across my radar back in the late 1950s and early 1960s.

One might say that my experience with respect to Harvard could be put forth as a new kind of proof concerning the existence of God ... because, quite frankly, I would have a tough time explaining how I got into and out of Harvard without presupposing the existence of God.

Technological Reflections

However, that entails a set of events that would take us beyond the thrust of this presentation.

I started out as a pre-theological student with the idea of working toward some kind of ministerial career. However, for a variety of reasons, I became dissatisfied with myself, and, as a result, I began to move in other directions – including physical science, philosophy, and finally, psychology – or, more specifically, Social Relations – an interdisciplinary course covering topics in sociology, psychology, and anthropology. I wrote an undergraduate honors thesis which developed – or attempted to – a new theory concerning the phenomenon of anxiety.

After graduating college, I got a job at a youth detention center just outside of Boston. The Vietnam War had been heating up while I was going to college, and although the youth detention center job was a draft-deferrable kind of job, nevertheless, when the time came for my selective service physical exam, I refused to comply with a lot of the things that I was being asked to do by the military authorities during the physical exam process and, as a result, I ended up being interviewed by the FBI. Among other things, the FBI wanted to fingerprint me, but I refused, and, then, they wanted me to sign a card indicating that I refused to be fingerprinted, and I refused that as well.

When I showed up for work the next day, my employer (which was the State of Massachusetts) had already been contacted by the FBI. I was called into the supervisor's office and given an opportunity to sign a loyalty oath – which was done in those days in Massachusetts – and get back with the military program or I would be fired, so, I chose to be fired.

I had no intention of being disloyal to the Constitution of the United States or trying to overthrow the federal government. Nonetheless, I wasn't going to be bullied into signing such a document.

Three or four months later I left for Canada with $50.00 to my name, no job, and no place to live. Eventually, I got a job as co-director of a youth haven house in Toronto, and when the money for that project ran out, I was hired by the Counseling and Development Center at York University where I: Did some research, helped run some sensitivity training groups, and did a little counseling.

| Technological Reflections |

After the Counseling and Development Job ended, I taught a course on the psychology of learning for the Education Ministry in Ontario that was being given to prospective counselors in the Ontario provincial educational system. When the foregoing course ended, I taught a course in transpersonal psychology while serving as a college don at York University.

I started a graduate program in education at the University of Toronto, but before getting into this aspect of things a little, I should provide some context because it relates to the other part of your two-part question, Len, concerning my professional and spiritual background. I grew up in a Christian environment, and, indeed, as previously indicated, I began college with the idea of becoming a minister, however, I went through a period involving several years involving the dark night of the soul before finally beginning to pursue issues of spirituality once again.

I began to read widely about different mystical traditions. I was much taken with the work of Baba Ram Das – Richard Alpert – who had been a professor of psychology when I was at Harvard before he and Timothy Leary were fired from their professorships due to their activities involving psychotropic drugs. However, I also was intrigued by the writings of several of your former countrymen, Len, – P.D. Ouspensky and Georg Gurdjieff, and, eventually, I joined a Gurdjieff group in Toronto that was linked to Madam Walsh – whom I met -- whose husband had been the attending physician for Gurdjieff when he was in France.

When I was investigating different mystical traditions, there was a book store near the University of Toronto that was run by a couple who had converted to Buddhism. Initially, the store only carried works concerning different dimensions of the Buddhist spiritual tradition, but eventually, the store carried titles concerning all manner of mystical and spiritual issues.

I use to go there mainly to try to find books related to Gurdjieff, but, one day I came across a book by Rafael Lefort called: *The Teachers of Gurdjieff*. Among the teachers of Gurdjieff were individuals who were known as Sufis, a term that I had not heard of prior to reading the book ... in fact, prior to seeing the term "Sufi" in the aforementioned book, my only fleeting contact with Islam -- which is

| Technological Reflections |

the spiritual tradition in which the Sufi mystical path is rooted -- had been when I worked in a mental institution just outside of Boston when I was an undergraduate, and a Muslim had had a very short stay in the facility at which I worked.

Now, as it turns out, the name Rafael Lefort is a pseudonym for an individual whose identity was never known. However, after reading the book bearing his name, I began trying to find books on the Sufi tradition, and back in the late 1960s, early 1970s, this was not always easy to do ... and this is where the story gets a little interesting.

After the funding for the aforementioned youth haven in Toronto ran out, I applied for a similar job in a city that was a few miles outside of Toronto. I was called for an interview, and when I arrived at the potential job site, there were a lot of candidates waiting in line in front of me.

While waiting for my name to be called, I struck up a conversation with a young, extremely intelligent high school student who happened to be sitting next to me. He knew a great deal about mysticism, Gurdjieff, Ouspensky, and quite a few other topics. He was the sort of kid who belonged at Harvard rather than me.

Eventually, my name was called for an interview. Eventually, I found out that I didn't get the job.

However, following some gigs as an iterant bartender at different university functions, I began full-time employment at the bookstore at York University, and, a couple of years later became one of its textbook buyers. Whenever I got the chance, however, I would continue to return, on a fairly regular basis, to the Buddhist bookstore near the University of Toronto.

I had been frequenting that bookstore for several years, and would visit the store on different days of the week according to my work schedule. It was a relatively small, two room bookstore, and even on busy days – usually on Saturdays – there were rarely more than 6-10 people in the store.

I knew the owners and the clerks who worked there, often engaging them in conversation about various issues. One Saturday, some six months, or so, following my previously mentioned failed job interview in a near-by city, I went to the Buddhist bookstore on a

Saturday, and, surprisingly, no one, with the exception of me and another individual, the store clerk, was there.

The clerk who usually worked on Saturdays was not present. In his place was the young man with whom I had such a great conversation in another city prior to my failed interview. The usual clerk had been called away on some sort of family emergency and had asked the young man if he would fill in for the day.

He remembered me, and I remembered him. We struck up a conversation, and somewhere along the line I mentioned my budding influence in the Sufi mystical path.

He asked me if I wanted to meet a Sufi teacher. I answered affirmatively, and he wrote down a name and a number on a piece of paper before handing it to me.

We talked a bit longer, and, then, I left. The number and name I had been given led me to still another person with whom I met for a five or six hour meeting, and, while I was there his spiritual guide called. My name came up in the conversation, and a meeting with the teacher was arranged.

The second time that I interacted with the teacher was at a mosque during Ramadan, the month of fasting. It was also Christmas Eve.

The spiritual guide took me to a place in the middle of the mosque and instructed me on a zikr or chant. He started out, and I followed suit.

Not long after engaging the chant – or it engaging me -- a very pronounced state came over me. It continued on for a time even after the recitation came to a close, and, then, gradually, dissipated.

I stayed with the teacher for a while longer, and, then, asked for permission to leave, which was granted. A few months later, I became initiated into the Chishti Order of the Sufi mystical path, which I consider to be the servant's entrance to Islam, and, by the Grace of God, I have done my best to try to travel this path for the last 50-plus years.

I continued going to the Buddhist bookstore for several years following my Sufi initiation. I went to the store on different days and at different times of the day, but I never saw the young man in the store again who had sent me on a journey that led to the best Christmas gift that I had ever received.

Not too long after becoming initiated, three things happened over the course of the next few years. One, I began a doctoral program in education at the University of Toronto; two, I became involved in a textbook-bias campaign concerning Islam with respect to the problematic contents of the books that were being used in grade schools and high schools across the Province of Ontario; three, I became involved in a student group's empirically-documented case concerning plagiarism that had been committed by a faculty member in the Department of Middle East and Islamic Studies at the University of Toronto.

This is where my professional and spiritual journey began to merge. Indeed, the spiritual part of the journey had a significant, if not dominant, shaping influence on what did, and didn't happen, in my professional career.

Before recounting what happened in my life as a result of the interaction of the foregoing three dynamics, I would like to mention something that, initially, might seem counter-intuitive. More specifically, although people who are Targeted Individuals have undergone, and are continuing to undergo, extremely painful forms of physical, emotional, and mental abuse, their intense difficulties are, in a way, a tremendous gift because as a result of such experiences, Targeted Individuals have: Direct knowledge about, understanding of, and insight into just how corrupt and evil certain segments of government, corporations, the media, psychology, the military, and the medical community have become.

Unfortunately, there are many people in North American society who are oblivious to the presence of the evil, pathological, psychopathic forces that are actively present within many aspects of government and social institutions. As a result, all too many people have been unable to acquire and exercise the gift of fear which is necessary to be able to sense, detect, and respond to the dynamics of terrorism that daily are being inflicted on, among others, Targeted Individuals.

I went to two of the best academic institutions in the world. Very expensive forms of education, and, yet, I was kept in ignorance by those institutions and didn't begin to wake up to the way of power or the terror tactics that are employed by the way of power until I was brought into direct contact with how the way of power actually operates. The way of power that I experienced is not the same as what Targeted Individuals have had to endure, but, nonetheless, a certain amount of pain and difficulty still characterized my experiences.

Everything of value that I have learned in my life has come from outside of formal systems of education. As a result of such non-formal education, I have come to have an appreciation for, among other things, what Targeted Individuals have been, and are still, trying to tell people about what certain dimensions of the world are actually like, and, as a result of their testimonies concerning their experiences, I have developed some degree of a appreciation for the importance of the gift of fear in conjunction with the forms of terrorism directed toward Targeted Individuals and which are being exercised across many demographic strata of society … hearing the oral histories of Targeted Individuals has helped me to develop a healthy appreciation concerning the danger that exists amongst us.

By use of the term "fear" I am not alluding to some state of frenzied, unthinking panic, but, rather, I am alluding to people who have developed a deep, visceral and emotional understanding concerning the presence of evil in the world. For instance, Targeted Individuals have had considerable opportunity to acquire a justifiable sense of fear concerning the presence of evil and the sort of damage that such evil can inflict upon the lives of people.

When I use the term "gift of fear," I am talking about that term in the same way that Gavin de Becker. He wrote the book, *The Gift of Fear*, and he uses that phrase – that is, "the gift of fear" – to refer to the intuitive capabilities within human beings that are able – if we learn to listen to them -- to sense the presence of very real, and not imagined, dangers, and, as a result, try to develop methods for avoiding, escaping from, or surviving those dangers.

However, just as Targeted Individuals have had to pay a very difficult, painful – and, therefore, costly -- form of tuition in order to acquire insights concerning the methods of abuse, terrorism, and undue influence which are employed through the manner in which many governmental agencies, as well as many social, medical, media, and military institutions, operate, I have had my own non-formal mediums of educational tuition that have had to be paid.

Nonetheless, with respect to that which is about to be said, I am not trying to say that whatever pain or difficulties I have had to endure is anything like what Targeted Individuals go through on a daily basis. At the same time, there has been a price that has had to be paid for acquiring some taste for, or sense of, the gift of fear that has begun to become established within me.

For example, doctoral degrees usually take between three and seven years to obtain. It took me seventeen years to obtain my doctorate, and upon hearing the foregoing, one might well conclude that either I'm one dumb doctoral candidate or, perhaps, there is something more to the story.

The "something more" being alluded to here has to do with, among other things, my participation in the aforementioned textbook bias campaign concerning Islam as well as my participation involving the student group that brought charges of plagiarism against a professor of Middle East and Islamic Studies at the University of Toronto. I'm going to outline just a few aspects concerning the plagiarism case which took place in the late 1970's, more than fifty years ago, because the case helps to demonstrate some of the reasons why Targeted Individuals have such difficulty getting people to really listen to what they are saying.

The professor in question was the editor of a textbook consisting of a series of articles concerning Islam and Muslims that had been written by various professors at different universities in Canada, including several articles by the editor of the foregoing textbook. The student group to which I belonged had received a tip from another professor that the two articles by the editor of the textbook might contain plagiarized material.

As a result, members of the student group began to do some research concerning the issue. Eventually, we came across evidence indicating that there was considerable plagiarized material in the two articles that we had been investigating.

We wrote a short report on the matter and forwarded our findings to the President of the University of Toronto. In addition, we released a small newsletter covering the issue and hand-distributed the material to professors and students across the campus.

We also prepared a package which contained a copy of our report accompanied by a questionnaire that asked a variety of questions that probed a person's judgment concerning the claims of plagiarism that were in our report. Among other things, the report contained side-by-side comparisons of the source material that had been plagiarized and the passages from the articles in the textbook that contained such plagiarized material.

The foregoing package (i.e., report, questionnaire, and covering letter) was sent out to a number of professors across North America who specialized in the areas of Middle East and Islamic Studies. We received back about 25 of the questionnaires, and the vast majority of them agreed that the excerpts from the two articles being probed constituted instances of plagiarism when compared against the original source materials, and, in fact, one professor from a university in New York indicated that he had come across other evidence that the professor who had edited the textbook and who had contributed several articles to that same book also had committed plagiarism with respect to another article that had been written on another occasion.

The student group to which I belong prepared a second newsletter containing the results that we had received from professors working at other universities in North America as well as our comments concerning a letter that the President of the University of Toronto had written in response to our initial report on the matter. We distributed this second newsletter to members of the University of Toronto community, including the President of the University, and, in addition, we released the material to a number of media outlets in Toronto.

The media's initial response to our package was quite enthusiastic. In fact, a newspaper with national prominence wanted to have an exclusive to the issue.

However, a week, or so, later, none of the media outlets were interested in pursuing the plagiarism case. We learned from sources that some administrators and several professors from the University of Toronto had contacted the media to say that the student group to which I belonged was just a bunch of Muslims who were trying to create trouble for a respected member of the University of Toronto and that the media should drop the issue – which they did.

A short while after the plagiarism issue had been dropped, the professor who had committed plagiarism was appointed by the University to serve as faculty advisor to the university committee that investigated and made deliberations concerning potential violations -- such as plagiarism -- involving the student honor code. A little later on, I came across a newspaper story about some graduate student who had been denied his doctoral degree at the University of Toronto, or who had had the degree revoked, because, according to the aforementioned honor committee, that individual had committed plagiarism.

In the aftermath of the plagiarism case, the University did not withdraw administrative recognition from the student group to which I belonged. Furthermore, none of the individuals in our group were called before the university administration and officially reprimanded for our actions.

However, in its own underhanded manner, the University administration did find a way to exact punishment. Not too long after the foregoing events had transpired, I was approached by my thesis advisor. He wanted to know what I was up to because the Minister of Education for the Province of Ontario had contacted the Director of the Institute where I was enrolled and wanted to know why I was still being allowed to attend the University of Toronto.

Subsequently, whenever I tried to get together with my purported thesis advisor to discuss my dissertation, the professor was never available for consultation and discussion. This dynamic continued to take place for quite some time.

Eventually, the clock was run out on my doctoral program. Although, on my own – that is, without any help from my thesis advisor -- I had written a thesis and attempted to submit the document prior to the doctoral program deadline, my department wouldn't accept the dissertation, and, as a result, I entered what was called "lapsed candidacy status," and this status did not permit me to use university facilities or have access to faculty members, but it did carry the possibility of allowing me to re-enroll at some later time should I ever complete a dissertation and, thereby, be eligible to go through the oral examination process if I could get the appropriate people at the University to agree to what I was doing in the way of a dissertation.

To make a long story much shorter, it took me ten years to figure out a way to become re-enrolled in the doctoral program and be given the opportunity to formally defend my dissertation through the required oral examination. I had written another dissertation on the hermeneutics of understanding, and my oral examination committee consisted of: A quantum physicist; a biophysicist; several experts in the philosophy of science; a linguist; a historian, and a specialist in adult education.

The latter individual said that he had never previously encountered a dissertation like mine and hoped to never do so again, but he voted in favor of accepting the dissertation. In fact, every member of the oral examining committee voted in favor of accepting my dissertation.

Prior to going before the oral examination committee, I had met my previous thesis advisor – the one who always found a way, or excuse, for not being able to meet with me. He told me that a number of students prior to me had tried to do what I was trying to do and they had all failed.

After I successfully defended my dissertation, I went back to my academic department. There were a number of professors milling about and fully expecting my news to be that my dissertation had been rejected, and, when, I gave them the "good" news, their jaws visibly dropped.

Despite obtaining my doctorate, due to the period of 17 years that were required to get the degree, any potential career that I might have had was pretty much ruined. However, the looks of shock on the faces of the professors when they discovered that I had been successful in my oral defense was nearly worth the price that had to be paid for going through such a 17-year ordeal.

To add a further embellishing detail to the foregoing saga, I should indicate that when the time came for the diploma ceremonies to take place during which successful candidates would receive their signed doctoral degrees, the University library system in which I worked was on strike. As a result, I refused to cross the picket line and missed the diploma ceremonies despite having waited 17 years for such an opportunity.

In the end, all we really get to keep is the integrity with which we try to live life. As the Tracy Chapman song goes: "All you have is your soul," and for seventeen years I struggled to maintain some degree of integrity in the foregoing matter and to keep a tight watch over my soul.

Targeted Individuals face a problem that is very similar to the one which I have outlined in the foregoing account of my pursuit to get a doctorate – although – to be sure -- the problems which Targeted Individuals face are much more painful, difficult, and intense than my foregoing experiences. Nonetheless, on many levels, the lives of Targeted Individuals have been made extremely difficult and filled with one obstacle or attack after another.

As I discovered in my own case, government officials ignore the plight of Targeted Individuals. The media turns a blind eye to the abuses being perpetrated against Targeted Individuals. Academics refuse to carry out research which would demonstrate that the problems experienced by Targeted Individuals are real and not imagined. Finally, the general public is propagandized via government officials, so-called journalists, and academics to believe that all is well that and there is no malignant cancer eating away at the fabric of society.

Some people might wonder why I even bothered pursuing a doctorate for seventeen years – especially given that I earlier said that the most important facets of life are learned about outside of formal educational processes. There are two reasons.

The first reason had to do with the fact that my spiritual guide had wanted me to pursue such a degree, and he had helped me in a variety of ways to work toward realizing such a project. Although he had passed on before I got my doctorate, I wanted to complete the process he had encouraged me to pursue.

The second reason had to do with a certain stubborn streak that exists within me. I wasn't about to let educational psychopaths get away with trying to bully me into submission, and I suspect that there are a lot of people among Targeted Individuals who have similar feelings and aren't about to let psychopaths bully them and will find whatever way they can to fight back, and based on my own experience, I have a lot of respect for, and compassion for, such individuals.

I haven't had much of a career. As an adjunct professor in both Canada and the United States, I have had to scramble to be able to teach courses covering: Introductory psychology, abnormal psychology, social psychology, transpersonal psychology, philosophy, criminology, diversity, and life-span development. However, adjunct professors are the migrant workers of the educational system … they are very poorly paid, provided with no benefits, and have few, if any rights, within the academic community.

Eventually, I resigned from teaching and decided to concentrate on writing books. Some 45, or so, books have been written over the last two decades, and many of them are floating about somewhere in the Widener Library system at Harvard University.

The topics range from: Education, to: Evolution, philosophy, psychology, cosmology, religion, quantum physics, medicine, Tolstoy, constitutional philosophy, government, sovereignty, Islam, and the Sufi path. Although over the years, thousands of copies of the books have been sold, presently, all of the books are available for free at my web site.

Len – Second Question

2.) I learned that you consider the claims of Targeted Individuals to be legitimate from a preview of the book you are writing. It was mentioned in the chapter appropriately called "Phenomenology Hijacking". Not every day you meet a person who is not a Targeted Individual, but understands the reality of the Targeting Program. What events in your history led you to this belief, while most of the people do not take our claims seriously?

If there is one consistent theme in American history, the phenomenon of Targeted Individuals is it. What makes the Targeted Individuals of today different from Targeted Individuals of the past is the extensive role that technology plays in carrying out such a targeting process.

Indigenous peoples of North America were the original Targeted Individuals. They were abused in every possible way conceivable, and, yet, here we are today, many centuries later, and, for the most part, government officials, media representatives, religious authorities, academics, and large swaths of the general public still tend to resist listening to the litany of abuses which, for centuries, have been directed against indigenous peoples or resist acknowledging that every treaty ever signed with indigenous peoples has been broken by the United States.

The next set of Targeted Individuals in America were slaves – both black and white (many people forget that slavery did not involve just people of color) -- who were subject to all manner of physical, emotional, mental, financial, political, social, and spiritual abuse. Slavery might have officially ended, but a great deal of the aforementioned abuse continues against individuals who are targeted because they do not exhibit the right race, ethnicity, socio-economic status, or religious affiliation.

Throughout American history: The poor, women, as well as people of Hispanic, Irish, Chinese, Jewish, Japanese, Italian, East European, and Asian ancestry have all taken their turn as Targeted Individuals in America. Moreover, some members of the aforementioned groups continue to be targeted for abuse of one kind or another.

In the late 1800s and early 1900s, Smedley Butler, who -- until Audie Murphy came along in the Second World War – had been the most decorated soldier in U.S. military history, has written a book called: *War Is a Racquet*. Among other things, the book outlined his account of how his military service had largely been in the service of vested corporate and banking interests rather than in the service of the people of the United States.

Corporations and bankers identified individuals who stood in the way of their financial and economic agendas and, as a result, such individuals became Targeted Individuals. Consequently, thousands of people died in various parts of the world because the U.S. military was authorized to serve the interests of corporations and banks through eliminating Targeted Individuals who stood in the way of increased profits, greed, and control.

| Technological Reflections |

Smedley Butler also thwarted a plot by fascist-oriented business people in the United States to remove FDR from power in the early-to-mid 1930s. The business people disliked Roosevelt's New Deal and believed that there dislike entitled them to target individuals for the purpose of illicitly and illegally taking over the government of the United States.

With the full support of the United States government, Palestinians have been Targeted Individuals for 75 years. Indeed, the inhabitants of Gaza in occupied Palestine, as well as Palestinians in the West Bank, are serving as Targeted Individuals as we speak.

In 1953, the American CIA helped to finance a coup and to overthrow the democratically elected government of Mohammed Mossadeq in Iran. Thousands of people became Targeted Individuals and they were either killed or were: Tortured, imprisoned, or displaced as a result of the Shah of Iran having been placed in power.

In 1954, the CIA helped to overthrow the democratically elected government of Jacobo Árbenz Guzmán in Guatemala. Some 50,000 Guatemalans became Targeted Individuals and were killed during the coup.

Martin Luther King, whose memory was commemorated just a few days ago, was a Targeted Individual for much of his adult life. One of the reasons that he was targeted was not because he was black but because he was opposed to the Vietnam War and indicated in reference to the war that "the United States was the greatest purveyor of violence in the world."

The violence that was being committed by the United States in Vietnam was not just the result of collateral damage. There was a CIA- and military run-program of targeted killing which took place in Vietnam that was known as the Phoenix Program, and as a result hundreds of thousands of people were tortured and/or killed because they had become Targeted Individuals. Moreover, the many different highly toxic colored chemical compounds beside Agent Orange that were used in Vietnam have targeted many Vietnamese and either led to the death of such individuals or left them with incurable illnesses, disabilities, and birth defects.

| Technological Reflections |

From 1965 through 1973, Cambodia was bombed repeatedly. The U.S. war in Vietnam was not going well, and as a result, decisions were reached by U.S. officials which turned Cambodians into Targeted Individuals, and hundreds of thousands of people lost their lives due to the aforementioned bombing campaign, and, in addition, this helped set the stage for the Killing Fields involving individuals who had been targeted by Pol Pot's government a few years later.

In 1989, the U.S. government targeted individuals in Panama. As a result, hundreds of thousands of Panamanian people were killed, maimed, and displaced – not because the later individuals had done anything wrong but because the United States had a desire to be able to demonstrate full spectrum dominance over Panama in order to further America's political agenda in the region.

Former U.S. government officials Bill Richardson and Madeline Albright both said that despite the fact that 500,000 children had been killed during the first Gulf war which began in 1990-91 in Iraq and continued on, to some extent, during the Presidency of Bill Clinton, nonetheless, according to Albright and Richardson, the U.S.-led intervention had been worth it … but, worth it for whom? Millions of Iraqi people died, or were maimed, or were imprisoned, or tortured, or displaced because they had become Targeted Individuals as a result of a manufactured, false story by the daughter of a Kuwaiti government official concerning premature Kuwaiti babies that allegedly had been smashed on a hospital floor by Iraqi soldiers.

The Iraqi people again became Targeted Individuals beginning in 2003 and continuing to this day. This time, the sin of the Iraqi people was manufactured by American government officials who claimed – without verified evidence -- that Iraq had played a role in the September 11, 2001 tragedies in New York, Washington, and Pennsylvania, and as a result, millions more Iraqis were killed, maimed, imprisoned, tortured, robbed, and/or displaced through the targeted efforts of the United States government.

Beginning in 2014, the United States designated people of Yemen as Targeted Individuals du jour. As a result, more than 500,000 people from Yemen were killed over the next 6-7 years with the full support of the United States government.

The United States has identified a litany of Targeted Individuals in a variety of countries in Asia, Africa, the Middle East, and elsewhere. Drones have been dispatched -- in progressively increasing numbers -- by Presidents: Bush, Obama, Trump, and Biden to kill certain Targeted Individuals without due process, and, as a result, thousands of innocent individuals – many of them children -- have been killed.

Throughout many of the foregoing periods of time, mind-control programs like MK-Ultra were being run by the U.S. government. For instance, private individuals had been targeted by psychologists, government officials, and intelligence operatives in Canada and the United States to become unwitting participants in government-run experiments involving LSD and other psychotropic drugs.

I was familiar with many of the revelations that were made during the Church Hearings that took place in the mid-1970s which disclosed, with much fanfare, some of the programs and weapons that had been developed by the CIA and other intelligence or governmental agencies. Although the people who were killed, injured, or experimented on during such programs were not generally known as Targeted Individuals at that time, nonetheless, that is what they were.

In addition, people -- such as Cathy O'Brien, Janet Phelan, and others -- also provided considerable testimony concerning how, without their informed consent, they had been illegally forced to become Targeted Individuals within government-sanctioned and operated mind-control and behavior controlled programs.

Some time ago, I remember discovering Catherine Horton's testimony with respect to the way in which she had become a targeted individual, first in England and later in the United States. For a while, I followed her internet program which explored the topic of Targeted Individuals, but, then, lost track of her for a few years.

A number of months ago, I happened on an interview involving whistleblower Bill Binney and Katherine Horton. I was surprised to learn that Bill Binney, a man of considerable integrity, had also become a targeted individual, and I was even more surprised – and quite happy to discover – that Bill Binney and Katherine Horton – who is a woman of considerable integrity -- had somehow come together and become man and wife.

And, of course, Len, we can't leave your testimony out of the discussion. In fact, I first set eyes on you and listened to you when both you and Robert Duncan – a former creator of mind-control programs – did an interview about the issue of Targeted Individuals on the show that used to be known as Koncrete (now, the Danny Jones Podcast). I subsequently read Duncan's book *"Soul Catcher"* concerning the government's research and operation of programs involving Targeted Individuals.

A little while after listening to you and Robert Duncan, I stumbled upon – and, it was a matter of either blind luck or the result of forces above my pay grade – the work of Sabrina Wallace, another targeted individual. She has generated a lot of very highly intelligent, insightful technical information that delineates the research and implementation of programs over the last 25-plus years involving not only Targeted Individuals but, as well, how all of that research is in the process of being used to transform much of the rest of humanity into Targeted Individuals as well.

Late last year I finished a book: *David Icke's Perspective: A Sufi's Meditative Reflection* concerning the first 60, or so, pages of David's book entitled: *Everything You Need To Know But Have Never Been Told*, and in my book I talked a little about the issue of frequency following behavior that is at the heart of what is going on with Targeted Individuals. I was very surprised when you contacted me through academia.edu and expressed interest in some of the things that were said in the book. I was surprised with your interest in my work not only because I admired the testimony that you gave during the aforementioned interview on Koncrete, as well as some of the other research you have been doing with blood analysis involving nanotechnology, but, as well, here you were, making contact with me.

I just never imagined that such a meeting might take place. Usually, when it comes to the Internet, I watch the people on the screen, and the people on the screen don't tend to talk back to me … so to speak.

In any event, to sort of sum up my response to your earlier question, I became interested in the issue of Targeted Individuals through a variety of different research avenues and as a result of that research have come to understand that Targeted Individuals have been a common, persistent theme in American history. The biggest difference between the Targeted Individuals of the past and the Targeted Individuals of the present is the way in which technology is being used to try to interfere with, control, disable, or eliminate the lives of the individuals who are being targeted, and it is precisely because of the way in which technology has increased the scale level which is being applied to the phenomenon of Targeted Individuals that has set my Spider Man-like Sensors to begin tingling and sounding the alarm of danger with respect to what is going on not only in the United States but all around the world in conjunction with the Targeted Individual phenomenon.

3.) There are a lot of Targeted Individuals whose families, friends, colleagues, loved ones rejected them, don't believe them, consider them mentally off. Do you have any advice to TI's who are struggling from social isolation due to the problem that I just described?

Some singers put together two or more songs and refer to the bringing together of elements from different songs as a process of mashup. I'm not going to sing – and, believe me, I am doing everyone a favor by not singing – but rather, I'm just going to juxtapose or mashup a few lines from three different songs and throw out a few comments as a way of kicking off my response to your question, Len.

The first line comes from the work of the relatively recently deceased Canadian, Gordon Lightfoot which is entitled: 'The Wreck of the Edmund Fitzgerald' and provides an account concerning the sinking of a freighter ship during a storm that hit Lake Superior in 1975, with the loss of all 29 members of the crew. The line I have in mind is:

"Does anyone know where the love of God goes when the waves turn the minutes to hours?"

A second set of lines comes from the Tracy Chapman song that, earlier, I referred to in passing – namely,

"All you have is your soul." At one point in the song, she says:

Don't be tempted by the shiny apple; don't you eat of the bitter fruit;

Hunger only for a taste of justice, hunger only for a world of truth.

And, finally, I will add a couple of lines from one of my favorite Paul Simon songs:

We're working our jobs; collect our pay.

Believe we're gliding down the highway

When in fact we're slip-sliding away.

What do we make of the events of life? If an individual believes in a Divinity of some kind, then, such a person tends to hold to the idea that what takes place in life has value and meaning, even if one doesn't necessarily understand the nature of the value or meaning which is entailed by whatever events are taking place in one's life – especially if such events are painful and debilitating. On the other hand, if an individual does not believe in a Divinity of some kind, then, such a person might consider events to be random and, yet, still makes choices concerning what meaning and value the person feels should be assigned to life's events in a way that assists that individual to cope with "the slings and arrows of outrageous fortune."

Irrespective of whether, or not, a person believes in God, nevertheless, when, in Gordon Lightfoot's words: "the waves turn the minutes to hours" the question to ask is not: Where does the love of God go?, but, rather, the question becomes what is a person going to do "when the waves turn the minutes to hours." For those who do not have beliefs in a Divinity, the first part of the Gordon Lightfoot song line is a non-starter, but the last part of the foregoing question persists – namely, when the "waves turn the minutes to hours" how is one to proceed?

For those who do have a belief in God, then, one should know that one's existence, intelligence, and emotion have all been shaped by God and that they are gifts for which to be grateful and are manifestations of God's presence. Then, like the individual who does not believe in

God, the problem remains the same – when the waves turn the minutes to hours, how is one to proceed?

Whether we like it or hate it, life is full of trials. All trials are about a test of character, and this remains the case whether one believes in God or not.

Every day, Targeted Individuals – irrespective of their beliefs about God -- are faced with the question of what to do when the waves of strife, pain, and loss of control come crashing down on their lives, threatening to sink their existential ships in one of life's storms. So, what is one to do?

According to Tracy Chapman one should keep the following perspective in mind:

Don't be tempted by the shiny apple; don't you eat of the bitter fruit;

Hunger only for a taste of justice, hunger only for a world of truth.

The people who get paid to make the life of Targeted Individuals miserable or the people who have set AI programs running to make the lives of Targeted Individuals miserable are trying to break human beings. Seeking to break human beings is the purpose of every form of torture, abuse, and system of control.

Among other things, the computer program: Spells, demons or algorithmic protocols that are run against Targeted Individuals use the dynamics of classical conditional and operant conditioning, and, therefore, employ techniques of both negative and positive strategies of reinforcement in the attempt to induce people to move in different emotional and conceptual directions. Targeted Individuals are flooded with all manner of input that is intended to confuse and disorient them, to induce their minds to dissociate and, in the process, such minds become vulnerable to whatever ideas, thoughts, or emotions are being directed toward Targeted Individuals. During such a state of confusion, uncertainty and vulnerability, the purveyors of torture and abuse against Targeted Individuals want a person to either be tempted by whatever shiny apple is projected into one's consciousness or such purveyors of chaos want their targets to eat and consume, as well as be consumed by, the bitter fruit of the ordeal in which an individual, through no fault of one's own, has become entangled.

Tracy's advice – and it is good, sound advice – is to aspire to a quality of character that maintains that no matter how one is being treated – and Targeted Individuals are treated abysmally by people without conscience and by people without any regard for another human being. Nonetheless, Tracy says that one should: "hunger only for a taste of justice; hunger only for a world of truth." The advice is not easy to follow, but it is the only path forward.

To seek justice is to struggle toward coming to an understanding that justice can only be done when one chooses, as best one can, to live in accordance with the truth in relation to oneself and in relation to others. Alternatively, to seek truth is to struggle toward coming to an understanding about how truth can only be realized when one chooses, as best one can, to do justice to the evidence that is available … to be fair – and to keep working to refine one's sense of fairness – with respect to one's assessment and judgment concerning the nature of experience – whether one's own, or that of someone else.

Of course, every boxer has a plan going into a fight, but, often times, as someone has said, that plan goes out the window, the first time one gets hit with a solid left or right. Targeted Individuals are in the fight of their lives, and as the blows rain down on them on a daily basis, such individuals have to try to keep going back to the plan – keep hungering for character; keep hungering for justice; keep hungering for truth; keep hungering to be committed to one's essential identity.

The essential self – irrespective of whether, or not, one is a believer in God – is all about sovereignty … about the capacity to make choices that assist one to seek out truth, justice, character, and identity. Sovereignty is also about having the right to resist whatever seeks to interfere with one's essential desire to realize truth, justice, character, and essential identity in one's life. The purveyors of torture and abuse toward Targeted Individuals are trying to induce Targeted Individuals to cede their essential agency, their essential sovereignty, to the torture/abuse program of mind control that is being administered, and as Tracy Chapman points out, one needs to remember that in the final analysis of things – all a person has is one's soul.

Every day that an individual manages to struggle to survive to enable one to be able to fight another day against the slings and arrows of outrageous fortune is a victory. Irrespective of whether, or not, one is a Targeted Individual, the problem for all of us remains the same: What to do when the "waves turn the minutes to hours'.

Courage is not a function of the absence of fear. Rather, courage is the ability to cede one's agency to truth, justice, identity, character, and sovereignty while standing in one's fear.

I remember – although it is possible that in my old age I am mis-remembering things a little – that when I lived in Canada years ago and was working on this or that project late at night, in the background I would hear an American television station sign off in a manner which often included lines from a poem by Eva Merriam which goes:

"Frightened, you are my only friend. And frightened we are everyone. Someone must take a stand. Come coward, take my coward's hand."

Many individuals who are not Targeted Individuals have lost contact with the nature and purpose of life – that is, the need: To seek the truth; to seek justice; to seek character; to seek sovereignty; to seek essential identity. Targeted Individuals are brought face-to-face with the importance of the foregoing needs every single day of their lives, and this brings us to the aforementioned lines from Paul Simon's song:

"We're working our jobs; collect our pay.
Believe we're gliding down the highway
When in fact we are slip-slidin away."

Having a job at which to work is important, and having some pay to collect is also important, and there have been times in my life when

I have had neither a job nor pay, and, there also were a few times when I was homeless. However, if our lives are nothing more than working our jobs and collecting our pay, then, there is a very good chance that we are, in fact, slip-slidin away even as we believe we're gliding down life's highway.

The people who are responsible for the torture and abuse of Targeted Individuals are working their jobs and collecting their pay and believe that they are gliding down the highway, when, in fact, they are slip slidin away. They have ceded their essential agency to the most despicable dimensions of human potential, and irrespective of whether, or not, one believes in God, every day that the purveyors of torture and abuse cede their agency to their most despicable dimensions and potential, they have abandoned truth, justice, character, identity, as well as the principles of sovereignty and, as a result, their essential selves are slip-slidin away, and, consequently, they are losing everything of value entailed by the opportunity that life affords a human being.

Targeted Individuals might be the ones whose lives are in pain and turmoil. Yet, however small and limited the knowledge of such individuals might be, they know far more about the importance of the principles that are given expression through the essence and constructive potential of life than do those who are occupied with bringing misery into the lives of their fellow human beings.

The experience of being a Targeted Individual tends to be inherently isolating. This is because part of the experience of being Targeted is fraught with difficulty involving the problem of how to go about finding people that one can trust because of the way the targeting programs are set up – that is, part of the targeting process is often intended to instill paranoia and/or distrust of not only other human beings but of oneself, and, of course, this leads to being isolated ... being isolated from others and being isolated from oneself.

Unfortunately, a lot of the general public has been programmed by: The media, the government, the medical system, and academia to cede their agency to a condition of "willful blindness" in which despite having a subliminal sense of the truth of things, many members of the general public will deny, or fiercely resist acknowledging, the presence of the terrifying truth – which is the evidence to which the experience of Targeted Individuals is giving expression -- that one's government is not dedicated to one's well being and, in fact, it is busily engaged in taking away everyone's: Sovereignty, truth, justice, identity, and all semblance of character ... such a possibility is very traumatic and threatening for many people because the educational system has failed to provide human beings with the kinds of social, emotional or psychological skills that are necessary to deal with such difficulties.

The foregoing sort of willful blindness also tends to isolate Targeted Individuals because many people really don't want to know the truth of things. As a result, they will try to remove themselves as far as possible from the experiences and testimonies of Targeted Individuals.

All a person can do is to stand in one's: Essential truth, justice, character, identity, and sovereignty as best one can. Don't let others gaslight one, but don't permit or enable yourself to gaslight yourself either.

The people who are around Targeted Individuals tend to need as much help, if not more so, than is needed by those who have been targeted. Being in a condition of willful blindness is a very debilitating condition in which to be, and, the advantage that Targeted Individuals have in this regard is that notwithstanding the pain and other difficulties that go with being targeted, Targeted Individuals are more intimately connected to certain truths than are the people who are not targeted. However, due to the manner in which the latter individuals have ceded their agency to a condition of willful blindness, they are deeply mired in a false existence.

Targeted Individuals should have compassion for their own condition and the condition of other Targeted Individuals but they should also have compassion for the condition of those who are thoroughly entangled in a web of willful blindness. One should try to help such people if one can, but one might keep in mind a principle that athletes often mention.

More specifically, one has to wait for the game to come to you and, then, one needs to learn how to recognize what the game offers and, then, go with what one is given. But, if one tries to force oneself on the game, the game will always be beyond one's reach.

The foregoing dynamic requires patience and discernment. These are not easy qualities of character for any of us to acquire, but one has to keep trying to develop such qualities as best one can because these sorts of qualities of character are among the keys that will help one to struggle in a more effective way toward realizing one's essential potential.

4.) What would be your message to people who do not take TI claims seriously?

This is a hard question to try to answer simply because there are so many dynamics in play that seek to control what people think or what they think about. In this respect, some observers speak of the "Overton Window" which alludes to the way in which discourse is permitted to take place only within prescribed limits of discussion.

Within the Overton Window – which is set and shaped by the media, corporations, government agencies, financial interests, schooling, academia, and politicians -- people are permitted to say whatever they like – pro or con – concerning a given topic. However, once someone begins to color outside the lines set by the Unofficially Official Overton Window that governs thought and speech, then, terms such as "conspiracy theory," "disinformation," "anarchist," "trouble maker," "anti-democratic," "demagogue," "insurrectionist," "breach of national security," and so on, begin to be directed toward whomever doesn't wish to be controlled by the way in which people with self-serving agendas want to control thought, speech, or what is written.

All one has to do is think about the cases of William Binney, Julian Assange and Chelsea Manning to begin to have a sense of what is at stake when Overton Windows are set by those in control and who are maneuvering to enforce what can and can't be communicated. Overton Windows are tactics of control, and when one complies with those tactics and does not raise questions about their legitimacy, then, pretty soon, one can't distinguish between truth and falsehood.

Targeted Individuals who have spoken out have violated the Overton Window that has been established for handling such topics. The powers that be simply can't have citizens talking about the possibility that the government has taken tax payer money and used it to do research – such as is the case with DARPA (the Defense Advance Research Agency Projects Agency) – that will enable the government to enslave its citizens by controlling what people think, say, and do.

When Targeted Individuals speak up, they are like the Toto-character in *The Wizard of Oz*. Toto had the gift of fear and also was sufficiently intelligent, insightful, courageous, and protective of his companions that he was able to pull back the curtain to reveal what was actually taking place. The operator of the controls – that is, the master of the Overton Window that had been established in the *Wizard of Oz* – tries to save the situation and says: "Pay no attention to the man behind the screen."

This is the kind of situation with which Targeted Individuals are faced. They have tried, as best they can, to pull back the curtain in relation to government duplicity, and the guardians of the Overton Window concerning Targeted Individuals have said to the public: "Pay no attention to the man behind the curtain," and, unfortunately, most people have paid attention to what the "Wizard" said rather than what is being revealed by the pulling back of the curtain of secrecy with respect to government corruption and its programs of abuse, torture, and control.

George Orwell used another term in his novel *1984* to describe what is going on – namely, Newspeak. The whole idea of Newspeak is a way of referring to a psychological dynamic in which language can be used as a weapon that undermines, and interferes with, the process of thought altogether.

For example, if whenever the term "peace" is used one means "war" or "violence" or "subjugation," then, a person begins to have difficulty trying to figure out what someone is actually talking about. If a person is exposed to this psychological dynamic long enough, eventually, the individual loses the ability to think about peace in any other way than as a vehicle of violence, war, and subjugation.

In a sense, Newspeak is a way of narrowing the Overton Window. By setting words against themselves, then, thoughts soon are set against themselves and emotions are set against themselves, and, as a result, an individual becomes psychologically incapable of thinking about things in any other way than the confused, self-contradictory dynamic which has been brought about through the mind-killing and soul-killing rules of syntax and semantics to which Newspeak gives expression ... all contrary thoughts and alternative ways of thinking have been eliminated and have disappeared into the black hole of Newspeak.

So, what happens when the government is successful in establishing the kind of Overton Window or form of Newspeak that has been weaponized against the American people? Despite considerable evidence to the contrary, the events that took place in places such as Maui, Hawaii or Paradise, California are nothing more than unfortunate sets of circumstances and have nothing to do with the use of directed energy weapons ... move along folks, there is nothing to see here. Or, notwithstanding the considerable documented evidence brought forth by Katherine Watt and Sasha Latypova which demonstrates how public health has been weaponized by the military against the American people, instead, any discussion of evidence concerning such information is labeled as propaganda, misinformation or disinformation or mal-information.

The term mal-information is an interesting expression of the Overton Window and the active presence of Newspeak. Something constitutes mal-information when it is true but steps on the toes of vested interests and, therefore, runs the risk of threatening those interests and, consequently, should not be permitted.

Julian Assange and Chelsea Manning were guilty of spreading mal-information. The problem with their actions wasn't that what they were revealing was untrue, but, rather, what they were disclosing was entirely true and for that reason had to be shut-down ... it was mal-information.

In 1948, Harry Truman signed into law the Smith-Mundt Act which originally had been introduced into Congress in 1945. The provisions of the Act were intended to: (a) establish a framework for regulating how the State Department would be permitted to disseminate broadcast information to foreign countries; (b) prohibit the American government from broadcasting such information to the citizens of the United States.

In 2012, the Smith-Mundt Modernization Act removed the prohibition against the American government propagandizing

Americans in the same way that people in other countries are propagandized. To refer to the Smith-Mundt Act of 2012 as a matter of "modernization" rather than a repealing of the prohibition against propagandizing Americans is another expression of the Overton Window and Newspeak at work.

Most of the people who interact with, and surround, Targeted Individuals are all influenced by the ramifications of the Smith-Mundt Modernization Act of 2012. Most of the people who interact with and surround Targeted Individuals have been exposed to the gaslighting dynamic set in motion by the aforementioned Modernization Act in which actual evidence is turned into some sort of "conspiracy theory" or "mal-information."

As a matter of public record, conspiracy theories are introduced into federal and state courts by prosecutors every week of the year. All R.I.C.O. cases – that is, cases which are advanced under the Racketeer Influenced and Corrupt Organizations Act -- are conspiracy theories.

The fact that the government gets to say what is, and what is not, a prosecutable conspiracy theory is part of the Overton Window and also an expression of Newspeak. Conspiracies both exist and do not exist at the same time.

When government officials speak in terms of conspiracies then conspiracies are real. When anyone else other than the government introduces the idea of a conspiracy, then, conspiracies are mere fantasies.

The notion of conspiracy theory was initially introduced by a CIA agent acting on behalf of a government agency that wanted to weaponize the idea of conspiracy and induce people to dismiss any research which had to do with alternative accounts of what happened in Dealey Plaza in Dallas on November 22, 1963. Of course, if the foregoing account is true, then the CIA agent who leaked the idea on behalf of his superiors is, along with his controllers, guilty of violating the law which prevents CIA agents from operating within the United States.

William Colby, former director of the CIA, intimated during the Church Senate Committee Hearings in 1975 that, at the very least, the CIA often plants stories with domestic media people ... stories that are intended to shape the understanding of the American public. Colby also has stated that the CIA owns anyone of any significance within the American media.

This sort of assertion seems to indicate that CIA agents are carrying out assignments within the territorial United States in order to influence the American public. If so, then, those kinds of actions are in violation of the laws that supposedly govern where and with whom the CIA can conduct its activities.

Many people have been so indoctrinated and propagandized that if one were to mention to them the names: Frank Olson, John Kennedy, John Kennedy Junior, Robert Kennedy, Sirhan Sirhan, Fred Hampton, John Hinckley, John Lennon, Mark Chapman, Paul Wellstone, Bruce Ivins, Danny Casolaro, Malcolm X, Marvin Gaye, Sam Cook, Gary Webb, Jamal Khashoggi, Qassem Soleimani, Vince Foster, Barry Seal, Udo Ulfkotte, Julian Assange, Chelsea Manning, Seth Rich, Andreas Noack, as well as 16 year old American, Abdulrahman al-Aulaqi -- and assuming the person to whom the foregoing names have been mentioned had even heard of some of those people, then, the circumstances surrounding the foregoing names tend to be perceived by many, if not most individuals, as being unrelated to one another rather than, possibly, serving as narratives which have been clothed in ways that often are nothing more than what are termed by intelligence agencies as "limited hangouts" – that is, stories developed by government officials and released to the media to be sold to the public as something relatively innocuous and peripheral in order to try to forestall or discourage most people from looking more deeply and carefully into the lives of people who have been targeted for assassination or people who have had their lives turned upside down by governments, corporations, and intelligence agencies that feel threatened by the activities of the foregoing individuals.

Most people in the United States do not know that the third leading cause of death – and, according to some measures, constitutes the leading cause of death in the United States -- is the result of preventable medical errors. Every year between 300,000 and 600,000 people die due to iatrogenic causes – that is, preventable but medically induced deaths..

In other words, each decade, somewhere between 3 million and 6 million people die unnecessarily at the hands of the medical industry. This has been going on for decades.

19 Arabs were held responsible for the tragedies that took place on September 11, 2001 which resulted in the death of over 2,000 people. As a result, two countries – Afghanistan and Iraq -- which had nothing to do with the September 11th events were attacked by the United States and decimated, with millions of people being killed, maimed, displaced, imprisoned, or tortured.

However, when the medical system is shown to be responsible for the unnecessary deaths of thousands of times as many individuals as died on 9/11, nothing is done. All one has to do is look at who the advertisers are for news programs on television or what vested interests contribute money to various news programs, and one understands why the media is relatively silent about the third leading cause of death in America year after year after year, decade after decade.

Moreover, given the foregoing considerations, no one should be surprised that the National Childhood Vaccine Injury Act of 1986 was signed into law by Ronald Regan. This Act not only removed the issue of liability from the process of manufacturing vaccines, but, as well, turned the United States Justice Department into an agency, paid for by taxpayers, whose primary mission turned out to be a process of placing all manner of legal and financial obstacles in the way of citizens who were seeking compensation, under the law, for possible vaccine-caused injuries.

The liability issues that were removed from the table in 1986 were further expanded through the PREP Act of 2005. According to this legislation, when a health emergency is declared by the Federal government, then, no one who is operating under the provisions of emergency authorization can be held liable – either financially or criminally -- for what they do, even if what they do causes death or injury.

I could go on, but I believe the gist of my position is clear. Given the tremendous forces of propaganda, censorship, indoctrination, intimidation, media manipulation, and so on that are in play with respect to Targeted Individuals, finding effective leverage points through which to pry open the informational bubbles in which so many people are wrapped becomes akin to Hercules' task of cleaning out the Augean stables. However, I believe that more programs like the one we are doing – involving a variety of other individuals -- might have some degree of constructive impact on the foregoing problem

-----

5.) Any predictions about where this is going, at the level of the general population, and with the Targeting Individuals in particular?

There is a short answer and a long answer that can be given to your question, Len. I'll try to provide you with both.

The short answer is of a religious, spiritual, or mystical nature – some might wish to describe it as a theological sort of response. I suspect that your audience consists of people who operate out of a variety of backgrounds, not all of which are religious or spiritual in nature, and, consequently, this part of my answer is not intended for them. I do believe, however, that they might be much more interested in the second, longer part of my response and, so, I will ask for their patience while I outline my initial perspective.

I am not a Christian, but I have love for Jesus or Isa (peace be upon him), and, in many ways, he – not the New Testaments account -- has helped shape my life. I am deeply inspired by his example and his character. Furthermore, along with Christians, Muslims believe there will be a second coming of Jesus (peace be upon him), and during this second coming, all outstanding accounts will be settled, and, as a result, ultimately, evil will not prevail.

When that time will arrive, no one knows. I live in the here and now, and should the second coming not occur in my lifetime then I will have to deal with whatever comes my way as best I can.

My efforts might succeed in some ways, and they might fail in some ways. However my actions are evaluated, I'm likely going to die -- sooner rather than later, and to use a sport's analogy, my mission or task or challenge is to try to leave everything that I have to offer – which might not be all that much -- on the playing floor of life.

There is no shame in losing. There is only shame in not trying as best one can, and, so win or lose, I know that evil has been set loose in

Technological Reflections

the world, and I know that Targeted Individuals have sort of been canaries in the coal mine in this respect, and they have helped to warn me concerning one of the faces of the hydra-headed monster that walks among us.

What, if anything, I might be able to do about the foregoing problem remains to be seen. One of the reasons why I agreed to speak with you, Len, on this program is because I wanted to try to do something rather than nothing, small though that "something" might be.

Did I have a certain amount of trepidation concerning appearing on the show? Yes, I did, but if what various members of the Targeted Individuals Community are saying is true – individuals such as you, Len, Sabrina Wallace, Ana Mihalcea, Katherine Horton, and Bill Binney -- then, really, there is no such thing as being able to hide from the evil that is stalking us, and since I am inclined to accept their perspective on this issue, then, whether I appeared on this show or I didn't appear, nevertheless, in many ways, the problems that I will face in the future are likely to be pretty much the same.

The foregoing considerations remind me of a fairly well-known story involving a man who had been told that as long as he stayed away from the city of Samarkand he would be able to continue to live. Consequently, the man arranged his life in a manner that was designed to keep him far from the aforementioned city.

One day, however, he saw Death in his vicinity and Death gave him a very strange look. The man panicked and began riding blindly just to get away from Death.

Somehow, he ended up in Samarkand where Death was waiting for him. Before Death took him away, the man asked about the strange look that had been on the face of Death when the two met in another city, and Death replied that since he had a fast-approaching appointment with the man in Samarkand, he was surprised to see the man in another city.

Now, I can follow the example of the man in the story and become panicked and begin galloping every which way in an attempt to escape what cannot be escaped. Or, I can accept that my time of death has already been arranged, and, consequently, I need to try to work my way toward that date with as much character as I can muster ... which, sometimes, doesn't seem all that much.

I see hopeful signs concerning some people's willingness to take on the evil that is polluting our world, but I also see some very troubling signs in that regard as well. As a result, I am uncertain about how things will turn out in the short run, but I am very confident that in the longer run – that is, whenever Jesus (peace be upon him) might return – then, at that time, evil will be dealt with appropriately in one way or another.

My longer answer begins with something that might appear to be religiously oriented. Nevertheless, in reality, as I hope soon will become clear, that which is being alluded to here is a point of view that is quite different from what first impressions might conclude.

So, let's begin with a definition of religion. Religion is a process of searching for the truth concerning the nature of one's relationship with Being or Reality.

If one looks at the etymological roots of the term religion, there are certain themes which have prominence. First, the dynamics of religion are such that there is a dimension of conceptual and emotional binding which tends to tie one to whatever one considers the truth concerning the nature of one's relationship with Reality to be.

Secondly, in addition to a conceptual and emotional bond that ties one to a particular way of engaging what one considers to be the truth concerning the nature of one's relationship with reality, there is also some sort of moral compass that is present in such a perspective which addresses the issue of what one considers to be the truth with respect to how a person should conduct one's relationship with whatever one considers the truth to be.

Irrespective of whether one is a believer, agnostic, or atheist, I find it interesting that when matters of character are to be reflected upon there seems to be a great deal of overlap among the different positions. On the constructive side of the ledger, most people, irrespective of their hermeneutical orientation concerning the nature of life, would consider qualities of: Honesty, sincerity, patience, courage, generosity, gratitude, kindness, humility, perseverance, integrity, compassion, love, friendship, discipline, forgiveness, nobility, tolerance, fairness, and equanimity to be desirable qualities, whereas on the negative side of the ledger, most people, irrespective of their hermeneutical orientation concerning the nature of life, would consider qualities of: Dishonesty, insincerity, cowardice, unfriendliness, meanness, arrogance, flightiness, animosity, intolerance, hard-heartedness, indifference, stinginess, ungratefulness, intemperateness, ignobility, impatience, sloppiness, unfairness, and a tendency to hold grudges to be undesirable qualities.

People might disagree about how to go about giving expression to constructive qualities or avoid giving vent to negative qualities. However, there are degrees of freedom surrounding what might be acceptable examples of either various constructive or problematic qualities.

For example, how to give expression to the quality of love has been addressed in very different ways through poetry, literature, philosophy, and psychology. There is no one way to give expression to love, humility, courage, compassion, and so on, just as there is no one way to indicate that certain acts necessarily give expression to meanness, or arrogance, or cowardice, or dishonesty. Qualities of character are principle-governed and not rule-based.

Having said the foregoing, consider the following. The first amendment says that:

"Congress shall make no law respecting an establishment of religion, or prohibiting the free exercise thereof."

What does this mean?

Before attempting to address the foregoing question, one should know that George Mason, a delegate from Virginia, argued during the Philadelphia Constitutional Convention of 1787 that some sort of a Bill of Rights should be introduced into the document that was being constructed, and he made some concrete proposals in this regard. His suggestions were all turned down by the other delegates, and as a result, he voted against the Constitution prior to its release, first, to the Continental Congress, and, then, subsequently, to the people in the 13 states for purposes of being discussed in different sessions of the ratification conventions that were held.

During the ratification meetings that took place in various states between 1787 and 1790, there were repeated calls from delegates to add some sort of Bill of Rights to be included in the Constitution prior to its being ratified. These overtures were repeatedly frustrated and rejected by federalist forces who also were serving as delegates during the ratification conventions.

After the Constitution was ratified by the different states and Congress had begun its first session, James Madison was approached by various individuals and reminded of promises which had been made during different ratification conventions that a Bill of Rights would be added to the Constitution once it was ratified. Initially, Madison resisted these reminders, but, eventually, he relented and put together a series of proposals that were brought before Congress, discussed, rewritten somewhat, and, then, approved.

What did the people in Congress mean by the notion of religion that appears in the first amendment? Some people in Congress were Christians, but there were different denominations of Christians. Some people in Congress were Deists. Some people in Congress were not all that religiously oriented.

Many of the people in Congress were sufficiently educated, well-read and worldly to be aware of the existence of Jews, Buddhists, Hindus, Muslims, and, as well, to be aware that indigenous peoples had a variety of religious orientations. Consequently, one might suppose that the general sense of the term religion in the first amendment that was acknowledged by the members of Congress was likely to be fairly broad, and, in fact one might suppose that their understanding of the term could be similar to the definition which I outlined earlier – namely, religion gives expression to an individual's search concerning the nature of one's relationship with Being or Reality.

I feel that anyone who would like to dispute the foregoing contention is going to have a very difficult time demonstrating that some other notion of religion was intended by the members of Congress who voted on, among other things, the first amendment, and which was signed into law by a President who also was a Freemason, which has its own notion of divinity. If the foregoing contention turns out to be true, then, the first amendment raises some very difficult questions.

For example, if religion gives expression to a person's search for the truth concerning the nature of one's relationship with Reality or Being, then, economics, politics, philosophy, science, and law all satisfy the conditions that constitute religion as previously defined. This means that almost everything that Congress does tends to be a violation of the first amendment because virtually all Congressional legislative acts are either engaging in a process of establishing a religion or prohibiting the free exercise thereof.

Moreover, all of the legislation that is advanced for purposes of creating different departments – from: Defense, to: the Interior, Treasury, Energy, Environment, Education, Immigration, Health, Justice, Housing, as well as subsets of those departments such as the CIA, NSA, FBI, CDC, FDA, FEMA, and the EPA – have questionable constitutional provenances because every governmental department and subset agency is seeking to put forth a perspective that gives expression to one, or more, person's search for the truth concerning the putative nature of a human being's relationship with Reality or Being.

Like religion, laws are meant to be conceptually and emotionally binding. Like religion, laws possess a moral compass that is intended to direct how people are to live their lives.

The Department of Defense, DARPA, the CIA, NSA, and the FBI are government organizations which have helped – each in its own inimitable style -- to make the lives of thousands of Targeted Individuals a living hell. In effect, those agencies have sought to impose their form of religion onto Targeted Individuals and, as well, have prohibited Targeted Individuals from being able to freely exercise their own approach to religion, and, as such, all of the foregoing government agencies have been permitted to violate the first amendment rights of Targeted Individuals.

Let's take a look at the Judiciary. For instance, there is nothing in the 1787 Constitution which entitles or requires that the members of the judiciary should be the ones who determine what the Constitution, or any of its amendments, means. One cannot possibly have three equal but separate branches of government as long as only one of those branches gets to say what the Constitution supposedly means.

The Constitution indicates that power is to be invested in the judiciary in conjunction with all cases of law and equity that arise under: The Constitution; the laws of the United States; treaties that are made; cases involving ambassadors, public ministers, consuls, as well as cases touching upon matters of admiralty and maritime jurisdiction. In addition, Constitutional power is invested in the judiciary to deal with cases of controversy involving: The United States; disputes between two, or more, states, or between a state and one or more citizens of another state, or between citizens of different states, as well as between a state or the citizens of a state and one, or more, foreign governments.

According to the Constitution, the judiciary shall have original jurisdiction with respect to those cases that concern ambassadors, public ministers, consuls, as well as states. In all other cases, the judiciary shall have appellate jurisdiction both with respect to fact and law unless some other kind of alternative arrangement is established through congressional action.

Given the foregoing guidelines, an appropriate question to ask is the following: Whether power is exercised through original or appellate jurisdiction, how is that power to be exercised? In other words, what principles should serve as the metric or standard for evaluating and deciding cases?

The only directional guidance that is given in the Constitution concerning the power of the judiciary is found in Article IV, Section 4 of that document. The aforementioned section stipulates that the United States government guarantees a republican form of government to the states and their citizens.

Republicanism was a moral philosophy that emerged during the Enlightenment. This philosophical perspective attracted a great deal of interest and many adherents among Americans throughout the 1700s.

Republicanism required those individuals who wished to comply with that moral, philosophical framework to operate through principles of: Integrity, honesty, impartiality, humility, financial independence, objectivity, non-partisanship, honor, compassion, reason, judiciousness, egalitarianism, and a willingness to avoid circumstances in which one would be serving as a judge in matters that involved one's own causes.

The moral philosophy of republicanism was at the heart of a revolutionary approach to the idea of governance that was being discussed in the homes, taverns, and tea houses throughout the colonies. Under republicanism, government officials would be required to act in accordance with the moral principles that were at the heart of that philosophical orientation.

In other words, republicanism required that those with political authority could not conduct themselves according to their own personal likes, dislikes, and/or interests as, generally, had been the case in most political environments throughout history. Instead, public officials would be required to abide by a set of moral principles that actually would serve the public rather than the self-serving machinations of government officials. (If interested, one can learn more about the origins, development and impact which republicanism had on colonists with respect to their way of life in Gordon Wood's Pulitzer Prize-winning book: *The Radicalism of the American Revolution*).

Given the foregoing considerations, the power that is invested in the judiciary by the Constitution is predicated on the idea of acting in accordance with the principles of republicanism. As a result, the sole focus of the federal judiciary should be to ensure that the behavior of public officials – whether state or federal – which involved cases that came to the courts through original or appellate jurisdiction would be judged in accordance with the principles of republicanism that had been guaranteed to the states and the citizens of those states by the Constitution.

For members of the judiciary to busy themselves with discerning, or trying to discern, the meaning of the Constitution would be to engage in something that was antithetical to republicanism – namely, that the courts would be acting in a manner which involved the members of the judiciary serving as judges in their own causes. After all, whatever the meaning of the Constitution that was being advanced by members of the judiciary might be, such an interpretation would not give expression to anything but their own causes concerning their beliefs about the nature of the Constitution.

The possible meanings of the Constitution are not what should be the concern of the judiciary. Instead, what should have been at issue in any case before the judiciary is whether or not government officials had been complying with the moral requirements of republicanism that were constitutionally guaranteed to the people of the United States.

Consequently, the hundreds of books that contain judicial rulings concerning the alleged meanings as well as the decisions that established arbitrary precedents concerning such Constitutional meanings are, for the most part, null and void. The application of judicial power only extends to ensuring that the guarantee of republican government which is specified in Article IV, section 4 is being observed in the cases that the judiciary takes on through either original or appellate jurisdiction. Any other kind of judicial consideration or focus besides serving the requirements of the guarantee that is indicated in Article IV, section 4 is nothing but invented legal fictions that have no actual standing or authorization within the Constitution.

For 236 years, the judiciary has continually exercised a form of power – involving meanings and precedents that shift with assumptions, values, and beliefs – to which it – that is, the judiciary -- is not constitutionally entitled. Moreover, like the Golum in J.R.R. Tolkien's *Lord of the Rings* trilogy, once members of the judiciary put on the ring of power, they become reluctant to take that ring of power off irrespective of what the corrupting ramifications of that ring might be for them or for others.

I attended the Zoom-meeting on Friday, January 12, 2024 concerning the Targeted Individuals legal case that is now waiting for the 5th Court of Appeals to set a date for hearing arguments concerning the illegality of the Terror Watch List. I also noted that a reference was made during the meeting concerning the existence of several Secret Categories of the Terror Data Base which also exist and do not seem to be covered by the present case, indicating that the underlying problem being faced by both Targeted Individuals and the rest of the citizenry might be systemic rather than being limited to a single agency or department of government.

My heart hopes that the foregoing legal case will be successful. Following 9/11, I was reported to the FBI by someone that I had thought was a friend.

My sins were that I was Muslim, had an as-seen-on-TV computer (with which to write books), and kept to myself because I had just moved to the area and didn't know very many people. There is a good chance that my name is in one, or more, of the data bases that were referenced during the aforementioned Zoom meeting, and, therefore, a victory in the foregoing legal case could have positive ramifications for me.

Notwithstanding the foregoing considerations, I believe that the problems facing the community of Targeted Individuals, as well as the rest of the general public, are not going to be resolved by a business as usual approach to such legal issues ... that is, taking individual cases through the Appeal Courts, and, then, to the Supreme Court. There is a fundamental need for a constitutional re-visioning along the lines that have been expressed in the foregoing comments on the judiciary.

For example, the Ninth Amendment indicates that:

"The enumeration in the Constitution, of certain rights, shall not be construed to deny and disparage others retained by the people."

Yet, for 236 years, Congress, the judiciary, as well as the states (and state judiciaries) have been denying and disparaging the rights that are retained by the people even if such rights are not specifically enumerated in the Constitution but, as noted earlier, are alluded to by the word: "others" – that is, other rights – in the text of the Ninth Amendment.

For example, considerations of health, education, sovereignty, conscription, and religion are not among the enumerated rights that have been accorded to Congress. Therefore, every attempt by Congress to introduce legislation concerning such issues constitutes an attempt to deny and disparage the unenumerated rights of the people that are entailed by the Ninth Amendment.

Moreover, when state governments, via their legislatures and judiciaries, seek to co-opt issues involving, for example, health, education, sovereignty, conscription, and/or religion, then, state governments also are engaged in acts which seek to deny and disparage the unenumerated rights of the people. For example, the Tenth Amendment indicates that:

"The powers not delegated to the United States by the Constitution, nor prohibited by it to the states, are reserved to the states respectively, or to the people."

Consequently, the Tenth Amendment clearly indicates that states are not the only ones with Constitutional standing with respect to powers that have not been delegated to the United States, nor prohibited by the Constitution to the states. If this were not the case, then, there would have been no point for Roger Sherman to add the phrase "or to the people" to the original wording of that amendment.

In addition, seeking to withhold Constitutional standing from the people in conjunction with the sorts of powers that are being alluded to in the Tenth Amendment, would be another way of trying to deny and disparage the unenumerated rights of the people. After all, citizens have a right – unenumerated though it might be -- to have access to the sorts of reserved, but unspecified, powers being alluded to in the Tenth Amendment which would enable those individuals to be able to actively realize their unenumerated rights under the Ninth Amendment.

The guarantee that is present in Article IV, section 4 of the Constitution not only requires the judiciary to ensure that all members of the federal government are acting in accordance with the moral principles of republicanism, but the array of cases which the judiciary has been given power to engage via Article III, section 2 of the Constitution indicates that the judiciary has the authority to ensure that cases involving states and citizens will be conducted in accordance with the requirements of the moral philosophy of republicanism as well. Consequently, for the last 236 years, the federal judiciary should have been actively restraining state governments from denying and decrying the unenumerated rights of citizens as well as actively upholding the Constitutional standing of the people concerning those powers that have not been delegated to the United States nor prohibited to the states and which, therefore, have been "reserved to the states respectively, or to the people."

Unfortunately, for some 236 years, the federal judiciary has, by and large, failed in its fiduciary responsibilities to the citizens of America when it comes to the issue of ensuring that no branch of government, whether federal or state, denies and disparages the unenumerated rights of individual citizens that are established through the Ninth Amendment. Furthermore, the judiciary has also failed to actively protect the Constitutional standing of individual citizens by reminding the federal and state actors in the cases before them about the unspecified, reserved powers under the Tenth Amendment that have not been delegated to the United States nor prohibited to the states or to the people.

Article IV, section 4 also requires the United States to protect the states against invasion. Yet, despite the fact that corporations were an anathema to the colonialists who were engaging in a revolution against not only England but the activities of the East India Company, nonetheless, the judiciary and members of Congress have enabled corporations to invade the lives of people and to acquire substantial influence, if not control, over the lives of those citizens.

Corporations are legal fictions. Legal fictions are arbitrary ways that the courts invent in order to, supposedly, solve legal problems, with a wink and a nod, that could not be resolved if one were to abide by the law as it is written.

Corporations exist as a result of charters that give expression to a limited and temporary set of permissions which are granted by governments, and such charters set forth the understandings that are supposed to regulate the existence of those temporary and limited entities. However, starting with the 'Dartmouth College v. Woodward' decision handed down in 1819 by the Marshall Court (a decision that the judiciary was not constitutionally authorized to make), corporations began to be treated as entities that had a form of life which had contractual rights independent of whatever charter permissions existed.

As a result, via the *'Dartmouth College v Woodward'* decision, the first will-'o-the-wisp apparition of the corporation as a shadowy, person-like entity with certain constitutional protections was, like Frankenstein's monster, given life. One might note in passing that John Marshall had an array of corporate entanglements in his legal past which induced him to look on corporations with favor and, therefore, aside from the fact that the Court had no authority to interpret the Constitution's meaning, he also was violating Article IV, section 4 of the Constitution in the *'Dartmouth College v Woodward'* decision because he was rendering a decision that allowed him to serve as a judge in his own cause – namely, his favorable opinion concerning the existence of corporations.

Corporations have no reality other than the fictional narrative or legal fiction that has been unconstitutionally assigned to them by the judiciary. Consequently, when the judiciary fails to observe its fiduciary responsibilities to the states and the people under Article IV, section 4, then, corporations are allowed to become person-like entities with rights rather than being restricted to being mere charters with limited and temporary permissions that, under the Ninth and Tenth Amendments, are subservient to the unenumerated rights and powers of the people, as well as the unspecified powers of the states.

Every policy of federal and state governments that seeks to deny and disparage the unenumerated rights of the people under the Ninth Amendment constitutes an act of violence against the people. As such, these acts violate Article IV, section 4 of the Constitution because the United States government is supposed to protect the states and their people against all forms of domestic violence, and, yet, neither the legislature nor the executive will make an application to the judiciary to protect the people in this regard, nor does the judiciary, on the authority of its own original jurisdiction, serve as protectors of, and advocates for, the unenumerated rights of the people under the Ninth Amendment.

Finally, the Executive branch of the United States is also constrained by the guarantee of republican government inherent in Article IV, section 4 of the Constitution. This means that whatever: Executive Orders, fast-tracked treaties, calls for martial law, national security directives, intelligence operations, and/or security classification schemes that are initiated, knowingly or unknowingly, through the Office of the President, or the President's representatives, all of the foregoing practices must (according to the guarantee of the Constitution) be in compliance with the principles to which the moral philosophy of republicanism gives expression.

The judiciary has original jurisdiction when it comes to the behavior of ambassadors, public officials, and consuls as well as cases in which states are involved. With respect to the issue of original jurisdiction, the Supreme Court does not have to be referred cases by lower courts to be able to investigate the conduct of federal employees but has the authority to do so without any such request in order to determine whether ambassadors, officials, consuls, and states are conducting themselves in accordance with the provisions of Article IV, section 4 of the Constitution.

Unfortunately, the Supreme Court has rarely exercised its fiduciary responsibility in matters of original jurisdiction when it comes to ensuring that ambassadors, public officials, consuls, and states are complying with the moral requirements of republican philosophy that are guaranteed to the states and the people by Article IV, section 4 of the Constitution. As a result, the CIA, the FBI, the NSA, the military, the IRS, the NIH, the CDC, the FDA, and an array of intelligence agencies associated with different departments in the federal government have never been called to task for a multiplicity of breaches concerning the aforementioned Constitutional guarantee.

All branches and departments of the federal government as well as the branches and departments of many states have colluded, if not conspired, with one another to try to prevent the people from truly understanding: (1) the nature of the obligations that government officials have under the principles of the moral philosophy of republicanism which have been guaranteed to the states and their people in Article IV, section 4 of the Constitution; (2) the constraints involving religion that restrict the legislative activities of Congress under the First Amendment, and (3) the unenumerated and unspecified rights and powers that have been extended to the people through the Ninth and Tenth Amendments respectively.

However, as remiss as federal and state governments have been in attending to their fiduciary responsibilities to the people for 236 years, the people, themselves, have not made the effort or taken the time to properly understand the nature of the circumstances, opportunities, rights, and powers that have the potential to enable the people to realize their own sovereignty quite independently of federal and state governments. Neither the federal nor state governments have the Constitutional standing to deny and disparage the unenumerated rights and reserved, yet unspecified, powers of the Ninth and Tenth Amendments respectively, but people are going to have to actively seek the realization of such unenumerated rights and unspecified powers because, as history has clearly demonstrated, federal and state officials tend to become drunk on the power and rights that have been usurped from the people and, as a result, such officials will resist the people taking back what has belonged to the latter individuals since the amended Constitution came into existence in 1791.

Seeking the realization of unenumerated rights and unspecified powers is not a call for anarchy but a demand for sovereignty. Sovereignty is not about the unrestrained exercise of freedom that some libertarians might suppose is the case but, rather, sovereignty is about having the protected opportunity to seek to discover and realize the nature of one's essential nature.

Sovereignty is about decentralization of power rather than the centralization of power. However, sovereignty is also about ensuring that such decentralized power is capable of protecting everyone's opportunity to realize their unenumerated rights and unspecified powers in a manner that is mutually consonant with one another.

In whatever manner the foregoing issues are tackled, there is going to have to be some sort of institutional medium or dynamic through which people can come together to have an opportunity to explore, discuss, formulate, and actuate possible ways of resolving those matters. Whether this is in the form of grand jury-like bodies or is in the form of some kind of healing-circles, or in the form of some other alternative possibility, the institutional format or dynamic will be independent of federal and state governments but, at the same time, will have to find ways of working with those levels of governance.

The federal and state governments can help people with the sovereignty project. Nonetheless, those forms of governance cannot solve the challenges that are entailed by that project.

The sovereignty challenge can only be resolved by the people themselves. That challenge cannot be resolved through: Voting, elected representation, or the activities of various branches of government but, instead, must be engaged by the people themselves through: Discussion, debate, critical reflection, constructive exercises of character, reciprocity, compromise, and fairness in conjunction with the aspirations of the participants.

It is not enough for people to speak about freedoms and liberties. The people must come together in an array of settings to actively engage in the difficult, nuanced work that is entailed by the challenge of developing an understanding about what freedom looks like – in actual lived terms – within the context of a multiplicity of people that are each seeking and have a right to conditions and principles of sovereignty being applied to their lives.

The current Constitution does not have to be jettisoned to accomplish the foregoing project. Nonetheless, constitutional provisions that are present in Article IV, section 4, along with the First Amendment's restrictions concerning the establishment or prohibition of religion by Congress, as well as the authority inherent in the Ninth and Tenth amendments concerning the sovereignty of the people must be acknowledged, honored, and judiciously protected as well as supported by federal and state forms of governance.

Unfortunately, for a variety of reasons, time is running out. If we, the people, do not act on the aforementioned sovereignty project soon, we might well lose the capacity to do so altogether or have that opportunity taken away from us by parties that have no interest in the people becoming truly sovereign.

Pursuit of the sovereignty project is the only way in which a sense of duty and obligation might arise in the context of the Constitution. Absent such a project, the potential of the Constitution that was introduced in 1787, ratified over the next several years, and amended in 1791, will continue to erode as it has been doing for the last 236 years.

If things continue on in the way they are going, then, at some point, a tipping point involving the American republic is going to be reached. When that happens, the promise and guarantee of abiding by the principles of republican moral philosophy will disappear and, as a result, complete tyranny or complete arbitrariness will reign.

We have a quickly evaporating opportunity to stop such a tipping point from taking place. The choice is ours, but without the establishment of an authentic sovereignty project, whatever decisions are made will come to nothing and our choices will do nothing but increase the distance between our existential circumstances and the possibility of leading sovereign lives.

12. Some Evolutionary Considerations

Evolution is a technological tool that seeks to use the technology of the legal system to validate its use as a tool of undue influence within a technological framework known as "education".

In the preface to *But is it Science? : The Philosophical Question in the Creation/Evolution Controversy* edited by Robert T. Pennock and Michael Ruse, the two editors indicate that while the U.S. Constitution prohibits the teaching of religion - since doing so gives expression to a form of establishing a system of religious belief and, thereby, contravenes the 1st Amendment - nevertheless, that same fundamental document does not prohibit the teaching of science, even if the quality of the latter should be bad. Over a period of several decades, at least three cases wormed their way through various facets of the legal system and each of those cases led to judicial decisions that, apparently, verified the perspective that was being advanced by Pennock and Ruse.

Among the cases that seem to confirm the foregoing claim of Pennock and Ruse are: *McLean v. Arkansas,* 1982, as well as the 1987 *Edwards v. Aguillard* decision that took place in Louisiana and, eventually, went to the U.S. Supreme Court. In addition, the *Kitzmiller et al v. Dover Area School Board* judgment was rendered in Pennsylvania around 2005.

However, upon examination, the idea that science does not violate provisions of the U.S. Constitution seems fraught with difficulties. Indeed, the title of the book of readings edited by Pennock and Ruse might be focusing on the wrong philosophical question.

More specifically, instead of asking whether or not creationist science or the doctrine of intelligent design qualify as science - even bad science - perhaps the philosophical question that needs to be asked is: 'But is it true?' In this instance, the "it" that is being questioned with respect to some degree of truth could either be, on the one hand, creation science and the thesis of intelligent design, or, on the other hand, evolution ... or, perhaps, both sides of that controversy need to be engaged in a critically reflective manner.

Let us suppose that one accepts the collective conclusions of the aforementioned three legal proceedings. In other words, let us assume that creation science and the thesis of intelligent design do not qualify as science but give expression - each in its own way -- to the teaching of religion and, as well, that the theory of evolution does qualify as being scientific in nature. Does this end the matter?

Not necessarily! The theory of evolution might satisfy the conditions of being scientific, but if essential features of that theory cannot be shown to be true, then one might wonder why students should be required to learn its details.

Of course, an obvious response to the foregoing issue would be to point out that science is a methodological process that historically can be shown to have assisted human beings to establish better and better understandings concerning the nature of certain aspects of reality. Consequently, a student should be exposed to scientific methods, together with the results arising from those methods, so that an individual can gain facility and competence with respect to being able to critically engage both scientific methods and results, thereby, enhancing a person's chances of being able to deal with various facets of life in a constructive, rational, informed, and insightful fashion.

Nonetheless, even though there is plenty of historical evidence to indicate that a great many truths have been established through the process of science, there is also considerable historical evidence to demonstrate that an array of false ideas have populated the annals of science. Among the false theories that were accepted by a majority of the scientific community - sometimes for substantial periods of time - were: Ptolemaic astronomy; phlogiston theory; Caloric theory of chemistry; spontaneous generation; Lamarckian evolution; the blank slate (tabula rasa) model of mind; Phrenology; steady state theory of the universe (or, possibly, the Big Bang ... depending on which cosmological version of the universe turns out to be correct); and various editions of string theory.

Moreover, even if we leave aside issues concerning the manner in which certain false theories have dominated the practice of science from time to time, and even though scientific methodology offers a means through which to constantly seek to improve one's understanding of some given phenomenon, the fact of the matter is that scientists tend to be wrong more often than they are right. Indeed, the history of science provides an account of how researchers - both individually and collectively - struggle to escape from a condition of ignorance concerning various physical phenomena and work their way through resolving an array of problems that - hopefully - eventually puts them in a position to fashion a tenable understanding concerning such phenomena that, in time, gets modified or overthrown to better reflect empirical observations, both old and new.

Over the years, human understanding concerning quantum physics, chemistry, gravitation, thermodynamics, materials science, biology, astrophysics, mathematics and a host of other disciplines have all gone through a series of changes - some small and some quite considerable. Our current grasp of the foregoing areas - and many others -- is built on a multiplicity of mistaken ideas that were reshaped or replaced by a series of insights and discoveries that appeared to bring us closer to certain truths than previous ways of understanding were able to do that were, in turn, replaced and reshaped by an array of subsequent insights, discoveries, and observations.

An essential part of science revolves about becoming involved in a rigorous process of discernment in which that which is true or truer must be differentiated from that which is false. This is accomplished through observation, measurement, experimentation, analysis, critical reflection and so on.

Given the foregoing considerations, one might ask: Is evolutionary theory an example of a science that leads to a true or a false understanding of reality? Although the vast majority of scientists in the world today accept one version, or another, of a neo-Darwinian evolutionary model, I believe that enough problematic features have been put forth in my book: *Evolution Unredacted* to, at the very least, call into question the tenability of many facets of evolutionary theory, and, as a result, lend some degree of legitimacy to the idea that a student might have a right to resist, and not be subjected to, the doctrinaire teachings of evolutionary theory.

Among other things, the theory of evolution cannot provide a step-by-step account concerning: The emergence of the first protocell; the origins of the genetic code; the transition from: Chemotrophs to cyanobacteria and/or Archaea organisms (many of the latter life forms are extremophiles) - or vice versa; the transition from: Anaerobic to aerobic organisms; the transition from: Prokaryotic to Eukaryotic life forms; the origins of metabolic systems specializing in, for example, respiration, endocrine activity, immune responses, nervous functioning, sexual reproduction, consciousness, memory, reason, intelligence, language, and creativity.

Does the theory of evolution offer accounts that purport to explain all of the above sorts of transitions? Yes, it does.

However, none of those accounts has been proven to be true. All of those accounts are missing key pieces of evidence that are capable of substantiating that those models, hypotheses, and ideas are unquestionably true.

On the one hand, evidence exists that supports the possibility that in certain cases, species might have been formed through a process of, say, isolating different portions of a population that, over time, leads to the appearance of new variations that are no longer able to produce viable offspring with members of the original population. Nonetheless, one cannot demonstrate with real scientific rigor that the sorts of processes be alluded to above are responsible for the origins of all species.

The theory of evolution encompasses a great many factual observations and discoveries. Yet, at the same time, it gives expression to a model in which speculation and assumption continue to play a major role, and, as a result, despite all of the propaganda being issued by various evolutionary scientists, many facets of the theory of evolution are a long way from having been verified and, quite frankly, might never be capable of being verified.

Moreover, even if one puts aside all of the scientific inadequacies of the theory of evolution, there are a variety of constitutional issues that need to be explored. In other words, although evolutionary theory might be classified as a science, nevertheless, there might be a partisan quality to its framework that could be at odds with the requirements of Article IV, Section 4 of the United States Constitution (more on this shortly). In addition, one could raise the possibility that there also is a religious dimension to the theory of evolution (more on this shortly) and, if so, then, science, or not, such a theory might well be in contravention of the establishment clause of the 1st Amendment.

Article IV, Section 4 of the U.S. Constitution indicates that the federal government "shall guarantee to every state a republican form of government, and shall protect each of them against invasion;" Republicanism is a moral philosophy of the Enlightenment that generated a great deal of interest within colonial America and helped shape the fabric of the Constitutional process.

In order to qualify as being republican in nature, judgments and actions had to exhibit a variety of qualities. More specifically, to be considered republican in nature, actions and judgments had to exhibit:

Integrity, objectivity, independence, non-partisanship, equitability, fairness, disinterestedness, nobility, and be devoid of elements that served the individual interests of the person performing a given action or making a particular judgment rather than serving the collective interests of society.

The collective interests of society are summed up in the Preamble to the Constitution. Those collective interests include: Forming a more perfect union; establishing justice; insuring domestic tranquility; providing for the common defense, promoting the general welfare, and securing the blessings of liberty for ourselves and our posterity.

The theory of evolution fails to be objective, independent, and nonpartisan in a variety of ways. More specifically, that theory is being advanced as a true account concerning the random, material origins of species despite the fact that: (1) no one has been able to prove that <u>all</u> species (as opposed to <u>some</u> species) are the result of neo-Darwinian dynamics; (2) no one has been able to demonstrate that reality is inherently random, and (3) no one has been able to prove that consciousness, reason, memory, logic, intelligence, understanding, language, creativity, talent (e.g., musical, artistic, mathematical, etc.), and spirituality are purely material phenomena.

Furthermore, the theory of evolution is replete with elements having to do with notions of randomness and the material basis of reality that might be serving the hermeneutical and political interests of those who are propagating the theory of evolution rather than the collective interests of society, and, therefore, are not necessarily promoting the general welfare of the country ... especially if the aforementioned elements involving randomness turn out to be wrong. While such ideational elements have not, yet, been proven to be incorrect, they also have not, yet, been demonstrated to be a correct description of reality, and, therefore, requiring students to learn the theory of evolution would appear to undermine principles of equitability and fairness that constitute integral dimensions of the principle of republicanism that has been guaranteed to each state of the union, and, therefore, under the provisions of the 9th and 10th Amendments, to all the people of those states.

As noted previously, Article IV, Section 4 of the Constitution not only guarantees a republican form of government to every state but, as well, promises to "... protect each of" the states from invasion. Presumably, the protections to which the Constitution might be alluding do not involve just physical threats but could also be extended to protections against certain kinds of philosophical, hermeneutical, and conceptual systems that seek to invade the minds and hearts of the people of the United States through institutions of learning and, thereby, acquire political and legal control of the citizenry and, in the process, undermine the guarantee of a republican form of government.

Notwithstanding the foregoing considerations, teaching the theory of evolution in public schools might also be in contravention of the establishment clause of the 1st Amendment. After all, some individuals have traced the etymological roots of the word religion back to a Latin word - re-li-gare -- that conveys a process of binding or tying.

Any conceptual system constitutes a way of binding or tying a person's understanding to one, or another, understanding of reality. Consequently, the theory of evolution is a conceptual system that tends to tie and bind a person's understanding to various kinds of assumptions, ideas, beliefs, and values in an organized fashion.

Other individuals feel that the notion of religion might also be etymologically linked to another Latin word: "re-li-gi-o-nem". This latter term gives expression to a sense of reverence toward whatever might be considered to be sacred in nature - E.g., the truth, or qualities of compassion, love, forgiveness, meaning, purpose, and so on.

The sacred need not be tied to the notion of Divinity. For instance, Buddhism is considered to be a religion, yet that spiritual tradition often is understood to be based on teachings that tend not to be God-centric in character but, instead, embrace an array of methods, principles, and values that are engaged in a reverential, and, therefore, sacred fashion.

Those who are proponents of evolutionary theory tend to defend their perspective as being inviolable, true, sacrosanct, as well as being worthy of commitment and deep respect. Moreover, such individuals tend to treat the principles, values, and ideas of evolution with attitudes and behaviors that appear to be indistinguishable from individuals who have reverence toward certain religious ideas, principles, or values and consider those themes to be sacred and inviolable.

Referring to the theory of evolution in terms of science does not extinguish the qualities of: Reverence, sacredness, commitment, binding, and tying that are present in the understanding of many of those who are advocates for that theory. Placing the theory of evolution under the rubric of science does not remove the properties of assumption, speculation, belief, interpretation, faith (sometimes referred to as a degree of confidence), and philosophy that tend to flow through that theory.

Given the foregoing considerations, then, surely, teaching the theory of evolution would seem to qualify as an attempt to establish a religious-like belief system. All of the elements of religion - namely, a sense of: Reverence, sacredness, faith, interpretation, inviolability, the sacrosanct, commitment, binding, universality, essentialness, and so on - are present in those who are proponents of, and advocates for, the theory of evolution.

There are several other possible etymological dimensions in the notion of religion that potentially tie that word to the theory of evolution. One of these dimensions is linked to Cicero's way of using the term 're-legere', while another etymological derivation of religion gives emphasis to an Old French sense in which the notion of religion refers to a process through which a community exhibits collective devotion to certain ideas.

Cicero's aforementioned manner of engaging the idea of "re-le-gere" involves a methodology through which an individual goes over a given text on a number of different occasions. Presumably, the process of reading and re-reading a given text is a way of exercising due diligence with respect to trying to determine, among other things, the truth concerning the meaning of that text.

Similarly, proponents of evolutionary theory also tend to go over, again and again, the observations, measurements, experiments, and so on associated with that theory in order to try to determine the meaning and truth that might be entailed by those activities. Whether the text being studied is a book or the language of nature seems irrelevant.

Furthermore, Cicero's manner of approaching the process of "re-legere" tends to imply that the process of critically reflecting on the meaning of a given text - whether written or having to do with the nature of reality -- is intended to serve as a way of providing one with an opportunity to work toward distinguishing between, on the one hand, the actual meaning of something and, on the other hand, meanings that might be arbitrarily imposed on a text by the individual engaging that material. If so, then, this also reflects the tendency of science to go over something again and again in order to try to discern the difference between, on the one hand, the actual truth of something and, on the other hand, false beliefs concerning the nature of some aspect of experience and, consequently, appears to bind the theory of evolution to religion in, yet, another way.

Moreover, just as religious communities tend to be devoted to the principles, values, and practices which bind the members of that community together in relation to what they believe constitutes the truth of Being, so too, the members of those communities that accept the theory of evolution reflect many of the qualities that characterize the Old French etymological derivation of the term religion. In other words, members of a community of believers involving evolutionary theory are tied together by a common sense of purpose, meaning, valuation, understanding, belief, and truth concerning the principles, ideas, values, and practices entailed by the theory of evolution in ways that parallel what goes on within so-called religious communities.

Therefore, one cannot automatically assume that just because the theory of evolution is referred to as being, or categorized as being, scientific, then, this kind of classification prevents that theory from also giving expression to a variety of religious-like qualities. To whatever extent the theory of evolution entails the foregoing sorts of religious elements, then, that theory also would appear to contravene the establishment clause of the 1st Amendment.

Thus, there seems to be a conflict between the theory of evolution and the U.S. Constitution not only in relation to the 1st Amendment, but, as well, in relation to Article IV, Section 4 of that document. As a result, the editors of: *But Is It Science? -- The Philosophical Question In the Creation/Evolution Controversy* - have put things in a misleading manner since the issue is not whether one can consider the theory of evolution to be scientific in nature - which, in certain ways, it might be - but, instead, the issue is whether, or not, a person recognizes the religious and non-republican elements that are present in the theory of evolution and, as a result, one is prepared to remain consistent by seeking to ensure that such a theory - along with other religious-like systems of thought – are prevented from being taught in public schools because that theory is in contravention of various provisions of the U.S. Constitution.

The previously mentioned *McLean v. Arkansas Board of Education* legal proceeding arose in conjunction with Act 590 that the governor of Arkansas had signed into law on March 19, 1981. The title of that act was: "Balanced Treatment for Creation Science and Evolution Science," and as the act's name suggests, the law required public schools in Arkansas to offer programs that provided balanced treatments of creation science and evolutionary science.

A number of individuals and organizations joined together to bring suit against: (1) the Arkansas Board of Education, (2) the director for the Arkansas Department of Education, and (3) the State Textbooks and Instructional Materials Selecting Committee that, collectively, were responsible for translating Act 590 into active educational policy. Among the individuals and organizations that are being represented through the plaintiff side of the case were: The National Association of Biology Teachers, the Arkansas Education Association, the American Jewish Congress, various churches in Arkansas from different denominational backgrounds, as well as a biology teacher from Arkansas and an array of individuals who were parents or friends of students in Arkansas public schools.

The *McLean v. Arkansas Board of Education* trial took place from December 7, 1981 to December 17, 1981. Judge William R. Overton presided over the proceedings and issued his decision on January 5, 1982.

The suit was first filed on May 27, 1981. The complaint maintained that Act 590 was in contravention of the U.S. Constitution because, among other things, that law violated the establishment clause of the First Amendment - which, according to Judge Overton, is made applicable to the states by the way of the 14th Amendment, but, one should point out that the Amendments extend to the people of any given state independently of the 14th Amendment due to the guarantee of a republican form of government in Article IV, Section 4 of the Constitution.

The aforementioned complaint filed by the plaintiffs contained two other charges as well. More specifically, Act 590 denies teachers and students their right to academic freedom by undermining the Free Speech Clause of the 1st Amendment and, in addition, Act 590 is excessively vague and, therefore, violates the Due Process Clause of the 14th Amendment.

In his January 5, 1982 decision, Judge Overton provides a certain amount of legal background to help frame some of the issues in the *McLean v. Arkansas Board of Education dispute.* For instance, he quotes from Justice Black's 1947 decision concerning the *Everson v. Board of Education* case:

"The 'establishment of religion' clause of the First Amendment means at least this: Neither a state nor the Federal Government can set up a church. Neither can pass laws which aid one religion, aid all religions, or prefer one religion over another. Neither can force nor influence a person to go to or to remain away from church against his will or force him to profess a belief or disbelief in any religion ... No tax, large or small, can be levied to support any religious activities or institutions, whatever they may be called, or whatever form they may adapt to teach or practice religion."

The notion of "church" in Justice Black's foregoing statement is used as a representative term that applies to a wide variety of religious institutions that, presumably, is intended to include (despite not being specifically mentioned): Temples, synagogues, mosques, abbeys, cathedrals, meeting halls, houses of worship, spiritual sanctuaries, and the like. The foregoing presumption is strengthened when Justice Black subsequently indicates that the underlying principle extends to: "religious activities or institutions, whatever they may be called, or whatever form they may adapt to teach or practice religion."

However, although Justice Black seems to assume that everyone will understand what is meant by the idea of a religion or church (including its extended sense noted above), nonetheless, there is considerable vagueness that surrounds and permeates his foregoing statement. As pointed out earlier, the notion of religion might be applicable to almost any conceptual system that involves qualities of: Tying or binding someone to a set of values, teachings, ideas, values, practices, purposes, meanings, methods, understandings, theories, and/or attitudes that are engaged repetitively because they generate a sense of reverence, sacredness, and commitment that orients individuals and/or communities concerning the nature of the truth about an individual's or a community's relation with Being.

Therefore, if a church - irrespective of whatever it might be called or whatever form it might assume - revolves around, in part or in whole, the foregoing set of qualities, properties, and activities, then, Justice Black - possibly without fully understanding the implications of his words -- might be referring to a great deal more than he - or Judge Overton - believes is being claimed in the *Everson v. Board of Education* case. Indeed, any set of practices, ideas, beliefs, values, theories, principles, methods, and so on that one considers to be inviolable, sacrosanct, sacred, and worthy of reverence -- but which cannot necessarily be demonstrated to be true - begins to be indistinguishable from the usual senses associated with terms such as "church" or "religion".

Thomas Jefferson maintained that the "Establishment Clause" of the First Amendment erected a wall of separation between church and State. Yet, depending on what the State holds to be true, one might contend that the policies of the State could give expression to a set of values, ideas, beliefs, principles, methods, and practices that are difficult, if not impossible, to distinguish from religious activities when construed in the broader sense outlined above. If so, then, the so-called wall of separation that, supposedly, was put in place through the "Establishment Clause" of the First Amendment and which was intended to differentiate between church and state tends to dissolve before our eyes.

Judge Overton's decision in *McLean v. Arkansas Board of Education* also cites the words of Justice Felix Frankfurter with respect to the latter's 1948 judgment concerning *McCollum v. Board of Education*. According to Justice Frankfurter:

"Designed to serve as perhaps the most powerful agency for promoting cohesion among a heterogeneous democratic people, the public school must keep scrupulously free from entanglements in the strife of sects. The preservation of the community from divisive conflicts, of Government from irreconcilable pressures by religious groups, of religion from censorship and coercion however subtly exercised, requires strict confinement of the State to instructions other than religious ..."

The idea that public schools should be an agency "for promoting cohesion among heterogeneous democratic people" is put forward as a truism in the foregoing decision. Consequently, Justice Frankfurter does not explore whether, or not, public schools should be an agency "for promoting cohesion", nor does he critically reflect on what might be meant by the notion of cohesion.

Justice Frankfurter wants the instruction that takes place in public schools to be "other than religious," but he doesn't explain precisely what he means by this allusion. Furthermore, although he is clear that public schools should remove themselves "from entanglements in the strife of sects," and although Justice Frankfurter is clear that he is referring to the strife that tends to arise in conjunction with religious sects, he, apparently, fails to consider the possibility that strife also arises in conjunction with all manner of philosophical, scientific, and political sectarian thought and activity, and, as a result, one is thrown deeper into uncertainty concerning the manner of the instruction that is "other than religious" and, therefore, should be adopted by public schools to promote the sort of cohesion he seems to have in mind (at least in a vague sense) for "a heterogeneous democratic people."

During the course of rendering his decision for *McLean v. Arkansas School Board*, Judge Overton makes reference to the opinion of Justice Clark that was issued in conjunction with the 1963 case of *Abbington School District v. Schempp*. In the latter case, Justice Clark maintained that in order to be able to comply with the requirements of the Establishment Clause of the First Amendment, "... there must be a secular legislative purposed and a primary effect that neither advances nor inhibits religion."

The secular constraint upon legislative activity was again affirmed in the 1973 decision concerning *Lemon v. Kurtzman*. In that case, a tripartite set of conditions was established to serve as guidance for trying to parse such matters - namely, (1) the legislation must serve a secular purpose; (2) the primary effect of the legislation must be to neither inhibit nor advance religion, and, finally, (3) such legislation should not encourage or generate excessive government entanglement in religious matters.

Notwithstanding the rather amorphous cloud of meaning in which condition (3) tends to be enveloped as a result of the presence of the term "excessive" (and, therefore, becomes a possible focus for future objections under the Due Process provisions of the 14th Amendment), one might question the requirement that legislation must serve a secular purpose since those purposes not only are fraught with all manner of strife (and, according to Justice Frankfurter, isn't one of the reasons for pursuing secular rather than religious systems of thought is to be able to avoid sectarian strife?) but, perhaps, more importantly, despite the lack of religious vocabulary associated with various notions of secularism, nonetheless, that sort of approach to governance tends to promote views of reality that cannot be proven to be true - anymore than religious models can be proven to be true to everyone's satisfaction - and secular approaches to governance also require citizens to treat legislation as being: Inviolable, sacrosanct, sacred, deserving of reverence, and capable of binding or tying individuals and the community to sectarian theories (of a philosophical kind) concerning the nature of reality?

Is secularism really any less sectarian than overtly religious systems of thought are? Is secularism really any less entangled in issues of strife than are religious sects with respect to disputes about what values, beliefs, ideas, practices, principles, and so on should be treated reverentially and considered to be inviolable, sacrosanct, or sacred and, therefore, worthy of obligating individuals and the community in one way rather than another?

The foregoing considerations are not an attempt to put forth some post-modernist, relativistic deconstruction of the legal system. Rather, an attempt is being made to indicate that there is considerable amorphousness at the heart of the U.S. Constitution as well as in many subsequent judicial decisions concerning the supposed nature of that document.

For instance, if the republican form of government that is guaranteed in Article IV, Section 4 of the U.S. Constitution requires federal government officials - including justices -- to act and make decisions in accordance with republican qualities of: Objectivity, integrity, impartiality, equitability, fairness, independence, disinterestedness, and not being judges in their own affairs, then, why are secular theories of reality being given preference to religious theories of reality? Moreover, displaying a differential preference for secular ideas very likely will not only serve to inhibit the observance, practice, and pursuit of religious values, ideas, practices and so on, but, as well, encourages and promotes secular ideas as if they were religious in nature ... that is, the sort of ultimate views of reality that should be taught in schools and toward which students should develop the requisite reverence and learn how to treat such ideas as being sacred, inviolable, and sacrosanct in nature?

After running through a few relevant aspects of legal history (noted previously in this chapter) in order to provide a context for his decision, Judge Overton's ruling in *McLean v. Arkansas Board of Education* proceeds to offer an extended historical analysis of religious fundamentalism and its decades-long conflict with the theory of evolution. However, Judge Overton does not make any comparable effort to put forth a critical review concerning the theory of evolution and whether, or not, there is a form of fundamentalism to which the theory of evolution might give expression.

Judge Overton does indicate - with a hint of approval -- that the Biological Sciences Curriculum Study (BSCS), which is a non-profit organization that works with scientists and teachers, has developed a series of biology texts that give emphasis to the theory of evolution. He also notes that those texts are being used by 50 percent of the children in American public school systems.

However, Judge Overton, apparently, has nothing to say about whether, or not, requiring school children to use the BSCS books might constitute a contravention of either the Establishment Clause of the First Amendment or the Guarantee Clause of Article IV, Section 4 in the

Constitution. After all, the sectarian nature of the theory of evolution and its claim to constitute a scientific portrait concerning the nature of reality has not been proven to be true and, perhaps, can never be shown to be true.

Judge Overton's ruling also makes reference to the history of fundamentalist opposition toward the theory of evolution when he notes that such a history is documented in Justice Fortas' Supreme Court opinion in *Epperson v. Arkansas*. This latter legal decision rescinded the Arkansas legislative Act 1 of 1929 that prohibited the teaching of evolution in public schools.

In each of the foregoing decisions, reasons are given about why fundamentalist views concerning the issue of origins should not be taught in public schools. However, none of those legal decisions explores whether, or not, there might be reasons why the theory of evolution also should not be taught to public school children, and one can't help but wonder whether any of the jurists who were (or are) making decisions concerning the teaching of evolution know much, if anything, about what they are advocating ... or whether their rulings are in compliance with the republican qualities of impartiality, objectivity, integrity, independence, equitability, disinterestedness, and fairness that are guaranteed through Article IV, Section 4 of the Constitution.

After providing an overview of religious fundamentalism and its history of conflict with the theory of evolution, Judge Overton's decision in *McLean v. Arkansas Board of Education* cites some of the evidence that he feels demonstrates the religious intent underlying Act 590 that, supposedly, calls for a balanced treatment of Creation Science and the theory of evolution in the classrooms of public schools. While one is inclined to agree with Judge Overton's assessment of the foregoing evidence, nonetheless, one should keep in mind that there doesn't seem to be any comparable effort on the part of Judge Overton to critically reflect on the possibility that many facets of the theory of evolution also give expression to a religious-like, fundamentalist orientation.

A distinction is made in Judge Overton's decision between, on the one hand, some of the scientific elements that are present in the theory of evolution and, on the other hand, the relative absence of - or the presence of problematic facets of -- scientific rigor in creation science. However, such a distinction tends to obscure the issue that should have been at the heart of the *McLean v. Arkansas Board of Education* case.

In other words, rather than drawing a distinction between what is science and what is not science, Judge Overton should have better delineated the full nature of the Establishment Clause as well as explored the relevance of Article IV, Section 4 to the matter before his court. As a result, Judge Overton does not appear to issue a ruling that complies with the requirements that are entailed by the guarantee of a republican form of government that is given in the U.S. Constitution.

On the one hand, there is nothing in the Constitution that is functionally dependent on being able to make a distinction between science and non-science. On the other hand, there is a great deal - constitutionally speaking -- that rests on the issue of what constitutes a religion and that rests on the issue of what constitutes establishing a religion.

When the pursuit of scientific methodology leads to the rise of a hermeneutical system like the theory of evolution that has not - and, perhaps, cannot -- be proven to be true (i.e., that the origin of <u>all</u> species is a function of neo-Darwinian dynamics) and which claims that the ultimate nature of reality is both random and material in nature (again, neither of which has been proven to be true, and, perhaps, cannot be proven to be true), then, such a system of hermeneutics becomes indistinguishable from religious systems that seek to impose a sectarian way of thinking on citizens. Consequently, the presence of the foregoing elements in the theory of evolution contravenes both the Establishment Clause of the 1st Amendment, as well as the requirements of Article IV, Section 4 of the Constitution.

According to Judge Overton - and he is basing the following criteria on the testimony of witnesses who participated in the *McLean v. Arkansas Board of Education* trial proceedings - science has five essential properties. (1) Science seeks to discover the nature of the natural laws that govern phenomena; (2) the explanations offered by science are couched in terms of natural laws; (3) the tenets of science can be empirically tested; (4) its conclusions are provisional and, as a result, might change over time; and, (5) the principles of science are capable of being falsified.

Shortly after stating the foregoing characteristics of science, Judge Overton proceeds to point out that Section 4(a) of Act 590 fails to qualify as being scientific because that section depends on the idea that the origin of life arose as a sudden creation "from nothing." Judge Overton claims that such a contention is not scientific because it requires some form of "supernatural intervention that is not guided by natural law", and, consequently, entails an explanation that is not an expression of natural laws, and, in addition, such a thesis is not testable, and cannot be falsified.

In 2012, Lawrence M. Krauss released a book entitled: *A Universe from Nothing.* The author is an atheist, and, therefore, he is not trying to sneak the realm of the supernatural into the discussion by introducing the possibility of something arising from nothing.

The foregoing book is considered to be a book of science. The contents of his book weave together elements from quantum physics, particle physics, astrophysics, thermodynamics, and cosmology to support the idea that the singularity out of which our universe might have arisen could have been an unstable quantum state that spontaneously gave expression to the universe we have inherited and which made life possible.

Of course, whether the foregoing ideas of Lawrence Krauss are correct, or not, is a separate issue. Nonetheless, irrespective of whether his thesis is, or is not, true, the fact that such ideas are considered to be scientific indicates that, contrary to the claim of Judge Overton, the possibility that something might arise out of nothing does not necessarily depend on supernatural intervention.

In any event, insisting on a distinction between natural and supernatural might be something of a snipe hunt. There is nothing that we know of that precludes the possibility that the so-called natural laws of the universe give expression to God's presence in the operations and dynamics that govern that universe, and, as such, God is free to maintain or make exceptions with respect to how those laws unfold in any given case.

If God maintains (or conserves) natural law, this is not supernatural intervention in a natural phenomenon, but, rather, natural law merely becomes a way of marking God's presence in the process of directing physical phenomena. If God makes an exception in the manner in which natural laws are manifested in any given set of circumstances, then, this also would not constitute a supernatural intervention in a natural process but, instead, would merely reflect that God, by virtue of Divine Presence, was modulating the way in which natural law was being manifested in such events.

Judge Overton's perspective concerning the foregoing issues suggests he believes that supernatural events are neither testable nor falsifiable. Notwithstanding the potentially false dichotomy between the natural and the supernatural that is present in Judge Overton's perspective, for thousands of years, mystics from a variety of spiritual traditions have indicated otherwise.

One can elect to dismiss, out of hand, the foregoing claims of the mystics, but doing so seems to exhibit a considerable resonance with the actions of religious clerics who refused to look through Galileo's telescope when given the opportunity to do so. After all, the mystics contend that mysticism is an empirical science in which one is constantly engaged in a process of testing and falsifying various ideas concerning the nature of the mystical path.

One might also point out in passing that at the present time the heart of Lawrence Krauss's perspective concerning the possibility of a universe arising from nothing is neither testable nor falsifiable. Yet, he is considered to be a scientist and his ideas are considered to be scientific even as his colleagues understand that the ideas of Lawrence Krauss concerning the possibility of the universe arising from nothing might not be correct.

Also, one might want to keep in mind that like many claims in science, the statements of mystics (as opposed to theologians) also often tend to be tentative in nature. For example, and as touched upon in the opening chapter of this book, the dissertation that my spiritual guide wrote to satisfy one of the conditions of his doctorate program was considered by A.J. Arberry - an eminent scholar of Islam and the Sufi mystical tradition - to be one of the best treatises on the Sufi path to have been written in the English language.

Early on in his academic career, my spiritual guide would update the foregoing dissertation so that it would better reflect what he experienced and discovered during one, or another, of his 40-day periods of seclusion. However, after a while, he gave up on the idea of modifying the contents of his dissertation because the lived experience generated through his many periods of seclusion were constantly outstripping the written words of his dissertation in too dynamic, rigorous, and ineffable a manner.

The foregoing considerations tend to muddy the waters a little as far as the issue of distinguishing between science and religion is concerned (especially in conjunction with religion's mystical dimension). However, irrespective of whether, or not, one accepts Judge Overton's manner of bringing specific criteria to bear on the problem of distinguishing between science and non-science, none of this is germane to the real issue at the center of *McLean v. Arkansas Board of Education* - namely, whether creation science and the theory of evolution (each in its own way) are, among other things, in contravention of the Establishment Clause of the First Amendment, or the Guarantee Clause of Article IV, Section 4 of the basic Constitution.

Judge Overton provided evidence in his ruling (for example, among, other things, he quoted a statement to this effect from the writing of Duane Gish, a prominent proponent of creation science) that the judge was aware of the claim that the theory of evolution was religious in nature. Yet, he did not seem to pursue this issue and, instead, appeared to accept, at face value, the idea that the theory of evolution was scientific in nature while creation science was not scientific in character.

Conceivably, defense counsel might have done an inadequate job of inducing various witnesses to develop, and elaborate on, the religious-like features that are present in the theory of evolution. Nevertheless, there was enough evidence presented in the *McLean v. Arkansas Board of Education* case to indicate that Judge Overton might not have exercised due diligence with respect to pursuing this facet of the proceedings - especially given that the foregoing issue is far more relevant to the central legal themes of the case (e.g., the Establishment Clause of the First Amendment and Article I, Section 4 of the Constitution) than is the process of trying to differentiate between what is science and what is not science.

Judge Overton was justified in striking down Act 590 of the

Arkansas legal code because that piece of legislation clearly violates the prohibitions inherent in the Establishment Clause of the First Amendment, as well as being in contravention of the provisions inherent in Article IV, Section 4 of the Constitution. However, Judge Overton's ruling missed the opportunity to truly deliver a balanced decision (and, therefore, one done in accordance with republican principles) when he failed to overturn the 1968 Supreme Court decision in *Epperson v. Arkansas* that vitiated the Initiated Act of 1929 prohibiting the theory of evolution from being taught in public schools because irrespective of however scientific the theory of evolution might be considered to be, nonetheless, that theory contains an array of elements that render it sectarian in a manner that is indistinguishable from religious theories and, therefore, constitutes a violation of the Establishment Clause of the First Amendment and, in addition, is in contravention of Article IV, Section 4.

Finally, toward the end of his ruling for *McLean v. Arkansas Board of Education*, Judge Overton states:

"Implementation of Act 590 will have serious and untoward consequences for students, particularly those planning to attend college. Evolution is the cornerstone of modern biology ... Any student who is deprived of instruction as to the prevailing scientific thought on these topics will be denied a significant part of science education."

The foregoing warning sounds an awful lot like it is alluding to some sort of a religious-like litmus test for higher education. In other words, Judge Overton's foregoing words seem to be suggesting that unless a person can demonstrate that one is a true believer in the theory of evolution and, as a result, has been thorough indoctrinated into the catechism of evolutionary principles concerning the nature of reality, then that individual risks being thrown into the higher education equivalent of hell or purgatory where such an individual will have to endure boiling in mental anguish for an eternity or, at least, for the duration of one's college career ... and, possibly, longer.

I remember reading Theodosius Dobzhansky's 1973 essay from the *American Biology Teacher* entitled: "Nothing in Biology Makes Sense Except in the Light of Evolution." I thought at the time when I read the foregoing essay that it was an exercise in hyperbole since a great deal of - if not most of - the material in biology makes considerable sense independently of the theory of evolution.

To be sure, the theory of evolution does provide one with a hermeneutical way to tie the phenomena of biology together in a tidy little package that lends more sense to those phenomena than they might have if the theory of evolution is not true. Nevertheless, one can easily jettison the theory of evolution (but not population genetics) and still understand a great deal about the marvelous phenomena to which the study of biology gives expression.

Contrary to what Judge Overton claims in the foregoing quote, evolution is not the cornerstone of biology. The cornerstone of biology is biology.

One doesn't need evolution to understand the principles of photosynthesis, the Krebs cycle, nervous functioning, metabolic pathways, cellular physiology, membrane dynamics, motility, molecular genetics, or a litany of other biological functions and principles. The theory of evolution might tell one - correctly or incorrectly - what purposes and functions are served through various biological processes, but that theory contributes little, or nothing, toward the process of revealing the nuts and bolts of how cells and organisms operate.

At best, the theory of evolution enables biologists to speculate about why cells and organisms might operate in the way they do or why, in certain limited cases, new species might form due to factors such as isolation. But, if someone were to wave a wand that erased the ideas of evolutionary theory from our collective memory banks, human beings would still have discovered a great deal that makes sense with respect to biological processes under a variety of different circumstances.

Nearly a quarter century later, many of the foregoing issues resurfaced again in the 2004-2005 legal proceedings known as *Tammy Kitzmiller, Et Al. v. Dover Area School District Et Al.* The basis for the Pennsylvania case was rooted in an October 18, 2004 memorandum issued by the Dover Area School Board of Directors which announced that students would be required to not only learn about various problems that were entailed by Darwin's theory of evolution, but, as well, students would be required to learn about "other theories of evolution including, but not limited to, intelligent design."

The forgoing resolution was followed a month later by a November 19, 2004 press release from the Dover Area School District stipulating that teachers at Dover High School would be required to read a statement to 9th grade biology students that identified a number of principles. Included in the press release were statements claiming that: There were gaps in the theory of evolution; the theory of evolution was not a fact; the idea of intelligent design provides an account for the origin of life that is different from the theory of evolution, and the book - *Of Pandas and People* - was a resource that students might use in order to learn more about the intelligent design perspective.

A little less than a month later, a suit was filed in U.S. District Court on December 14, 2004. The suit alleged that both the October 18, 2004 resolution of the Dover Area School Board of Directors as well as the November 19, 2004 press release of the Dover Area School District contravened the Establishment Clause of the First Amendment.

The trial began on September 26, 2005. It concluded a little over a month later on November 4, 2005.

The judge presiding over the case was John E. Jones II. He concluded that it was: "...unconstitutional to teach ID [i.e., Intelligent Design] as an alternative to evolution in a public school science classroom."

Like the legal decision in the McLean v. Arkansas Board of Education that was handed down in the 1980s, Judge Jones' judicial decision in the *Kitzmiller, et al v. Dover Area School District et al* case engages in a lengthy discussion that explores a variety of both legal and scientific issues concerning the attempt of Christian fundamentalists to oppose the teaching of the theory of evolution. Such opposition assumed the form of either trying to ban the teaching of the theory of evolution or seeking to have creationist or intelligent design alternatives to the theory of evolution be given equal time in public school classrooms.

During his historical review, Judge Jones II refers to the 1975 Tennessee case of *Daniel v. Waters*. In that dispute, the Sixth Circuit Court of Appeals concluded the legislation at issue gave a "...

preferential position for the Biblical version of creation 'over' any account of the development of man based on scientific research and reasoning" and, therefore, was in contravention of the Establishment Clause of the First Amendment.

Although the Sixth Circuit Court of Appeals rightly pointed out that the Tennessee statute that was being explored in the *Daniel$ v.$ Waters* case violated the Establishment Clause, the Court failed to indicate that the Tennessee statute also constituted a violation of Article IV, Section 4 of the Constitution because the disputed legislation undermined the principle of republican government that had been guaranteed to each of the states. Extending a preferred position to a Biblical version of creation relative to other non-Biblical accounts concerning the development of human beings that were based on scientific research and reasoning demonstrates that the Tennessee statute was not drawn up in an: Objective, impartial, disinterested, non-partisan, equitable, or fair manner, and, as a result, is inconsistent with the qualities of republicanism.

The Sixth Circuit Court of Appeals does not raise questions in its judicial decision about whether, or not, the theory of evolution should be given a preferred position in public schools. Although the members of the Sixth Circuit Court of Appeals might have felt - if they even considered the matter - that such issues were irrelevant to determining the Constitutional status of the Tennessee statute that was being called into question, the case offered an opportunity for the Court to explore the nature of the Establishment Clause, the Preamble to the Constitution, and Article IV, Section 4 of the Constitution in an equitable, fair, non-partisan, independent, and disinterested fashion, but they failed to do so.

If it is unconstitutional to assign a preferred position to the teaching in public schools of a Biblical account concerning the origins of life or the development of human beings, is it also unconstitutional to assign a preferred position to the teaching of a scientific researched and reasoned theory concerning the evolution of life or the evolution of human beings? Identifying the theory of evolution as being a function of science does not automatically serve to justify why such a theory should be considered to be incumbent on students to learn.

Naturally, those who consider the theory of evolution to be a true account concerning the origins of species believe it is in the best interests of students to be exposed to the research and reasoning that they feel substantiates their evolutionary perspective. However, those who consider the Biblical account concerning the origins of life and the nature of human development also believe the best interests of students are served by exposing students to the research and reasoning that the advocates of creationism feel substantiate their Biblical perspective.

Both the theory of evolution and the creationist approach to origins and human development are sectarian in nature. Why should one suppose that a sectarian position that is claimed to be scientific will be any less likely to violate the Establishment Clause of the First Amendment or to be in contravention of Article IV, Section 4 than is a Biblical approach to those same issues?

By failing to raise the foregoing sort of questions, the Sixth Circuit Court of Appeals is, itself, not only guilty of violating the requirements of Article IV, Section 4 of the Constitution, but, as well, the Court is helping to establish a sectarian framework. As pointed out earlier in this chapter -and notwithstanding the fact that the theory of evolution does not employ an overtly religious lexicon -- one encounters considerable difficulty avoiding the conclusion that the theory of evolution is, in many ways, virtually indistinguishable from a religious-like framework because the "facts" that it cites are not capable of demonstrating that the theory of evolution is a correct explanation for the origin of all species.

While stating his judicial opinion in the *Kitzmiller et al v. Dover Area School District et al* case, Judge Jones II cites the findings of Judge Overton in *McLean v. Arkansas Board of Education*. More specifically, Judge Jones II summarizes the legal opinion of the earlier case by stating:

"... the United States District Court of Arkansas deemed creation science as merely biblical creationism in a new guise and held that Arkansas's balanced-treatment statute could have no valid secular purpose or effect, served only to advance religion, and violated the First Amendment."

How does one determine what constitutes a "valid secular purpose"? What are the criteria that determine what constitutes a "valid secular purpose"?

More importantly, perhaps, one wonders why secular ideas should be accorded preferential consideration to non-secular ideas in the legal opinion of Judge Jones II. Even if one were to ignore all of the considerations explored earlier in this chapter concerning the religious-like nature of the theory of evolution, as well as ignore the possibility that the theory of evolution might violate the Establishment Cause of the First Amendment when considered from the perspective of a deeper analysis involving a more inclusive notion of religion, nonetheless, the theory of evolution tends to violate the principles inherent in Article IV, Section 4 of the Constitution because that theory cannot necessarily be shown to be true in an objective, impartial, non-partisan, disinterested, equitable, and fair manner by individuals who are not already committed to that theory.

In addition, the District Court of Arkansas seemed to be immune to the irony inherent in their previous quoted words since the theory of evolution serves only to advance the philosophy of evolutionism. This might constitute a secular purpose, but it is not a <u>valid</u> secular purpose because the sectarian nature of the theory of evolution tends to violate the Establishment Clause of the First Amendment as well as contravene the requirements of Article IV, Section 4.

If a person would like to ask whether, or not, the theory of evolution is a scientific theory, then, by all means, ask scientists - and such questions were asked in both *McLean v. Arkansas Board of Education* as well as in *Kitzmiller et al v. Dover School District et al.* However, scientists are not necessarily the people who should be consulted if one is trying to determine the extent to which the theory of evolution constitutes an objective, equitable, fair, independent, impartial, non-partisan, disinterested account of the nature of reality or our relationship to Being and, thereby, is capable of serving a "valid secular purpose" ... that is, one that is capable of satisfying the degrees of freedom and constraints that are set forth in the Constitution (including: The Preamble; the Establishment Clause of the First Amendment; the 9th and 10th Amendment, as well as Article IV, Section 4 of the Constitution).

Judge Jones II commits the same error in his decision concerning *Kitzmiller et al v. Dover Area School District* legal proceedings that

Judge Overton committed in the latter's judgment in the *McLean v. Arkansas Board of Education* case. More specifically, each of the foregoing justices spends a great deal of time in their respective decisions making distinctions between science and non-science but spend relatively little time on exploring the nature of the Establishment Clause of the First Amendment, or on analyzing the nature of Article IV, Section 4 of the Constitution, or reflecting on whether, or not -- under the 9th and 10th Amendment -- either secular or non-secular agencies (or neither) should have control of the educational process, or whether, or not, either Federal or State agencies (or neither) should assume control of the educational process.

Both Judge Overton and Judge Jones II make the same point in their respective legal proceedings - namely, that finding fault with the theory of evolution does not necessarily constitute evidence in favor of some edition of creation science or intelligent design. Consequently, each of those judges should have understand that there is a similar logical error present when the two jurists find fault with creationist science or intelligent design and, then proceed to conclude that some form of a secular conceptual system -- such as the theory of evolution or science -- must, necessarily, constitute the de facto default system that should govern citizens or be taught in public schools.

If Judge Jones II is going to spend an extended period of time pointing out the many problems that permeate the notion of intelligent design and how that notion gives expression to a religious point of view, then, Article IV, Section of the Constitution demands that Judge Jones II also spend an extended period of time exploring the many problems that permeate the theory of evolution and how that theory tends to violate the Establishment Clause of the First Amendment, as well as tends to be in contravention of the 9th and 10th Amendments along with Article IV, Section 4 of the Constitution. By failing to pursue the foregoing sorts of issues in his judicial decision, Judge Jones II was not exhibiting the necessary qualities of: Objectivity, disinterestedness, impartiality, independence, equitability, and fairness that are required by Article IV, Section 4 of the Constitution and which, supposedly, are guaranteed to the people of each of the states.

Judge Jones II describes how five years after the *McLean v.*

Arkansas Board of Education decision vacated Act 590 in Arkansas, the Supreme Court of the United States struck down a similar law in Louisiana. The majority opinion in the 1987 decision for *Edwards v. Aguillard* stipulated that Louisiana's Creationism Act" contravened the Establishment Clause of the First Amendment because the aforementioned Act amounted to "...restructuring the science curriculum to conform with a particular religious viewpoint."

Yet, if one were to retain the logic inherent in the foregoing way of describing the conflict between creationism and evolutionism in *Edwards$ v. Aguillard,* a person could easily - and justifiably - argue in parallel fashion that the theory of evolution constitutes a restructuring of the science curriculum to conform with a particular sectarian - if not religious-like - viewpoint that seeks to promote an evolutionary philosophy that is dressed up in scientific language. Referring to the theory of evolution as being scientific does not make it any less sectarian, or religious-like in the manner in which it seeks to impose a certain way of thinking on students and, in the process, attempts to induce the latter individuals to consider such a theory to be inviolable, sacrosanct, sacred, and deserving of a reverential-like commitment that should shape a person's understanding and engagement of reality.

Both Judge Overton in *McLean v. Arkansas Board of Education,* as well as Judge Jones II in *Kitzmiller et al v. Dover Area School District et al* seem to be oblivious to the manner in which they each tend to filter the information in their respective cases through the presumptive lenses of science and the theory of evolution rather than filter information through a process of reflecting on that information in a truly objective, impartial, independent, non-partisan, fair, and equitable fashion that tends to lead to the conclusion that, on the one hand, <u>neither</u> creation science or its update counterpart, intelligent design should be taught in public schools, <u>nor</u>, on the other hand, should the theory of evolution be taught in public schools. In fact, the extent to which each of the aforementioned judges seems to be blind to the conceptual dynamic through which their respective cases are being framed and filtered in a manner that give unquestioned priority to science and the theory of evolution indicates just how problematic the issue of establishing a "valid secular purpose" can be if one is going to, simultaneously, try to reconcile such purposes with, say, the requirements of Article IV, Section 4.

Secular purposes are not necessarily the de facto solution for avoiding violations of the Establishment Clause of the First Amendment or transgressions against the requirements of Article IV, Section 4 of the Constitution. Purposes that are neither secular nor non-secular should be sought ... purposes that require an on-going process of critical reflection intended to ascertain that neither secular nor non-secular perspectives that have sectarian, religious-like features are permitted to be imposed on citizens, and, in addition, to ascertain that the actions and decisions of government officials are in compliance with the requirements of a republican form of government.

During his decision for *Kitzmiller et al v. Dover Area School District et al*, Judge Jones II states:

"We are in agreement with plaintiff's lead expert, Dr. Miller, that from a practical perspective, attributing unsolved problems about nature to causes and forces that lie outside the natural world is a 'science stopper'. As Dr. Miller explained, once you attribute a cause to an untestable supernatural force, a proposition that cannot be disproven, there is no reason to continue seeking natural explanations as we have our answer."

Although the term "natural world" is used in the foregoing excerpt from the legal decision of Judge Jones II, no definition is given for that phrase.

How does one determine what forces and causes lay within, or beyond, the purview of the natural world? How does one prove what forces and causes lay within the boundaries of the natural world?

Just because one has methods at one's disposal that are capable of detecting certain kinds of forces or causal relations in observed phenomena does not mean that other kinds of forces and causes aren't also present that fall beyond the capacity of one's methods for detecting phenomena, forces, and causes. Moreover, forces and causes that cannot be engaged or measured by our current methodology are not necessarily supernatural.

The neutrino is calculated to measure 10^{-24} meters (.000000000000000000000001) or 10 yoctometers. The Planck length is 10^{-35} meters or in the vicinity of .0000000001 yoctometers.

The Planck length tends to mark a boundary for classical ideas concerning the nature of space-time and gravity. Consequently, we have no idea what, if anything, lies on the other side of that boundary marker or how what transpires in that realm of the Universe affects what transpires on the level of the Planck length or larger.

For example, we don't know why constants -- e.g., the mass of an electron which is $9.10938356 \times 10^{-31}$ kilograms -- have the values they do. The Higgs field might have something to do with the mass value of an electron, but if so, at the present time, we do not know what the nature of the dynamics are between the structural properties of the electron and the structural properties of the Higgs field that would result in electrons having such a constant value.

We know that the Higgs field exists because CERN has been able to detect that field through the presence of the Higgs boson. However, we do not know what -- if anything -- makes the Higgs field possible, but irrespective of whatever might make the Higgs field possible and even though we do not, yet, fully understand the properties of that field, we assume that those dynamics are natural in character.

Natural forces and causes are whatever makes observable phenomena possible irrespective of whether, or not, we can detect them, measure them, or understand them. Advances in methodology, measurement, and instrumentation often expand the horizons of the observable and detectible, but, currently, we do not know whether, or not, we will reach a point in the future when we might encounter some sort of inherent limitation to what can be observed or measured through our physical methods and instruments.

If such a limit should be reached, this does not mean that we have exhausted what the natural world has to offer. Instead, what it means is that we will have reached a terminal point for what our methods and instruments can reveal about the character of the natural world.

Conceivably, God operates in the interstitial spaces that cannot be accessed by our methods and instruments. This would not make such dynamics supernatural but, rather, those dynamics would merely give expression to a species of natural phenomena that are beyond our ability to observe, detect, or measure.

Judge Jones II - as well as Dr. Miller, the lead witness for the plaintiff - maintains that: "once you attribute a cause to an untestable supernatural force, a proposition that cannot be disproven, there is no reason to continue seeking natural explanations as we have our answer." Yet, the theory of evolution constantly makes reference to the idea of random, chance events that cannot be proven to be truly - that is, ontologically, rather than just methodologically -- random, chance phenomena, and, as a result, the foregoing perspective has tended to stop scientists from looking for natural explanations that transcend the idea of randomness but still fall within the realm of the natural world even though the properties and characteristics of that natural world might fall beyond the capacity of our present (and, possibly, future) methods, measurements, and instruments to be able to detect.

Neither Judge Jones II nor Dr. Kenneth Miller (the lead witness for the plaintiff) - nor anyone else -- knows how the first protocells came into existence or how the genetic code came into existence. Neither of those individuals knows how consciousness, intelligence, memory, reason, language, or creativity came into being or what made them possible.

They assume that the aforementioned sorts of phenomena are part and parcel of the natural world. Nonetheless, they know almost nothing about the underlying dynamics or causal forces that give expression to those sorts of qualities or properties and, quite possibly, they will never be able to prove or test what, ultimately, is responsible for those phenomena.

In short, neither Judge Jones II nor Dr. Kenneth Miller has defensible grounds for claiming that the natural world is a realm that necessarily excludes the presence of God. Indeed, the nature of God's activity in the natural world might just be among those phenomena that are beyond the capacity of our physical methods and instruments to be able to detect or measure.

When Judge Jones II and Dr. Miller refer to the idea of the supernatural as being a "science stopper", they seem to be blind to the parallel possibility that approaching reality in the way they do could be something of a "soul or spirit stopper". By insisting that: Public schools, their teachers, and their students must adopt a scientific approach to reality that promotes the theory of evolution, they are advocating a policy that, in many respects, cannot be tested or proven to be true, and, therefore, is as much a sectarian system as any religion and, as such, becomes an oppressive force that interferes with the opportunity of individuals to freely seek natural explanations for phenomena - such as life - that fall beyond the limitations of the theory of evolution.

Judge Jones II indicated in his decision that during Dr. Miller's testimony the professor maintained that just because researchers cannot explain all the details of evolutionary theory, this, in and of itself, does not necessarily invalidate the theory of evolution. Perhaps this is true, but, nonetheless, such a claim does tend to lead to the emergence of questions about where and how one should draw the line that enables one to differentiate between problematic speculations and substantiated theories.

The foregoing contention takes place during a section in the judicial decision of Judge Jones II that critically analyzes some of the ideas of Professor Michael Behe concerning the issue of 'irreducible complexity'. Dr. Behe is of the opinion that there are many processes within organisms involving phenomena such as motility, blood clotting, and the immune response that exhibit structural properties of sufficient complexity whose origins, or way of coming together, cannot be explained adequately by the theory of evolution.

Taking issue with the foregoing position of Professor Behe, Judge Jones II cites the testimony of Dr. Miller and Dr. Padian indicating that Dr. Behe's perspective fails to take into consideration well known mechanisms of evolutionary dynamics. For example, Judge Jones II states:

"In fact, the theory of evolution proffers exaptation as a well-recognized, well-documented explanation for how systems with multiple parts could have evolved through natural means."

Exaptation is a process in which biological systems acquire functions that those systems did not originally possess. To illustrate the foregoing issue, Judge Jones II refers to an example provided by Dr. Padian during the latter's testimony indicating that the middle ear bones of mammals arose, over time, from the mammalian jawbone.

Judge Jones II proceeds to claim that the foregoing evidence demonstrates that Professor Behe's notion of 'irreducible complexity' excludes such data from consideration and, therefore, refutes the professor's argument. Yet, Judge Jones II fails to indicate what the set of step-by-step processes was that led the middle ear bones of mammals to arise from and become differentiated from mammalian jawbones.

Consequently, neither Judge Jones II nor Dr. Padian have provided a step-by-step map that plots out how one goes from mammalian jawbones to the emergence of mammalian middle ear bones. Apparently, this is one of the evolutionary details that - according to Judge Jones II and Dr. Kenneth Miller - evolutionary theory is not required to explain but which - quite incredibly -- does not cause the theory of evolution to lose any sense of validity.

Yet, if one were to say that God were responsible for the transition from mammalian jawbones to mammalian middle ear bones, evolutionary scientists would demand that the proponents of that kind of a theory to provide a step-by-step account of how God made such a transition possible. However, if the proponents of that kind of a theory could not provide evidence capable of substantiating their claim, then, evolutionary scientists would very likely argue that the absence of such evidence undermines the validity of a creationist theory of origins.

None of the examples of exaptation that Judge Jones II mentioned in his decision or that Dr. Miller ran through during his testimony provide the step-by-step evidence that is needed to demonstrate that their claims are warranted. They both allude to the possibility of exaptation with respect to the emergence of complex systems of motility, blood clotting, and the immune system, but, apparently, those possibilities are supposed to be accepted without having to present any detailed evidence capable of demonstrating that exaptation correctly (and not just possibly or theoretically) accounts for the emergence of complex systems over time.

Judge Jones writes in his decision that:

"... Dr. Miller presented peer-reviewed studies refuting Professor

Behe's claim that the immune system was irreducibly complex. Between 1996 and 2002, various studies confirmed each element of the evolutionary hypothesis explaining the origin of the immune system"

Moreover, on cross-examination Dr. Behe was presented with 58 publications that had been peer-reviewed, along with nine books and a number of chapters from several textbooks on immunology that explored the evolution of the immune system.

To begin with, one might ask if any of the people who were among the peers who reviewed the aforementioned studies on the evolution of the immune system were, or were not, individuals who accepted the theory of evolution. If all of them were proponents of the theory of evolution, then, perhaps, one should not be too surprised that the studies being alluded to might have been acceptable to the peers who reviewed them as long as those studies exhibited the sort of characteristics that would have resonated - to varying degrees -- with the sensibilities of the individuals who were reviewing that material.

Consequently, the foregoing alliance of studies and peers might only indicate that the peers, along with the people who conducted the studies, operated out of a similar world-view. If so, then, the evidence being cited by Judge Jones II or Dr. Miller does not necessarily constitute evidence that the theory of evolution has been shown to be true in some independent fashion.

Secondly, what does it mean to say that a study confirms a given theory? What are the criteria of confirmation? What justifies such criteria?

Since none of the individuals who wrote: Those 58 studies, or nine books, or several textbooks on immunology were present when immune systems began to emerge in various organisms and also were not present when new wrinkles might have been introduced to those systems, I can pretty much guarantee that none of the individuals to whom Judge Jones II or Professor Miller are referring would be able to specify the precise set of steps that led to the appearance of those systems or to their development. Unfortunately, Judge Jones II seems to exhibit little common sense and ask: How do either the authors of those studies and books or the peers who are reviewing that material know that things happened in the way that is being claimed in their studies.

Judge Jones II seems to be treating informed speculation concerning the possible emergence of immune systems as if it were established truth. Furthermore, rather inexplicably, he appears to be claiming that such informed speculation is capable of disproving Dr. Behe's ideas concerning irreducible complexity.

Professor Behe's notion of irreducible complexity might, or might not, be true. However, speculation about what could have happened in the past is not necessarily the same thing as being able to produce step-by-step, verifiable evidence indicating what actually did happen in the past. Therefore, even if all of those 58 studies, 9 books, and assorted chapters that allegedly were considered to confirm the theory of evolution's account concerning the development of immune systems, nevertheless, until one closely and critically examines what is meant by the notion of 'confirmation' and reflects on the criteria that are being used to establish that supposed confirmation (and whether such criteria are justified), one can't really be sure what, if anything, has been demonstrated by the studies and books to which Judge Jones II is alluding.

I'm pretty sure that Judge Jones II did not review the 58 studies, nine books, and chapters in several textbooks of immunology that are being referred to in his legal decision. Instead, he seemed to merely accept, at face value, the testimony of Dr. Miller and several other witnesses for the plaintiff that the foregoing material proved what they claimed it did.

Throughout his decision, Judge Jones II seems to exhibit the same sort of inclination that is being noted above with respect to appearing to be positively deposed toward the idea of the theory of evolution without exhibiting any sort of countering critical reservation concerning that theory. As such, he seems to be in contravention of Article IV, Section 4 of the Constitution because he has failed to act in an: Objective, impartial, non-partisan, independent, equitable, and fair fashion, and, as a result, he is helping to establish the theory of evolution as a sectarian system that is difficult, if not impossible, to differentiate from religious-like systems and, as such, violates the

Establishment Clause of the First Amendment.

The way to resolve the issues that arise in *McLean v. Arkansas Board of Education* or in *Kitzmiller et al v. Dover Area School District et al* (or any of the other legal proceedings that have dealt with those issues) is neither to accept the theory of evolution while rejecting some variation on creationist theory, nor should one attempt to resolve the foregoing matters by accepting creation science or intelligent design while rejecting the theory of evolution, nor should one try to resolve those problems by trying to provide a balanced treatment of the two competing visions. Rather, one should proceed with the understanding that creation science, intelligent design, and the theory of evolution all violate the Establishment Clause of the First Amendment, as well as Article IV, Section 4 of the Constitution, and, therefore, should not be permitted to shape educational policy in the public school system.

13. The Sovereignty Project

What is the nature of a person's obligation or duty today with respect to the Constitutional arrangements that were initiated through the Philadelphia Convention of 1787 and which were further realized by means of the ratification conventions that were held during the several years following the foregoing gathering in Philadelphia? The only honest and defensible answer is: None.

The 1787 Constitutional Convention was entirely extra-legal. In other words, not only did those proceedings fail to abide by -- as well as went beyond -- the provisions and requirements inherent in the Articles of Confederation but, in addition, the 1787 meetings in Philadelphia generated a document which sought to supplant those Articles in a manner that was not recognized as being an expression of the rule of law that had been established by means of the Articles of Confederation.

Of course, one might note in passing, that the aforementioned Articles of Confederation were provisions for governance that had not been agreed to by the American people either, but, instead, those principles constituted a system of power that was imposed on the general colonial populations that, under the control of vested financial and political interests, were turning themselves into self-proclaimed sovereign states that ruled over populations according to the likes and dislikes of a group of political elites with entrenched interests. Both the Articles of Confederation and the 1787 Constitution were arbitrary ways of organizing a system of governance, and this quality of self-serving arbitrariness is just one of the factors which tend to undermine anyone's attempt to claim that the 1787 Philadelphia Constitution and associated ratification conventions possess any sort of moral authority over the people of the United States.

The 1787 Philadelphia Convention, along with the ensuing ratification conventions, served as the Trojan horse through which a coup of the American people was engineered. Indeed, many tricks were played on the American people by way of the ratification process (For example, read Pauline Maier's work: *Ratification*), and this all resulted in a "way of power" taking control of the United States rather than resulting in the founding of a republic which, according to Ben Franklin, supposedly had been established ... if we could keep it, and, as it turns out, almost from the very beginning, the republic has been lost.

The claims of the foregoing paragraphs are stated as declarative sentences. However, the arguments and evidence in support of those claims can be found in a number of books (e.g., *Beyond Democracy*, *Quest for Sovereignty*, *Sovereignty and the Constitution*, *Sovereignty: A Play in Three Acts*, as well as *The People Amendments*) that have been written and which are available for free at https://www.billwhitehouse.com/press.htm .)

The primary means through which the American people are currently attached to the Constitution is by an array of stick-and-carrot inducements that are applied in the form of: Judicial force, political force, economic force, religious force, educational force, corporate force, media force, institutional force, military force, medical force, and/or the force of incarceration. One is required to comply with the so-called "rule of law" that has official oversight concerning behavior in the United States not because anyone (including lawyers, jurists, or politicians) can plausibly or justifiably demonstrate why the people of today have an indisputable duty and obligation to subjugate themselves to the alleged rule of law that was set loose in 1787, but, rather, one is required to comply with the legal fiction known as the "rule of law" because, if one does not do as one is told, one is likely to become the focus of the way of power's inclination to resolve all of its problems via violence of one kind or another (i.e., force) instead of by means of critical reasoning, fairness, character, and a recognition that all human beings have an inherent sovereignty that cannot be abrogated by any form of governance.

America does not operate in accordance with the rule of law but via the rule of force. Indeed, the notion of the rule of law is just a euphemistic cover-story which is intended to veil the wielding of violent power, and this has been true since the founding of America.

In response to the foregoing considerations, the ensuing discussion will be restricted to topics and issues concerning the First, Ninth, and Tenth Amendments. In addition, the provisions of Article IV, section 4 of the Constitution will be critically reflected upon ... at least to a degree.

To begin with, we will assume – for the sake of argument – that the 1787 Philadelphia Constitution, along with the Bill of Rights, has some sort of moral claim on the people of today. What follows is a brief overview which indicates that almost nothing that is being done today within the halls of American governance can be reconciled with the original Philadelphia document and its first ten amendments.

Therefore, even if there were some dimension of the 1787 Constitution plus the Bill of Rights that had a moral claim on our allegiance (and, as individuals such as Lysander Spooner and others have pointed out, there is no such dimension), nonetheless, what has been transpiring in government for the last 236 years, or so, has no demonstrable moral or constitutional standing and, consequently, cannot be justified or defended as a basis for governance of sovereign individuals. What is being presented here are just a few of the most important considerations which, for those who are willing to take the time, can be explored in more detail via the list of books that were mentioned previously.

Let's start the discussion by taking a look at the judiciary. For instance, there is nothing in the 1787 Constitution which entitles or requires that the members of the judiciary should be the ones who determine what the Constitution, or any of its amendments, means. One cannot possibly have three equal but separate branches of government as long as only one of those branches gets to say what the Constitution supposedly means.

The Constitution indicates that power is to be invested in the judiciary in conjunction with all cases of law and equity that arise under: The Constitution; the laws of the United States; treaties that are made; cases involving ambassadors, public ministers, consuls, as well as cases touching upon matters of admiralty and maritime jurisdiction. In addition, Constitutional power is invested in the judiciary to deal with cases of controversy involving: The United States; disputes between two, or more, states, or between a state and one or more citizens of another state, or between citizens of different states, as well as between a state or the citizens of a state and one, or more, foreign governments.

According to the Constitution, the judiciary shall have original jurisdiction with respect to those cases that concern ambassadors, public ministers, consuls, as well as states. In all other cases, the judiciary shall have appellate jurisdiction both with respect to fact and law unless some other kind of alternative arrangement is established through congressional action.

Given the foregoing guidelines, an appropriate question to ask is the following: Whether power is exercised through original or appellate jurisdiction, how is that power to be exercised? In other words, what principles should serve as the metric or standard for evaluating and deciding cases?

The only directional guidance that is given in the Constitution concerning the power of the judiciary is found in Article IV, Section 4 of that document. The aforementioned section stipulates that the United States government guarantees a republican form of government to the states and their citizens.

Republicanism was a moral philosophy that emerged during the Enlightenment. This philosophical perspective attracted a great deal of interest and many adherents among Americans throughout the 1700s. Republicanism required those individuals who wished to comply with that moral, philosophical framework to operate through principles of: Integrity, honesty, impartiality, humility, financial independence, objectivity, non-partisanship, honor, compassion, reason, judiciousness, egalitarianism, and a willingness to avoid circumstances in which one would be serving as a judge in matters that involved one's own causes.

The moral philosophy of republicanism was at the heart of a revolutionary approach to the idea of governance that was being discussed in the homes, taverns, and tea houses throughout the colonies. Under republicanism, government officials would be required to act in accordance with the moral principles that were at the heart of that philosophical orientation.

In other words, republicanism required that those with political authority could not conduct themselves according to their own personal likes, dislikes, and/or interests as, generally, had been the case in most political environments throughout history. Instead, public officials would be required to abide by a set of moral principles that actually would serve the public rather than the self-serving machinations of government officials. (If interested, one can learn more about the origins, development and impact which republicanism had on colonists with respect to their way of life in Gordon Wood's Pulitzer Prize-winning book: *The Radicalism of the American Revolution*).

Given the foregoing considerations, the power that is invested in the judiciary by the Constitution is predicated on the idea of acting in accordance with the principles of republicanism. As a result, the sole focus of the federal judiciary would be to ensure that the behavior of public officials – whether state or federal – which involved cases that came to the courts through original or appellate jurisdiction would be judged in accordance with the principles of republicanism that had been guaranteed to the states and the citizens of those states by the Constitution.

For members of the judiciary to busy themselves with discerning, or trying to discern, the meaning of the Constitution would be to engage in something that was antithetical to republicanism – namely, that the courts would be acting in a manner which involved the members of the judiciary serving as judges in their own causes. After all, whatever the meaning of the Constitution that was being advanced by members of the judiciary might be, such an interpretation would not give expression to anything but their own causes concerning their beliefs about the nature of the Constitution.

The possible meanings of the Constitution are not what should be the concern of the judiciary. Instead, what should have been at issue in any case before the judiciary is whether or not government officials had been complying with the moral requirements of republicanism that were constitutionally guaranteed to the people of the United States.

Consequently, the hundreds of books that contain judicial rulings concerning the alleged meanings as well as the decisions that established arbitrary precedents concerning such Constitutional meanings are, for the most part, null and void. The application of judicial power only extends to ensuring that the guarantee of republican government which is specified in Article IV, section 4 is being observed in the cases that the judiciary takes on through either original or appellate jurisdiction. Any other kind of judicial consideration or focus besides serving the requirements of the guarantee that is indicated in Article IV, section 4 is nothing but invented legal fictions that have no actual standing or authorization within the Constitution.

For 236 years, the judiciary has continually exercised a form of power – involving meanings and precedents that shift with assumptions, values, and beliefs – to which it is not constitutionally entitled. Moreover, like the Golum in J.R.R. Tolkien's *Lord of the Rings* trilogy, once members of the judiciary put on the ring of power, they were reluctant to take that ring of power off irrespective of what the corrupting ramifications of that ring might be for them or for others.

Let's consider, for a moment, or so, the powers of Congress. For example, the First Amendment stipulates that: "Congress shall make no law respecting an establishment of religion, or prohibiting the free exercise thereof …" Although there might be many ways to talk about religion, in essence, religion appears to refer to any conceptual-emotional undertaking that seeks to determine – and, then, as a matter of duty or obligation, require one to act in accordance with -- what one considers to be the truth concerning the nature of one's relationship with Being or Reality.

Notwithstanding the manner in which any given individual might conceive of the notion of a Divinity, religion doesn't require that individuals believe in such a notion. Religion is the existential orientation which generates one's sense of duty and obligation in relation to whatever it is that one considers the truth to be concerning the alleged nature of one's relationship to reality or ontology.

Although words such as: Economics, politics, law, physics, cosmology, philosophy, technology, psychology, morality, evolution, epistemology, education, mythology, history, and medicine are used as if they were referring to fields of study that are quite apart from the idea of religion, nonetheless, such a perspective does not really seem to be all that tenable. Each of the words which were mentioned earlier entails conceptual and methodological activities that purport to map out the alleged truth concerning the relationship between, on the one hand, individuals and, on the other hand, the nature of reality.

Furthermore, the sub-text of those sorts of perspectives tends to be that one should act in a manner that reflects, or is consonant with, those alleged truths. Consequently, practices that pursue issues of truth and that entail a sense of obligation concerning those truths but which go by any name other than religion would not only smell as sweet but would, as well, tend to satisfy the essential conditions that constitute what makes a rose a rose or makes a religion a religion.

Therefore, any legislation that is introduced into Congress which seeks to induce citizens to pursue: A particular course of action, a set of policies, or a way of life that gives expression to what members of Congress believe to be the truth concerning the nature of an individual's relationship with Reality is a violation of the First Amendment. Such legislation is both an attempt to make laws "respecting the establishment of religion" – that is, to impose a conception of truth and obligation onto citizens -- as well as an attempt to "prohibit the free exercise thereof" in the case of individuals who do not agree with the notion of reality that is being proposed by government officials.

In light of the foregoing considerations, almost all legislation that has been introduced and passed by one congressional session or another across the 236-plus years of the American republic has been in violation of the First Amendment. In addition, if the judiciary had been doing the one job that its members actually had been authorized to do by the Constitution, then, over the years, the members of Congress would have told, time and time again, by the judiciary that Article IV, section 4 of the Constitution prohibits such congressional actions – that is, the members of Congress have been violating the guarantee of republicanism that had been given to the states and its citizens by the Constitution when Congress seeks to impose on citizens ideas which the members of Congress believe to be the nature of truth -- and, therefore, the source of obligation or duty -- because by passing such legislation the members of Congress are seeking to be judges in their own causes ... actions that are inconsistent with the moral philosophy of republicanism that has been guaranteed to the states and their people.

Congress is not free to do whatever it would like to do. Rather, the activities of Congress are constrained by the moral requirements of republican government that have been constitutionally vouchsafed to the states and their citizens and, as well, Congress is constrained by the very clear prohibitions that are stated in the opening part of the

First Amendment concerning the establishment of religion or the prohibition of the free exercise thereof.

In addition, the Ninth Amendment indicates that "The enumeration in the Constitution, of certain rights, shall not be construed to deny and disparage others retained by the people." Yet, for 236 years, Congress, the judiciary, as well as the states (and state judiciaries) have been denying and disparaging the rights that are retained by the people even if such rights are not specifically enumerated in the Constitution but, as noted above are alluded to by the word: "others" – that is, other rights – in the text of the Ninth Amendment.

For example, considerations of health, education, sovereignty, conscription, and religion are not among the enumerated rights that have been accorded to Congress. Therefore, every attempt by Congress to introduce legislation concerning such issues constitutes an attempt to deny and disparage the unenumerated rights of the people that are entailed by the Ninth Amendment.

Moreover, when state governments, via their legislatures and judiciaries, seek to co-opt issues involving, for example, health, education, sovereignty, conscription, and/or religion, then, state governments also are engaged in acts which seek to deny and disparage the unenumerated rights of the people. For example, the Tenth Amendment indicates that: "The powers not delegated to the United States by the Constitution, nor prohibited by it to the states, are reserved to the states respectively, or to the people." Consequently, the Tenth Amendment clearly indicates that states are not the only ones with Constitutional standing with respect to powers that have not been delegated to the United States, nor prohibited by the Constitution to the states. If this were not the case, then, there would have been no point for Roger Sherman to add the phrase "or to the people" to the original wording of that amendment.

In addition, seeking to withhold Constitutional standing from the people in conjunction with the sorts of powers being alluded to in the Tenth Amendment, would be another way of trying to deny and disparage the unenumerated rights of the people. After all, citizens have a right – unenumerated though it might be -- to have access to the sorts of reserved, but unspecified, powers being alluded to in the

Tenth Amendment which would enable those individuals to be able to actively realize their unenumerated rights under the Ninth Amendment.

The guarantee that is present in Article IV, section 4 of the Constitution not only requires the judiciary to ensure that all members of the federal government are acting in accordance with the moral principles of republicanism, but the array of cases which the judiciary has been given power to engage via Article III, section 2 of the Constitution indicates that the judiciary has the authority to ensure that cases involving states and citizens will be conducted in accordance with the requirements of the moral philosophy of republicanism as well. Consequently, for the last 236 years, the federal judiciary should have been actively restraining state governments from denying and decrying the unenumerated rights of citizens as well as actively upholding the Constitutional standing of the people concerning those powers that have not been delegated to the United States nor prohibited to the states and which, therefore, have been "reserved to the states respectively, or to the people."

Unfortunately, for some 236 years, the federal judiciary has, by and large, failed in its fiduciary responsibilities to the citizens of America when it comes to the issue of ensuring that no branch of government, whether federal or state, denies and disparages the unenumerated rights of individual citizens. Furthermore, the judiciary has also failed to actively protect the Constitutional standing of individual citizens by reminding the federal and state actors in the cases before them about the unspecified, reserved powers that have not been delegated to the United States nor prohibited to the states or to the people.

Article IV, section 4 also requires the United States to protect the states against invasion. Yet, despite the fact that corporations were an anathema to the colonialists who were engaging in a revolution against not only England but the activities of the East India Company, nonetheless, the judiciary and members of Congress have enabled corporations to invade the lives of people and to acquire substantial influence, if not control, over the lives of those citizens.

Corporations are legal fictions. Legal fictions are arbitrary ways that the courts invent in order to, supposedly, solve legal problems, with a wink and a nod, that could not be resolved if one were to abide by the law as it is written.

Corporations exist as a result of charters that give expression to a limited and temporary set of permissions which are granted by governments, and such charters set forth the understandings that are supposed to regulate the existence of those temporary and limited entities. However, starting with the *'Dartmouth College v. Woodward'* decision handed down in 1819 by the Marshall Court (a decision that the judiciary was not constitutionally authorized to make), corporations began to be treated as entities that had a form of life which had contractual rights independent of whatever charter permissions existed.

As a result, via the *'Dartmouth College v Woodward'* decision, the first will-'o-the-wisp apparition of the corporation as a shadowy, person-like entity with certain constitutional protections was, like Frankenstein's monster, given life. One might note in passing that John Marshall had an array of corporate entanglements in his legal past which induced him to look on corporations with favor and, therefore, aside from the fact that the Court had no authority to interpret the Constitution's meaning, he also was violating Article IV, section 4 of the Constitution in the *'Dartmouth College v Woodward'* decision because he was rendering a decision that allowed him to serve as a judge in his own cause – namely, his favorable opinion concerning the existence of corporations.

Corporations have no reality other than the fictional narrative or legal fiction that has been unconstitutionally assigned to them by the judiciary. Consequently, when the judiciary fails to observe its fiduciary responsibilities to the states and the people under Article IV, section 4, then, corporations are allowed to become person-like entities with rights rather than being restricted to being mere charters with limited and temporary permissions that, under the Ninth and Tenth Amendments, are subservient to the unenumerated rights and powers of the people, as well as the unspecified powers of the states.

Every policy of federal and state governments that seeks to deny and disparage the unenumerated rights of the people under the Ninth Amendment constitutes an act of violence against the people. As such, these acts violate Article IV, section 4 of the Constitution because the

United States government is supposed to protect the states and their people against all forms of domestic violence, and, yet, neither the legislature nor the executive will make an application to the judiciary to protect the people in this regard, nor does the judiciary, on the authority of its own original jurisdiction, serve as protectors of, and advocates for, the unenumerated rights of the people under the Ninth Amendment.

Finally, the Executive branch of the United States is also constrained by the guarantee of republican government inherent in Article IV, section 4 of the Constitution. This means that whatever: Executive Orders, fast-tracked treaties, calls for martial law, national security directives, intelligence operations, and/or security classification schemes that are initiated, knowingly or unknowingly, through the Office of the President, or the President's representatives, all of the foregoing practices must (according to the guarantee of the Constitution) be in compliance with the principles to which the moral philosophy of republicanism gives expression.

The judiciary has original jurisdiction when it comes to the behavior of ambassadors, public officials, and consuls as well as cases in which states are involved. With respect to the issue of original jurisdiction, the Supreme Court does not have to be referred cases by lower courts to be able to investigate the conduct of federal employees but has the authority to do so without any such request in order to determine whether ambassadors, officials, consuls, and states are conducting themselves in accordance with the provisions of Article IV, section 4 of the Constitution.

Unfortunately, the Supreme Court has rarely exercised its fiduciary responsibility in matters of original jurisdiction when it comes to ensuring that ambassadors, public officials, consuls, and states are complying with the moral requirements of republican philosophy that are guaranteed to the states and the people by Article IV, section 4 of the Constitution. As a result, the CIA, the FBI, the NSA, the military, the IRS, the NIH, the CDC, the FDA, and an array of intelligence agencies associated with different departments in the federal government have never been called to task for a multiplicity of breaches concerning the aforementioned Constitutional guarantee.

All branches and departments of the federal government as well as the branches and departments of many states have colluded, if not conspired, with one another to try to prevent the people from truly understanding: (1) the nature of the obligations that government officials have under the principles of the moral philosophy of republicanism which have been guaranteed to the states and their people in Article IV, section 4 of the Constitution; (2) the constraints involving religion that restrict the legislative activities of Congress under the First Amendment, and (3) the unenumerated and unspecified rights and powers that have been extended to the people through the Ninth and Tenth Amendments respectively.

However, as remiss as federal and state governments have been in attending to their fiduciary responsibilities to the people for 236 years, the people, themselves, have not made the effort or taken the time to properly understand the nature of the circumstances, opportunities, rights, and powers that have the potential to enable the people to realize their own sovereignty quite independently of federal and state governments. Neither the federal nor state governments have the Constitutional standing to deny and disparage the unenumerated rights and reserved, yet unspecified, powers of the Ninth and Tenth Amendments respectively, but people are going to have to actively seek the realization of such unenumerated rights and unspecified powers because, as history has clearly demonstrated, federal and state officials tend to become drunk on the power and rights that have been usurped from the people and, as a result, such officials will resist the people taking back what has belonged to the latter individuals since the amended Constitution came into existence in 1791.

Seeking the realization of unenumerated rights and unspecified powers is not a call for anarchy but a demand for sovereignty. Sovereignty is not about the unrestrained exercise of freedom that some libertarians might suppose is the case but, rather, sovereignty is about having the protected opportunity to seek to discover and realize the nature of one's essential nature.

Sovereignty is about decentralization of power rather than the centralization of power. However, sovereignty is also about ensuring that such decentralized power is capable of protecting everyone's opportunity to realize their unenumerated rights and unspecified powers in a manner that is mutually consonant with one another.

One way of engaging the foregoing issues can be accessed for free through https://www.billwhitehouse.com . Just go toward the bottom of that web page and click on the link entitled "Sovereignty".

In whatever manner the foregoing issues are tackled, there is going to have to be some sort of institutional medium or dynamic through which people can come together to have an opportunity to explore, discuss, formulate, and actuate possible ways of resolving those matters. Whether this is in the form of grand jury-like bodies or is in the form of some kind of healing-circles, or in the form of some other alternative possibility, the institutional format or dynamic will be independent of federal and state governments but, at the same time, will have to find ways of working with those levels of governance.

The federal and state governments can help people with the sovereignty project. Nonetheless, those forms of governance cannot solve the challenges that are entailed by that project.

The sovereignty challenge can only be resolved by the people themselves. That challenge cannot be resolved through: Voting, elected representation, or the activities of various branches of government but, instead, must be engaged by the people themselves through: Discussion, debate, critical reflection, constructive exercises of character, reciprocity, compromise, and fairness in conjunction with the aspirations of the participants.

It is not enough for people to speak about freedoms and liberties. The people must come together in an array of settings to actively engage in the difficult, nuanced work that is entailed by the challenge of developing an understanding about what freedom looks like – in actual lived terms – within the context of a multiplicity of people that are each seeking and have a right to conditions and principles of sovereignty being applied to their lives.

The current Constitution does not have to be jettisoned to accomplish the foregoing project. Nonetheless, constitutional provisions that are present in Article IV, section 4, along with the First Amendment's restrictions concerning the establishment or prohibition of religion by Congress, as well as the authority inherent in the Ninth and Tenth amendments concerning the sovereignty of the people must be acknowledged, honored, and judiciously protected as well as supported by federal and state forms of governance.

Unfortunately, for a variety of reasons, time is running out. If we, the people, do not act on the aforementioned sovereignty project soon, we might well lose the capacity to do so altogether or have that opportunity taken away from us by parties that have no interest in the people becoming truly sovereign.

Pursuit of the sovereignty project is the only way in which a sense of duty and obligation might arise in the context of the Constitution. Absent such a project, the potential of the Constitution that was introduced in 1787, ratified over the next several years, and amended in 1791, will continue to erode as it has been doing for the last 236 years.

If things continue on in the way they are going, then, at some point, a tipping point involving the American republic is going to be reached. When that happens, the promise and guarantee of abiding by the principles of republican moral philosophy will disappear and, as a result, complete tyranny or complete arbitrariness will reign.

We have a quickly evaporating opportunity to stop such a tipping point from taking place. The choice is ours, but without the establishment of an authentic sovereignty project, whatever decisions are made will come to nothing and our choices will do nothing but increase the distance between our existential circumstances and the possibility of leading sovereign lives.

Principles of Sovereignty: Some Food For Thought

Many people - on all sides of the issue - have been consumed with the: 'Who', 'why', and 'how' of the events on 9/11, but some twenty-two years later those questions are not foremost on my mind. Instead, I am concerned with what the events of 9/11 have set in motion with respect to the systematic stripping of rights, freedoms, and sovereignty that occurred in relation to American citizens, not to mention the millions of individuals who were adversely affected elsewhere in the world due to the collateral damage that ensued due to the forces given expression through the events of 9/11.

Americans - as well as individuals and communities elsewhere in the world -- have been swindled out of sovereignty by an array of scoundrels both known and unknown. America has become a failed nation because none of its essential institutions -- such as the three branches of federal government, the military, the Federal Reserve Bank, the media, and academia -- have, for the most part, done anything to prevent tyranny, oppression, and injustice from conducting a blitzkrieg of America, as well as communities elsewhere in the world.

While the events of 9/11 helped pave the road to the foregoing sort of dissolution, the problem actually began more than 225 years ago with the coup d'etat that was set in motion in the summer of 1787 in Philadelphia when a group of people -- sometimes referred to as the 'Founding Fathers' or 'Framers' -- decided to swindle Americans out of the opportunity to work toward establishing something that was far better than a republic or a democracy. Those individuals helped to establish a republic, and, unfortunately, almost from the very beginning, they began to betray the idea of a republic by failing to live in accordance with the moral principles of republicanism that are at the heart of the form of governance that was manipulated into existence through the process of ratification by the 'Founding Fathers.'

From there, things went from bad to worse. The so-called 'Founding Fathers' -- especially James Madison who came up with the Virginia Plan that served as the template for the Constitution - were appalled by the idea of democracy because, among other things, that mode of government often tended to oppress minorities in order to appease majorities who were inclined to operate out of arbitrary, volatile perspectives. Indeed, it is important to understand that the mode of government known as a republic is not at all synonymous with the notion of a democracy ... representative or otherwise.

However, by the mid-to-late 1790s, democracy had overrun republicanism as the form of governance that became dominant in America, and one of the signs of this transition was the formation of political parties ... something that was actually inconsistent with the moral principles of republicanism (enshrined in Article IV, section 4 of the Constitution) that required people in government to be impartial, objective, and unbiased in their deliberations and, therefore, indicates that belonging to a political party constitutes a conflict of interest with the moral duties of someone in government as far as the political philosophy of republicanism is concerned.

Relevant to the foregoing considerations is something that might be referred to as: The *Anaconda Principle.* This notion refers to the way in which most, if not all, governments engage in a process of increasingly and progressively squeezing the political, emotional, spiritual, social, educational, economic, and physical life out of citizens over a period of time. More specifically, each time the citizenry exhales in relief from having survived some arbitrary, unjustified, problematic exercise in public policy that was imposed on those citizens by government, the coils of power become wrapped even more tightly about the people through the next round of arbitrary and unjustified policies that are leashed upon the people.

Since 9/11, we have witnessed the introduction of: The Patriot Act (2001 - plus its reauthorization in 2005 that made many of its provisions permanent); The John Warner Authorization Act (2006); the Military Commissions Act (2006); as well as the National Defense Authorization Acts of 2010, 2011, 2012, 2013 and continuing on. In addition, there have been a slew of Executive Orders (e.g.,10990, 10995, 10997, 10998, 10999, 11000, 11001, 11002, 11003, 11004, 11005, 11921, and more) that authorize the government to control virtually every aspect of American society whenever the government deems this to be appropriate.

The Anaconda Principle is being applied ever more rigorously and persistently to the American people. In the process whatever constructive elements of republicanism and democracy that still were hanging on for dear life after several hundred years of abuse have been squeezed, for the most part, from political existence.

The following set of principles outline a possible social/political framework of self-governance that goes beyond the possibilities inherent in tyrannies, republics, and democracies. The time for change is upon us, and I believe that the kind of change to which I am alluding - monumental though it might be - can be accomplished peacefully and without violence.

I invite you to reflect on the principles of sovereignty that are briefly noted below. Then, I invite you to reflect on the form of governance in existence today and compare it with the principles of sovereignty.

Sovereignty does not require force. It requires the broadening and deepening of understanding concerning the human condition, and when understood, sovereignty has a natural appeal to human beings because it reflects something that is integral to their own identity and sense of being human.

There is a significant difference between, on the one hand, the ways of republicanism, democracy or power and, on the other hand, the way of sovereignty. We each have a duty of care to carefully and critically reflect on the nature of the choices we might make with respect to the foregoing possibilities.

The following principles are in response to a question that someone once asked me - namely, "What is sovereignty?"

(1) Sovereignty is indigenous to, and inherent in, the potential of human beings. It is not derived from society or governments but, in fact, exists prior to, and independently of, the formation of society and governments.

(2) Sovereignty is the right to realize essential identity and constructive potential in ways that are free from techniques of undue influence (which seek to push or pull individuals in directions that are antithetical to the realization of sovereignty) but, as well, in ways that do not infringe on the like rights of others.

(3) Sovereignty entails the human capacity (and corresponding duties of care) to be able to push back the horizons of ignorance concerning the nature of reality.

(4) Sovereignty encompasses the right to the quality of food, shelter, clothing, education, and medical care that are minimally necessary to realize identity and constructive potential through the process of pushing back the horizons of ignorance.

(5) Sovereignty is rooted in the duties of care that are owed to others to ensure that those sovereignty rights are established, protected, and nurtured.

(6) Sovereignty is the right to choose how to engage the dynamics of: 'neither control, nor be controlled'.

(7) Sovereignty entails establishing local councils that constructively promote and develop principles of sovereignty and, if necessary, those councils would help mediate disputes that arise along the boundary dynamics involving the principle of: 'Neither control nor be controlled'. The composition, selection, and nature of the council would be similar to that of a grand jury.

In other words, council members would not be elected but chosen through an agreed-upon random-like process and, then, subject to a vetting process to determine the suitability of a given individual for taking on the responsibilities of the aforementioned council ... much like prospective jurors go through a voir dire process. In addition, the length of service would be for a limited time (6 months to a year) before new members would be selected through the sort of non-manipulated manner and vetting process that was noted earlier. Like a grand jury, the members of a local sovereignty council would be empowered to investigate whatever issues and problems seem relevant, but, unlike a grand jury, that council would have the authority to research issues, subpoena witnesses, and present their results directly to the community for further deliberation without having to go through the office of a prosecutor or attorney general.

(8) Sovereignty is the responsibility of individuals to work toward realizing their own individual sovereignty within a collective context that gives expression to the idea of sovereignty being writ large for the community as a whole.

(9) Sovereignty is rooted in economic activity that serves the principles of sovereignty, not vice versa. Corporations should be permitted to exist only as temporary charter arrangements devoid of any claims of personhood and they should be designed to serve specific purposes of value to both individual and collective sovereignty. Whatever profits accrue from corporate activity should be shared with the communities in which the corporation operates.

(10) The constructive value of money is a function of its role in advancing the principles of sovereignty for everyone. The destructive value of money is a function of the way it undermines, corrupts, and obstructs the principles of sovereignty.

Money acquires its value through the service it provides in relation to the establishment, enhancement, and protection of sovereignty. The money-generating capacity of banks should serve the purposes of sovereignty both individually and collectively. Banks should be owned and regulated by local communities as public utilities. Moreover, whatever profits are earned in conjunction with bank activities should be reinvested in the community.

(11) Capital refers primarily to the constructive potential inherent in human beings and only secondarily to financial resources. The flow of capital (in both human and financial terms) should serve the interests of sovereignty, both individually and collectively.

(12) Sovereignty is not a zero-sum game. It is about co-operation, not competition.

(13) Sovereignty is rooted in the acquisition of personal character traits involving: Honesty, compassion, charitableness, benevolence, friendship, objectivity, equitability, tolerance, forgiveness, patience, perseverance, nobility, courage, kindness, humility, integrity, independence and judiciousness.

(14) Sovereignty is not imposed from the outside in but is realized from the inside out through struggle by the individual to come to grips with the meaning of the idea of: 'Neither control nor be controlled'.

(15) Sovereignty is rooted in struggling against: Dishonesty, bias, hatred, jealousy, greed, anger, selfishness, intolerance, arrogance, apathy, cowardice, egocentrism, duplicity, exploitation, and cruelty.

(16) Sovereignty is the process of struggling to learn how not to cede one's moral and intellectual agency to anything but: Truth, justice and character in the service of realizing one's identity, and constructive potential, as well as in the service of assisting others to realize their identity and constructive potential.

(17) Sovereignty can never be defended, protected, or enhanced by diminishing, corrupting, co-opting, or suspending the conditions necessary for the pursuit, practice, and realization of sovereignty. Sovereignty should not be subject to the politics of fear.

(18) Sovereignty is rooted in the principle that no person can represent the sovereign interests of another individual unless the sovereign interests of everybody are equally served at the same time.

(19) The activities and purposes of: Governments, nations,

institutions, and corporations should always be capable of being demonstrated -- beyond a reasonable doubt - to be the service of the sovereignty of the people, taken both collectively and individually.

(20) Sovereignty is rooted in the principle of decentralization whenever doing so would serve the interests of sovereignty better than some form of centralization would be able to accomplish in a clearly demonstrable manner.

(21) Efficiency and wealth should be measured in terms that enhance the way of sovereignty, not the way of power.

(22) The principles of sovereignty should be rooted in the notion of sustainability, and those principles should not be pursued or realized at the expense of destroying the environment ... either with respect to the short term or in conjunction with the long term.

(23) Sovereignty is rooted in the cautionary principle. In other words, if there is a reasonable doubt about the safety, efficiency, judiciousness, or potential destructive ramifications of a given activity, then that activity should be suspended until a time when those doubts have been completely, successfully, and rigorously addressed.

(24) The defense of sovereignty is best served through the cooperation of de-centralized communities of sovereign individuals ... with only occasional, limited, and secondary assistance from centralized institutions and groups.

(25) Standing armies do not serve the interests of sovereignty but, rather, serve the interests of the bureaucracies that organize, fund, equip, and direct those standing armies. Being able to defend one's country and communities from physical attack does not require standing armies but, instead, requires sovereign individuals who understand the value of defending the principles of sovereignty that help a community and network of communities to flourish.

(26) The police should serve and protect both individual, as well as collective, sovereignty. The police should not be the guardians and enforcers of arbitrary laws that are designed to protect centralized governments, corporations, institutions, and other bodies that tend to operate in accordance with the way of power and, therefore, in opposition to the way of sovereignty.

(27) When done correctly, the practice of sovereignty creates a

public space or commons that is conducive to the pursuit and realization of the principles of sovereignty by everyone who is willing to struggle toward that end.

(28) Sovereignty is rooted in the principle that the commons - that is, the resources of the Earth, if not the Universe - cannot be proven, beyond a reasonable doubt, to belong to anyone. Therefore, the commons should be shared, conserved, and protected by all of us rather than be permitted to be treated as individual, institutional, corporate, or government forms of private property.

(29) Whatever forms of private property are considered to be permissible by general consensus, that property should serve the establishment, enhancement, and protection of the principles of sovereignty, both individual and collective.

(30) Aside from what is necessary to operate a business in an effective and productive manner, as well as what is necessary in the way of resources to be able to improve that business through research and development, and/or is necessary to provide a fair return for the employees of such a business for their collective efforts, then any profits that are generated by a business should be shared with the community or communities in which that business resides. The shareholders of a business should always be the entire community in which a business is located and not just a select number of private shareholders.

In exchange for foregoing kind of arrangement, there should be no taxes assessed in conjunction with businesses. At the same time, both businesses and the community become liable for whatever damages to individuals, the environment, or other parts of the community that are adversely affected by the activities of those businesses.

(31) A market in which all of its participants are not sovereign individuals is not a free market. Markets that exploit the vulnerabilities of participants are not free. Markets that are organized by the few in a way that undermines, corrupts, or compromises the principles of sovereignty are not free.

Markets in which the participants are all equally sovereign are free. Nonetheless, the freedom inherent in those markets should serve the interests of sovereignty for those who are both inside and outside of those markets.

(32) Sovereignty is only realizable when it is rooted in a collective, reciprocal, guarantee that we will all treat one another through the principles of sovereignty.

(33) Violations of sovereignty are an impediment to the full realization of the principles of sovereignty. However, those violations should not be primarily or initially be subject to punitive forms of treatment.

Instead, violations of sovereignty should be engaged through a process of mediated, conflict resolution and reconciliation intended to restore the efficacious and judicious functioning of sovereignty amongst both individuals and the collective. This mediated process is, first and foremost, rooted in a rigorous effort to determine the facts of a given situation before proceeding on with the process of mediation, conflict resolution, or reconciliation.

A community has the right to defend itself against individuals who violate, and show a disregard for, the sovereignty rights of other individuals. The aforementioned right to self protection might assume the form of: Treatment, exile, incarceration, paroled supervision, community service, and other forms of negotiated settlement with respect to those who undermine the principles of sovereignty.

(34) Alleged scientific and technical progress that cannot be rigorously demonstrated beyond a reasonable doubt to enhance the pursuit and realization of principles of sovereignty by everyone is subject to being governed by the precautionary principle.

(35) Sovereignty is not a form of democracy in which the majority rules on any given issue. Rather, sovereignty is a process of generating consensus within a community that can be demonstrated, beyond a reasonable doubt, to serve the sovereignty interests of everyone.

(36) Sovereignty is rooted in the principle that with respect to any given practice, then, before making a community decision concerning that practice, then a community should take into consideration what the impact of that practice is likely to be on generations seven times removed from the current one.

(37) Everyone should underwrite the costs of pursuing,

establishing, enhancing, realizing, and protecting sovereignty - both individually and collectively -- according to his or her capacity to do so.

(38) Sovereignty is not a function of political maneuvering, manipulations, or strategies. Rather, sovereignty is a function of the application of: Reasoned discussion, critical reflection, constructive reciprocity, creative opportunities, and rigorous methodology in the pursuit of pushing back the horizons of ignorance and seeking to establish, enhance, realize, and protect sovereignty, both individually and collectively.

(39) Sovereignty is not about hierarchy or leadership. Advisors and technical consultants who are capable of lending their expertise and experience to a given project that serves the interests of sovereignty in a community are temporary facilitators whose responsibilities do not extend beyond a given project or undertaking. Those facilitators often tend to arise in the context of a given need and, then, are reabsorbed into the community when a given need has been met.

(40) Education should serve the interests of establishing, developing, enhancing and protecting the principles of sovereignty - both individually and collectively - and not serve the interests of the way of power. Education should not use techniques of undue influence that push or pull individuals toward accepting, or rejecting, specific philosophical, political, economic, or religious perspectives.

(41) To whatever extent taxes are collected (and the issue of taxes needs to be considered and justified - to the extent that this can be accomplished - in a critically, rigorous fashion), those taxes should be assessed only on a local basis and only after all sovereignty needs of an individual for a given period of time have been addressed. Those taxes should be proportional -- within generally agreed upon specific limits -- to a person's capacity to pay those taxes without undermining a person's ability to fully pursue realizing the principles of sovereignty.

Whatever taxes are collected can only be used in conjunction with projects of which the individual taxpayer approves. Disputes concerning the issue of taxation should be handled through mediated discussions and not through punitive or coercive policies.

The foregoing statements of principle concerning the idea of sovereignty mark the beginning of the exploratory process, not the end. We all need to critically reflect on the foregoing set of principles because what we have today is working for just a very small number of individuals that follow the way of power and, as a result, seek to prevent people in general from being able to pursue, establish, enhance, realize, and protect the principles of sovereignty.

Sovereignty is not something new. The idea of sovereignty has been inherent in human beings for a very, very long time, but, unfortunately, as events have demonstrated again and again for thousands of years, people's aspirations for sovereignty have been thwarted persistently and rigorously by the way of power at nearly every juncture of history.

A person can commit one's moral and intellectual agency to the cause of sovereignty or an individual can cede that moral and intellectual agency to those who belong to the power elite - economically, militarily, socially, intellectually, politically, and religiously. A great deal hangs on the nature of the judgments one makes with respect to the issue of how one decides to cede one's moral, intellectual, and spiritual agency.

The following books are available for free in PDF format at: https://www.billwhitehouse.com/press.htm

Sovereignty and the Constitution

Beyond Democracy

Quest for Sovereignty

The People Amendments

Sovereignty: A Play in Three Acts

Searching For Sovereignty

Educational Horizons

www.ingramcontent.com/pod-product-compliance
Lightning Source LLC
Chambersburg PA
CBHW071909210526
45479CB00002B/348